# 3, 2, 1...
# DRAW!

ARCTURUS

This edition published in 2014 by Arcturus Publishing Limited
26/27 Bickels Yard, 151–153 Bermondsey Street, London SE1 3HA

Editors: Samantha Hilton, Joe Harris, Kate Overy and Joe Fullman
Illustrations: Dynamo Limited
Design concept: Keith Williams
Design: Dynamo Limited and Notion Design

ISBN: 978-1-78212-287-6
CH003656UK
Supplier: 29, Date 0914, Print run 3249

Printed in China

# CONTENTS

# ART MATERIALS

Before you begin drawing all the amazing characters in this book, you will need a few important pieces of equipment.

## PENS AND PENCILS

You can use a variety of drawing tools including pens, chalks, pens and paints. But to begin with use an ordinary HB pencil.

## PAPER

Use a clean sheet of paper for your final drawings. Scrap paper is useful and cheap for your practice work.

## ERASERS

Everyone makes mistakes which is why every artist has a good eraser. When you rub out a mistake, do it gently. Scrubbing hard at your paper will ruin your drawing and possibly even rip it.

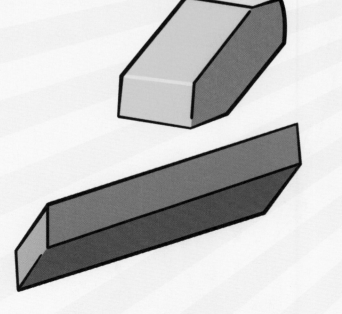

## RULER

Always use a ruler to draw straight lines.

## COMPASS

You can use a compass to draw a perfect circle but it can be tricky to use at first. For small circles, try using a coin, bottle top or any other small, round item you can find.

## INK PENS

The drawings in this book have been finished with an ink line to make them sharper and cleaner. You can get the same effect by using a ballpoint or felt-tip pen.

## PAINT

Adding colour to your drawing brings it to life. You can use felt-tip pens, coloured pencils or water-based paints like poster paint to make cleaning up easier.

5

# GETTING STARTED

In this book we use a simple two-colour system to show you how to draw a picture. Just remember: new lines are blue lines!

### STARTING WITH STEP 1

The first lines you will draw are very simple shapes. They will be shown in blue, like this. You should draw them with a normal pencil.

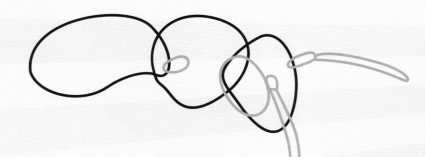

### ADDING MORE DETAIL

As you move on to the next step, the lines you have already drawn will be shown in black. The new lines for that stage will appear in blue.

### FINISHING OFF

When you reach the final stage you will see the image in full colour with a black ink line. 'Inking' a picture means tracing the main lines with a black pen. After the ink dries, use your eraser to remove all the pencil lines before adding your colour.

## MAKING CHANGES

If you want to make a change to your drawing but are not sure if it will work, you can lay a thinner piece of paper over the top of it. Then draw the change on the new piece of paper and lay it over the first one to see both drawings together.

## PRACTICE SHAPES

All good artists will tell you that practice is very important. Practise drawing flat shapes such as triangles, circles and squares. Then try making them into pyramids, spheres and cubes by drawing extra lines and then colouring them in with your colouring pencils.

## DON'T SMEAR

It's easy to mess up your drawing by smearing the lines you have just drawn with your hand. If this keeps happening, place a piece of paper over your drawing to protect it. But remember not to drag the piece of paper across your drawing as this will smear it too.

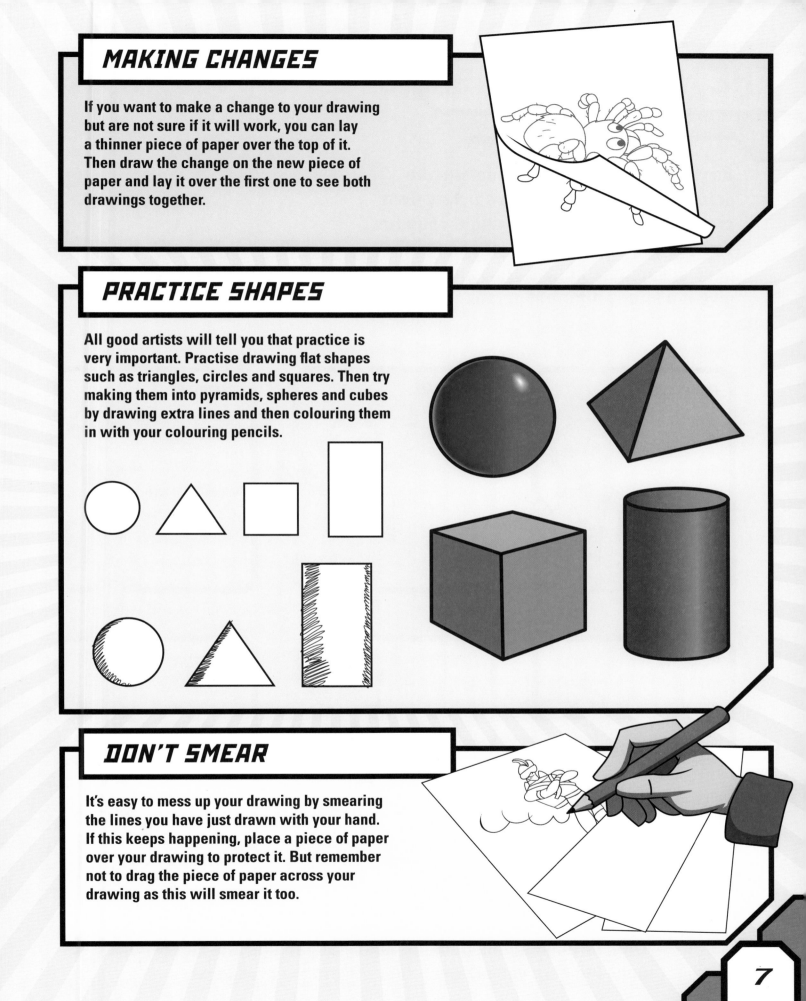

# THE NEXT STEP

As you improve, you can transform the drawings in this book into your very own creations by making a few slight changes. You can use other colours, or change the pose of your character's arms and legs to give it a totally different personality.

## RUNNING

Tuck one leg back and angle the arms and suddenly your robot is running.

## WAVING

Change the angle of the head and one of the arms and it looks like the robot is waving.

## JUMPING

Raise one leg and both arms to make him look like he is jumping.

## POSING

By raising both arms a bit our little metal friend is posing away and showing off with the best of them.

## UPSET

By lowering his eyes and turning his mouth the other way up, you can make your robot look as though he's upset.

## COLOUR

You don't have to stick to our colours either. Choose what you want and go crazy with your colours.

Look throughout the book for handy Super Tips and Fun Feature pages to help you take your drawing to the next level.

# DRAWING ANIMALS

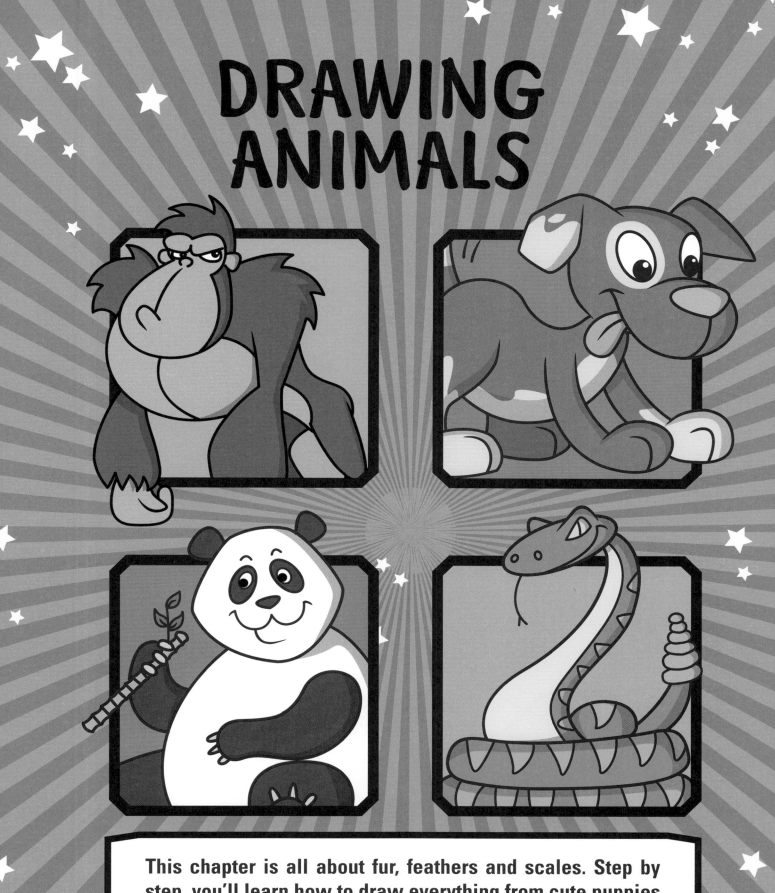

This chapter is all about fur, feathers and scales. Step by step, you'll learn how to draw everything from cute puppies and parrots to slithering snakes and fearsome gorillas.

# KITTEN

**Let's start by drawing a playful kitten. Give your pet a large head, big eyes and a long tail so it looks really cute.**

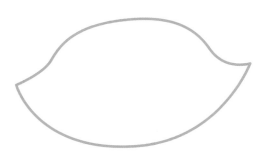

## STEP 1

First, draw a shape a bit like a lemon. A kitten's head is big compared to the rest of its body.

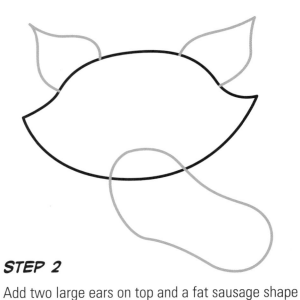

## STEP 2

Add two large ears on top and a fat sausage shape to create your kitten's body.

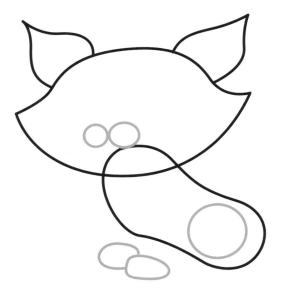

## STEP 3

Next, add a large circle for the back leg, two small ones for the face and two ovals for the front paws.

## STEP 4

Draw two large eyes. Then, add a little nose and complete the back leg and front legs.

## STEP 5

Now fill in the final details. Add eyes, eyebrows, a small mouth, fur around the ears and cheeks, and don't forget a long, swishy tail.

## SUPER TIP!

Your kitten doesn't have to be the same colour as this one. As you can see, a simple colour change gives your furry friend a completely different look.

Why not colour a few of them in different colours and have a whole litter of cuddly, fluffy kittens?

## STEP 6

Your cat can be any colour. Adding small white spots in the eyes will give them a cute, shiny effect.

# PUPPY

When a puppy is happy or excited, it wags its tail from side to side. Try to show this in your drawing by using movement lines (see page 48).

### STEP 1

Start by drawing a simple circle. If you like, you could trace around a coin.

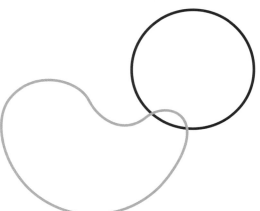

### STEP 2

Then, add a big, squashy jelly-bean shape to make the puppy's body.

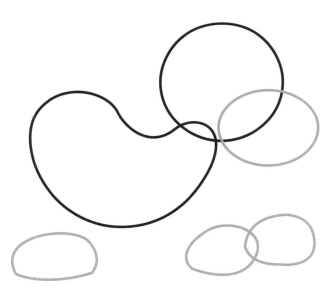

### STEP 3

Four more circular shapes will make the muzzle and feet.

### STEP 4

Draw curved front legs to make it look as if your puppy is about to jump up. Add a back leg. Draw big floppy ears and a large nose on its muzzle.

## STEP 5

Next, draw on its big eyes and its mouth with a slobbery tongue. Then, complete the paws and other back leg. Finally, don't forget its waggly tail!

## STEP 6

You can choose any pattern you like for your puppy's body. You could try some large patches, or small spots, like you see on Dalmatians.

# PONY

Follow these step-by-step instructions to create your very own pony. Give it a strong, stocky body, short legs, and a long mane and tail of flowing hair.

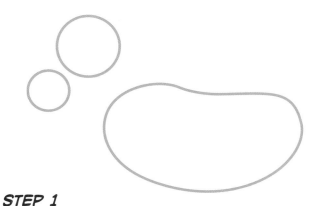

### STEP 1

Start with two circles and a jelly bean shape to give you the pony's head and body.

### STEP 2

Link the three shapes together and add a circle and an oval shape for the tops of the pony's legs.

### STEP 3

Next, add six small circles for the leg and hoof joints. Draw an ear and the top of the pony's mane.

### STEP 4

Draw lines to link the leg and hoof joints to create the pony's legs. Add nostrils, an eyelid and the front part of the mane.

## STEP 5

Draw the long bushy mane and tail. Add hooves, complete its eye and eyebrow, and add its other ear.

## STEP 6

You can colour your pony any shade you like. Dapples, as shown here, are a nice touch.

# PARROT

**Try to capture this parrot's brightly coloured feathers and large, curved beak and claws.**

### STEP 1

First, draw a slightly wobbly pear shape to make the parrot's body.

### STEP 2

Next, add simple wing shapes and a large hooked beak.

### STEP 3

Add the long curved claws and a large eye. Then draw some plumage on top of your parrot's head.

### STEP 4

Add in the branch and a bit more detail on the eye.

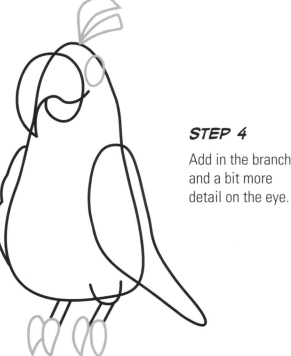
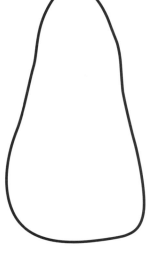

## STEP 5

Give the parrot some long tail feathers. Then add more feathers over the body. They look a bit like the number '3' lying on its side.

## STEP 6

Now you can colour your parrot in nice, bright colours.

### SUPER TIP!

You don't have to draw every feather on a parrot's body. If you want to make it look like it has feathers all over, just draw some little patches of feather shapes. They should be spaced out over its body and wings.

# PANDA

You'll use plenty of rounded shapes when drawing this large black and white bear. Be sure to add a stick of bamboo, its favourite food.

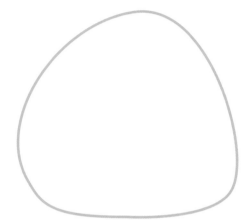

## STEP 1

Draw a large oval shape, slightly narrower at the top, to make your panda's body.

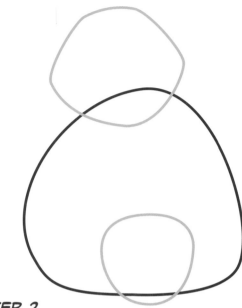

## STEP 2

Add one oval shape to make the panda's head and another for its leg.

## STEP 3

Next, add curved lines to make the panda's arms, ears and an outstretched leg.

## STEP 4

A panda's feet look a lot like shoes. Large circles on its face make the eye patches. Add a small nose.

## STEP 5

Add a smiling face, eyebrows, eyes, claws and its favourite snack – a stick of bamboo. See the Super Tip to find out how to draw bamboo.

### SUPER TIP!

**A stick of bamboo is very simple to draw.**

- Draw a straight-edged rectangle like this.

- Pencil in the lines for the bamboo segments.

- When you ink the picture, add curves between the lines. This will make the bamboo look bumpy and ridged.

## STEP 6

Real pandas are black and white… but who says yours has to be? Why not try some other colours – purple and pink, or green and orange?

19

# GORILLA

**Make sure that your gorilla has a large head and arms that are longer than its legs. It should also walk on all fours.**

### STEP 1

First, draw a simple shape that looks like a table tennis bat.

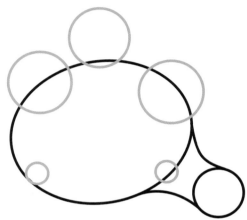

### STEP 2

Next, add five circles to form the base for the gorilla's shoulders and elbows.

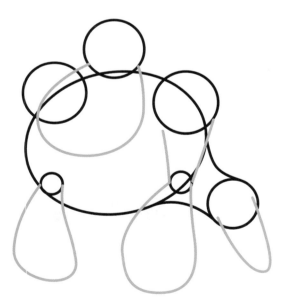

### STEP 3

Now, add five more shapes to make the powerful arms, one leg and large jaw.

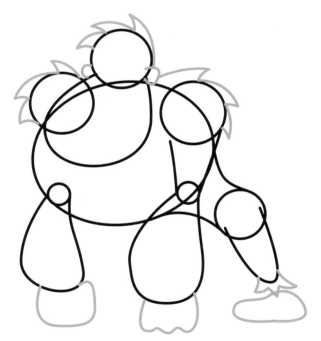

### STEP 4

Draw small spikes to create the hair on the gorilla's head and shoulders. Don't forget to draw its hands and feet.

## STEP 5

Add more fur to the arms. Draw simple lines for your gorilla's face, lip, chest, toes and back leg.

### SUPER TIP!

The gorilla's face may look complicated but it starts with three simple steps...

- The eyebrows

- The eyes

- The nose

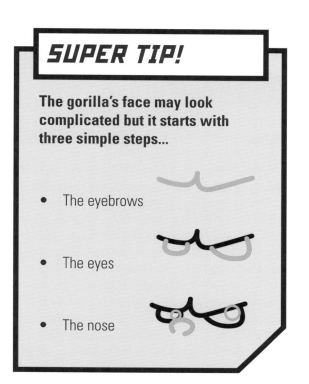

## STEP 6

Colour in your gorilla using two shades of the same colour. You could use blue, grey or brown.

# TIGER

It's time to tackle the tiger, the largest of all the big cats. Carefully colour its orange and black stripes, which help it to blend in with its jungle surroundings.

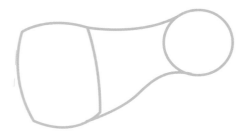

### STEP 1

Start by drawing a rectangle and a circle. Link them together with two curved lines.

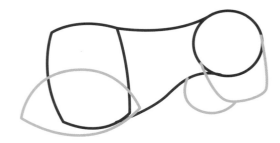

### STEP 2

Add these three shapes to create the main part of the tiger's head and its back legs.

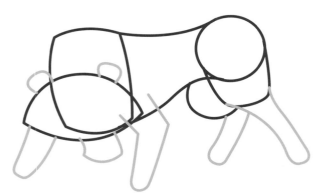

### STEP 3

Add a pair of ears to the top of its head and draw in the legs. The small shape at the bottom of the tiger's head will be its lower jaw.

### STEP 4

Next, draw the eyes, nose, muzzle, feet and tail. Make sure you draw its tail using curved lines with no sharp angles.

Start the tiger's stripes with simple single lines. You can use straight lines, curved lines or zigzags. Then draw lines on either side of that first line to make the shapes shown here.

### STEP 5

Add eyelids and eyes to complete the tiger's face. If you want your tiger to look more friendly, draw the eyelids higher up its face. Draw simple lines for its stripes. See the Super Tip to find out how to make them work.

### STEP 6

Colour your tiger a nice bright orange and strong black.

# RATTLESNAKE

**Start with a couple of simple sausage shapes and soon you'll have a deadly rattlesnake – coiled and ready to strike.**

## STEP 1

First, draw two long, squashed sausage shapes to make the coils of your rattlesnake's body.

## STEP 2

Add two curved lines that meet at the top to make the rattlesnake's long neck.

## STEP 3

For the rattlesnake's head, draw a wide, oval shape. Then add a long, pointy tail.

## STEP 4

Next, add two 'eyebrow' shapes on its head. Draw a line down one side of its neck and a small circle to create an extra coil.

## STEP 5

Complete its face and add a long, forked tongue.
Draw V-shapes to show the snake's markings. You
can colour these in a different shade.

## SUPER TIP!

A really simple way to draw the snake's
famous rattle is to build it from squashed
sausages (just like its body).

Add sausage shapes to the tail, making
each one smaller as you get closer to the
tip of the rattlesnake's tail.

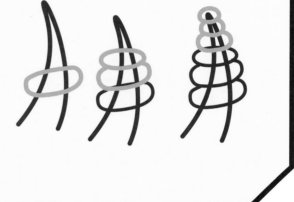

## STEP 6

To make the eye look
really snake-like, simply
draw a vertical line inside
the eyeball. Then add
some colours.

The final animal in this chapter is the deadliest of them all – a scary shark. Take your time getting those sharp teeth just right.

### STEP 1

Draw a large teardrop shape to make the shark's sleek body.

### STEP 2

Add pointy fins and a nose. At this stage, your shark could be mistaken for a friendly dolphin!

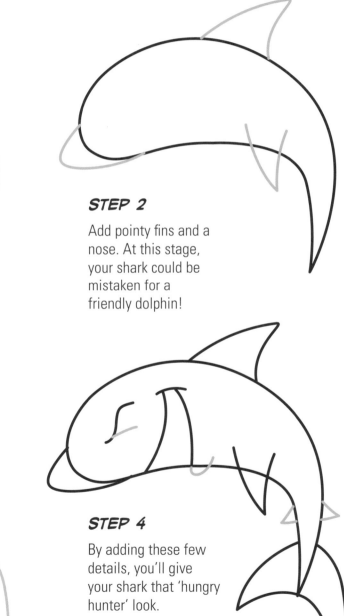

### STEP 3

Next, draw a large, wide mouth, a squiggle for its eye and a large tail fin.

### STEP 4

By adding these few details, you'll give your shark that 'hungry hunter' look.

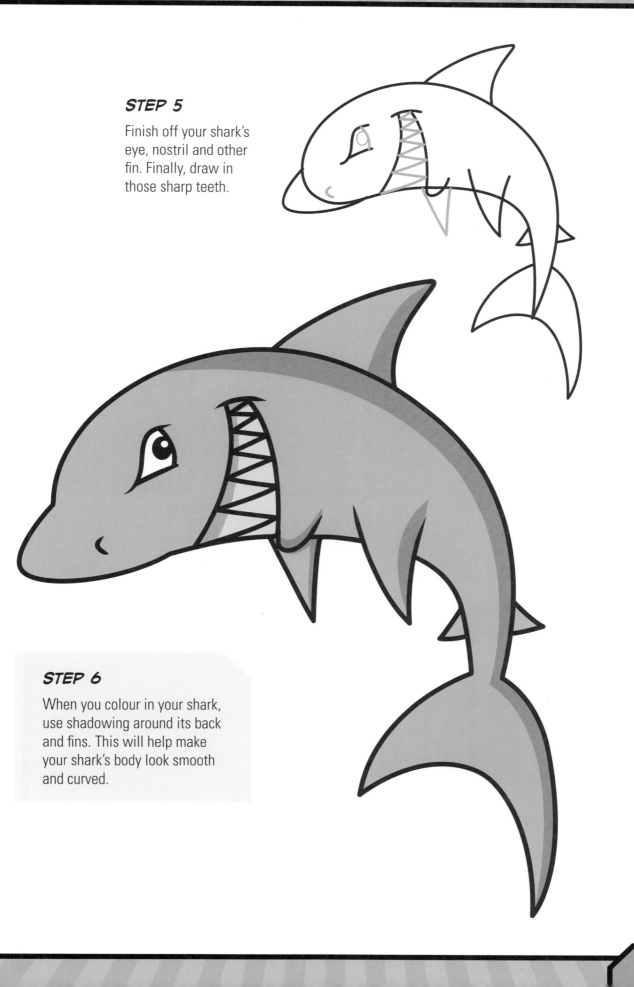

## STEP 5

Finish off your shark's eye, nostril and other fin. Finally, draw in those sharp teeth.

## STEP 6

When you colour in your shark, use shadowing around its back and fins. This will help make your shark's body look smooth and curved.

# CREATING EMOTIONS

FUN FEATURE

Once you've learned how to draw the animals in this book, you might want to try drawing them with different expressions. They could look happy, sad, angry or even puzzled.

## HAPPY

Draw wide-open eyes and raised eyebrows to create a happy face.

## ANGRY

Add straight lines for eyebrows, an open mouth and a jagged line for teeth. Now he looks angry!

## SURPRISED

Big eyes, one raised eyebrow and a round mouth help your character to look surprised.

## SAD

By curving your character's eyebrows and mouth down you can make him look sad.

## THINKING

A pointed eyebrow and a slightly wobbly mouth make him look as if he is thinking about something.

## EYES

As you can see, it's very easy to change expressions with a few tweaks. You can completely alter your character by just changing the eyes and eyebrows.

Here are a few to try. From the top, these eyes are: surprised, sleepy, scared, angry and sneaky.

# DRAWING BUGS

This chapter explores the stinging, biting, scuttling world of bugs. With their long legs, scary pincers and bulging eyes, these mini-beasts make great subjects for icky drawings!

# RHINOCEROS BEETLE

Let's start by drawing this unusual-looking beastie. Make sure its two large horns look sharp and dangerous and that its armoured body is shiny.

### STEP 1

First, draw the horns. Follow the shape on the right and then add a long oval for the beetle's body.

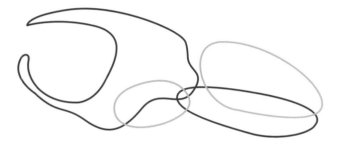

### STEP 2

Next, add two oval shapes to create the beetle's wing cover and face.

### STEP 3

Draw some fine details on the horns and add three oval shapes to begin the beetle's legs.

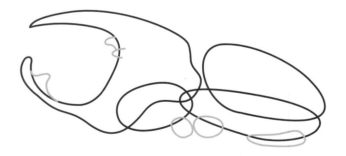

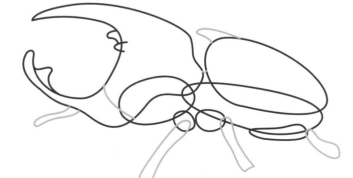

### STEP 4

Add the legs and the spike on the beetle's body. Then add a curved line across the horns.

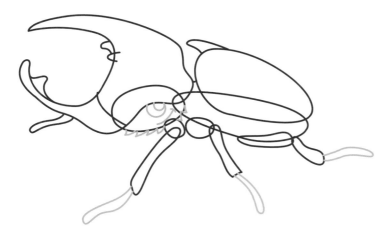

### STEP 5

Finally, add the last part of the legs and complete the outline of the head as shown. Then add its eye.

### STEP 6

A rhinoceros beetle may look fierce but it's actually harmless. To make its body look super shiny, add a white line across its back as shown below.

# SCORPION

For this scorpion, you'll need to draw eight legs – not to mention a huge pair of claws. It also has a thin tail curving over its back… with a nasty sting at the end of it!

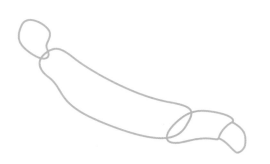

### STEP 1

Begin to draw the scorpion's body by linking together these four shapes.

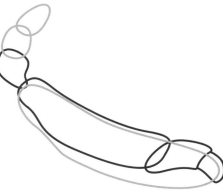

### STEP 2

Draw over the first outline with these three shapes. The two small ovals mark the start of its famous tail.

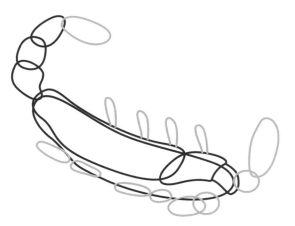

### STEP 3

These small loops are the start of the legs. There are four on each side and two for each of the claws at the front. Add another oval to the tail.

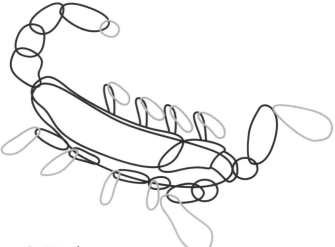

### STEP 4

Add some more loops to form the next segments of the legs, claws and tail. A 'segment' is part of an insect's body.

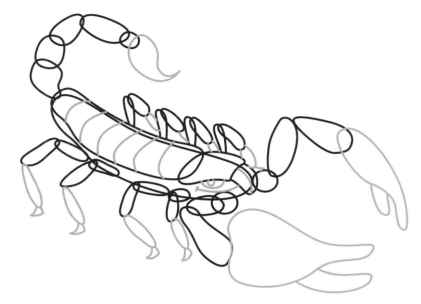

## STEP 5

Draw the last segments of the legs and add six stripy lines across the main body. Then, add the large, snappy claws and the sharp sting in the tail. Lastly, draw the scorpion's face.

## STEP 6

Colour your scorpion red. It may have a smiling face, but don't be fooled. The sneaky glint in its eye suggests that it may be about to strike!

# PRAYING MANTIS

**Take your time drawing this rather strange insect! It has a triangular head, a long body and large front legs. The front legs are folded in a way that makes the bug look like it's praying.**

## STEP 1

Draw the insect's three main body parts – its small, triangular head and two longer shapes.

## STEP 2

Link the head to the main body and then add two narrow shapes to form its wings.

## STEP 3

Now, add its eyes and long antennae. Three small shapes begin the middle and back legs and a shape like the letter 'J' is the start of its front legs.

## STEP 4

Next, add the insect's long, thin back legs and its bent middle legs. Finish off the large front legs.

## STEP 5

Add two lines to divide up the wings. Then give it eyes and a smile to make this insect look like a cute little guy.

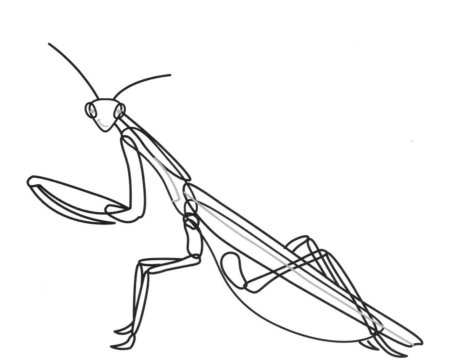

## STEP 6

When you colour in your insect, use light and dark shades of green to highlight the different parts of its body.

# RED ANT

Like all insects, red ants have six legs, which can be tricky to draw. They also have sharp pincers and are sometimes known as fire ants because of their reddish colour.

### STEP 1

First, make up the ant's body from these bean-like shapes. Make sure the head is slightly flattened.

### STEP 2

Next, add two sharp pincers and long antennae. Draw three ovals for the start of the leg joints.

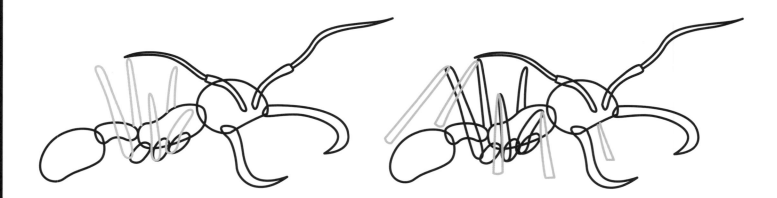

### STEP 3

Add long segments to the ant's skinny legs, as shown here.

### STEP 4

Add another set of segments to the legs, so they point downwards.

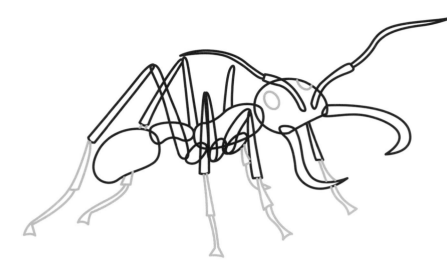

## STEP 5

Draw the final segments of the ant's six legs and add a pair of eyes.

## STEP 6

Red ants spend most of their time on the forest floor. Colour them with reddish-brown colours to keep them hidden!

# BUTTERFLY

**Butterflies come in many different colours and patterns. This one is yellow and orange… but you could choose any colours you like.**

### STEP 1

First, draw a small, round head, a sausage shape for the body and two antennae.

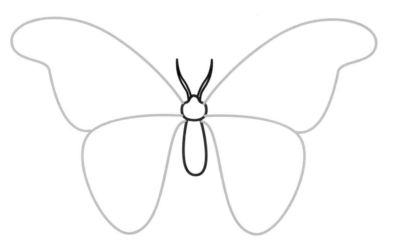

### STEP 2

Draw the butterfly's large and beautiful wings next. Try to make the two wings exactly the same size and shape.

### STEP 3

Add some markings to the wings. Then draw some stripy lines on to the insect's body.

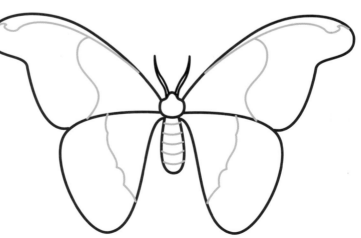

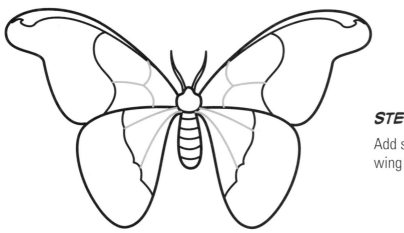

## STEP 4

Add some more details to its wing markings.

## STEP 5

Finally, add more shapes to the wings and draw on its mouth and big eyes.

## STEP 6

Time for colouring. Why not look at other butterflies or moths and try your own markings and colours?

# TARANTULA

The tarantula's plump body is made of two round shapes and is quite simple to draw. However, you'll need to take more care with all those legs. Each one is made of four sections.

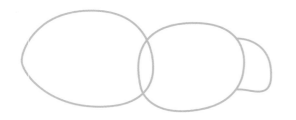

## STEP 1

First, draw two overlapping oval shapes to make the body and head. Add a smaller shape to make the mouth at the front.

## STEP 2

Next, draw four ovals and five sausage shapes to begin to form the spider's eight legs and one of its feelers.

## STEP 3

Now, add some more segments to the spider's long, thin legs and its feeler.

## STEP 4

Next, add more oval-shaped leg segments and the outline of the other feeler.

## STEP 5

Complete the legs, then add curved zigzags along the outline of its head and body to make it furry. Add large eyes and a line down the spider's mouth.

## SUPER TIP!

**Tarantulas are covered in tiny hairs that give them a slightly furry appearance.**

- Draw the main body shape and colour it in.

- Then add short lines dotted around. Only use a few to make it slightly furry, rather than completely hairy like a bear!

## STEP 6

We've coloured our spider using black and orange. Each segment of the legs is a different colour, to make a stripy pattern.

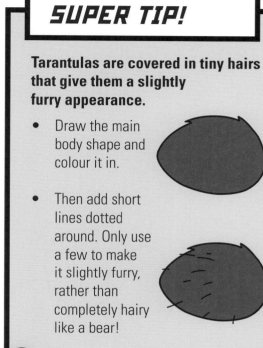

# HORNET

A hornet looks a bit like a wasp, only bigger. It has large eyes, a smooth body, long wings and bold, black and yellow markings.

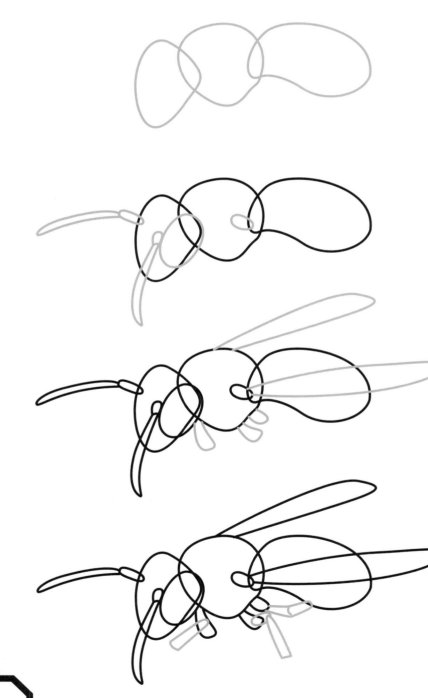

### STEP 1

First, draw three oval shapes to make the hornet's head and body.

### STEP 2

Next, add the long antennae and eye. Draw a small circle on the middle part of the hornet. This is where the wing joins on.

### STEP 3

Next come the long and very thin wings. Add three ovals to begin its legs.

### STEP 4

Add more segments to create the hornet's long legs.

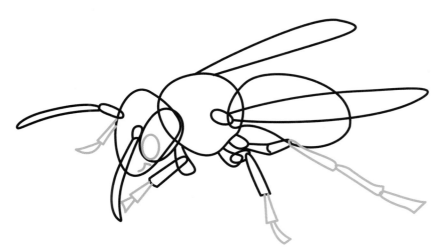

### STEP 5

Finish the legs as shown above. Add a pupil to the insect's eye and a little, smiling mouth.

## *SUPER TIP!*

- To create see-through wings for bugs such as hornets, wasps and bees, first draw vein lines.

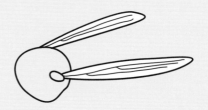

- Colour the wings in a very light shade. Pale blue works best.

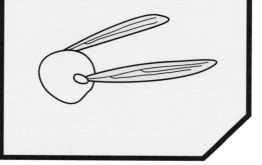

### STEP 6

Yellow and black warn you to keep your distance from this super-sized stinger!

# CENTIPEDE

**The centipede's body is made up of lots of little, round segments. You'll need to carefully draw 20, each one larger than the last and with a little leg attached.**

### STEP 1

First, draw a long curved line. You can make it any shape you want as long as you keep it slightly curved.

### STEP 2

Starting at the back of your centipede, draw a very small egg shape. Move along the line drawing the same shape again and again. Make each one slightly larger as you go.

### STEP 3

Draw a small curved line where each circle joins to start the legs.

## STEP 4

Now you have made a start on all the legs, go over them again and thicken them up.

## STEP 5

Add the centipede's tail and antennae. Don't forget some nice big eyes so your centipede can see where it's going.

## SUPER TIP!

**We've drawn our centipede in a straight line to show you how to do it, but you can pose yours any way you want to.**

- Sketch your first line in any shape you want. Here, we've drawn a more curved line.

- Then, start building your circle shapes along the line like this.

## STEP 6

Add a darker shade to the bottom edge of the circles when you're colouring. This will give the body a nice rounded shape.

# LOCUST

This member of the grasshopper family has a very distinctive shape. Make sure its back legs are much longer than the others.

### STEP 1

First, draw a long, curving body that leads up to a chunky neck. Add a teardrop-shaped head.

### STEP 2

Next, add a wing case and the start of a long back leg. Then draw two ovals. They will turn into the two front legs.

### STEP 3

Draw a pair of short antennae. Add big eyes, an eyebrow and a mouth. Draw more leg segments. Its long legs will help it to hop!

## STEP 4

Finish the strong back legs and add more segments to the other legs and detail to the eyes.

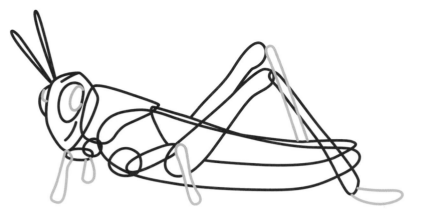

## STEP 5

Draw the feet, and add some lines on the wing case and lower body.

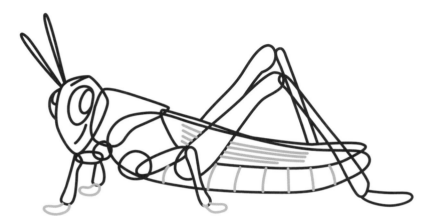

## STEP 6

Choose some different shades of yellow and orange for your locust. Now it's ready to hop off the page!

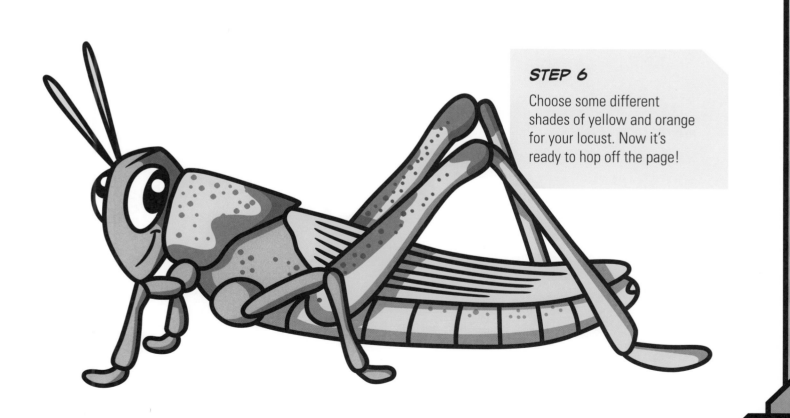

# ADDING MOVEMENT

## FUN FEATURE

Here are some fun ways to make your bugs look as though they're really moving. Follow these tips and pretty soon they'll be crawling or buzzing off your page.

## FLOATY MOVEMENT

Show how a butterfly flutters through the air by adding a small dotted line that traces the path it has flown.

## SPEED LINES

To make it look as if your bug is moving quickly, add simple lines coming away from its back end. Draw a puff of smoke and it will really zoom along.

## VIBRATION LINES

You can easily make the wings of your bug look as though they are moving back and forth. Just add simple vibration lines that follow the line of the edges of the wings, as shown here.

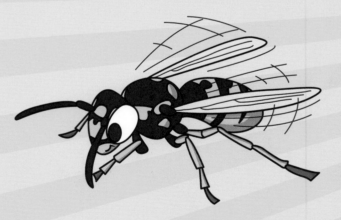

## SNAP, SNAP!

A sudden movement, such as a fierce snap from a claw, can be shown by adding a cartoon flash. This spiky shape will give your drawing some extra drama. Look out!

# DRAWING
# FAIRIES AND PRINCESSES

There are many different magical characters to draw in this chapter, from a colourful rainbow fairy to a proud Native American princess. But they're all super cute and fun!

# WOOD FAIRY

The first character for you to draw is a mischievous wood fairy. She has pointy ears and delicate wings that help her to flutter from tree to tree.

### STEP 1

First, draw the shape above to make the main body of the fairy.

### STEP 2

Next, add arms, legs and a simple circle to start the fairy's head.

### STEP 3

Draw a pointed shape on the circle for her chin. Carefully draw her hands and add her lower legs.

### STEP 4

Now add her hair, a pointy ear, a neck and some feet. Her hair can be any style but this pixie cut looks best.

## STEP 5

After you have added her clothes and face, draw on her beautiful fairy wings.

## STEP 6

You can make your fairy any colour you want. Just remember that she should look at home among the flowers and trees.

# FAIRYTALE PRINCESS

This happy fairytale princess wears a long, flowing gown and a golden crown. Her dress should sparkle as if it's been sprinkled with fairy dust.

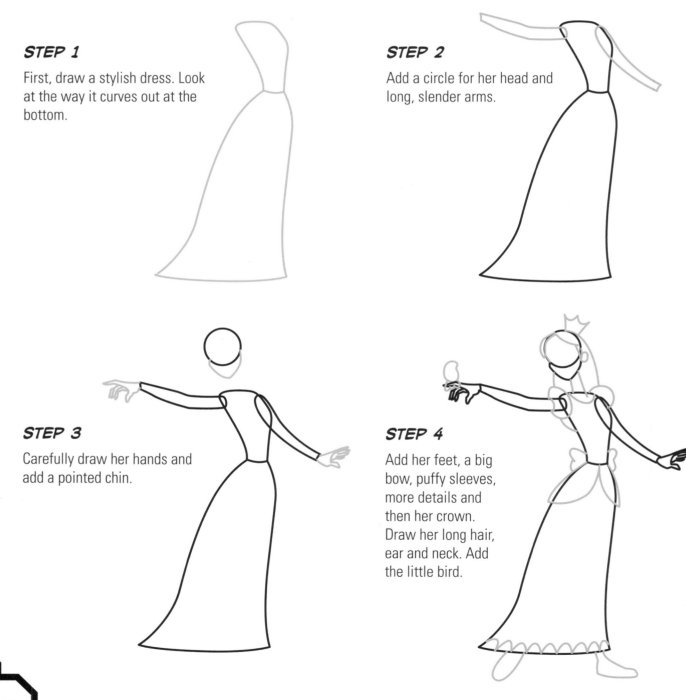

### STEP 1

First, draw a stylish dress. Look at the way it curves out at the bottom.

### STEP 2

Add a circle for her head and long, slender arms.

### STEP 3

Carefully draw her hands and add a pointed chin.

### STEP 4

Add her feet, a big bow, puffy sleeves, more details and then her crown. Draw her long hair, ear and neck. Add the little bird.

### STEP 5

Finish her pretty face, shoes and the little bird. Then, add more details to the dress as shown.

### STEP 6

Time to add colour! We've chosen blue but you could use any colour.

## SUPER TIP!

An easy way to add sparkle to the princess's dress is to leave small dots of the picture without colour.

Another way to make the small white sparkles is to add little dots of white poster paint.

Keep them spread out – don't bunch them up in one place.

# SKY FAIRY

**Sky fairies have hair and clothes that make them look a bit like fluffy clouds. Their soft, rounded wings are the colour of the sky.**

## STEP 1

First, draw two shapes that look like a lower-case letter 'i'.

## STEP 2

Add her arms, chin and her floaty cloud skirt.

## STEP 3

Carefully add her hand and the top of her legs.

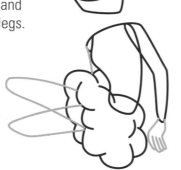

## STEP 4

Finish off her legs, then draw her mouth and ear. Add a big fluffy hairstyle, rather like candyfloss!

## STEP 5

Now it's time to add her eyes and her other hand. Soft, rounded wings complete the picture.

## SUPER TIP!

It's very easy to change the sky fairy into a storm fairy, just by changing the colours of her clothes, hair and face.

We've used dark blue and purple to make her a storm fairy. Why don't you use other colours to make her into another type of fairy?

## STEP 6

She could be a bright sky fairy like this one. Or you could use darker colours to make her a storm fairy. See the Super Tip on the left.

# NATIVE AMERICAN PRINCESS

This Native American princess is wearing her traditional dress. Decorate her outfit with plenty of tassels and feathers.

## STEP 1

First, draw these shapes to make her body.

## STEP 2

Next, add a circle for her head. Draw her arms and the tops of her legs.

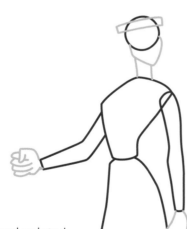

## STEP 3

Draw a tilted and pointed shape at the bottom of the circle. Then, add her neck and her headband. Carefully draw her hands and lower legs.

## STEP 4

Add the staff, her hair, her cuffs and her feet. Her dress needs a little more detail too.

## STEP 5

Draw feathers on her staff and her headband. Add lots of fringing to her dress. Finish her face and shoes.

## STEP 6

Her clothes are made from animal skins, but you could decorate them with fabulous jewels if you want to.

# FLAME FAIRY

**Bright red hair, flaming wings and an orange dress tell you that this fairy is hot stuff. She really looks like she's made of fire!**

## STEP 1

First, draw the top of her dress and then add her fire skirt. Use pointy shapes to give it movement.

## STEP 2

Next, add a circle for her head. Then, draw her long arms and the top parts of her legs.

## STEP 3

Now add a pointy chin and a hand. Finish her legs.

## STEP 4

Add her ears, flaming hair, wings and pointy feet.

## STEP 5

Now draw her face and add
some simple lines
for her dress and shoes.

## STEP 6

Choose hot colours like orange
and red to make a flame fairy.
Use shades of blue and white if
you want to make an ice fairy.

# AFRICAN PRINCESS

This African princess's dress may look simple, but its bright colours and her pretty jewels and feathered headband make her look truly royal.

### STEP 1

Start by drawing her long dress to make a simple body shape.

### STEP 2

Now add her head, long neck and arms to give her a royal look.

### STEP 3

Add her pointed chin, her hands and her bare feet.

## STEP 4

Draw her pretty headband with its feathers. Add her earrings, cuffs and a fold in her dress.

## STEP 5

Now draw her face, necklace and add the stripes to her dress.

## STEP 6

Use bright colours to help this princess pop off the page!

# FAIRY GODMOTHER

**A fairy godmother is a kind, simply dressed character who uses her trusty magic wand to sort out problems.**

### STEP 1

Use these two round shapes to begin her body.

### STEP 2

Add a circle for her head and draw her arms.

### STEP 3

Draw her hair and face. Her hands and little legs come next.

### STEP 4

She needs some fairy wings, so that she can take flight. Don't forget that magic wand!

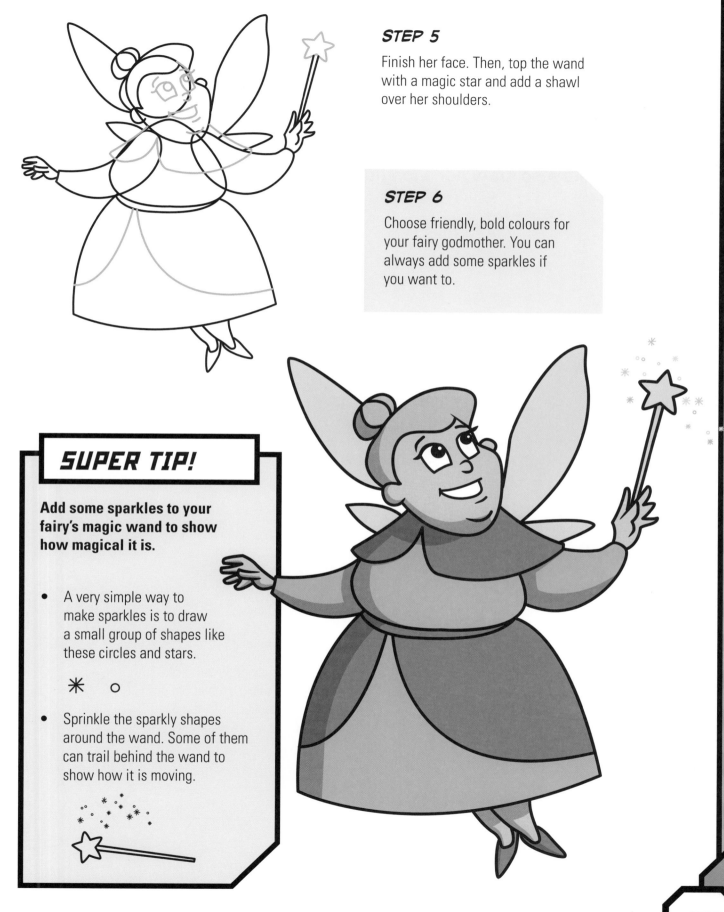

## STEP 5

Finish her face. Then, top the wand with a magic star and add a shawl over her shoulders.

## STEP 6

Choose friendly, bold colours for your fairy godmother. You can always add some sparkles if you want to.

## SUPER TIP!

Add some sparkles to your fairy's magic wand to show how magical it is.

- A very simple way to make sparkles is to draw a small group of shapes like these circles and stars.

- Sprinkle the sparkly shapes around the wand. Some of them can trail behind the wand to show how it is moving.

# ARABIAN PRINCESS

This Arabian princess looks fabulous in her pink two–piece outfit and sparkling jewels. You could also draw her a magic carpet!

## STEP 1

First, draw a simple body shape made up of trousers and a top.

## STEP 2

Next, add an oval shape for her head. Then draw her arms and feet.

## STEP 3

Draw a simple line across the shoulders. Then add her neck, ear and hands. Sketch some more details around her waist.

## STEP 4

Carefully draw her face. Then add a simple fold on her trouser leg and a line at the top of her shoes.

## STEP 5

Add her long hair and crown. Then draw sparkling jewels around her waist.

## STEP 6

We've coloured her outfit in shades of pink, but you can choose any colours you like.

# RAINBOW FAIRY

This fairy loves bright colours. Even her skirt is like a beautiful rainbow. With a wave of her magic wand, she can paint an arch of colours across the sky.

### STEP 1

First, draw a simple shape for her curved skirt and top.

### STEP 2

Next, draw her head, slightly tilted. Draw a bent leg, a straight leg and then her arms.

### STEP 3

Now, sketch in her fluttering wings and carefully draw her hands.

### STEP 4

Add feet, hair, dress detail and a magic wand.

## STEP 5

Now finish her face. Then add the rainbow. You could trace around a cup to get the curve just right.

## STEP 6

Time to colour. Remember, she's a rainbow fairy... so use as many different colours as possible!

# EXPERT COLOURING

## LIGHT AND SHADE

If you want to make your picture look 3–D, start thinking about light and shade. Decide which side of your picture is in shadow, and make the colours darker along either the left or right edge. Just use a darker version of the colour you have already used in that area.

## FELT--TIP PENS

You can create bold colours and strong lines with felt–tip pens. However, it's not easy to correct mistakes that you've made with a pen. So start off with a pencil sketch first! Add the felt–tip colours once you're happy with the result.

## COLOURING PENCILS

These create a paler and calmer look than felt–tips. Colouring pencils are also easier to blend together. Sketch your drawing first with an HB pencil. Then, gently layer your colour, making it as light or as dark as you like.

## WATERCOLOURS

Watercolours are easy to blend together and you can create beautiful pictures. First, sketch your drawing with a waterproof pen. Then, add water to your paint, but don't add too much. If you do, it might spoil your paper.

# DRAWING
# HEROES AND VILLAINS

Now it's time to create some fantastic superheroes – and
their arch enemies, of course. Each one has a special power
that you'll need to bring out in your drawing.

# THE FIREFLY

The Firefly is a bug-eyed hero who can control fire. Red-hot flames leap out from his hands and body to capture criminals.

### STEP 1

First, copy these shapes to create his head, torso and superhero underwear.

### STEP 2

Next, add these long, thin shapes for his long arms and thighs.

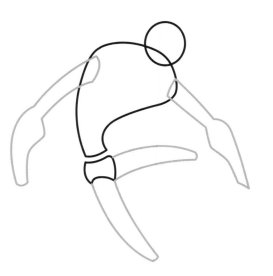

### STEP 3

Give your superhero a pointy chin, clenched fists and curved lower legs.

### STEP 4

Now it is time to add those flames. You can also draw bulging muscles on his upper arms. Add two lines to join his torso and underwear.

## STEP 5

Then draw two big bug eyes and add a flame pattern to his chest.

## STEP 6

Finally, bring your hero to life by adding flames to his head. Use bright colours such as yellow and red for his body.

# MISS MIRACLE

With her long, flowing cape, Miss Miracle is ready to fly into action. She keeps her true identity a secret with her green eye mask.

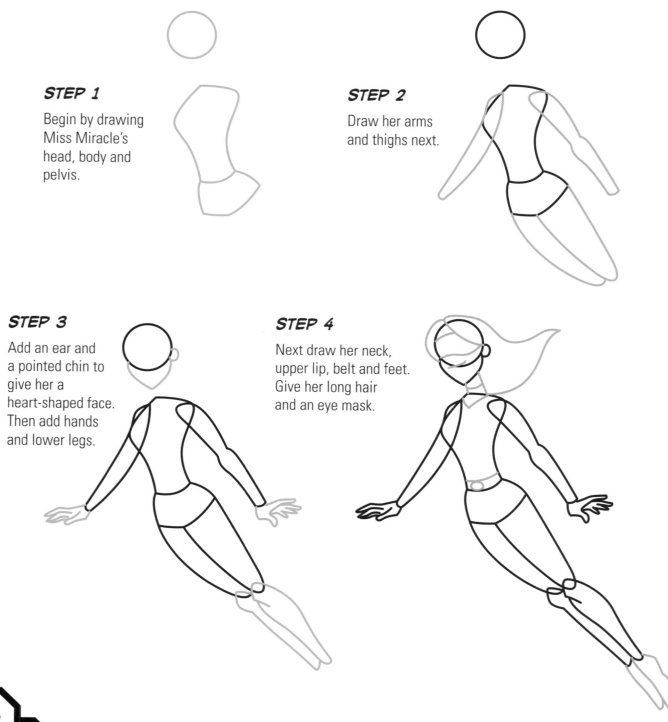

### STEP 1

Begin by drawing Miss Miracle's head, body and pelvis.

### STEP 2

Draw her arms and thighs next.

### STEP 3

Add an ear and a pointed chin to give her a heart-shaped face. Then add hands and lower legs.

### STEP 4

Next draw her neck, upper lip, belt and feet. Give her long hair and an eye mask.

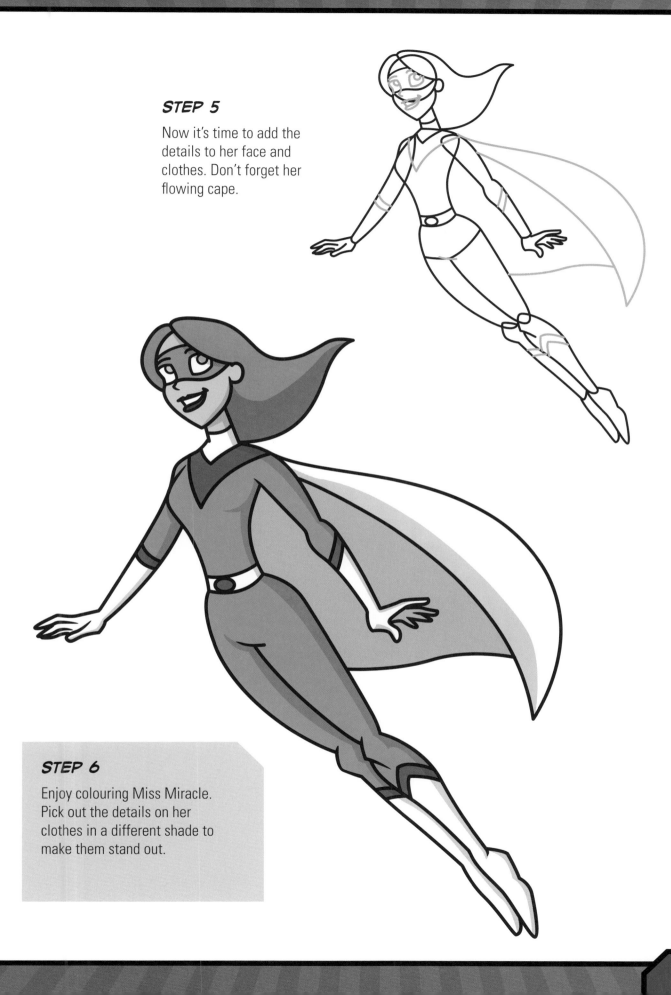

**STEP 5**

Now it's time to add the details to her face and clothes. Don't forget her flowing cape.

**STEP 6**

Enjoy colouring Miss Miracle. Pick out the details on her clothes in a different shade to make them stand out.

# WHIZZ-KID

**Whizz-Kid is a teenager who can move with lightning speed. Remember to add some speed lines to show her zipping along.**

### STEP 1

First, draw a peanut shape for Whizz-Kid's torso, then a circle for her head.

### STEP 2

Next, add carrot shapes for her upper arms and thighs.

### STEP 3

Add her chin and ear. Then draw her lower arms and legs to make it look as if she is racing to the rescue.

### STEP 4

Draw her feet, hands, neck, hair and eyes. Then add other details to her outfit as shown here.

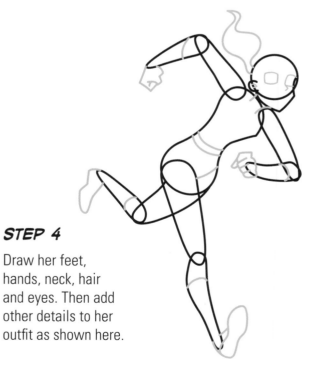

## STEP 5

Finish sketching her face, eye mask and hair. Add the sharp, jagged lines to her costume.

## STEP 6

Don't forget the lines and puffs of smoke to show that she is zooming into action. Then colour her however you like.

## SUPER TIP!

**Puffs of smoke show sudden movement. They are easy to draw:**

- In pencil, draw circles of different sizes. Overlap them until you have the shape and size of puff you want.

- Ink round the edge of the shape. Then rub out the inner parts to finish your puff of smoke.

# DOC PARADOX

**This evil scientist spends all day in his laboratory thinking of nasty ways to take over the world. His latest invention, the Impossi-tron, might help him do just that!**

### STEP 1

Start by drawing the Doc's lab coat.

### STEP 2

Next, add a big, round head, sleeves and trousers.

### STEP 3

Now draw his ear and big chin, hands and feet.

### STEP 4

Enjoy drawing that crazy hair. Then add his neck, the front of his lab coat and the bottom of the Impossi-tron.

## STEP 5

Next, draw the Doc's mad, googly eyes and face. Add the shirt details and the rest of the Impossi-tron.

## STEP 6

Draw energy waves coming from the top of the Impossi-tron. Then colour the Doc in. You could add a faint scar on this head.

# CAPTAIN FANTASTIC

**Captain Fantastic has everything a superhero needs. He's got super-strength, super-speed, super-good looks and a really super hairstyle.**

### STEP 1

First, draw the Captain's wide body and head. Then add a vertical line to find the centre of his head and neck. This will help you get everything in the right place.

### STEP 2

Draw two more lines from the top of his head to make a triangle. Then, add the bulging arms, legs and feet.

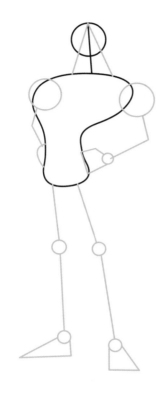

### STEP 3

Complete the arms and start to flesh out his legs. Add a mop of hair and a strong chin. Draw his belt and a line to form the bottom of his cape.

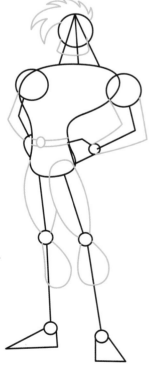

### STEP 4

Draw the rest of the cape. Add the eye mask, sloping shoulders and shins.

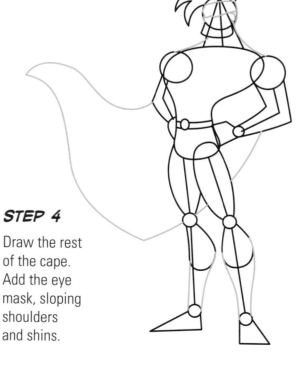

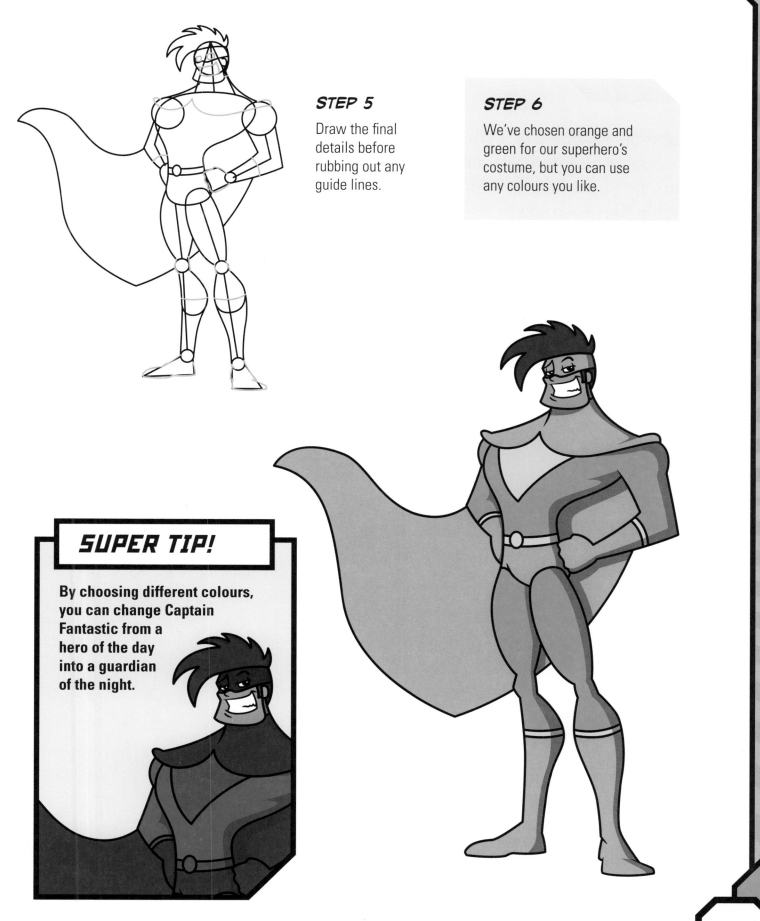

### STEP 5

Draw the final details before rubbing out any guide lines.

### STEP 6

We've chosen orange and green for our superhero's costume, but you can use any colours you like.

## SUPER TIP!

By choosing different colours, you can change Captain Fantastic from a hero of the day into a guardian of the night.

# MADAM MAYHEM

**Madam Mayhem is a villain who likes to cause chaos. She zooms along on her flying surfboard, making mischief wherever she goes.**

### STEP 1

Copy these shapes to make her body and head.

### STEP 2

Use two sausage shapes for her thighs and add a short line from her head to her body.

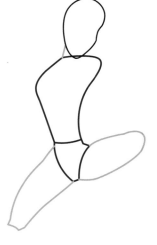

### STEP 3

Add her arms, lower legs and wing-like collar.

### STEP 4

Now it's time to draw her nose, spiky helmet, clenched fists and belt. Don't forget the all-important surfboard.

## STEP 5

Complete the surfboard. Draw her face and add the details to her gloves and boots. Draw a big cloud of smoke.

## STEP 6

Finally, bring your flying villain to life with spooky colours.

# THE CRUNCHER

This metal-jawed villain is super-mean.
The Cruncher's powerful body and deadly
jaws will crush anything in sight!

### STEP 1

First, draw his
big torso and his
pelvis. Add a small
circle for his head.

### STEP 2

Then draw his
chunky arms and
thighs like this.

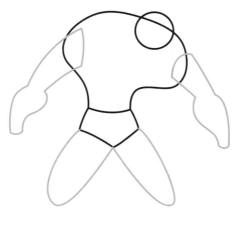

### STEP 3

Next, finish the
legs of his jeans and
add a belt buckle.
Draw clenched fists
before adding his
savage jaws.

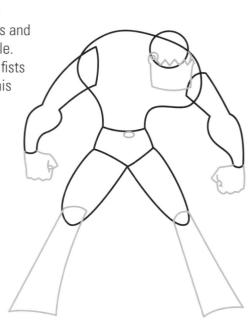

### STEP 4

Now give him spiky
hair and add the
details to his clothes.

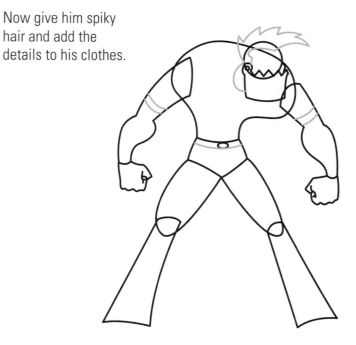

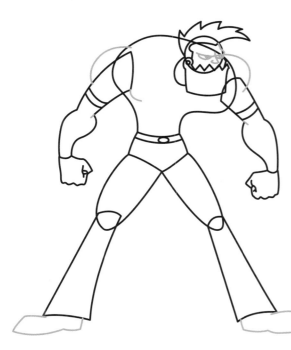

## STEP 5

Draw his face, giving him a heavy brow to make him look mean. Then, add bulging arm muscles and big feet.

## STEP 6

Now you can add colour. Use shading to show off his large chest and arm muscles.

# GALAXY GIRL

**Galaxy Girl is a daring space traveller. Armed with a cosmic wand, her mission is to protect the world from alien attack.**

## STEP 1

Begin by drawing Galaxy Girl's head, torso and thighs.

## STEP 2

Next, draw her arms and lower legs like this, so it looks as if she is floating in space.

## STEP 3

Draw a circle around her head for the space helmet. Then add shoulder and knee pads. Don't forget her hands, and her other foot.

## STEP 4

Add the cosmic wand before drawing her hairline, nose and the details to her outfit. Draw an oxygen pack on her back.

## STEP 5

Draw her face and the curved breathing tube. Add oval reflection shapes to her helmet. Draw some curved lines to show the cosmic wand sending a signal.

## STEP 6

Finally, add some cool colours that will make Galaxy Girl look out of this world.

## SUPER TIP!

Giving your heroes cool space helmets is easy if you follow these simple steps:

- Draw a simple circle around your character's head.

- Add small circles or blob shapes on one side to hint at reflections.

- Add a small curved shape on the other side to show the shape of the helmet.

# ROCKET RACER

Rocket Racer wears roller blades and a rocket backpack to blast him along at super-speed. He's so fast that bad guys don't even see him coming!

### STEP 1

Draw a rounded shape like a balloon for his head. Add a powerful torso and superhero underwear.

### STEP 2

Next, add his thighs and folded arms.

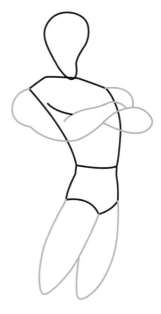

### STEP 3

Add a neck line. Then draw a large pair of cool goggles and muscly lower legs.

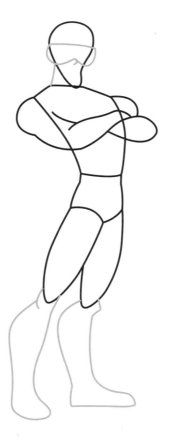

### STEP 4

Draw a helmet fin and add the straps for his backpack. Then begin to draw his roller blades.

## STEP 5

Complete his backpack and roller blades. Then add the final details to his costume.

## STEP 6

Use bright red and yellow details to bring your hero to life.

# ACTION POSES

The methods shown in this chapter are perfect if you want to draw a character in the same pose every time. But what if you want to draw the same character in lots of different poses?

## STEP 1: START WITH A STICKMAN

Place a piece of paper over a character you like and trace it as a stickman. How big or long are the arms, legs, head and body?

## STEP 2: STRIKE A POSE!

Draw a new stickman in a different position, making sure that the arms, legs, head and body are exactly the same size as in your first traced picture.

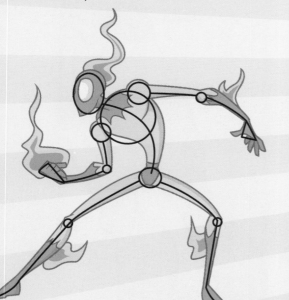

## STEP 3: ACTION!

Now you can flesh out your character in the new pose. Once you are happy with what you have drawn in pencil, add inks and colours.

# DRAWING MANGA

Manga is a style of drawing from Japan. Manga artists create lots of unusual characters and monsters to tell their stories. This chapter will show you how to draw some for yourself.

# VILLAIN

**There's no doubt that this guy is a villain. His pale, sneering face and red robotic eye make him look really scary!**

### STEP 1

Start by drawing the shape of your villain's long body and legs. Add a head with a pointy chin.

### STEP 2

Then draw two straight lines to make his legs and waist.

### STEP 3

Next, draw his arms and feet. Add two ears and two lines for his nose. Join the head to the body with a neck. Draw two short lines for the collar of his jacket.

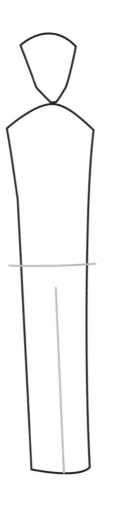

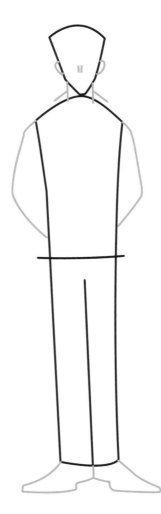

## STEP 6

Colour him in using shades such as purple, red, black and blue. Use shading around the edges so that he looks 3-D.

## STEP 4

Add long, curved lines to make the shape and folds of his suit. Don't forget his hairline and that scary robotic eye.

## STEP 5

Now you can add the crazy hair, shirt, tie and suit outlines. Add the rest of the robotic eye and a small mouth. Finally, finish his trousers.

## SUPER TIP!

**You can make your villain look even more scary by giving him incredible mind powers.**

- Draw a scribbly semi-circle around his head. Then add long, wavy lines, spreading outwards.

# GIRL GENIUS

With her big glasses and white lab coat, Girl Genius looks super brainy. You could give her more 'clever' accessories, such as books, if you want.

### STEP 1

First, draw the girl's white lab coat and her head.

### STEP 2

Next, draw two sausage shapes for the tops of her arms.

### STEP 3

Add forearms, wide trousers and the outline of her hair.

### STEP 4

Draw her face and neck. Add hands, feet, and the opening of her lab coat.

## STEP 5

Add her glasses, the two flasks and the details on her face and coat.

## STEP 6

Finally, colour her in. Leave her jacket white so that it looks like a scientist's lab coat.

# FIRE SPIRIT

The Fire Spirit is an evil creature who can use his magical powers to control fire. He has a long face, pointy ears and a nasty grin.

### STEP 1

First, draw a tall shape like this for the spirit's robe.

### STEP 2

Add his pointy head and the wide sleeves of his robe.

### STEP 3

Draw those long, pointy ears, his neck, claw-like fingers, and flames of fire around his feet.

### STEP 4

Now draw the flames shooting out of his hands and around his feet. The flames should curl upwards.

## STEP 5

Draw his evil eyes, tiny nose and sneaky smile. Give his eyes tiny black pupils to make him look really wicked. Then add lines to suggest the folds in his long, flowing robe.

## STEP 6

Colour your villain with spooky purple, hot red and yellow.

## SUPER TIP!

- When colouring in flames, start with a yellow colour in the middle parts of the flame.

- Add red and orange colours as you move towards the outside of your flames.

# MARTIAL ARTIST

This martial artist is crouching low to the ground, ready to attack. His special pose and determined face show us he's a skilled fighter.

### STEP 1

First, draw a peanut shape for his body and a pot shape for his hips. Add a small circle for his head.

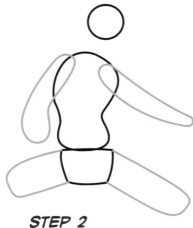

### STEP 2

Add sausage shapes for his arms and thighs.

### STEP 3

Draw a pointed chin, graceful hands and flowing lower legs.

### STEP 4

Carefully draw feet, cuffs and hair.

## STEP 5

Add his narrow eyes, nose and serious mouth. Then draw the final details of his clothing.

## SUPER TIP!

**The strapping on this martial artist's leg is easy to draw. Just follow these steps:**

- First draw your straps as simple crosses down his leg.

- Add lines on either side.

- Erase the cross you started with and colour in the straps.

## STEP 6

Colour your character. Use shading to make him stand out from the page.

# MINI MONSTER

The big-eyes of this mini monster make him look cute. But who is he? Does he fight other mini monsters in an arena, or is he a pet? You decide!

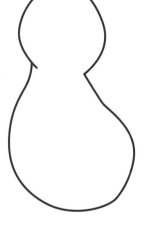

### STEP 1

Firstly, draw a shape like a wobbly peanut.

### STEP 2

Draw two large leaf-shaped ears, a curve for a nose, and two club-like arms.

### STEP 3

Add a long curved tail, back legs and a pointy forehead.

### STEP 4

Now it's time to draw his big eyes, small mouth, and claws. Sketch in details for the ear on the left and the back paws.

## STEP 5

Add long whiskers. Then cover your mini monster's body in spots… or stripes if you prefer.

## STEP 6

Now colour your mini monster in any shade you like. When it comes to monsters, there are no rules. Anything goes!

# SAMURAI

Samurai were brave Japanese warriors. This one is tall with a square jaw, which makes him look proud. He wears a green robe and clogs, and carries a long samurai sword.

### STEP 1

First, draw a long, curved rectangle shape for the samurai's robe. Add a small circle for his head.

### STEP 2

Draw a square jaw and two lines for his neck. Then draw sausage shapes for his arms.

### STEP 3

Next, add his shoulders and the gaping sleeves of his robe. Draw a belt and his feet.

## STEP 4

Draw his hairline, hands and wooden clogs. Add the edging to his robe.

## STEP 5

Draw his face, long sword, and topknot. Finish off the wooden clogs.

## STEP 6

Finally, colour in your samurai. A strong green colour makes his robe stand out.

# LITTLE OLD LADY

This lady is so happy. Her round body makes her look very cuddly and kind. Her wide open mouth and closed eyes show that she's really laughing.

### STEP 1

Draw a mushroom shape for her upper body and a pebble shape for her head.

### STEP 2

Draw a thick shape for her lower body.

### STEP 3

Add her hairline and mouth. Then draw the wide sleeves of her robe.

### STEP 4

Carefully draw her hands, hair, tiny nose and belt.

## STEP 5

Add the final details, including curves for her eyes and the bowl of noodles.

## STEP 6

Colour the little old lady in nice soft colours.

# CAT GIRL

**This manga character has a cat's furry tail, big ears and long whiskers. She also has a playful expression – just like a cat!**

### STEP 1

First, draw an oval for her head, and this curved, pointy shape for her body.

### STEP 2

Draw two sausage shapes for her legs and long arms.

### STEP 3

Add her cat-like ears and the rest of her legs.

### STEP 4

Her 'S'-shaped tail comes next. Then add her neck, the details of her clothing, her hands, feet and face. Don't forget those big manga eyes!

## STEP 5

Draw her shaggy hair wrapping round the front of her ears. That way she looks more like a cat. Add details to her cuff and shoes.

## STEP 6

You could add multicoloured streaks to her hair or leave it bright pink like this. Her whiskers are the finishing touch!

# SUMO WRESTLER

Sumo wrestlers are very large and heavy. This one squats down low as he faces his opponent. During fights, a sumo wears a silk loincloth called a 'mawashi'.

### STEP 1

Sumos are large so start the body and head with these big round shapes.

### STEP 2

Add the very rounded arms and legs, and his mawashi.

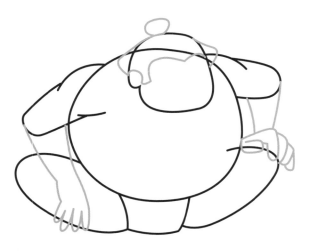

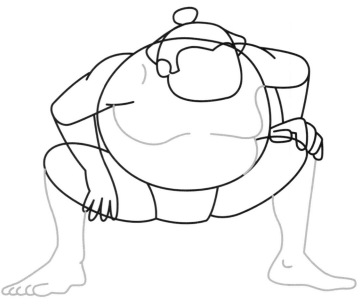

### STEP 3

Add the rest of his arms and hands. Then draw the sumo's hairstyle.

### STEP 4

Add details to his chest. Finish off the legs and feet.

## STEP 5

Draw his face and hair. He has heavy eyebrows, a wide mouth and a fierce expression. Add the pieces hanging down from his mawashi. They are called 'sagari'.

## STEP 6

Sumo wrestlers believe the colour of their mawashi affects their luck in matches. Red must be this sumo's lucky colour!

# SPECIAL EFFECTS

## FUN FEATURE

You can make your drawings more exciting by adding special effects. It will also make your stories more fun if your characters have special powers. Here are some basic effects you can use on your creations:

### LIGHTNING BLAST

Give your characters lightning powers! Add blue-coloured jagged lines coming from their hands or weapons. This will make it look like they are shooting lightning bolts.

### SPARKLE-RIFFIC

Why not give some characters magical powers? Add sparkles of different-sized stars around their hands, like this.

### HEATING IT UP

Give your characters fire power by adding flames. Flames are rounded at the bottom but shaped like wavy spikes at the top. Colour the centre of the flames in a light yellow.

# DRAWING
# ROBOTS AND MONSTERS

In the final chapter you'll learn how to draw lots of scary robots and monsters. You can then use these techniques to create some weird and wonderful characters of your own.

# MEGAMORPH

**Megamorph has huge metal wings and mighty arms and legs. This giant robot is easy to draw, but use a ruler as there are lots of straight lines.**

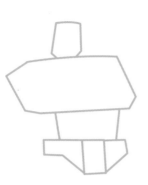

### STEP 1

First, draw Megamorph's chest and lower body. Then add his small square head.

### STEP 2

Now carefully draw Megamorph's shoulders and upper legs. Add ears and chest details.

### STEP 3

Next, add his big shoulder guards and neck. Draw his rounded knees and chunky lower legs.

### STEP 4

Add his arms, feet and mighty fists. Don't forget the line that goes down the middle of his chest.

## STEP 5

The final details are his face and those big pointed wings.

## STEP 6

Colour him using a mixture of blues, greys and bright colours. Add some details to the wings.

# DRAGON

Dragons are huge, fire-breathing monsters that look a lot like dinosaurs. Try to make yours look as terrifying as possible.

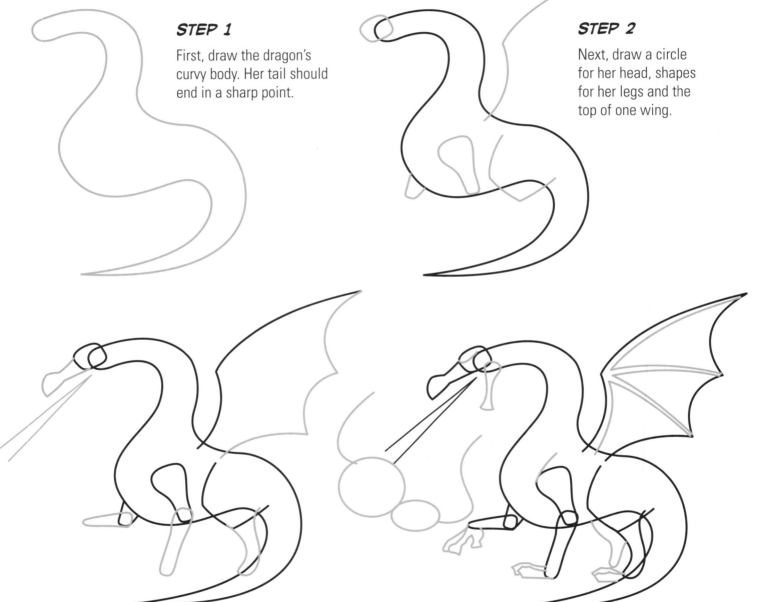

**STEP 1**

First, draw the dragon's curvy body. Her tail should end in a sharp point.

**STEP 2**

Next, draw a circle for her head, shapes for her legs and the top of one wing.

**STEP 3**

Add her long jaw, curves to the wing, and her lower legs. The two lines coming from her head are the beginning of her fiery breath.

**STEP 4**

Draw her lower jaw, clawed feet and details to her wing. Add two circles and wavy lines for her fiery breath.

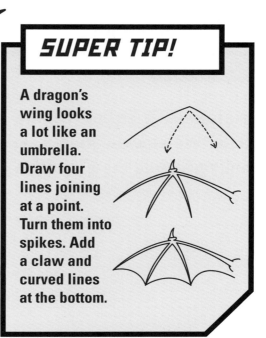

## SUPER TIP!

A dragon's wing looks a lot like an umbrella. Draw four lines joining at a point. Turn them into spikes. Add a claw and curved lines at the bottom.

## STEP 5

Bring your dragon to life by adding her razor-sharp teeth, claws, her second wing and the details to her head. Don't forget the claw on her wing. Then, finish her dragon breath.

## STEP 6

Add the triangular spines that run along the dragon's back. Then finish her off in bold, bright colours.

# FUNNY ALIEN

**This creature is called 'Blinky'. He is an alien monster with seven googly eyes. He has a big, friendly grin and thick, orange fur.**

### STEP 1

First, draw this shape to make your monster's body.

### STEP 2

Add Blinky's wide head. Then draw his arms – one long and one curved.

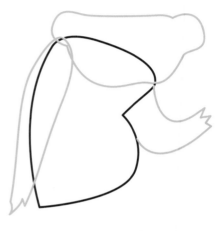

### STEP 3

Now it's time to add lots of circles for his eyes. Then draw his legs, leaving a jagged line for his fur.

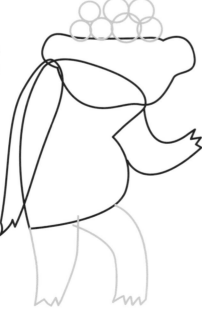

### STEP 4

Add big, chunky hands and feet. Draw on claws. Give him a tuft of hair on top of his head.

### STEP 5

Dot his body with shaggy tufts of fur. Then give him a wide, toothy grin. Draw black pupils on his eyes. Put them in different positions to make him look really monstrous.

### STEP 6

Finish off your monster by colouring him in. The brighter, the better!

# RETRO ROBOT

**Retro Robot is a happy, shiny robot with a slightly old-fashioned look. Use your pencils and pens to capture his wide toothy smile, bendy arms and large, clunky feet.**

### STEP 1

Start by copying these shapes for your robot's head and body.

### STEP 2

Add small circles for his shoulders and hips, before drawing his long, skinny legs.

### STEP 3

Draw his big eyes and wide mouth. Then add his long, bendy arms.

### STEP 4

Give him an antenna, hands and feet. Don't forget that toothy grin.

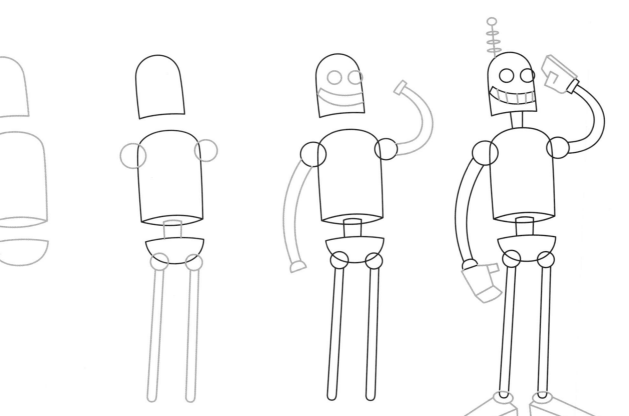

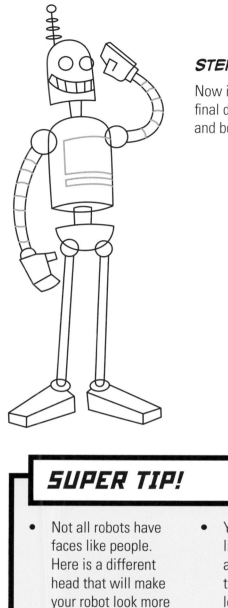

## STEP 5

Now it's time to add the final details to his arms and body.

## STEP 6

Finally, add big black dots to give him googly eyes, before colouring him in.

## SUPER TIP!

- Not all robots have faces like people. Here is a different head that will make your robot look more like a machine.

- You can add little cameras and lights like this. He doesn't look so friendly now, does he?

# FRANKENSTEIN'S MONSTER

**This monster is a crazy science experiment gone wrong! Dr Frankenstein made this creature by joining bits of bodies together with metal bolts. Now it's your turn to make him!**

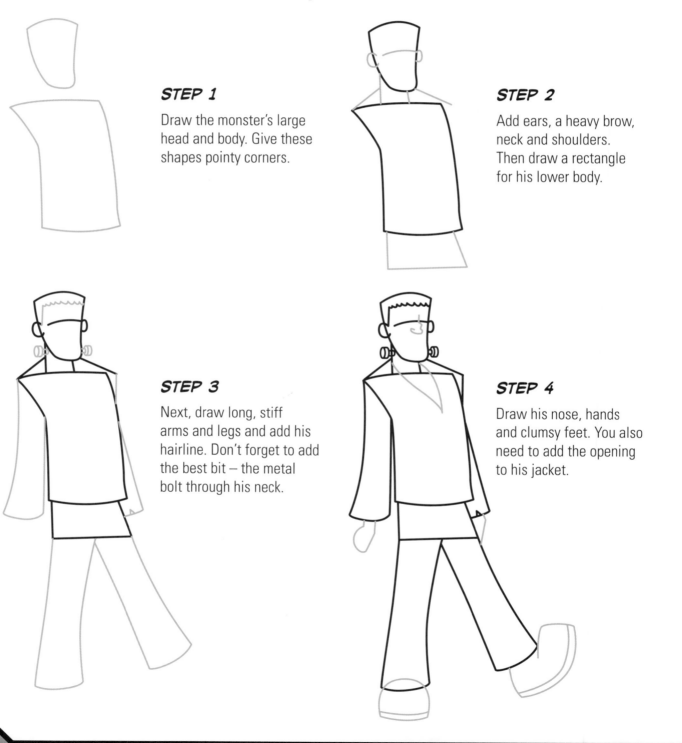

### STEP 1

Draw the monster's large head and body. Give these shapes pointy corners.

### STEP 2

Add ears, a heavy brow, neck and shoulders. Then draw a rectangle for his lower body.

### STEP 3

Next, draw long, stiff arms and legs and add his hairline. Don't forget to add the best bit — the metal bolt through his neck.

### STEP 4

Draw his nose, hands and clumsy feet. You also need to add the opening to his jacket.

## STEP 5

Draw his fingers, before adding the details to his face and clothes. Don't forget the big scar across his forehead.

## STEP 6

Your monster is now ready to colour. Use a gross green colour for his skin. GRRRRR!

# COMPACTO THE CRUSHERBOT

**Compacto moves around on big, rolling caterpillar tracks. He has huge, crushing plates instead of hands. His mission? To crush anything that gets in his way!**

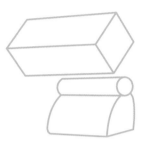

### STEP 1

Begin by drawing a large block for his chest, a tube shape for his waist and curved shape for his lower body.

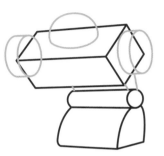

### STEP 2

Next, draw his head and round shoulders. Then add lines to join the two parts of his body.

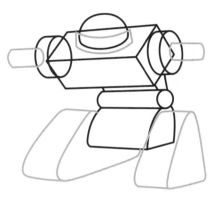

### STEP 3

Draw a caterpillar track on either side of his body. Add upper arms and a neckband.

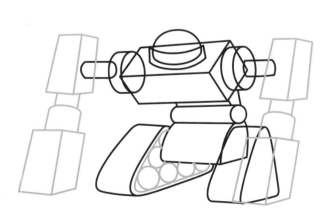

### STEP 4

Add the circles that turn the track around. Then draw his heavy metal arms.

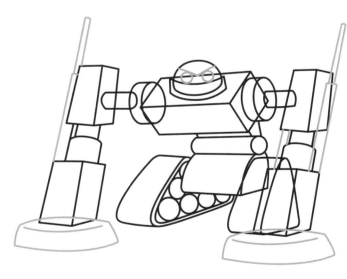

### STEP 5

Now it's time to add the eyes and other details, including the heavy crushing plates.

## STEP 6

Add the final details to the tracks and other parts of the Crusherbot. He's now ready to colour in.

## SUPER TIP!

**Follow these instructions to make your robot look like he's really pounding the ground:**

- Start with your basic crushing plate shape. Add some small lines to show the impact on the ground.

- If you want to show even more destruction, add some long cracks between the lines.

- You can even add some small puffs of smoke to really finish it off.

# Q-T BOT

**Q-T Bot is the perfect robot friend. His special antennae mean you can call him any time you need help. This cheerful robot may be small, but he's stronger than he looks!**

## STEP 1

Use a coin to draw a big circle for his head. Then use a ruler to copy these shapes for his body and thighs.

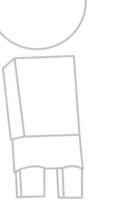

## STEP 2

Take your time to draw his upper arms and lower legs. Don't forget to leave room for his big robot feet.

## STEP 3

Now add lower arms, feet and big googly eyes. You also need to draw a line down the side of the leg on the right.

## STEP 4

Give Q-T Bot a little mouth and helmet. Then draw shoulders, arm joints and a line for his waist.

## STEP 5

Add chunky fingers, earphones and antennae. Draw a line down the side of his pants.

## STEP 6

Finally, draw a planet on his chest and colour him in. We've used blue, but you could choose any colour you like.

# WEREWOLF

In horror stories, a werewolf is a creature that's part human, part wolf. He has a man's body and wolf-like features such as a long bushy tail and razor-sharp teeth.

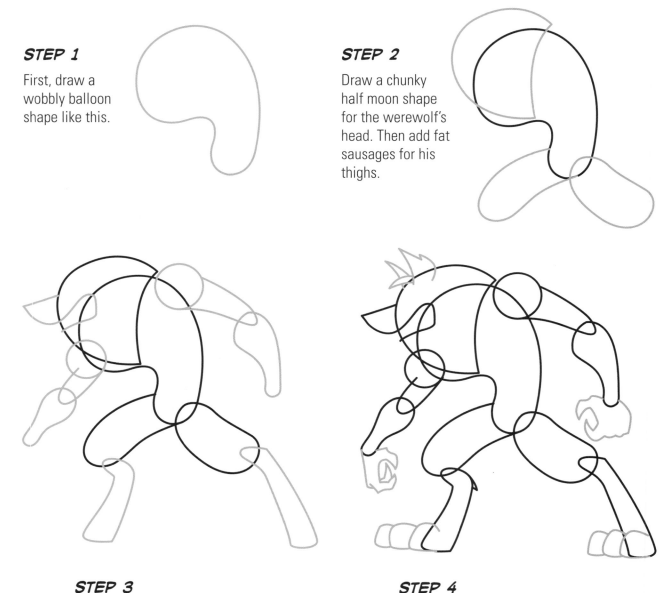

**STEP 1**

First, draw a wobbly balloon shape like this.

**STEP 2**

Draw a chunky half moon shape for the werewolf's head. Then add fat sausages for his thighs.

**STEP 3**

Draw his long muzzle and mouth, his shoulders and arms, and lower legs.

**STEP 4**

Next, draw his hairy ears, hands and big wolf feet.

## STEP 5

Now it's time to add his long tail, eyes and ragged trousers. Then add lots of tufty bits of fur.

## STEP 6

When you colour in your werewolf, remember to add lots of shading to make him really stand out. AWOOOOOOOO!

# VAMPIRE GIRL

With her well-cut suit and shiny black hair, Vampire Girl looks chic and stylish. But stay away from those fangs... because this girl bites!

### STEP 1

Begin by drawing her slim body and head. Add a pointed ear.

### STEP 2

Draw long legs followed by her thin arms.

### STEP 3

Join her head and body with a neck. Continue the lines of her neck to make the front opening of her jacket, and add her hands.

## STEP 4

Give her a wide collar, large cuffs and a belt buckle. Then add her long, straight hair.

## STEP 5

Finish off your drawing with her vampire face and hairline. Don't forget her fangs and the bat necklace.

## STEP 6

Now colour Vampire Girl using dark, dangerous colours!

# DRAWING TEXTURES

## FUN FEATURE

A texture is the way a surface looks and feels. It can be rough, smooth, shiny, dull, furry or scaly. Here are some simple tips to help you give your drawings texture:

### OLD AND RUSTY

To make a robot look old and rusty, add dirty streaks of oil and patches of rust. Use green and brown pens or paint.

### SHINY AND NEW

To make a robot shine, add white highlights to one side of every edge. Then draw white patches with star shapes on them. Now your robot looks as if it's brand new!

### HAIRY AND SCARY

To make a monster look furry, draw rough zigzags along the outline. Then, add more zigzag shapes to the body here and there.

### SMOOTH AND SCALY

Add patches of small half circles at different points all over the monster's body. This will make the monster look scaly all over.

# Holt Literature & Language Arts

**Fourth Course**

## UNIVERSAL ACCESS Interactive Reading

- **Word Analysis, Fluency, and Systematic Vocabulary Development**
- **Reading Comprehension**
- **Literary Response and Analysis**

**HOLT, RINEHART AND WINSTON**

A Harcourt Education Company

**Austin** • Orlando • Chicago • New York • Toronto • London • San Diego

# Credits

## Editorial

**Project Directors:** Kathleen Daniel, Juliana Koenig
**Editor:** Amy Fleming
**Managing Editor:** Mike Topp
**Manager of Editorial Services:** Abigail Winograd
**Senior Product Manager:** Don Wulbrecht
**Editorial Staff:** Susan Kent Cakars, Susan Joseph, Brenda Sanabria, Sari Wilson, Michael Zakhar
**Project Administration:** Elizabeth LaManna
**Editorial Support:** Renée Benitez, Louise Fernandez, Laurie Muir
**Editorial Permissions:** David Smith, Carrie Jones
**Conceptual Framework and Writing:** e2 Publishing Services, Inc.

## Art, Design, and Production

**Director:** Athena Blackorby
**Senior Design Director:** Betty Mintz
**Series Design:** Proof Positive/Farrowlyne Associates, Inc.
**Design and Electronic Files:** Proof Positive/Farrowlyne Associates, Inc.
**Photo Research:** Proof Positive/Farrowlyne Associates, Inc.
**Production Manager:** Catherine Gessner
**Production Coordinator:** Myles Gorospe

Printed in the United States of America
ISBN 0-03-065032-1

17  082  11 10 09 08

# Contents

## • PART ONE •
## LITERARY RESPONSE AND ANALYSIS . . . . . . . . . . . . . . . . . . . . . . . . 1

## CONSUMER, WORKPLACE, AND PUBLIC DOCUMENTS

## CHAPTER 8:
## LITERARY CRITICISM: EVALUATING STYLE

**Reading Standard 1.1** Identify and use the literal and figurative meanings of words and understand word derivations.

**Reading Standard 3.11** Evaluate the aesthetic qualities of style, including the impact of diction and figurative language on tone, mood, and theme, using the terminology of literary criticism. (Aesthetic approach)

## CHAPTER 9: LITERARY CRITICISM:
## BIOGRAPHICAL AND HISTORICAL APPROACH

**Reading Standard 1.2** Distinguish between the denotative and connotative meanings of words and interpret the connotative power of words.

**Reading Standard 1.3 (Grade 8 Review)** Use word meanings within the appropriate context and show ability to verify those meanings by definition, restatement, example, comparison, or contrast.

**Reading Standard 3.7 (Grade 8 Review)** Analyze a work of literature, showing how it reflects the heritage, traditions, attitudes, and beliefs of its author. (Biographical approach)

**Reading Standard 3.12** Analyze the way in which a work of literature is related to the themes and issues of its historical period. (Historical approach)

## CHAPTER 10: DRAMA

**Reading Standard 1.2** Distinguish between the denotative and connotative meanings of words and interpret the connotative power of words.

**Reading Standard 1.2 (Grade 8 Review)** Understand the most important points in the history of English language and use common word origins to determine the historical influences on English word meanings.

**Reading Standard 3.1** Articulate the relationship between the expressed purposes and the characteristics of different forms of dramatic literature (e.g., comedy, tragedy, drama, dramatic monologue).

**Reading Standard 3.10** Identify and describe the function of dialogue, scene designs, soliloquies, asides, and character foils in dramatic literature.

## • PART TWO •
## READING COMPREHENSION

**Reading Standard 2.1** Analyze the structure and format of functional workplace documents, including the graphics and headers, and explain how authors use the features to achieve their purposes.

**Reading Standard 2.2** Prepare a bibliography of reference materials for a report using a variety of consumer, workplace, and public documents.

**Reading Standard 2.3** Generate relevant questions about readings on issues that can be researched.

**Reading Standard 2.4** Synthesize the content from several sources or works by a single author dealing with a single issue; paraphrase the ideas and connect them to other sources and related topics to demonstrate comprehension.

**Reading Standard 2.5** Extend ideas presented in primary or secondary sources through original analysis, evaluation, and elaboration.

**Reading Standard 2.6** Demonstrate use of sophisticated learning tools by following technical directions (e.g., those found with graphic calculators and specialized software programs and in access guides to World Wide Web sites on the Internet).

**Reading Standard 2.7** Critique the logic of functional documents by examining the sequence of information and procedures in anticipation of possible reader misunderstandings.

**Reading Standard 2.8** Evaluate the credibility of an author's argument or defense of a claim by critiquing the relationship between generalizations and evidence, the comprehensiveness of evidence, and the way in which an author's intent affects the structure and tone of the text (e.g., in professional journals, editorials, political speeches, primary source material).

# To the Student

## A Book for You

*Teachers open the door, but you must enter by yourself.*
—Chinese Proverb

Reading is an interactive process. The more you put into it, the more you get out of it. This book is designed to do just that—help you interact with the selections you read by marking them up, asking your own questions, taking notes, recording your own ideas, and responding to the questions of others.

## A Book Designed for Your Success

*Interactive Reading* goes hand-in-hand with *Holt Literature and Language Arts.* It is designed to help you interact with the selections and master the California Language Arts Standards.

To do this, the book has two parts that each follow a simple format:

### Part 1    Literary Response and Analysis

Increasing your understanding of literature is a major goal of the California Language Arts Standards. To help you master how to respond to, analyze, evaluate, and interpret literature, *Interactive Reading* provides—

For each chapter:
- The academic vocabulary you need to know to master the literature standards for the chapter, defined for ready reference and use.
- The first selection from the corresponding chapter in *Holt Literature and Language Arts* reprinted in an interactive format to support and guide your reading.
- A new selection for you to read and respond to, enabling you to apply and extend your skills and build toward independence.

For each selection:
- A Before You Read page that preteaches the literary focus and provides a reading skill to help you comprehend the selection.
- A Vocabulary Development page that preteaches selection vocabulary and provides a vocabulary skill to use while reading the prose selections.
- Literature printed in an interactive format to guide your reading and help you respond to text.
- A graphic organizer that helps you understand the literary focus of the selection.
- Standards Review pages that help you practice test-taking skills while applying the standards.

## Part 2    Reading Comprehension

Reading informational texts and documents is another major thrust of the California Language Arts Standards. To help you master how to read informational materials, this book contains—

For Informational Materials:
- The academic vocabulary you need to know to master the informational standards, defined for ready reference and use.
- New informational selections for each standard in interactive format to guide your reading and help you respond to the text.
- A Before You Read page that preteaches the informational focus and provides a reading skill to help you comprehend the selection.
- A graphic organizer that helps you understand the informational focus of the selection.
- Standards Review pages that help you practice test-taking skills while applying the standards.

For Consumer, Workplace, and Public Documents:
- The academic vocabulary you need to know to master the standards, defined for ready reference and use.
- New documents for each standard in interactive format to guide your reading and help you respond to the text.
- A Before You Read page that preteaches the document focus and defines specialized terms.
- A Standards Review page that helps you practice test-taking skills while applying the standard.

## A Book for Your Own Thoughts and Feelings

Reading is about *you*. It is about connecting your thoughts and feelings to the thoughts and feelings of the writer. Make this book your own. The more you give of yourself to your reading, the more you will get out of it. We encourage you to write in it. Jot down how you feel about the selection. Question the text. Note details you think need to be cleared up or topics you would like to learn more about.

Keep track of what you have learned and what you have read with the following tools at the back of the book:
- A Word List
- A Checklist for Standards Mastery

# A Walk Through the Book

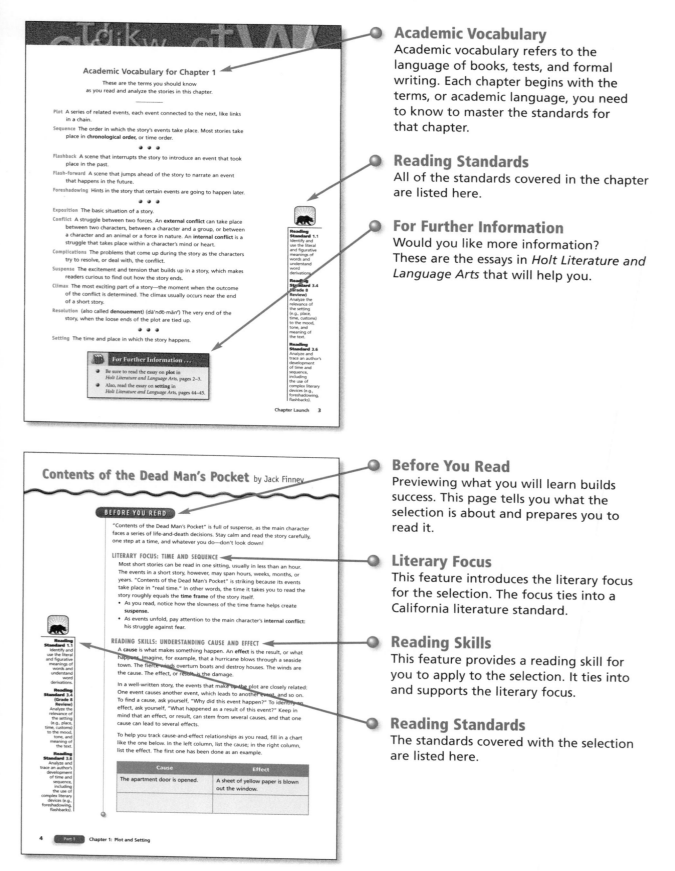

## Academic Vocabulary
Academic vocabulary refers to the language of books, tests, and formal writing. Each chapter begins with the terms, or academic language, you need to know to master the standards for that chapter.

## Reading Standards
All of the standards covered in the chapter are listed here.

## For Further Information
Would you like more information? These are the essays in *Holt Literature and Language Arts* that will help you.

## Before You Read
Previewing what you will learn builds success. This page tells you what the selection is about and prepares you to read it.

## Literary Focus
This feature introduces the literary focus for the selection. The focus ties into a California literature standard.

## Reading Skills
This feature provides a reading skill for you to apply to the selection. It ties into and supports the literary focus.

## Reading Standards
The standards covered with the selection are listed here.

## Vocabulary Development

Vocabulary words for the selection are pretaught. Each entry gives the pronunciation and definition of the word as well as a context sentence.

## Vocabulary Skills

When you read, you not only have to recognize words but also decode them and determine meaning. This feature introduces a vocabulary skill to use to understand words in the selection. It ties into and supports the vocabulary standard.

---

**SHORT STORY**

### VOCABULARY DEVELOPMENT

**PREVIEW SELECTION VOCABULARY**
Preview the following words from the story before you begin reading.

**projection** (prō·jek′shən) n.: something that juts out from a surface.

Tom's paper was trapped between the ledge and the decorative **projection** sticking out from the wall.

**discarding** (dis·kärd′iŋ) v. used as adj.: abandoning; getting rid of.

He rejected one plan after another, **discarding** all useless ideas.

**confirmation** (kän′fər·mā′shən) n.: proof.

As **confirmation** that he could walk on the ledge, he made sure that it was wide enough to fit his shoe.

**exhalation** (eks′hə·lā′shən) n.: something breathed out; breath.

After holding his breath, Tom felt an **exhalation** of air as he breathed again.

**imperceptibly** (im′pər·sep′tə·blē) adv.: in such a slight way as to be almost unnoticeable.

Tom moved along the ledge **imperceptibly**, taking tiny, cautious steps.

**rebounded** (ri·bound′id) v.: bounced back.

After he broke the window, Tom's arm **rebounded**, bouncing backward from the force of the blow.

**interminable** (in·tur′mi·nə·bal) adj.: endless.

Although the time seemed **interminable**, Tom had been on the ledge only a few minutes.

**irrelevantly** (i·rel′ə·vənt·lē) adv.: in a way not relating to the point or situation.

Tom thought **irrelevantly** about the apartment furnishings, as if the cozy rooms could stop him from plunging to his death.

**incomprehensible** (in·käm′prē·hen′sə·bal) adj.: not understandable.

The puzzling sheet of paper in his pocket would be **incomprehensible** to anyone who found his body.

**unimpeded** (un′im·pēd′id) adj.: not blocked; unobstructed.

With nothing blocking it, the yellow paper flew **unimpeded** out the window.

### PREFIXES

Just by adding a few letters up front, you can turn *appear* into *reappear*, *likely* into *unlikely*, and *freezing* into *subfreezing*. *Re–*, *un–*, and *sub–* are **prefixes**, word parts that attach to the front of a word or word root to change its meaning. *Re–* means "again"; *un–* means "not"; *sub–* means "below."

As you read, look for words with these or other prefixes. Use your knowledge of prefixes to help you figure out the meanings of some unfamiliar words.

Contents of the Dead Man's Pocket **5**

---

## Side-Column Notes

Each selection is accompanied by notes in the side column that guide your interaction with the selection. Many notes ask you to underline or circle in the text itself. Others provide lines on which you can write your responses to questions.

## Types of Notes

The different types of notes throughout the selection help you—

- Focus on literary elements
- Apply the reading skill
- Apply the vocabulary skill
- Think critically about the selection
- Develop word knowledge
- Build vocabulary
- Build fluency

---

# Contents of the Dead Man's Pocket

### Jack Finney

**WORD STUDY**

*Portable* is usually an adjective, meaning "able to be carried." Here, in line 3, the word is a noun, naming a thing. Read on, and circle what *portable* refers to.

At the little living-room desk Tom Benecke rolled two sheets of flimsy[1] and a heavier top sheet, carbon paper sandwiched between them, into his portable. *Interoffice Memo*, the top sheet was headed, and he typed tomorrow's date just below this; then he glanced at a creased yellow sheet, covered with his own handwriting, beside the typewriter. "Hot in here," he muttered to himself. Then from the short hallway at his back he heard the muffled clang of wire coat hangers in the bedroom closet, and at this reminder of what his wife was doing he thought: hot, no—
10 guilty conscience.

He got up, shoving his hands into the back pockets of his gray wash slacks, stepped to the living-room window beside the desk and stood breathing on the glass, watching the expanding circlet of mist, staring down through the autumn night at Lexington Avenue,[2] eleven stories below. He was a tall, lean, dark-haired young man in a pullover sweater, who looked as though he had played not football, probably, but basketball in college. Now he placed the heels of his hands against the top edge of the lower window frame and shoved upward. But as
20 usual the window didn't budge, and he had to lower his hands and then shoot them hard upward to jolt the window open a few inches. He dusted his hands, muttering.

**SETTING**

Setting is the time and place of a story. Underline the words in line 15 that tell how far above the street Tom's apartment is.

---

1. **flimsy** n.: thin paper used for typing carbon copies. Before computers and copying machines, copies of business communications were made with carbon paper.
2. **Lexington Avenue:** one of the main streets in New York City.

"Contents of the Dead Man's Pocket" by Jack Finney. Copyright © 1956 by Crowell-Collier Company, copyright renewed © 1984 by Jack Finney. Reprinted by permission of Don Congdon Associates, Inc.

**6** Part 1 Chapter 1: Plot and Setting

## Vocabulary

The vocabulary words that were pretaught are defined in the side column and set in boldface in the selection, allowing you to see them in context.

---

VOCABULARY

**projection** (prō-jĕk′shən) *n.*: something that juts out from a surface.

*Pro–* is a Latin prefix meaning "forward"; the root *ject* means "throw" or "thrust."

**discarding** (dĭs-kärd′ĭŋ) *v.* used as *adj.*: abandoning; getting rid of.

IDENTIFY

Pause at line 124. Why is the yellow paper so important to Tom? Underline the details that tell you why.

PREDICT

After reading lines 125–141, what do you predict Tom will do?

_____

_____

_____

_____

_____

_____

_____

_____

_____

ornament of the ledge by the breeze that moved past Tom Benecke's face.

100    He knelt at the window and stared at the yellow paper for a full minute or more, waiting for it to move, to slide off the ledge and fall, hoping he could follow its course to the street, and then hurry down in the elevator and retrieve it. But it didn't move, and then he saw that the paper was caught firmly between a **projection** of the convoluted⁴ corner ornament and the ledge. He thought about the poker from the fireplace, then the broom, then the mop—**discarding** each thought as it occurred to him. There was nothing in the apartment long enough to reach that paper.

110    It was hard for him to understand that he actually had to abandon it—it was ridiculous—and he began to curse. Of all the papers on his desk, why did it have to be this one in particular! On four long Saturday afternoons he had stood in supermarkets, counting the people who passed certain displays, and the results were scribbled on that yellow sheet. From stacks of trade publications, gone over page by page in snatched half hours at work and during evenings at home, he had copied facts, quotations, and figures onto that sheet. And he had carried it with him to the Public Library on Fifth Avenue, where he'd spent a dozen

120    lunch hours and early evenings adding more. All were needed to support and lend authority to his idea for a new grocery-store display method; without them his idea was a mere opinion. And there they all lay, in his own improvised shorthand—countless hours of work—out there on the ledge.

For many seconds he believed he was going to abandon the yellow sheet, that there was nothing else to do. The work could be duplicated. But it would take two months, and the time to present this idea was now, for use in the spring displays. He struck his fist on the window ledge. Then he shrugged. Even though his

130    plan was adopted, he told himself, it wouldn't bring him a raise

---

4. **convoluted** (kän′və-lōōt′ĭd) *adj.*: intricate; coiled or twisted.

---

## Fluency

Successful readers are able to read fluently—clearly, easily, quickly, and without word identification problems. In most selections, you'll be given an opportunity to practice and improve your fluency.

---

IDENTIFY CAUSE & EFFECT

What causes the "barrier" to break (lines 337–339)?

_____

_____

_____

_____

_____

_____

_____

CLARIFY

Re-read lines 340–354. What is the "sheer emptiness" Tom encounters? Explain what happens next.

_____

_____

_____

_____

_____

_____

_____

FLUENCY

Read the boxed passage aloud twice. On your second read, focus on your pacing and delivery.

utter safety, the contrast between it and where he now stood, was more than he could bear. And the barrier broke then, and the fear of the awful height he stood on coursed through his nerves and muscles.

340    A fraction of his mind knew he was going to fall, and he began taking rapid blind steps with no feeling of what he was doing, sliding with a clumsy, desperate swiftness, fingers scrabbling along the brick, almost hopelessly resigned to the sudden backward pull and swift motion outward and down. Then his moving hand slid onto not brick but sheer emptiness, an impossible gap in the face of the wall, and he stumbled.

His right foot smashed into his left ankle bone; he staggered sideways, began falling, and the claw of his hand cracked against glass and wood, slid down it, and his fingertips were pressed

350    hard on the puttyless edging of his window. His right hand smacked gropingly beside it as he fell to his knees; and, under the full weight and direct downward pull of his sagging body, the open window dropped shudderingly in its frame till it closed and his wrists struck the sill and were jarred off.

For a single moment he knelt, knee bones against stone on the very edge of the ledge, body swaying and touching nowhere else, fighting for balance. Then he lost it, his shoulders plunging backward, and he flung his arms forward, his hands smashing against the window casing on either side and—his body moving

360    backward—his fingers clutched the narrow wood stripping of the upper pane.

For an instant he hung suspended between balance and falling, his fingertips pressed onto the quarter-inch wood strips. Then, with utmost delicacy, with a focused concentration of all his senses, he increased even further the strain on his fingertips hooked to these slim edgings of wood. Elbows slowly bending, he began to draw the full weight of his upper body forward, knowing that the instant his fingers slipped off these quarter-inch strips he'd plunge backward and be falling. Elbows

## Contents of the Dead Man's Pocket

**Story Map** Review the sequence of events in "Contents of the Dead Man's Pocket." Then, fill in the Story Map below.

| Title |
|---|
| |

| Setting |
|---|
| |

| Characters |
|---|
| |

| Problem |
|---|
| |

↓

| Event 1 |
|---|
| |

| Event 2 |
|---|
| |

| Event 3 |
|---|
| |

| Event 4 |
|---|
| |

| Event 5 (Climax) |
|---|
| |

↓

| Resolution |
|---|
| |

Contents of the Dead Man's Pocket **27**

**Own the Story**
Graphic organizers help reinforce your understanding of the literary focus in a highly visual and creative way.

---

## Standards Review

**LITERATURE**

**Test Practice**

### Contents of the Dead Man's Pocket

Complete the sample test item below. The box at the right explains why three of these choices are not correct.

| Sample Test Item | Explanation of the Correct Answer |
|---|---|
| One **conflict** of the story takes place between— <br><br> A  Tom and his boss <br> B  Tom and his own ambition <br> C  Tom and his wife <br> D  Tom and a book of matches | The correct answer is *B*. <br><br> *A* is incorrect because Tom's boss is not mentioned in the story. *C* is incorrect because Tom and his wife haven't argued. *D* is also incorrect; Tom has trouble lighting the matches, but the matches present only a minor difficulty. |

**DIRECTIONS:** Answer the following questions by circling the letter of the best response.

**Reading Standard 3.4 (Grade 8 Review)** Analyze the relevance of the setting (e.g., place, time, customs) to the mood, tone, and meaning of the text.

**Reading Standard 3.6** Analyze and trace an author's development of time and sequence, including the use of complex literary devices (e.g., foreshadowing, flashbacks).

1. The **setting** of "Contents of the Dead Man's Pocket" provides—
   A  beauty
   B  humor
   C  suspense
   D  romance

2. All of the following describe Tom's **internal conflicts** except—
   F  deciding between work and the movies
   G  overcoming his fear
   H  fighting the temptation to look down
   J  rescuing the paper from the ledge

3. In the story's sequence of events, which event happens last?
   A  Tom breaks the window.
   B  Tom lights the matches.
   C  Clare goes to the movies.
   D  Tom steps out onto the ledge.

4. The author slows down time by—
   F  using flashback and foreshadowing
   G  describing the events moment by moment
   H  setting the story on the eleventh-floor ledge
   J  focusing on one character

5. At the **resolution** of "Contents of the Dead Man's Pocket" Tom realizes that—
   A  work is less important
   B  work is more important
   C  family and work are of equal importance
   D  family is less important

**28** Part 1  Chapter 1: Plot and Setting

**Standards Review: Literature**
This feature helps you practice for the state-wide tests by asking questions about the literary focus.

**Sample Test Item**
For a multiple-choice question, you have to choose the one—and only one—correct answer. This feature models the thinking involved in making such choices.

**Questions**
These questions test your mastery of the standard, while mirroring the type of questions you will find on the state-wide tests.

## Standards Review

VOCABULARY DEVELOPMENT

**TestPractice** **Contents of the Dead Man's Pocket**

### Prefixes

**DIRECTIONS:** Match each prefix with its definition by writing the correct letter on the line.

1. _____ re–         a. no; not

2. _____ un–         b. forward

3. _____ sub–        c. again

4. _____ pro–        d. below

**Reading Standard 1.1**
Identify and use the literal and figurative meanings of words and understand word derivations.

### Vocabulary in Context

**DIRECTIONS:** Complete the paragraph by writing a word from the word box to fit in each sentence below. Not all words will be used.

**Word Box**

projection
discarding
confirmation
exhalation
incomprehensible
rebounded
unimpeded
irrelevantly
interminable
imperceptibly

Tom crept on the ledge, holding his breath, then let out a great (1) _____ of air. So (2) _____ did he move that Tom felt as if he were standing still. He had been on the ledge, he thought, an (3) _____ length of time. However, his burning cigarette was (4) _____ that he had actually been there only a few minutes. Staring at his unreadable, (5) _____ scrawl on the sheet of paper, he wondered why the work had seemed so important.

✓ **Before You Go On . . .**
Check your Standards Mastery at the back of this book.

---

## Standards Review: Vocabulary
This feature helps you practice for the state-wide tests by asking questions about the vocabulary skill and the specific vocabulary words taught with the selection.

## Questions
The first part of the practice test asks questions about the vocabulary skill.

## Vocabulary in Context
The second part of the practice test assesses your mastery of the vocabulary words by asking you to put them in context.

# Part One

## Literary Response and Analysis

# Plot and Setting

# Academic Vocabulary for Chapter 1

These are the terms you should know
as you read and analyze the stories in this chapter.

---

**Plot** A series of related events, each event connected to the next, like links in a chain.

**Sequence** The order in which the story's events take place. Most stories take place in **chronological order,** or time order.

• • •

**Flashback** A scene that interrupts the story to introduce an event that took place in the past.

**Flash-forward** A scene that jumps ahead of the story to narrate an event that happens in the future.

**Foreshadowing** Hints in the story that certain events are going to happen later.

• • •

**Exposition** The basic situation of a story.

**Conflict** A struggle between two forces. An **external conflict** can take place between two characters, between a character and a group, or between a character and an animal or a force in nature. An **internal conflict** is a struggle that takes place within a character's mind or heart.

**Complications** The problems that come up during the story as the characters try to resolve, or deal with, the conflict.

**Suspense** The excitement and tension that builds up in a story, which makes readers curious to find out how the story ends.

**Climax** The most exciting part of a story—the moment when the outcome of the conflict is determined. The climax usually occurs near the end of a short story.

**Resolution** (also called **denouement**) (dā'noo·män') The very end of the story, when the loose ends of the plot are tied up.

• • •

**Setting** The time and place in which the story happens.

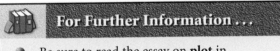

### For Further Information . . .

- Be sure to read the essay on **plot** in *Holt Literature and Language Arts,* pages 2–3.
- Also, read the essay on **setting** in *Holt Literature and Language Arts,* pages 44–45.

**Reading Standard 1.1** Identify and use the literal and figurative meanings of words and understand word derivations.

**Reading Standard 3.4 (Grade 8 Review)** Analyze the relevance of the setting (e.g., place, time, customs) to the mood, tone, and meaning of the text.

**Reading Standard 3.6** Analyze and trace an author's development of time and sequence, including the use of complex literary devices (e.g., foreshadowing, flashbacks).

# Contents of the Dead Man's Pocket by Jack Finney

"Contents of the Dead Man's Pocket" is full of suspense, as the main character faces a series of life-and-death decisions. Stay calm and read the story carefully, one step at a time, and whatever you do—don't look down!

### LITERARY FOCUS: TIME AND SEQUENCE

Most short stories can be read in one sitting, usually in less than an hour. The events in a short story, however, may span hours, weeks, months, or years. "Contents of the Dead Man's Pocket" is striking because its events take place in "real time." In other words, the time it takes you to read the story roughly equals the **time frame** of the story itself.

- As you read, notice how the slowness of the time frame helps create **suspense**.
- As events unfold, pay attention to the main character's **internal conflict:** his struggle against fear.

### READING SKILLS: UNDERSTANDING CAUSE AND EFFECT

A **cause** is what makes something happen. An **effect** is the result, or what happens. Imagine, for example, that a hurricane blows through a seaside town. The fierce winds overturn boats and destroy houses. The winds are the cause. The effect, or result, is the damage.

In a well-written story, the events that make up the plot are closely related: One event causes another event, which leads to another event, and so on. To find a cause, ask yourself, "Why did this event happen?" To identify an effect, ask yourself, "What happened as a result of this event?" Keep in mind that an effect, or result, can stem from several causes, and that one cause can lead to several effects.

To help you track cause-and-effect relationships as you read, fill in a chart like the one below. In the left column, list the cause; in the right column, list the effect. The first one has been done as an example.

| Cause | Effect |
| --- | --- |
| The apartment door is opened. | A sheet of yellow paper is blown out the window. |
|  |  |

**Reading Standard 1.1** Identify and use the literal and figurative meanings of words and understand word derivations.

**Reading Standard 3.4 (Grade 8 Review)** Analyze the relevance of the setting (e.g., place, time, customs) to the mood, tone, and meaning of the text.

**Reading Standard 3.6** Analyze and trace an author's development of time and sequence, including the use of complex literary devices (e.g., foreshadowing, flashbacks).

## VOCABULARY DEVELOPMENT

### PREVIEW SELECTION VOCABULARY

Preview the following words from the story before you begin reading.

**projection** (prō·jek′shən) *n.:* something that juts out from a surface.

*Tom's paper was trapped between the ledge and the decorative **projection** sticking out from the wall.*

**discarding** (dis·kärd′iŋ) *v.* used as *adj.:* abandoning; getting rid of.

*He rejected one plan after another, **discarding** all useless ideas.*

**confirmation** (kän′fər·mā′shən) *n.:* proof.

*As **confirmation** that he could walk on the ledge, he made sure that it was wide enough to fit his shoe.*

**exhalation** (eks′hə·lā′shən) *n.:* something breathed out; breath.

*After holding his breath, Tom felt an **exhalation** of air as he breathed again.*

**imperceptibly** (im′pər·sep′tə·blē) *adv.:* in such a slight way as to be almost unnoticeable.

*Tom moved along the ledge **imperceptibly**, taking tiny, cautious steps.*

**rebounded** (ri·bound′id) *v.:* bounced back.

*After he broke the window, Tom's arm **rebounded**, bouncing backward from the force of the blow.*

**interminable** (in·tur′mi·nə·bəl) *adj.:* endless.

*Although the time seemed **interminable**, Tom had been on the ledge only a few minutes.*

**irrelevantly** (i·rel′ə·vənt·lē) *adv.:* in a way not relating to the point or situation.

*Tom thought **irrelevantly** about the apartment furnishings, as if the cozy rooms could stop him from plunging to his death.*

**incomprehensible** (in·käm′prē·hen′sə·bəl) *adj.:* not understandable.

*The puzzling sheet of paper in his pocket would be **incomprehensible** to anyone who found his body.*

**unimpeded** (un′im·pēd′id) *adj.:* not blocked; unobstructed.

*The yellow paper flew out the window; its progress was **unimpeded.***

### PREFIXES

Just by adding a few letters up front, you can turn *appear* into *reappear*, *likely* into *unlikely*, and *freezing* into *subfreezing*. *Re–*, *un–*, and *sub–* are **prefixes**, word parts that attach to the front of a word or word root to change its meaning. *Re–* means "again"; *un–* means "not"; *sub–* means "below."

As you read, look for words with these or other prefixes. Use your knowledge of prefixes to help you figure out the meanings of some unfamiliar words.

# Contents of the Dead Man's Pocket

## Jack Finney

### WORD STUDY

*Portable* is usually an adjective, meaning "able to be carried." Here, in line 3, the word is a noun, naming a thing. Read on, and circle what *portable* refers to.

_____

_____

_____

_____

_____

_____

_____

_____

_____

_____

_____

_____

At the little living-room desk Tom Benecke rolled two sheets of flimsy[1] and a heavier top sheet, carbon paper sandwiched between them, into his portable. *Interoffice Memo,* the top sheet was headed, and he typed tomorrow's date just below this; then he glanced at a creased yellow sheet, covered with his own handwriting, beside the typewriter. "Hot in here," he muttered to himself. Then, from the short hallway at his back, he heard the muffled clang of wire coat hangers in the bedroom closet, and at this reminder of what his wife was doing he thought: hot

10  guilty conscience.

He got up, shoving his hands into the back pockets of his gray wash slacks, stepped to the living-room window beside the desk and stood breathing on the glass, watching the expanding circlet of mist, staring down through the autumn night at Lexington Avenue,[2] eleven stories below. He was a tall, lean, dark-haired young man in a pullover sweater, who looked as though he had played not football, probably, but basketball in college. Now he placed the heels of his hands against the top edge of the lower window frame and shoved upward. But as

20  usual the window didn't budge, and he had to lower his hands and then shoot them hard upward to jolt the window open a few inches. He dusted his hands, muttering.

### SETTING

**Setting** is the time and place of a story. Underline the words in line 15 that tell how far above the street Tom's apartment is.

---

1. **flimsy** *n.:* thin paper used for typing carbon copies. Before computers and copying machines, copies of business communications were made with carbon paper.
2. **Lexington Avenue:** one of the main streets in New York City.

But still he didn't begin his work. He crossed the room to the hallway entrance and, leaning against the doorjamb, hands shoved into his back pockets again, he called, "Clare?" When his wife answered, he said, "Sure you don't mind going alone?"

"No." Her voice was muffled, and he knew her head and shoulders were in the bedroom closet. Then the tap of her high heels sounded on the wood floor, and she appeared at the end of 30    the little hallway, wearing a slip, both hands raised to one ear,

_____

_____

_____

_____

_____

CONFLICT

Underline the phrase in lines 50–53 that tells what Tom is *tempted* to do. Circle the sentence that tells what he "very much wanted" to do. How does Tom resolve this **internal conflict**?

_____

_____

_____

_____

_____

_____

_____

_____

_____

clipping on an earring. She smiled at him—a slender, very pretty girl with light brown, almost blond, hair—her prettiness emphasized by the pleasant nature that showed in her face. "It's just that I hate you to miss this movie; you wanted to see it, too."

"Yeah, I know." He ran his fingers through his hair. "Got to get this done, though."

She nodded, accepting this. Then, glancing at the desk across the living room, she said, "You work too much, though, Tom—and too hard."

40 He smiled. "You won't mind, though, will you, when the money comes rolling in and I'm known as the Boy Wizard of Wholesale Groceries?"

"I guess not." She smiled and turned back toward the bedroom.

At his desk again, Tom lighted a cigarette; then a few moments later, as Clare appeared, dressed and ready to leave, he set it on the rim of the ashtray. "Just after seven," she said. "I can make the beginning of the first feature."

He walked to the front-door closet to help her on with her 50 coat. He kissed her then and, for an instant, holding her close, smelling the perfume she had used, he was tempted to go with her; it was not actually true that he had to work tonight, though he very much wanted to. This was his own project, unannounced as yet in his office, and it could be postponed. But then they won't see it till Monday, he thought once again, and if I give it to the boss tomorrow he might read it over the weekend . . . "Have a good time," he said aloud. He gave his wife a little swat and opened the door for her, feeling the air from the building hallway, smelling faintly of floor wax, stream gently past his face.

60 He watched her walk down the hall, flicked a hand in response as she waved, and then he started to close the door, but it resisted for a moment. As the door opening narrowed, the current of warm air from the hallway, channeled through this

smaller opening now, suddenly rushed past him with accelerated force. Behind him he heard the slap of the window curtains against the wall and the sound of paper fluttering from his desk, and he had to push to close the door.

Turning, he saw a sheet of white paper drifting to the floor in a series of arcs, and another sheet, yellow, moving toward the
70  window, caught in the dying current flowing through the narrow opening. As he watched, the paper struck the bottom edge of the window and hung there for an instant, plastered against the glass and wood. Then as the moving air stilled completely, the curtains swinging back from the wall to hang free again, he saw the yellow sheet drop to the window ledge and slide over out of sight.

He ran across the room, grasped the bottom of the window and tugged, staring through the glass. He saw the yellow sheet, dimly now in the darkness outside, lying on the ornamental
80  ledge a yard below the window. Even as he watched, it was moving, scraping slowly along the ledge, pushed by the breeze that pressed steadily against the building wall. He heaved on the window with all his strength, and it shot open with a bang, the window weight rattling in the casing. But the paper was past his reach and, leaning out into the night, he watched it scud[3] steadily along the ledge to the south, half plastered against the building wall. Above the muffled sound of the street traffic far below, he could hear the dry scrape of its movement, like a leaf on the pavement.

90  The living room of the next apartment to the south projected a yard or more further out toward the street than this one; because of this the Beneckes paid seven and a half dollars less rent than their neighbors. And now the yellow sheet, sliding along the stone ledge, nearly invisible in the night, was stopped by the projecting blank wall of the next apartment. It lay motionless then, in the corner formed by the two walls a good five yards away, pressed firmly against the ornate corner

---

3. **scud** *v.:* glide or move swiftly.

IDENTIFY
CAUSE & EFFECT

Pause at line 76. What happens when the wind rushes through the apartment?

_____
_____
_____
_____
_____
_____
_____
_____
_____
_____

WORD STUDY

Circle the **prefix** in the word *invisible* (line 94). What does the prefix mean? What does *invisible* mean?

_____
_____
_____
_____
_____
_____
_____
_____

ornament of the ledge by the breeze that moved past Tom
Benecke's face.

100        He knelt at the window and stared at the yellow paper for a
full minute or more, waiting for it to move, to slide off the ledge
and fall, hoping he could follow its course to the street, and then
hurry down in the elevator and retrieve it. But it didn't move,
and then he saw that the paper was caught firmly between a
**projection** of the convoluted[4] corner ornament and the ledge.
He thought about the poker from the fireplace, then the broom,
then the mop—**discarding** each thought as it occurred to him.
There was nothing in the apartment long enough to reach
that paper.

110        It was hard for him to understand that he actually had to
abandon it—it was ridiculous—and he began to curse. Of all the
papers on his desk, why did it have to be this one in particular!
On four long Saturday afternoons he had stood in supermarkets,
counting the people who passed certain displays, and the results
were scribbled on that yellow sheet. From stacks of trade publications, gone over page by page in snatched half hours at work
and during evenings at home, he had copied facts, quotations,
and figures onto that sheet. And he had carried it with him to
the Public Library on Fifth Avenue, where he'd spent a dozen
120    lunch hours and early evenings adding more. All were needed to
support and lend authority to his idea for a new grocery-store
display method; without them his idea was a mere opinion. And
there they all lay, in his own improvised shorthand—countless
hours of work—out there on the ledge.

For many seconds he believed he was going to abandon the
yellow sheet, that there was nothing else to do. The work could
be duplicated. But it would take two months, and the time to
present this idea was *now,* for use in the spring displays. He struck
his fist on the window ledge. Then he shrugged. Even though his
130    plan was adopted, he told himself, it wouldn't bring him a raise

---

4.   **convoluted** (kän′və·loot′id) *adj.:* intricate; coiled.

## Sidebar

**projection** (prō·jek′shən) *n.:*
something that juts out from
a surface.

*Pro–* is a Latin prefix meaning
"forward"; the root *–ject–*
means "throw" or "thrust."

**discarding** (dis·kärd′iŋ) *v.*
used as *adj.:* abandoning;
getting rid of.

### IDENTIFY

Pause at line 124. Why is the
yellow paper so important to
Tom? Underline the details
that tell you why.

### PREDICT

After reading lines 125–141,
what do you predict Tom
will do?

_____

_____

_____

_____

_____

_____

_____

_____

_____

_____

_____

_____

in pay—not immediately, anyway, or as a direct result. It won't bring me a promotion either, he argued—not of itself.

But just the same—and he couldn't escape the thought—this and other independent projects, some already done and others planned for the future, would gradually mark him out from the score of other young men in his company. They were the way to change from a name on the payroll to a name in the minds of the company officials. They were the beginning of the long, long climb to where he was determined to be—at the very top. And

140  he knew he was going out there in the darkness, after the yellow sheet fifteen feet beyond his reach.

By a kind of instinct, he instantly began making his intention acceptable to himself by laughing at it. The mental picture of himself sidling along the ledge outside was absurd—it was actually comical—and he smiled. He imagined himself describing it; it would make a good story at the office and, it occurred

**INFER**

Re-read lines 133–141. What can you infer about Tom by his thoughts?

## VOCABULARY

**confirmation**
(kän′fər·mā′shən) *n.:* proof.

*Confirmation* comes from the
Latin word *firmus,* meaning
"strong." What other English
words are from this root?

_____

_____


## CLARIFY

Pause at line 176, and consider what has happened so far.
In your own words, explain
why Tom decides to go out
on the ledge.

_____

_____

_____

_____

_____

_____


## SETTING

Circle the words in lines
177–180 that describe the
second setting in the story.
How does the new setting
increase the suspense?

_____

_____

_____

_____

_____

to him, would add a special interest and importance to his memorandum, which would do it no harm at all.

150      To simply go out and get his paper was an easy task—he could be back here with it in less than two minutes—and he knew he wasn't deceiving himself. The ledge, he saw, measuring it with his eye, was about as wide as the length of his shoe, and perfectly flat. And every fifth row of brick in the face of the building, he remembered—leaning out, he verified this—was indented half an inch, enough for the tips of his fingers, enough to maintain balance easily. It occurred to him that if this ledge and wall were only a yard aboveground—as he knelt at the window staring out, this thought was the final **confirmation** of his intention—he could move along the ledge indefinitely.

160      On a sudden impulse, he got to his feet, walked to the front closet, and took out an old tweed jacket; it would be cold outside. He put it on and buttoned it as he crossed the room rapidly toward the open window. In the back of his mind he knew he'd better hurry and get this over with before he thought too much, and at the window he didn't allow himself to hesitate.

     He swung a leg over the sill, then felt for and found the ledge a yard below the window with his foot. Gripping the bottom of the window frame very tightly and carefully, he slowly ducked his head under it, feeling on his face the sudden change

170 from the warm air of the room to the chill outside. With infinite care he brought out his other leg, his mind concentrating on what he was doing. Then he slowly stood erect. Most of the putty, dried out and brittle, had dropped off the bottom edging of the window frame, he found, and the flat wooden edging provided a good gripping surface, a half inch or more deep, for the tips of his fingers.

     Now, balanced easily and firmly, he stood on the ledge outside in the slight, chill breeze, eleven stories above the street, staring into his own lighted apartment, odd and different-

180 seeming now.

First his right hand, then his left, he carefully shifted his fingertip grip from the puttyless window edging to an indented row of bricks directly to his right. It was hard to take the first shuffling sideways step then—to make himself move—and the fear stirred in his stomach, but he did it, again by not allowing himself time to think. And now—with his chest, stomach, and the left side of his face pressed against the rough cold brick—his lighted apartment was suddenly gone, and it was much darker out here than he had thought.

190 Without pause he continued—right foot, left foot, right foot, left—his shoe soles shuffling and scraping along the rough stone, never lifting from it, fingers sliding along the exposed edging of brick. He moved on the balls of his feet, heels lifted slightly; the ledge was not quite as wide as he'd expected. But leaning slightly inward toward the face of the building and pressed against it, he could feel his balance firm and secure, and moving along the ledge was quite as easy as he had thought it would be. He could hear the buttons of his jacket scraping steadily along the rough bricks and feel them catch momen-

200 tarily, tugging a little, at each mortared crack. He simply did not permit himself to look down, though the compulsion[5] to do so never left him; nor did he allow himself actually to think. Mechanically—right foot, left foot, over and again—he shuffled along crabwise, watching the projecting wall ahead loom steadily closer. . . .

Then he reached it, and at the corner—he'd decided how he was going to pick up the paper—he lifted his right foot and placed it carefully on the ledge that ran along the projecting wall at a right angle to the ledge on which his other foot rested. And now,

210 facing the building, he stood in the corner formed by the two walls, one foot on the ledging of each, a hand on the shoulder-high indentation of each wall. His forehead was pressed directly into the corner against the cold bricks, and now he carefully

---

5. **compulsion** *n.:* driving force.

You may know the term *trough* (trôf), meaning "a long, open container for pigs' food." In this context, however, *trough* (line 216) means "groove" or "long indentation."

IDENTIFY
CAUSE & EFFECT

In lines 224–230, underline the words that tell why Tom's fear suddenly increases.

IDENTIFY
CAUSE & EFFECT

Lines 241–247 tell about three events—one is a cause; the others are effects. Circle the cause, and underline the effects.

lowered first one hand, then the other, perhaps a foot farther down, to the next indentation in the rows of bricks.

Very slowly, sliding his forehead down the trough of the brick corner and bending his knees, he lowered his body toward the paper lying between his outstretched feet. Again he lowered his fingerholds another foot and bent his knees still more, thigh

220  muscles taut, his forehead sliding and bumping down the brick V. Half squatting now, he dropped his left hand to the next indentation and then slowly reached with his right hand toward the paper between his feet.

He couldn't quite touch it, and his knees now were pressed against the wall; he could bend them no farther. But by ducking his head another inch lower, the top of his head now pressed against the bricks, he lowered his right shoulder and his fingers had the paper by a corner, pulling it loose. At the same instant he saw, between his legs and far below, Lexington Avenue

230  stretched out for miles ahead.

He saw, in that instant, the Loew's theater sign, blocks ahead past Fiftieth Street; the miles of traffic signals, all green now; the lights of cars and street lamps; countless neon signs; and the moving black dots of people. And a violent, instantaneous explosion of absolute terror roared through him. For a motionless instant he saw himself externally—bent practically double, balanced on this narrow ledge, nearly half his body projecting out above the street far below—and he began to tremble violently, panic flaring through his mind and muscles,

240  and he felt the blood rush from the surface of his skin.

In the fractional moment before horror paralyzed him, as he stared between his legs at that terrible length of street far beneath him, a fragment of his mind raised his body in a spasmodic jerk to an upright position again, but so violently that his head scraped hard against the wall, bouncing off it, and his body swayed outward to the knife-edge of balance, and he very nearly plunged backward and fell. Then he was leaning far into the corner again, squeezing and pushing into it, not only his face but his chest and stomach, his back arching; and his fingertips

250 clung with all the pressure of his pulling arms to the shoulder-high half-inch indentation in the bricks.

He was more than trembling now; his whole body was racked with a violent shuddering beyond control, his eyes squeezed so tightly shut it was painful, though he was past awareness of that. His teeth were exposed in a frozen grimace, the strength draining like water from his knees and calves. It was extremely likely, he knew, that he would faint, slump down along the wall, his face scraping, and then drop backward, a limp weight, out into nothing. And to save his life he concentrated on

260 holding on to consciousness, drawing deliberate deep breaths of cold air into his lungs, fighting to keep his senses aware.

Then he knew that he would not faint, but he could not stop shaking nor open his eyes. He stood where he was, breathing deeply, trying to hold back the terror of the glimpse he had had of what lay below him; and he knew he had made a mistake in not making himself stare down at the street, getting used to it and accepting it, when he had first stepped out onto the ledge.

It was impossible to walk back. He simply could not do it. He couldn't bring himself to make the slightest movement. The

270 strength was gone from his legs; his shivering hands—numb, cold, and desperately rigid—had lost all deftness;[6] his easy ability to move and balance was gone. Within a step or two, if he tried to move, he knew that he would stumble clumsily and fall.

Seconds passed, with the chill faint wind pressing the side of his face, and he could hear the toned-down volume of the street traffic far beneath him. Again and again it slowed and then stopped, almost to silence; then presently, even this high, he would hear the click of the traffic signals and the subdued roar of the cars starting up again. During a lull in the street sounds,

280 he called out. Then he was shouting "*Help!*" so loudly it rasped his throat. But he felt the steady pressure of the wind, moving

---

6.  **deftness** *n.: skillfulness; coordination.*

PREDICT

Pause at line 273. Do you **predict** that Tom will make it to safety? Why or why not?

between his face and the blank wall, snatch up his cries as he uttered them, and he knew they must sound directionless and distant. And he remembered how habitually, here in New York, he himself heard and ignored shouts in the night. If anyone heard him, there was no sign of it, and presently Tom Benecke knew he had to try moving; there was nothing else he could do.

Eyes squeezed shut, he watched scenes in his mind like scraps of motion-picture film—he could not stop them. He saw
290 himself stumbling suddenly sideways as he crept along the ledge and saw his upper body arc outward, arms flailing. He saw a dangling shoestring caught between the ledge and the sole of his other shoe, saw a foot start to move, to be stopped with a jerk, and felt his balance leaving him. He saw himself falling with a terrible speed as his body revolved in the air, knees clutched tight to his chest, eyes squeezed shut, moaning softly.

Out of utter necessity, knowing that any of these thoughts might be reality in the very next seconds, he was slowly able to shut his mind against every thought but what he now began to
300 do. With fear-soaked slowness, he slid his left foot an inch or two toward his own impossibly distant window. Then he slid the fingers of his shivering left hand a corresponding distance. For a moment he could not bring himself to lift his right foot from one ledge to the other; then he did it, and became aware of the harsh **exhalation** of air from his throat and realized that he was panting. As his right hand, then, began to slide along the brick edging, he was astonished to feel the yellow paper pressed to the bricks underneath his stiff fingers, and he uttered a terrible, abrupt bark that might have been a laugh or a moan. He opened
310 his mouth and took the paper in his teeth, pulling it out from under his fingers.

By a kind of trick—by concentrating his entire mind on first his left foot, then his left hand, then the other foot, then the other hand—he was able to move, almost **imperceptibly,** trembling steadily, very nearly without thought. But he could feel the terrible strength of the pent-up horror on just the other

**exhalation** (eks′hə·lā′shən) n.: something breathed out; breath.

Change *exhalation* to its opposite by changing the prefix.

**imperceptibly**
(im′pər·sep′tə·blē) adv.: in such a slight way as to be almost unnoticeable.

Change *imperceptibly* to its opposite by dropping the prefix.

side of the flimsy barrier he had erected in his mind; and he knew that if it broke through he would lose this thin, artificial control of his body.

320     During one slow step he tried keeping his eyes closed; it made him feel safer, shutting him off a little from the fearful reality of where he was. Then a sudden rush of giddiness swept over him, and he had to open his eyes wide, staring sideways at the cold rough brick and angled lines of mortar, his cheek tight against the building. He kept his eyes open then, knowing that if he once let them flick outward, to stare for an instant at the lighted windows across the street, he would be past help.

    He didn't know how many dozens of tiny sidling steps he had taken, his chest, belly, and face pressed to the wall; but he 330 knew the slender hold he was keeping on his mind and body was going to break. He had a sudden mental picture of his apartment on just the other side of this wall—warm, cheerful, incredibly spacious. And he saw himself striding through it, lying down on the floor on his back, arms spread wide, reveling[7] in its unbelievable security. The impossible remoteness of this

---

**7. reveling** (rev'əl·iŋ) *v.* used as *adj.:* taking great pleasure or delight.

**INTERPRET**

Pause at line 319. What sort of **conflict** is Tom facing? Is it an **internal** or **external** conflict?

**IDENTIFY CAUSE & EFFECT**

Re-read lines 320–325. Circle what Tom tries to do as he walks the ledge. Then, underline two immediate effects of that action.

**IDENTIFY CAUSE & EFFECT**

What causes the "barrier" to break (lines 337–339)?

_____

_____

_____

_____

_____

_____

_____

_____

_____

**CLARIFY**

Re-read lines 340–354. What is the "sheer emptiness" Tom encounters? Explain what happens next.

_____

_____

_____

_____

_____

_____

_____

**FLUENCY**

Read the boxed passage aloud twice. On your second read, focus on your pacing and delivery.

utter safety, the contrast between it and where he now stood, was more than he could bear. And the barrier broke then, and the fear of the awful height he stood on coursed through his nerves and muscles.

340    A fraction of his mind knew he was going to fall, and he began taking rapid blind steps with no feeling of what he was doing, sidling with a clumsy desperate swiftness, fingers scrabbling along the brick, almost hopelessly resigned to the sudden backward pull and swift motion outward and down. Then his moving left hand slid onto not brick but sheer emptiness, an impossible gap in the face of the wall, and he stumbled.

His right foot smashed into his left anklebone; he staggered sideways, began falling, and the claw of his hand cracked against glass and wood, slid down it, and his fingertips were pressed
350 hard on the puttyless edging of his window. His right hand smacked gropingly beside it as he fell to his knees; and, under the full weight and direct downward pull of his sagging body, the open window dropped shudderingly in its frame till it closed and his wrists struck the sill and were jarred off.

For a single moment he knelt, knee bones against stone on the very edge of the ledge, body swaying and touching nowhere else, fighting for balance. Then he lost it, his shoulders plunging backward, and he flung his arms forward, his hands smashing against the window casing on either side; and—his body moving
360 backward—his fingers clutched the narrow wood stripping of the upper pane.

For an instant he hung suspended between balance and falling, his fingertips pressed onto the quarter-inch wood strips. Then, with utmost delicacy, with a focused concentration of all his senses, he increased even further the strain on his fingertips hooked to these slim edgings of wood. Elbows slowly bending, he began to draw the full weight of his upper body forward, knowing that the instant his fingers slipped off these quarter-inch strips he'd plunge backward and be falling. Elbows

370 imperceptibly bending, body shaking with the strain, the sweat starting from his forehead in great sudden drops, he pulled, his entire being and thought concentrated in his fingertips. Then, suddenly, the strain slackened and ended, his chest touching the windowsill, and he was kneeling on the ledge, his forehead pressed to the glass of the closed window.

Dropping his palms to the sill, he stared into his living room—at the red-brown davenport[8] across the room, and a magazine he had left there; at the pictures on the walls and the gray rug; the entrance to the hallway; and at his papers, type-

380 writer, and desk, not two feet from his nose. A movement from his desk caught his eye and he saw that it was a thin curl of blue smoke; his cigarette, the ash long, was still burning in the ashtray where he'd left it—this was past all belief—only a few minutes before.

His head moved, and in faint reflection from the glass before him, he saw the yellow paper clenched in his front teeth. Lifting a hand from the sill he took it from his mouth; the moistened corner parted from the paper, and he spat it out.

For a moment, in the light from the living room, he stared
390 wonderingly at the yellow sheet in his hand and then crushed it into the side pocket of his jacket.

He couldn't open the window. It had been pulled not completely closed, but its lower edge was below the level of the outside sill; there was no room to get his fingers underneath it. Between the upper sash and the lower was a gap not wide enough—reaching up, he tried—to get his fingers into; he couldn't push it open. The upper window panel, he knew from long experience, was impossible to move, frozen tight with dried paint.

400 Very carefully observing his balance, the fingertips of his left hand again hooked to the narrow stripping of the window

**PLOT**

The many details, or **complications,** of Tom's dangerous experience make it seem as if Tom had been on the ledge for a long time. Circle the words in lines 380–384 that tell how long he has really been on the ledge.

**PREDICT**

Pause at line 399. What might Tom do now?

_____

_____

_____

_____

_____

_____

_____

_____

_____

_____

_____

_____

_____

_____

_____

_____

_____

---

8. **davenport** (dav′ən·pôrt′) *n.:* large sofa or couch.

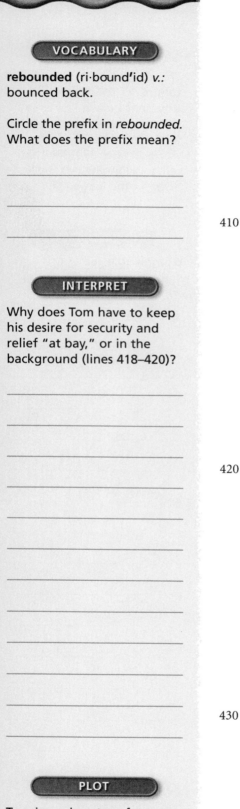

**rebounded** (ri·bound′id) *v.:*
bounced back.

Circle the prefix in *rebounded.*
What does the prefix mean?

_____

_____

_____


INTERPRET

Why does Tom have to keep
his desire for security and
relief "at bay," or in the
background (lines 418–420)?

_____

_____

_____

_____

_____

_____

_____

_____

_____

_____

_____

_____


PLOT

Tom is so close to safety, yet
so far away. In lines 421–431,
circle the three ways Tom
tries to get into the room.

casing, he drew back his right hand, palm facing the glass, and
then struck the glass with the heel of his hand.

His arm **rebounded** from the pane, his body tottering, and
he knew he didn't dare strike a harder blow.

But in the security and relief of his new position, he simply
smiled; with only a sheet of glass between him and the room
just before him, it was not possible that there wasn't a way past
it. Eyes narrowing, he thought for a few moments about what
410    to do. Then his eyes widened, for nothing occurred to him. But
still he felt calm; the trembling, he realized, had stopped. At the
back of his mind there still lay the thought that once he was
again in his home, he could give release to his feelings. He
actually *would* lie on the floor, rolling, clenching tufts of the rug
in his hands. He would literally run across the room, free to
move as he liked, jumping on the floor, testing and reveling
in its absolute security, letting the relief flood through him,
draining the fear from his mind and body. His yearning for this
was astonishingly intense, and somehow he understood that he
420    had better keep this feeling at bay.

He took a half dollar from his pocket and struck it against
the pane, but without any hope that the glass would break and
with very little disappointment when it did not. After a few
moments of thought he drew his leg up onto the ledge and
picked loose the knot of his shoelace. He slipped off the shoe
and, holding it across the instep, drew back his arm as far as he
dared and struck the leather heel against the glass. The pane
rattled, but he knew he'd been a long way from breaking it. His
foot was cold and he slipped the shoe back on. He shouted
430    again, experimentally, and then once more, but there was
no answer.

The realization suddenly struck him that he might have to
wait here till Clare came home, and for a moment the thought
was funny. He could see Clare opening the front door, with-
drawing her key from the lock, closing the door behind her, and
then glancing up to see him crouched on the other side of the

window. He could see her rush across the room, face astounded and frightened, and hear himself shouting instructions: "Never mind how I got here! Just open the wind—" She couldn't open it, he remembered, she'd never been able to; she'd always had to call him. She'd have to get the building superintendent or a neighbor, and he pictured himself smiling and answering their questions as he climbed in. "I just wanted to get a breath of fresh air, so—"

He couldn't possibly wait here till Clare came home. It was the second feature she'd wanted to see, and she'd left in time to see the first. She'd be another three hours or— He glanced at his watch; Clare had been gone eight minutes. It wasn't possible, but only eight minutes ago he had kissed his wife goodbye. She wasn't even in the theater yet!

It would be four hours before she could possibly be home, and he tried to picture himself kneeling out here, fingertips hooked to these narrow strippings, while first one movie, preceded by a slow listing of credits, began, developed, reached its climax, and then finally ended. There'd be a newsreel next, maybe, and then an animated cartoon, and then **interminable** scenes from coming pictures. And then, once more, the beginning of a full-length picture—while all the time he hung out here in the night.

He might possibly get to his feet, but he was afraid to try. Already his legs were cramped, his thigh muscles tired; his knees hurt, his feet felt numb, and his hands were stiff. He couldn't possibly stay out here for four hours or anywhere near it. Long before that his legs and arms would give out; he would be forced to try changing his position often—stiffly, clumsily, his coordination and strength gone—and he would fall. Quite realistically, he knew that he would fall; no one could stay out here on this ledge for four hours.

A dozen windows in the apartment building across the street were lighted. Looking over his shoulder, he could see the top of a man's head behind the newspaper he was reading; in

440

450

460

470

**IDENTIFY**

Circle the words in lines 445–450 that tell how long Clare has been gone. Underline the words in lines 451–455 that tell how long it will be before Clare gets home.

**VOCABULARY**

**interminable** (in·tur′mi·nə·bəl) *adj.:* endless.

another window he saw the blue-gray flicker of a television screen. No more than twenty-odd yards from his back were scores of people, and if just one of them would walk idly to his window and glance out. . . . For some moments he stared over his shoulder at the lighted rectangles, waiting. But no one appeared. The man reading his paper turned a page and then continued his reading. A figure passed another of the windows and was immediately gone.

480    In the inside pocket of his jacket he found a little sheaf of papers, and he pulled one out and looked at it in the light from the living room. It was an old letter, an advertisement of some sort; his name and address, in purple ink, were on a label pasted to the envelope. Gripping one end of the envelope in his teeth, he twisted it into a tight curl. From his shirt pocket he brought out a book of matches. He didn't dare let go the casing with both hands but, with the twist of paper in his teeth, he opened the matchbook with his free hand; then he bent one of the matches in two without tearing it from the folder, its red-tipped
490    end now touching the striking surface. With his thumb, he rubbed the red tip across the striking area.

He did it again, then again, and still again, pressing harder each time, and the match suddenly flared, burning his thumb. But he kept it alight, cupping the matchbook in his hand and shielding it with his body. He held the flame to the paper in his mouth till it caught. Then he snuffed out the match flame with his thumb and forefinger, careless of the burn, and replaced the book in his pocket. Taking the paper twist in his hand, he held it flame down, watching the flame crawl up the paper, till it flared
500    bright. Then he held it behind him over the street, moving it from side to side, watching it over his shoulder, the flame flickering and guttering in the wind.

There were three letters in his pocket and he lighted each of them, holding each till the flame touched his hand and then dropping it to the street below. At one point, watching over his

**PLOT**

Pause at line 502. How is Tom trying to solve his problem?

shoulder while the last of the letters burned, he saw the man across the street put down his paper and stand—even seeming, to Tom, to glance toward his window. But when he moved, it was only to walk across the room and disappear from sight.

510     There were a dozen coins in Tom Benecke's pocket and he dropped them, three or four at a time. But if they struck anyone or if anyone noticed their falling, no one connected them with their source, and no one glanced upward.

    His arms had begun to tremble from the steady strain of clinging to his narrow perch, and he did not know what to do now and was terribly frightened. Clinging to the window stripping with one hand, he again searched his pockets. But now—he had left his wallet on his dresser when he'd changed clothes—

**PREDICT**

Pause at line 509. At this point in the story, what possible events could happen next?

**irrelevantly** (i·rel′ə·vənt·lē)
*adv.:* in a way not related to
the point or situation.

**incomprehensible**
(in·käm′prē·hen′sə·bəl) *adj.:*
not understandable.

Pause at line 526. Why does
it matter to Tom that no one
would understand the yellow
sheet of paper?

_____

_____

_____

_____

_____

_____

_____

_____

_____

_____

Pause at line 553. What are
the possible effects of Tom's
plan?

_____

_____

_____

_____

there was nothing left but the yellow sheet. It occurred to him

520   **irrelevantly** that his death on the sidewalk below would be an
eternal mystery; the window closed—why, how, and from where
could he have fallen? No one would be able to identify his body
for a time, either—the thought was somehow unbearable and
increased his fear. All they'd find in his pockets would be the
yellow sheet. *Contents of the dead man's pockets,* he thought, *one
sheet of paper bearing penciled notations—**incomprehensible.***

    He understood fully that he might actually be going to die;
his arms, maintaining his balance on the ledge, were trembling
steadily now. And it occurred to him then with all the force of a

530   revelation that, if he fell, all he was ever going to have out of life
he would then, abruptly, have had. Nothing, then, could ever be
changed; and nothing more—no least experience or pleasure—
could ever be added to his life. He wished, then, that he had not
allowed his wife to go off by herself tonight—and on similar
nights. He thought of all the evenings he had spent away from
her, working; and he regretted them. He thought wonderingly
of his fierce ambition and of the direction his life had taken; he
thought of the hours he'd spent by himself, filling the yellow
sheet that had brought him out here. *Contents of the dead man's*

540   *pockets,* he thought with sudden fierce anger, *a wasted life.*

    He was simply not going to cling here till he slipped and
fell; he told himself that now. There was one last thing he could
try; he had been aware of it for some moments, refusing to think
about it, but now he faced it. Kneeling here on the ledge, the
fingertips of one hand pressed to the narrow strip of wood, he
could, he knew, draw his other hand back a yard perhaps, fist
clenched tight, doing it very slowly till he sensed the outer limit
of balance, then, as hard as he was able from the distance, he
could drive his fist forward against the glass. If it broke, his fist

550   smashing through, he was safe; he might cut himself badly, and
probably would, but with his arm inside the room, he would be
secure. But if the glass did not break, the rebound, flinging his
arm back, would topple him off the ledge. He was certain of that.

He tested his plan. The fingers of his left hand clawlike on the little stripping, he drew back his other fist until his body began teetering backward. But he had no leverage now—he could feel that there would be no force to his swing—and he moved his fist slowly forward till he rocked forward on his knees again and could sense that his swing would carry its greatest force. Glancing down, however, measuring the distance from his fist to the glass, he saw that it was less than two feet.

It occurred to him that he could raise his arm over his head, to bring it down against the glass. But, experimentally in slow motion, he knew it would be an awkward blow without the force of a driving punch, and not nearly enough to break the glass.

Facing the window, he had to drive a blow from the shoulder, he knew now, at a distance of less than two feet; and he did not know whether it would break through the heavy glass. It might; he could picture it happening, he could feel it in the nerves of his arm. And it might not; he could feel that, too—feel his fist striking this glass and being instantaneously flung back by the unbreaking pane, feel the fingers of his other hand breaking loose, nails scraping along the casing as he fell.

He waited, arm drawn back, fist balled, but in no hurry to strike; this pause, he knew, might be an extension of his life. And to live even a few seconds longer, he felt, even out here on this ledge in the night, was infinitely better than to die a moment earlier than he had to. His arm grew tired, and he brought it down and rested it.

Then he knew that it was time to make the attempt. He could not kneel here hesitating indefinitely till he lost all courage to act, waiting till he slipped off the ledge. Again he drew back his arm, knowing this time that he would not bring it down till he struck. His elbow protruding over Lexington Avenue far below, the fingers of his other hand pressed down bloodlessly tight against the narrow stripping, he waited, feeling the sick tenseness and terrible excitement building. It grew and

**PREDICT**

Pause at line 565. Will Tom be able to break the glass? Explain.

**WORD STUDY**

Examine the word *instantaneously* (line 571). Circle the smaller word within it that is familiar to you. Then, underline its suffix, or word ending. What does *instantaneously* mean?

**IDENTIFY**

Underline the sentence in lines 574–579 that explains why Tom hesitates.

**PLOT**

The **climax** is the most exciting part of a story. Underline the sentence in lines 588–593 that is the climax.

**VOCABULARY**

**unimpeded** (un'im·pēd'id) *adj.*: not blocked; unobstructed.

*Unimpeded* has the prefix *un–*, meaning "not." If you remove the prefix, you have the word *impeded*, meaning "blocked; obstructed." The Latin root *–pede–* means "foot." *Impede* comes directly from a Latin word meaning "to hold someone by the foot."

**INTERPRET**

At the end of the story, why does Tom laugh when he sees the yellow sheet of paper fly out the window?

_____

_____

_____

_____

_____

_____

_____

_____

_____

_____

_____

swelled toward the moment of action, his nerves tautening. He thought of Clare—just a wordless, yearning thought—and then 590 drew his arm back just a bit more, fist so tight his fingers pained him, and knowing he was going to do it. Then with full power, with every last scrap of strength he could bring to bear, he shot his arm forward toward the glass, and he said "Clare!"

He heard the sound, felt the blow, felt himself falling forward, and his hand closed on the living-room curtains, the shards and fragments of glass showering onto the floor. And then, kneeling there on the ledge, an arm thrust into the room up to the shoulder, he began picking away the protruding slivers and great wedges of glass from the window frame, tossing them in 600 onto the rug. And, as he grasped the edges of the empty window frame and climbed into his home, he was grinning in triumph.

He did not lie down on the floor or run through the apartment, as he had promised himself; even in the first few moments it seemed to him natural and normal that he should be where he was. He simply turned to his desk, pulled the crumpled yellow sheet from his pocket, and laid it down where it had been, smoothing it out; then he absently laid a pencil across it to weight it down. He shook his head wonderingly, and turned to walk toward the closet.

610 There he got out his topcoat and hat and, without waiting to put them on, opened the front door and stepped out, to go find his wife. He turned to pull the door closed and warm air from the hall rushed through the narrow opening again. As he saw the yellow paper, the pencil flying, scooped off the desk and, **unimpeded** by the glassless window, sail out into the night and out of his life, Tom Benecke burst into laughter and then closed the door behind him.

# Contents of the Dead Man's Pocket

**Story Map**    Review the sequence of events in "Contents of the Dead Man's Pocket." Then, fill in the Story Map below.

| Title |
| --- |
| |

| Setting |
| --- |
| |

| Characters |
| --- |
| |

| Problem |
| --- |
| |

↓

| Event 1 |
| --- |
| |

| Event 2 |
| --- |
| |

| Event 3 |
| --- |
| |

| Event 4 |
| --- |
| |

| Event 5 (Climax) |
| --- |
| |

↓

| Resolution |
| --- |
| |

# Standards Review

**LITERATURE**

## TestPractice — Contents of the Dead Man's Pocket

Complete the sample test item below. The box at the right explains why three of these choices are not correct.

| Sample Test Item | Explanation of the Correct Answer |
|---|---|
| One **conflict** of the story takes place between— <br><br> A  Tom and his boss <br> B  Tom and his own ambition <br> C  Tom and his wife <br> D  Tom and a book of matches | The correct answer is *B*. <br><br> *A* is incorrect because Tom's boss is not mentioned in the story. *C* is incorrect because Tom and his wife haven't argued. *D* is also incorrect; Tom has trouble lighting the matches, but the matches present only a minor difficulty. |

**DIRECTIONS:** Answer the following questions by circling the letter of the best response.

**Reading Standard 3.4 (Grade 8 Review)**
Analyze the relevance of the setting (e.g., place, time, customs) to the mood, tone, and meaning of the text.

**Reading Standard 3.6**
Analyze and trace an author's development of time and sequence, including the use of complex literary devices (e.g., foreshadowing, flashbacks).

1. The **setting** of "Contents of the Dead Man's Pocket" provides—

   A  beauty    C  suspense

   B  humor    D  romance

2. All of the following describe Tom's **internal conflicts** *except*—

   F  deciding between work and the movies

   G  overcoming his fear

   H  fighting the temptation to look down

   J  rescuing the paper from the ledge

3. In the story's sequence of events, which event happens last?

   A  Tom breaks the window.

   B  Tom lights the matches.

   C  Clare goes to the movies.

   D  Tom steps out onto the ledge.

4. The author slows down time by—

   F  using flashback and foreshadowing

   G  describing the events moment by moment

   H  setting the story on the eleventh-floor ledge

   J  focusing on one character

5. At the **resolution** of "Contents of the Dead Man's Pocket" Tom realizes that—

   A  work is less important

   B  work is more important

   C  family and work are of equal importance

   D  family is less important

# Standards Review

**TestPractice** | **Contents of the Dead Man's Pocket**

## Prefixes

**DIRECTIONS:** Match each prefix with its definition by writing the correct letter on the line.

1. _____ re–

2. _____ un–

3. _____ sub–

4. _____ pro–

a. no; not

b. forward

c. again

d. below

**Reading Standard 1.1** Identify and use the literal and figurative meanings of words and understand word derivations.

## Vocabulary in Context

**DIRECTIONS:** Complete the paragraph by writing a word from the word box to fit in each sentence below. Not all words will be used.

**Word Box**

projection
discarding
confirmation
exhalation
incomprehensible
rebounded
unimpeded
irrelevantly
interminable
imperceptibly

Tom crept on the ledge, holding his breath, then let out a great (1) _____ of air. So (2) _____ did he move that Tom felt as if he were standing still. He had been on the ledge, he thought, an (3) _____ length of time. However, his burning cigarette was (4) _____ that he had actually been there only a few minutes. Staring at his unreadable, (5) _____ scrawl on the sheet of paper, he wondered why the work had seemed so important.

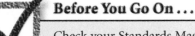

**Before You Go On . . .**

Check your Standards Mastery at the back of this book.

# The Love Letter by Jack Finney

Jake Belknap buys an old desk to use for writing to his family. Imagine his astonishment when the desk puts him in touch with a person from long ago.

## LITERARY FOCUS: TIME AND SEQUENCE

Most stories have a **plot,** a series of related events. In many of those stories, the plot is presented in chronological order: The events are told in the order in which they happen. The events in some stories, however, jump around in time. You may read of events happening in the present, then read of events that happened in the past. You might even read a story that takes place in two different **time frames**—with some events happening in the present at the same time other events are happening many years earlier or later.

- "The Love Letter" takes place in two different time frames. As you read, notice which character lives in 1959 and which character lives at an earlier time. How do they communicate?

- A **flashback** occurs when the narrator interrupts the story to tell about events that took place before the present action. Look for the flashback toward the beginning of "The Love Letter."

Keep track of the time frames in "The Love Letter" by filling out a chart like this one as you read. Write the event, and check which time frame it occurs in.

| Story Event | Time Frame: 1959 | Time Frame: Late 1800s |
|---|---|---|
|  |  |  |
|  |  |  |

## READING SKILLS: PARAPHRASE

Some of the letters within the story are written in a style that may be unfamiliar to you. The sentences are long, and the vocabulary is old-fashioned. To be sure you understand the text of each letter, read it through first. Then, **paraphrase** it—restate, in your own words, what you have read.

**Example from Text**
"Dearest! Papa, Mama, Willy, and Cook are long retired and to sleep."

**Sample Paraphrase**
"Sweetie! Dad, Mom, Willy, and the cook went to bed ages ago and are sound asleep."

**Reading Standard 1.1**
Identify and use the literal and figurative meanings of words and understand word derivations.

**Reading Standard 3.4 (Grade 8 Review)**
Analyze the relevance of the setting (e.g., place, time, customs) to the mood, tone, and meaning of the text.

**Reading Standard 3.6**
Analyze and trace an author's development of time and sequence, including the use of complex literary devices (e.g., foreshadowing, flashbacks).

## VOCABULARY DEVELOPMENT

### PREVIEW SELECTION VOCABULARY

Preview the following words from the story before you begin reading.

**premonition** (prem′ə·nish′ən) *n.:* feeling that something will happen.

*Jake has no **premonition**—no warning—that the desk contains a secret.*

**vaguely** (vāg′lē) *adv.:* in a way that is not definite or clear.

***Vaguely** he remembered the little drawer in the desk.*

**whimsical** (hwim′zi·kəl) *adj.:* impulsive; tending to act on sudden, fanciful ideas.

*Helen is serious, not **whimsical** and foolish.*

**indulgent** (in·dul′jənt) *adj.:* overly kind.

*Helen is tired of **indulgent** smiles from people with false manners.*

**rational** (rash′ən·əl) *adj.:* based on reasoning and logic rather than emotions.

*Although he is usually **rational,** Jake must also follow his heart.*

### CONTEXT CLUES

You can use **context clues** to help you figure out the meanings of some unfamiliar words. A word's **context** is the phrase or sentence it appears in.

For example, in "The Love Letter," Helen writes, "Papa, Mama, Willy, and Cook are long retired and to sleep." *Retired* has several different meanings. What does *retired* mean here? Look at the phrase *to sleep.* It indicates that in this context, *retired* means "gone to bed."

Later in the story, Jake tells the reader, "My parents sold their old home in New Jersey when my father retired two years ago, and now they live in Florida and enjoy it." Here *retired* means "gave up one's work because of age."

# The Love Letter

## Jack Finney

**PLOT**

Underline the detail in line 1 that **foreshadows,** or suggests, that something strange may happen with the desk.

**VOCABULARY**

**premonition** (prem′·ə·nish′ən) *n.:* feeling that something will happen.

**WORD STUDY**

Re-read lines 4–6. What is a *proprietor?* Underline the **context clues** that help you figure out the word's meaning.

_____

_____

_____

**WORD STUDY**

Circle the **context clue** that helps you understand what a *kitchenette* is (line 23).

**PLOT**

In lines 25–30, the narrator interrupts the present action to tell about events that happened earlier. Underline the sentence that begins the **flashback.**

I've heard of secret drawers in old desks, of course—who hasn't? But the day I bought my desk, I wasn't thinking of secret drawers, and I know very well I didn't have any least **premonition** or feel of mystery about it. I spotted it in the window of a secondhand store near my apartment, went in to look it over, and the proprietor told me where he got it. It came from one of the last of the big, old, mid-Victorian houses in Brooklyn; they were tearing it down over on Brock Place a few blocks away. He'd bought the desk along with some other furniture, dishes, glass-
10 ware, light fixtures, and so on. But it didn't stir my imagination particularly; I never wondered or cared who might have used it long ago. I bought it and lugged it home because it was cheap and because it was small. It was a legless little wall desk that I fastened to my living-room wall with heavy screws directly into the studding.

I'm twenty-four years old, tall and thin, and I live in Brooklyn to save money, and work in Manhattan to make it. When you're twenty-four and a bachelor, you usually figure you'll be married before much longer. I'm reasonably ambitious
20 and bring work home from the office every once in a while. And maybe every couple weeks or so I write a letter to my folks in Florida. So I'd been needing a desk; there's no table in my phone-booth kitchenette, and I'd been trying to work at a wobbly little end table I couldn't get my knees under.

So I bought the desk one Saturday afternoon, and spent an hour or more fastening it to the wall. It was after six when I finished. I had a date that night, and so I had time to stand and admire it for only a minute or so. It was made of heavy wood,

with a slant **top** like a kid's school desk, and with the same sort

30 of space **underneath** to put things into. But the back of it rose a good two **feet above** the desk top, and was full of pigeonholes like an old-style, roll-top desk. Underneath the pigeonholes was a row of three **brass**-knobbed little drawers. It was all pretty ornate; the **drawer** ends carved, some fancy scrollwork extending up over the back and out from the sides to help brace it against the wall. I dragged a chair up, sat down at the desk to try it for

WORD STUDY

The *pigeonhole* of a desk (line 31) is a small, open compartment used for filing papers. It gets its name from the fact that pigeons seek out similar small places to roost in.

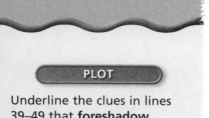

**PLOT**

Underline the clues in lines 39–49 that **foreshadow** what's to come.

**VOCABULARY**

**vaguely** (vāg′lē) *adv.:* in a way that is not definite or clear.

**PARAPHRASE**

Re-read lines 67–71. Paraphrase what Jake discovers.

height, then got showered, shaved, and dressed, and went over to Manhattan to pick up my date.

40     I'm trying to be honest about what happened, and I'm convinced that includes the way I felt when I got home around two or two-thirty that morning. I'm certain that what happened wouldn't have happened at all if I'd felt any other way. I'd had a good-enough time that evening. Roberta Haig is pretty nice— bright, pleasant, good-looking. But walking home from the subway, the Brooklyn streets quiet and deserted, it occurred to me that, while I'd probably see her again, I didn't really care whether I did or not. And I wondered, as I often had lately, whether I'd ever meet a girl I desperately wanted to be with— the only way a man can get married, it seems to me.

50     So when I stepped into my apartment I knew I wasn't going to feel like sleep for a while. I was restless, and I took off my coat and yanked down my tie, wondering whether I wanted some coffee. Then—I'd forgotten about it—I saw the desk I'd bought that afternoon, and I walked over and sat down at it, thoroughly examining it for the first time.

    I lifted the top, and stared down into the empty space underneath it. Lowering the top, I reached into one of the pigeonholes, and my hand and shirt cuff came out streaked with old dust; the holes were a good foot deep. I pulled open one of 60 the little brass-knobbed drawers, and there was a shred of paper in one of its corners, nothing else. I pulled the drawer all the way out and studied its construction, turning it in my hands; it was a solidly made, beautifully mortised[1] little thing. Then I pushed my hand into the drawer opening; it went in to about the middle of my hand before my fingertips touched the back. There was nothing in there.

    For a few moments I just sat at the desk, thinking **vaguely** that I could write a letter to my folks. And then it suddenly occurred to me that the little drawer in my hand was only half a

---

1.   **mortised** (môrt′ist) *v.* used as *adj.:* joined or fastened.

70   foot long, while the pigeonholes just above the drawer extended
     a good foot back.

         Shoving my hand in the opening again, exploring with my
     fingertips, I found a secret drawer which lay in back of the first.
     There was a little sheaf of folded writing paper, plain white, but
     yellow with age at the edges, and the sheets were all blank. There
     were three or four blank envelopes to match, and underneath
     them a small, round glass bottle of ink. There was nothing else
     in the drawer.

         And then, putting the things back into the drawer, I felt the
80   slight extra thickness of one blank envelope, saw that it was
     sealed, and I ripped it open to find the letter inside. The folded
     paper opened stiffly, the crease permanent with age, and even
     before I saw the date I knew this letter was old. The handwriting
     was obviously feminine, and beautifully clear—it's called
     Spencerian,[2] isn't it?—the letters perfectly formed and very
     ornate, the capitals, especially, being a whirl of dainty curlicues.[3]
     The ink was rust-black, the date at the top of the page was
     May 14, 1882, and, reading it, I saw that it was a love letter.
     It began:

90   *Dearest! Papa, Mama, Willy, and Cook are long retired[4] and to*
     *sleep. Now, the night far advanced, the house silent, I alone remain*
     *awake, at last free to speak to you as I choose. Yes, I am willing to*
     *say it! Heart of mine, I crave your bold glance, I long for the tender*
     *warmth of your look; I welcome your ardency,[5] and prize it; for*
     *what else should these be taken but sweet tribute to me?*

     I smiled a little; it was hard to believe that people had once
     expressed themselves in elaborate phrasings of this kind, but

IDENTIFY

Underline the details in lines
72–89 that indicate that the
contents of the desk are old.

IDENTIFY

Pause at line 90. Circle the
date the letter was written.

---

2.  **Spencerian** (spen·sir′ē·ən) *adj.:* characteristic of an elegant style
    of handwriting, with carefully formed letters.
3.  **curlicues** (kʉr′li·kyo͞oz) *n.:* fancy curves, as in a design or in handwriting.
4.  **retired** (ri·tīrd′) *v.:* gone to bed.
5.  **ardency** (är′dən·sē) *n.:* passion. The adjective form, *ardent,* appears
    in the letter's third paragraph.

they had. The letter continued, and I wondered why it had never been sent:

**PARAPHRASE**

Re-read lines 100–109, and restate the text in your own words.

**VOCABULARY**

**whimsical** (hwim′zi·kəl) *adj.:* impulsive; tending to act on sudden, fanciful ideas.

**indulgent** (in·dul′jənt) *adj.:* overly kind.

**WORD STUDY**

*Deride* (line 103) means "laugh at." Circle the **context clues** that help you figure out this word's meaning.

What does *figment* mean (line 113)? Underline the **context clues** you find.

100 *Dear one: Do not ever change your ways. Never address me other than with what consideration my utterances should deserve. If I be foolish and **whimsical**, deride me sweetly if you will. But if I speak with seriousness, respond always with what care you deem my thoughts worthy. For, oh my beloved, I am sick to death of the **indulgent** smile and tolerant glance with which a woman's fancies⁶ are met. As I am repelled by the false gentleness and nicety of manner which too often ill conceal the wantonness they attempt to mask. I speak of the man I am to marry; if you could but save me from that!*

110 *But you cannot. You are everything I prize; warmly and honestly ardent, respectful in heart as well as in manner, true, and loving. You are as I wish you to be—for you exist only in my mind. But, figment though you are, and though I shall never see your like, you are more dear to me than he to whom I am betrothed.*

*I think of you constantly. I dream of you. I speak with you, in my mind and heart; would you existed outside them! Sweetheart, good night; dream of me, too.*

*With all my love, I am,*
*your Helen*

120 At the bottom of the page, as I'm sure she'd been taught in school, was written, "Miss Helen Elizabeth Worley, Brooklyn, New York," and as I stared down at it now, I was no longer smiling at this cry from the heart in the middle of a long-ago night.

The night is a strange time when you're alone in it, the rest of your world asleep. If I'd found that letter in the daytime, I'd have smiled and shown it to a few friends, then forgotten it. But alone here now, a window partly open, a cool, late-at-night freshness stirring the quiet air—it was impossible to think of the girl who had written this letter as a very old lady, or maybe long

6. **fancies** (fan′sēz) *n.:* wishes; imaginary ideas.

130 since dead. As I read her words, she seemed real and alive to me, sitting—or so I pictured her—pen in hand at this desk, in a long, white, old-fashioned dress, her young hair piled on top of her head, in the dead of a night like this. Here in Brooklyn, almost in sight of where I now sat. And my heart went out to her as I stared down at her secret, hopeless appeal against the world and time she lived in.

I am trying to explain why I answered that letter. There, in the silence of a timeless, spring night, it seemed natural enough to uncork that old bottle, pick up the pen beside it, and then,
140 spreading a sheet of yellowing old notepaper on the desk top, to begin to write. I felt that I was communicating with a still-living young woman when I wrote:

> *Helen. I have just read the letter in the secret drawer of your desk, and I wish I knew how I could possibly help you. I can't tell what you might think of me if there were a way I could reach you. But you are someone I am certain I would like to know. I hope you are beautiful, but you needn't be; you're a girl I could like, and maybe ardently, and if I did, I promise you I'd be true and loving. Do the best you can, Helen Elizabeth Worley, in the time and place you*
> 150 *are; I can't reach you or help you. But I'll think of you. And maybe I'll dream of you, too.*
>
> *Yours,*
> *Jake Belknap*

I was grinning a little sheepishly as I signed my name, knowing I would read through what I had written, then crumple the old sheet and throw it away. But I was glad I'd written it—and I didn't throw it away. Still caught in the feeling of the warm, silent night, it suddenly seemed to me that throwing my letter away would turn the writing of it into a meaningless and foolish thing;
160 though maybe what I did seems more foolish still. I folded the paper, put it into one of the envelopes, and sealed it. Then I

ANALYZE

Underline what the narrator says about the night (lines 124–130). How does the setting—nighttime—affect the plot?

_____
_____
_____
_____
_____
_____
_____
_____

FLUENCY

Read the boxed letter aloud several times. Improve your speed and the smoothness of your delivery each time you read.

INFER

Why do you think Jake answers the letter?

_____
_____
_____
_____
_____

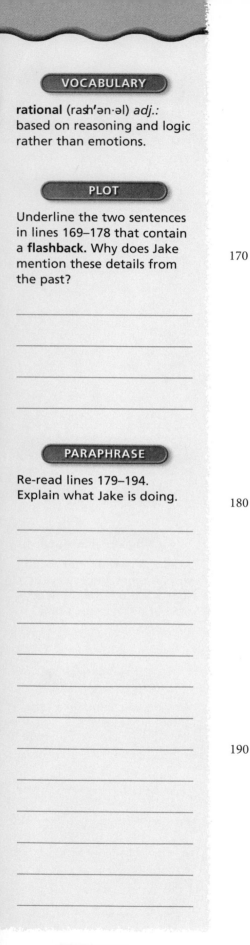

**VOCABULARY**

**rational** (rash′ən·əl) *adj.:*
based on reasoning and logic
rather than emotions.

**PLOT**

Underline the two sentences
in lines 169–178 that contain
a **flashback**. Why does Jake
mention these details from
the past?

_____

_____

_____

_____

**PARAPHRASE**

Re-read lines 179–194.
Explain what Jake is doing.

_____

_____

_____

_____

_____

_____

_____

_____

_____

_____

_____

_____

dipped the pen into the old ink, and wrote "Miss Helen Worley"
on the face of the envelope.

I suppose this can't be explained. You'd have to have been
where I was and felt as I did to understand it; but I wanted to
mail that letter. I simply quit examining my feelings and quit
trying to be **rational;** I was suddenly determined to complete
what I'd begun, just as far as I was able to go.

170   My parents sold their old home in New Jersey when my
father retired two years ago, and now they live in Florida and
enjoy it. And when my mother cleared out the old house I grew
up in, she packed up and mailed me a huge package of useless
things I was glad to have. There were class photographs dating
from grammar school through college, old books I'd read as a
kid, Boy Scout pins—a mass of junk of that sort, including a
stamp collection I'd had in grade school. Now I found these
things on my hall-closet shelf, in the box they'd come in, and I
found my old stamp album.

180   It's funny how things can stick in your mind over the years;
standing at the open closet door, I turned the pages of that beat-
up old album directly to the stamps I remembered buying from
another kid with seventy-five cents I'd earned cutting grass.
There they lay, lightly fastened to the page with a little gummed-
paper hinge; a pair of mint-condition,[7] two-cent, United States
stamps, issued in 1869. And standing there in the hallway looking down at them, I once again got something of the thrill I'd
had as a kid when I acquired them. It's a handsome stamp,
square in shape, with an ornate border and a tiny engraving in
the center: a rider on a galloping post horse. And for all I knew,
190   they might have been worth a fair amount of money by now,
especially an unseparated pair of stamps. But back at the desk,
I pulled one of them loose, tearing carefully through the
perforation, licked the back, and fastened it to the faintly
yellowing old envelope.

---

7.   **mint-condition:** like new or in its original form.

I'd thought no further than that; by now, I suppose, I was in almost a kind of trance. I shoved the old ink bottle and pen into a hip pocket, picked up my letter, and walked out of my apartment.

Brock Place, three blocks away, was deserted when I
200  reached it. Then, as I walked on, my letter in my hand, there stood the old house, just past a little shoe-repair shop. It stood far back from the broken, cast-iron fence, in the center of its wide, weed-grown lot, black-etched in the moonlight, and I stopped on the walk and stood staring up at it.

The high-windowed old roof was gone, the interior nearly gutted, the yard strewn with splintered boards and great chunks of torn plaster. The windows and doors were all removed, the openings hollow in the clear wash of light. But the high old walls, last of all to go, still stood, tall and dignified in their old-
210  fashioned strength and outmoded charm.

Then I walked through the opening where a gate had once hung, up the cracked and weed-grown brick pavement toward the wide old porch. I brought out my ink and pen, and copied

**INFER**

Pause at line 237. Why does Jake take the letter to the old Wister postal station?

_____

_____

_____

_____

_____

_____

_____

_____

_____

_____

_____

**PREDICT**

Pause at line 243. What do you predict will happen to the letter?

_____

_____

_____

_____

_____

_____

_____

the number carefully onto my envelope: _972_ I printed under the name of the girl who had once lived here, _Brock Place, Brooklyn, New York._ Then I turned toward the street again, my envelope in my hand.

There was a mailbox at the next corner, and I stopped beside it. But to drop this letter into that box, knowing in
220   advance that it could go only to the dead-letter office, would again, I couldn't help feeling, turn the writing of it into an empty, meaningless act. After a moment, I walked on past the box, crossed the street and turned right, suddenly knowing exactly where I was going.

I walked four blocks through the night. I turned left at the next corner, walked half a block more, then turned up onto the worn, stone steps of the Wister postal substation.

It must easily be one of the oldest postal substations in the borough; built, I suppose, not much later than during the
230   decade following the Civil War. And I can't imagine that the inside has changed much at all. The floor is marble; the ceiling high; the woodwork dark and carved. The outer lobby is open at all times, as are post-office lobbies everywhere, and as I pushed through the old swinging doors, I saw that it was deserted. As I walked across the worn stone of its floor, I knew I was seeing all around me precisely what Brooklynites had seen for no telling how many generations long dead.

I pushed the worn brass plate open, dropped my letter into the silent blackness of the slot, and it disappeared forever with
240   no sound. Then I turned and left to walk home, with a feeling of fulfillment, of having done, at least, everything I possibly could in response to the silent cry for help I'd found in the secrecy of the old desk.

Next morning I felt the way almost anyone might. Standing at the bathroom mirror shaving, remembering what I'd done the night before, I grinned, feeling foolish but at the same time secretly pleased with myself. I was glad I'd written and solemnly mailed that letter, and now I realized why I'd put no return

250 address on the envelope. I didn't want it to come forlornly back to me with NO SUCH PERSON, or whatever the phrase is stamped on the envelope. There'd once been such a girl, and last night she still existed for me. And I didn't want to see my letter to her—rubber-stamped, scribbled on, and unopened—to prove that there no longer was.

I was terrifically busy all the next week. I work for a wholesale-grocery concern; we got a big new account, a chain of supermarkets, and that meant extra work for everyone. More often than not I had lunch at my desk in the office and worked several evenings besides. I had dates the two evenings I was free.
260 On Friday afternoon I was at the main public library in Manhattan, at Fifth Avenue and Forty-second.

Late in the afternoon the man sitting beside me at the big reading-room table closed his book, stowed away his glasses, picked up his hat from the table, and left. I sat back in my chair, glancing at my watch. Then I looked over at the book he'd left on the table. It was a big, one-volume pictorial history of New York put out by Columbia University. I dragged it over, and began leafing through it.

I skimmed over the first sections on colonial and pre-
270 colonial New York pretty quickly, but when the old sketches and drawings began giving way to actual photographs, I turned the pages more slowly. I leafed past the first photos, taken around the mid-century, and then past those of the Civil War period. But when I reached the first photograph of the 1870's—it was a view of Fifth Avenue in 1871—I began reading the captions under each one.

I knew it would be too much to hope to find a photograph of Brock Place, in Helen Worley's time especially, and, of course, I didn't. But I knew there'd surely be photographs taken in
280 Brooklyn during the 1880's, and a few pages farther on I found what I'd hoped I might. In clear, sharp detail—and beautifully reproduced—lay a big, half-page photograph of a street less than a quarter mile from Brock Place; and, staring down at it there in

INFER

Pause at line 276. Circle the dates when the photographs were taken. Why is Jake interested in these photographs?

the library, I knew that Helen Worley must often have walked along this very sidewalk. "Varney Street, 1881," the caption said, "a typical Brooklyn residential street of the period."

Far down that lovely, tree-sheltered street—out of focus and distinct—walked the retreating figure of a long-skirted, puff-sleeved woman, her summer parasol[8] open at her back. Of the thousands of long-dead girls it might have been, I knew this could not be Helen Worley. Yet it wasn't completely impossible, I told myself; this was a street, precisely as I saw it now, down which she must often have walked. I let myself think that yes, this was she. Maybe I live in what is, for me, the wrong time. I was filled now with the most desperate yearning to be there, on that peaceful street—to walk off, past the edges of the scene on the printed page before me, into the old and beautiful Brooklyn of long ago. And to draw near and overtake that bobbing parasol in the distance; and then turn and look into the face of the girl who held it.

I worked that evening at home, sitting at my desk. Once more now, Helen Elizabeth Worley was in my mind. I worked steadily all evening, and it was around twelve-thirty when I finished; eleven handwritten pages which I'd get typed at the office on Monday. Then I opened the little center desk drawer into which I'd put a supply of rubber bands and paper clips, took out a clip and fastened the pages together, and sat back in my chair. The little center desk drawer stood half open as I'd left it, and then, as my eye fell on it, I realized suddenly that, of course, it, too, must have another secret drawer behind it.

I hadn't thought of that. It simply hadn't occurred to me the week before, in my interest and excitement over the letter I'd found behind the first drawer of the row; and I'd been too busy all week to think of it since. But now I pulled the center drawer all the way out, reached behind it and found the little groove in the smooth wood I touched. Then I brought out the second secret little drawer.

**PREDICT**

Pause at line 310. What do you think will happen next?

**PLOT**

Underline the words in lines 311–317 that tell how much time has passed since Jake found Helen's letter.

---

8. **parasol** (par′ə·sôl′) n.: small umbrella used as a sunshade.

The night is a strange time; things are different at night, as every human being knows somewhere deep inside him. And I

320 think this: Brooklyn has changed over seven decades; it is no longer the same place at all. But here and there, still, are little islands—isolated remnants[9] of the way things once were. And the Wister postal substation is one of them; it has changed, really, not at all. I think that there, in the dimness of the old Wister post office, in the dead of night, lifting my letter to Helen Worley toward the old brass door of the letter drop—I think that I stood on one side of that slot in the year 1959, and that I dropped my letter, properly stamped, written and addressed in the ink and on the very paper of Helen Worley's youth, into the

330 Brooklyn of 1882 on the other side of that worn, old slot.

I believe that—I'm not even interested in proving it—but I believe it. Because now, from that second secret little drawer, I brought out the paper I found in it, opened it, and, in rust-black ink on yellowing old paper, I read:

*Please, oh, please—who are you? Where can I reach you? Your letter arrived today in the second morning-post, and I have wandered the house and garden ever since in an agony of excitement. I cannot conceive how you saw my letter in its secret place, but since you did, perhaps you will see this one, too. Oh, tell me*

340 *your letter is no hoax or cruel joke! Willy, if it is you; if you have discovered my letter and think to deceive your sister with a prank, I pray you to tell me! But if it is not—if I now address someone who has truly responded to my most secret hopes—do not longer keep me ignorant of who and where you are. For I, too—and I confess it willingly—long to see you! and I, too, feel and am most certain of it, that if I could know you, I would love you. It is impossible for me to think otherwise.*

*I must hear from you again; I shall not rest until I do.*

*I remain, most sincerely,*

*Helen Elizabeth Worley*

350

---

9. **remnants** (rem′nənts) *n.:* leftovers; small remaining parts.

PLOT

Circle the date in line 327 that tells when Jake is living. Then, circle the date in line 330 that tells when Helen lived.

PLOT

Pause at line 348. Helen is living in the past, yet responding to a letter written in the present. What is Helen unaware of at this point in the story?

_____

_____

_____

_____

_____

_____

WORD STUDY

What is a hoax (line 340)? Circle the context clues that hint at the word's meaning.

_____

_____

_____

_____

_____

After a long time, I opened the first little drawer of the old desk and took out the pen and ink I'd found there, and a sheet of the notepaper.

For minutes then, the pen in my hand, I sat there in the night staring down at the empty paper on the desktop. Finally, then, I dipped the pen into the old ink and wrote:

*Helen, my dear: I don't know how to say this so it will seem even comprehensible to you. But I do exist, here in Brooklyn, less than three blocks from where you now read this—in the year 1959. We*
360 *are separated not by space, but by the years which lie between us. Now I own the desk which you once had, and at which you wrote the note I found in it. Helen, all I can tell you is that I answered that note, mailed it late at night at the old Wister station, and that somehow it reached you, as I hope this will, too. This is no hoax! Can you imagine anyone playing a joke that cruel? I live in a Brooklyn, within sight of your house, that you cannot imagine. It is a city whose streets are now crowded with wheeled vehicles propelled by engines. And it is a city extending far beyond the limits you know, with a population of millions, so crowded there is*
370 *hardly room any longer for trees. From my window as I write I can see—across Brooklyn Bridge, which is hardly changed from the way you, too, can see it now—Manhattan Island, and rising from it are the lighted silhouettes[10] of stone and steel buildings more than one thousand feet high.*

*You must believe me. I live, I exist, seventy-seven years after you read this; and with the feeling that I have fallen in love with you.*

I sat for some moments staring at the wall, trying to figure out how to explain something I was certain was true. Then I wrote:

380 *Helen: There are three secret drawers in our desk. Into the first you put only the letter I found. You cannot now add something to that*

---

10. **silhouettes** (sil'ə·wets') *n.:* dark shapes against a light background.

---

**IDENTIFY**

Underline the words in lines 357–374 that tell what Brooklyn was like in 1959.

_____

_____

_____

_____

_____

_____

_____

_____

*drawer and hope that it will reach me. For I have already opened*
*that drawer and found only the letter you put there. Nothing else*
*can now come down through the years to me in that drawer, for*
*you cannot now alter what you have already done.*

*In the second drawer, in 1882, you put the note which lies*
*before me, which I found when I opened that drawer a few minutes*
*ago. You put nothing else into it, and now that, too, cannot be*
*changed.*

390 *But I haven't opened the third drawer, Helen. Not yet! It is the*
*last way you can still reach me, and the last time. I will mail this as*
*I did before, then wait. In a week, I will open the last drawer.*

*Jake Belknap*


It was a long week. I worked. I kept busy daytimes; but at night,
I thought of hardly anything but the third secret drawer in my
desk. I was terribly tempted to open it earlier, telling myself that
whatever might lie in it had been put there decades before and
must be there now, but I wasn't sure, and I waited.

Then, late at night, a week to the hour after I'd mailed my
400 second letter at the old Wister post office, I pulled out the third
drawer, reached in, and brought out the last little secret drawer
which lay behind it. My hand was actually shaking, and for a
moment I couldn't bear to look directly—something lay in the
drawer—and I turned my head away. Then I looked.

I'd expected a long letter; very long, of many pages, her last
communication with me, and full of everything she wanted to
say. But there was no letter at all. It was a photograph, about
three inches square, a faded sepia in color, mounted on heavy,
stiff cardboard, and with the photographer's name in tiny gold
410 script down in the corner: Brunner & Holland, Parisian
Photography, Brooklyn, N.Y.

The photograph showed the head and shoulders of a girl
in a high-necked, dark dress with a cameo brooch at the collar.
Her dark hair was swept tightly back, covering the ears, in a style
which no longer suits our idea of beauty. But the stark severity

## CLARIFY

Re-read lines 380–385. Why
does Jake tell Helen not to
add anything to the first
drawer?

_____

_____

_____

_____

_____

_____

_____

_____

_____

## PLOT

Circle the words in line 392
that tell how much time will
pass before Jake opens the
third drawer.

## WORD STUDY

*Sepia* (line 408) means
"reddish-brown color."

_____

_____

_____

_____

_____

_____

**PLOT**

Circle the sentence in line 423 that Helen wrote at the bottom of her photograph. Circle the sentence in line 435 that was etched on her tombstone. What do the two sentences tell about the **time order** of the plot?

_____

_____

_____

_____

_____

_____

_____

_____

_____

_____

_____

_____

_____

_____

_____

_____

_____

_____

_____

_____

_____

_____

of that dress and hairstyle couldn't spoil the beauty of the face that smiled out at me from that old photograph. It wasn't beautiful in any classical sense, I suppose. The brows were unplucked and somewhat heavier than we are used to. But it is the soft,

420   warm smile of her lips, and her eyes—large and serene as she looks out at me over the years—that make Helen Elizabeth Worley a beautiful woman. Across the bottom of her photograph she had written, "I will never forget." And as I sat there at the old desk, staring at what she had written, I understood that, of course, that was all there was to say—what else?—on this, the last time, as she knew, that she'd ever be able to reach me.

It wasn't the last time, though. There was one final way for Helen Worley to communicate with me over the years, and it took me a long time, as it must have taken her, to realize it.

430   Only a week ago, on my fourth day of searching, I finally found it. It was late in the evening, and the sun was almost gone, when I found the old headstone among all the others stretching off in rows under the quiet trees. And then I read the inscription etched in the weathered old stone: Helen Elizabeth Worley— 1861–1934. Under this were the words, *I Never Forgot.*

And neither will I.

# The Love Letter

**Time Line**    "The Love Letter" tells of events that take place in two time periods. Clarify the sequence of events by filling in the Time Line below. Place the events in the order in which they actually happened. The first one is done for you.

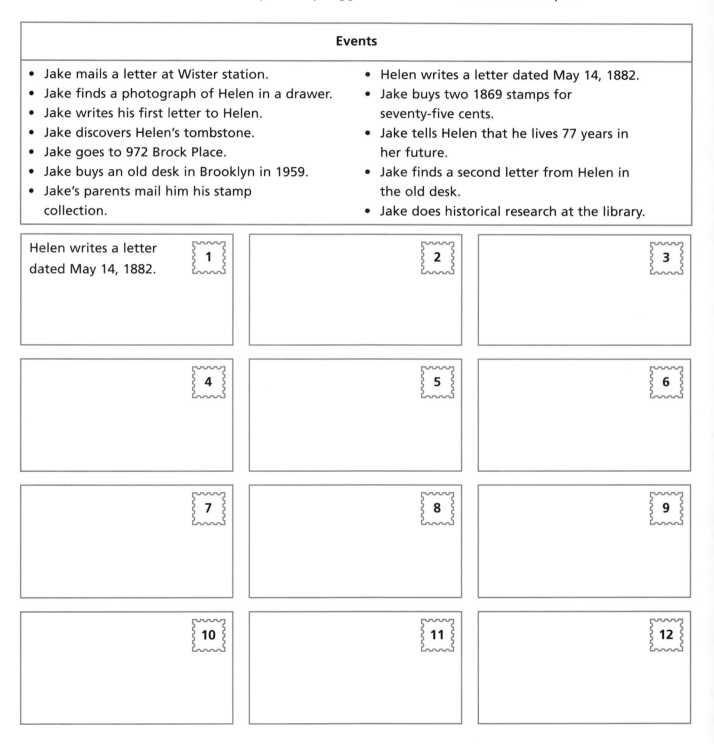

| Events |
|---|
|  |

- Jake mails a letter at Wister station.
- Jake finds a photograph of Helen in a drawer.
- Jake writes his first letter to Helen.
- Jake discovers Helen's tombstone.
- Jake goes to 972 Brock Place.
- Jake buys an old desk in Brooklyn in 1959.
- Jake's parents mail him his stamp collection.

- Helen writes a letter dated May 14, 1882.
- Jake buys two 1869 stamps for seventy-five cents.
- Jake tells Helen that he lives 77 years in her future.
- Jake finds a second letter from Helen in the old desk.
- Jake does historical research at the library.

**1** Helen writes a letter dated May 14, 1882.

**2**

**3**

**4**

**5**

**6**

**7**

**8**

**9**

**10**

**11**

**12**

# Standards Review

**TestPractice** : **The Love Letter**

Complete the sample test item below. Then, read the explanation at right.

| Sample Test Item | Explanation of the Correct Answer |
|---|---|
| The **setting** of this story is important because— <br><br> **A** Jake's last communication with Helen is in a graveyard. <br><br> **B** The two characters live in different times. <br><br> **C** Jake finds Helen's letter in an old desk. <br><br> **D** Helen's writing style is old-fashioned. | The correct answer is *B*. <br><br> *A* is a minor setting in the story. *C* is also incorrect, because the desk is only a way for Jake to find Helen's letters. *D* is not correct; although Helen's writing style *is* from another time, Jake can understand what she says. |

**DIRECTIONS:** Circle the letter of the best response.

**Reading Standard 3.4 (Grade 8 Review)**
Analyze the relevance of the setting (e.g., place, time, customs) to the mood, tone, and meaning of the text.

**Reading Standard 3.6**
Analyze and trace an author's development of time and sequence, including the use of complex literary devices (e.g., foreshadowing, flashbacks).

1. Which of the following is an example of **foreshadowing**?

   **A** Jake expects a long letter but receives a photograph instead.

   **B** Jake goes on an unsatisfying date with Roberta Haig.

   **C** Jake says that he didn't have a sense of mystery about the desk.

   **D** Jake buys the desk because it is inexpensive and small.

2. Which event happens first in the **plot**—in the story as the author tells it?

   **F** Jake finds a letter dated May 14, 1882.

   **G** Jake mails a letter in 1959.

   **H** Jake receives a photograph from Helen.

   **J** Jake buys an old desk.

3. In **chronological (time) order,** which event happens last?

   **A** Helen signs her photograph for Jake.

   **B** Helen writes a letter dated May 14, 1882.

   **C** Jake buys an old desk.

   **D** Jake finds the first letter.

4. How does Jake "visit" Helen's world of the 1870s?

   **F** He travels back to 1870 in a time machine.

   **G** He starts collecting antiques.

   **H** He leafs through a New York history book at the library.

   **J** He dreams about the 1870s in his sleep.

# Standards Review

**TestPractice** : **The Love Letter**

## Context Clues

**DIRECTIONS:** Circle the letter of the best response.

1. Identify the context clue for the **boldface** word in the following sentence:

   *Jake **leafed** through the book, looking at the photographs of Brooklyn taken when Helen was a child.*

   **A** turning the pages

   **B** photographs

   **C** Brooklyn

   **D** Helen was a child

2. Which item is *not* a context clue for the **boldface** word in the following sentence?

   *Tearing carefully along the **perforation**, Jake separated the two stamps.*

   **F** tearing

   **G** Jake

   **H** separated

   **J** two stamps

**Reading Standard 1.1** Identify and use the literal and figurative meanings of words and understand word derivations.

## Vocabulary in Context

**DIRECTIONS:** Complete the paragraph by writing a word from the word box to fit in each sentence below.

**Word Box**

rational

indulgent

whimsical

premonition

vaguely

Mr. Smish, a(n) (1) _____ father who often spoiled his son, bought the boy an unusual present. If he had been in a more (2) _____ state of mind and had been thinking more clearly, Mr. Smish would not have acted on impulse and bought such a(n) (3) _____ gift. Uncertain of his son's response, Mr. Smish was (4) _____ hoping that the boy would use the carrier pigeon to send letters to his grandparents. When he saw the boy's reaction, though, Mr. Smish had a(n) (5) _____ that, pretty soon, he would have to feed the bird and clean the cage himself.

✓ **Before You Go On . . .**
Check your Standards Mastery at the back of this book.

# Character

# Academic Vocabulary for Chapter 2

These are the terms you should know
as you read and analyze the stories in this chapter.

---

**Character traits**  The special qualities of a character, such as his or her behaviors, values, habits, likes, and dislikes.

**Characterization**  The way writers reveal how and why characters think, feel, and act. In **direct characterization,** the writer explains straight out, or directly, what the characters are like. In **indirect characterization,** the writer provides clues to what the characters are like. Clues are often found in the characters' words, private thoughts, and actions, as well as in the ways they look and dress.

**Motivation**  The reasons why a character acts or thinks in a certain way.

● ● ●

**Protagonist**  The main character in a story, usually the one who sets the action in motion.

**Antagonist**  The character or force that blocks the protagonist from achieving his or her goal.

**Subordinate characters**  Less-important characters.

● ● ●

**Flat character**  A character who has only one or two key personality traits.

**Round character**  A character who has many personality traits.

**Stock character**  A one-sided character whom we think of as a "type"— for example, the absent-minded professor.

● ● ●

**Dynamic character**  A character who changes in an important way during the story.

**Static character**  A character who is the same at the end of the story as at the beginning; static characters are most often subordinate characters.

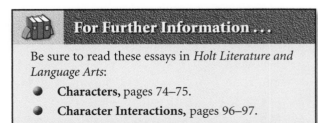

### For Further Information . . .

Be sure to read these essays in *Holt Literature and Language Arts*:

● **Characters,** pages 74–75.
● **Character Interactions,** pages 96–97.

**Reading Standard 1.3 (Grade 8 Review)** Use word meanings within the appropriate context and show ability to verify those meanings by definition, restatement, example, comparison, or contrast.

**Reading Standard 3.3** Analyze interactions between main and subordinate characters in a literary text (for example, internal and external conflicts, motivations, relationships, influences), and explain the way those interactions affect the plot.

**Reading Standard 3.4** Determine characters' traits by what the characters say about themselves in narration, dialogue, dramatic monologue, and soliloquy.

# Everyday Use by Alice Walker

## VOCABULARY DEVELOPMENT

### PREVIEW SELECTION VOCABULARY

The following words appear in "Everyday Use." Preview these words and their definitions before you begin reading.

**sidle** (sīd′'l) *v.:* move sideways, especially in a shy or sneaky manner.

*Try to walk with confidence rather than **sidle** up to people as if they scare you.*

**furtive** (fur′tiv) *adj.:* acting as if trying not to be seen. *Furtive* also means "done secretly."

*Boys followed her around in a **furtive** way, hoping not to be noticed.*

**cowering** (kou′ər·iŋ) *v.* used as *adj.:* drawing back or huddling in fear.

*The photograph showed me by the house, my frightened young daughter **cowering** behind my skirt.*

**oppress** (ə·pres′) *v.:* persecute; keep down by unjust use of power.

*Workers in dangerous, poorly paid jobs may feel that their bosses **oppress** them.*

**doctrines** (däk′trinz) *n.:* principles; teachings; beliefs.

*He agrees with many **doctrines** of that religion but disagrees with a few of the beliefs.*

**rifling** (rī′fliŋ) *v.* used as *n.:* searching thoroughly or in a rough manner.

*"The contents of that trunk are personal," I said. "Please stop **rifling** through it."*

### CONTEXT CLUES

When you come across an unfamiliar word, look at its **context**—the words and sentences surrounding it. You may find a definition, a restatement, or an example of the unknown word to help you unlock its meaning. In the examples below, the underlined words provide context clues for the boldface words.

DEFINITION: To **appreciate** the quilts, you must <u>understand their value</u> to the family.

RESTATEMENT: Suddenly Dee is **confronted** by her mother, who <u>challenges</u> her.

EXAMPLE: Maggie is ashamed of her **homely** features, including <u>the ugly scars on her legs</u>.

As you read "Everyday Use," look for other context clues in the form of examples, definitions, or restatements.

# Everyday Use

## For Your Grandmama

### Alice Walker

**CHARACTER**

In lines 8–13, the narrator, Mama, explains why Maggie will be nervous "until after her sister goes." Circle the disturbing detail that helps explain Maggie's lack of confidence. Underline the details that show how Maggie feels about her sister.

_____

_____

_____

_____

_____

_____

_____

**INFER**

In lines 22–30, Mama tells about a dream in which Dee embraces her on TV. What might Mama really want from Dee?

_____

_____

_____

_____

_____

I will wait for her in the yard that Maggie and I made so clean and wavy yesterday afternoon. A yard like this is more comfortable than most people know. It is not just a yard. It is like an extended living room. When the hard clay is swept clean as a floor and the fine sand around the edges lined with tiny, irregular grooves, anyone can come and sit and look up into the elm tree and wait for the breezes that never come inside the house.

Maggie will be nervous until after her sister goes: She will stand hopelessly in corners, homely and ashamed of the burn
10 scars down her arms and legs, eyeing her sister with a mixture of envy and awe. She thinks her sister has held life always in the palm of one hand, that "no" is a word the world never learned to say to her. You've no doubt seen those TV shows where the child who has "made it" is confronted, as a surprise, by her own mother and father, tottering in weakly from backstage. (A pleasant surprise, of course: What would they do if parent and child came on the show only to curse out and insult each other?) On TV mother and child embrace and smile into each other's faces. Sometimes the mother and father weep; the child wraps them in
20 her arms and leans across the table to tell how she would not have made it without their help. I have seen these programs.

Sometimes I dream a dream in which Dee and I are suddenly brought together on a TV program of this sort. Out of a dark and soft-seated limousine I am ushered into a bright room filled with many people. There I meet a smiling, gray, sporty man like Johnny Carson who shakes my hand and tells me what a fine girl I have. Then we are on the stage, and Dee

is embracing me with tears in her eyes. She pins on my dress a
large orchid, even though she had told me once that she thinks
30  orchids are tacky flowers.

   In real life I am a large, big-boned woman with rough,
man-working hands. In the winter I wear flannel nightgowns
to bed and overalls during the day. I can kill and clean a hog as
mercilessly as a man. My fat keeps me hot in zero weather. I can
work outside all day, breaking ice to get water for washing; I can
eat pork liver cooked over the open fire minutes after it comes
steaming from the hog. One winter I knocked a bull calf straight
in the brain between the eyes with a sledgehammer and had the
meat hung up to chill before nightfall. But of course all this
40  does not show on television. I am the way my daughter would
want me to be: a hundred pounds lighter, my skin like an
uncooked barley pancake. My hair glistens in the hot bright
lights. Johnny Carson has much to do to keep up with my
quick and witty tongue.

**CHARACTER**

In lines 31–44, circle
Mama's description of her
appearance. Put a star next
to details describing what
the mother does. Then,
underline the details showing
how Dee would like her
mother to be.

**FLUENCY**

Read the boxed text aloud
two times. Improve your
speed and smoothness of
delivery in your second
read-through.

**COMPARE & CONTRAST**

Re-read lines 45–51. Circle how Mama describes her own behavior with white people. Underline Mama's description of Dee's behavior.

**CHARACTER**

Pause at line 61. Underline Mama's description of the way Maggie walks. What event caused her to walk that way?

_____

_____

_____

_____

_____

_____

_____

_____

_____

**VOCABULARY**

**sidle** (sīd′'l) *v.:* move sideways, especially in a shy or sneaky manner.

**CHARACTER**

In lines 62–73, Mama remembers seeing her daughters during the fire. Circle what she remembers about Maggie. Underline what she remembers about Dee.

But that is a mistake. I know even before I wake up. Who ever knew a Johnson with a quick tongue? Who can even imagine me looking a strange white man in the eye? It seems to me I have talked to them always with one foot raised in flight, with my head turned in whichever way is farthest from them. Dee, though. She would always look anyone in the eye. Hesitation was no part of her nature.

"How do I look, Mama?" Maggie says, showing just enough of her thin body enveloped in pink skirt and red blouse for me to know she's there, almost hidden by the door.

"Come out into the yard," I say.

Have you ever seen a lame animal, perhaps a dog run over by some careless person rich enough to own a car, **sidle** up to someone who is ignorant enough to be kind to him? That is the way my Maggie walks. She has been like this, chin on chest, eyes on ground, feet in shuffle, ever since the fire that burned the other house to the ground.

Dee is lighter than Maggie, with nicer hair and a fuller figure. She's a woman now, though sometimes I forget. How long ago was it that the other house burned? Ten, twelve years? Sometimes I can still hear the flames and feel Maggie's arms sticking to me, her hair smoking and her dress falling off her in little black papery flakes. Her eyes seemed stretched open, blazed open by the flames reflected in them. And Dee. I see her standing off under the sweet gum tree she used to dig gum out of, a look of concentration on her face as she watched the last dingy gray board of the house fall in toward the red-hot brick chimney. Why don't you do a dance around the ashes? I'd wanted to ask her. She had hated the house that much.

I used to think she hated Maggie, too. But that was before we raised the money, the church and me, to send her to Augusta[1] to school. She used to read to us without pity, forcing words, lies, other folks' habits, whole lives upon us two, sitting

---

1. **Augusta:** city in Georgia.

trapped and ignorant underneath her voice. She washed us in
a river of make-believe, burned us with a lot of knowledge we
80    didn't necessarily need to know. Pressed us to her with the
serious ways she read, to shove us away at just the moment,
like dimwits, we seemed about to understand.

Dee wanted nice things. A yellow organdy dress to wear to
her graduation from high school; black pumps to match a green
suit she'd made from an old suit somebody gave me. She was
determined to stare down any disaster in her efforts. Her eyelids
would not flicker for minutes at a time. Often I fought off the
temptation to shake her. At sixteen she had a style of her own:
and knew what style was.

90    I never had an education myself. After second grade the school
closed down. Don't ask me why: In 1927 colored asked fewer
questions than they do now. Sometimes Maggie reads to me.
She stumbles along good-naturedly but can't see well. She knows
she is not bright. Like good looks and money, quickness passed
her by. She will marry John Thomas (who has mossy teeth in an
earnest face), and then I'll be free to sit here and I guess just sing
church songs to myself. Although I never was a good singer.
Never could carry a tune. I was always better at a man's job. I
used to love to milk till I was hooked in the side in '49. Cows are
100   soothing and slow and don't bother you, unless you try to milk
them the wrong way.

I have deliberately turned my back on the house. It is three
rooms, just like the one that burned, except the roof is tin; they
don't make shingle roofs anymore. There are no real windows,
just some holes cut in the sides, like the portholes in a ship, but
not round and not square, with rawhide holding the shutters up
on the outside. This house is in a pasture, too, like the other one.
No doubt when Dee sees it she will want to tear it down. She
wrote me once that no matter where we "choose" to live, she
110   will manage to come see us. But she will never bring her friends.

INFER

Pause at line 82. From
Mama's description of Dee's
behavior, what can you infer
about her feelings toward
Dee?

_____

_____

_____

_____

_____

_____

CHARACTER

Circle details about Maggie
given in lines 92–95.

INFER

In lines 96–97, underline
what Mama says she will do
after Maggie marries John
Thomas. How does Mama
feel about Maggie?

_____

_____

_____

_____

_____

_____

_____

## CHARACTER

In lines 111–112, circle what Maggie says about Dee.

## VOCABULARY

**furtive** (fur′tiv) *adj.:* acting as if trying not to be seen. *Furtive* also means "done secretly."

## INFER

Pause at line 121. Why did Jimmy T marry somebody other than Dee?

_____

_____

_____

_____

_____

## COMPARE & CONTRAST

In lines 129–134, circle Mama's description of the man's appearance. Then, underline Mama's description of Dee's appearance (lines 135–145). How do Dee and her boyfriend contrast with Mama and Maggie?

_____

_____

_____

_____

_____

_____

Maggie and I thought about this and Maggie asked me, "Mama, when did Dee ever *have* any friends?"

She had a few. **Furtive** boys in pink shirts hanging about on washday after school. Nervous girls who never laughed. Impressed with her, they worshiped the well-turned phrase, the cute shape, the scalding[2] humor that erupted like bubbles in lye. She read to them.

When she was courting Jimmy T, she didn't have much time to pay to us but turned all her faultfinding power on him.
120 He *flew* to marry a cheap city girl from a family of ignorant, flashy people. She hardly had time to recompose herself.

When she comes, I will meet—but there they are!

Maggie attempts to make a dash for the house, in her shuffling way, but I stay her with my hand. "Come back here," I say. And she stops and tries to dig a well in the sand with her toe.

It is hard to see them clearly through the strong sun. But even the first glimpse of leg out of the car tells me it is Dee. Her feet were always neat looking, as if God himself shaped them with a certain style. From the other side of the car comes a
130 short, stocky man. Hair is all over his head a foot long and hanging from his chin like a kinky mule tail. I hear Maggie suck in her breath. "Uhnnnh" is what it sounds like. Like when you see the wriggling end of a snake just in front of your foot on the road. "Uhnnnh."

Dee next. A dress down to the ground, in this hot weather. A dress so loud it hurts my eyes. There are yellows and oranges enough to throw back the light of the sun. I feel my whole face warming from the heat waves it throws out. Earrings gold, too, and hanging down to her shoulders. Bracelets dangling and
140 making noises when she moves her arm up to shake the folds of the dress out of her armpits. The dress is loose and flows, and as she walks closer, I like it. I hear Maggie go "Uhnnnh" again. It is

---

2. **scalding** (skôld′iŋ) *v.* used as *adj.:* burning hot; here, biting or stinging.

her sister's hair. It stands straight up like the wool on a sheep. It is black as night and around the edges are two long pigtails that rope about like small lizards disappearing behind her ears.

"Wa-su-zo-Tean-o!" she says, coming on in that gliding way the dress makes her move. The short, stocky fellow with the hair to his navel is all grinning, and he follows up with "Asalamalakim,[3] my mother and sister!" He moves to hug

150 Maggie but she falls back, right up against the back of my chair. I feel her trembling there, and when I look up I see the perspiration falling off her chin.

"Don't get up," says Dee. Since I am stout, it takes something of a push. You can see me trying to move a second or two before I make it. She turns, showing white heels through her sandals, and goes back to the car. Out she peeks next with a Polaroid. She stoops down quickly and lines up picture after picture of me sitting there in front of the house with Maggie **cowering** behind me. She never takes a shot without making

160 sure the house is included. When a cow comes nibbling around in the edge of the yard, she snaps it and me and Maggie *and* the house. Then she puts the Polaroid in the back seat of the car and comes up and kisses me on the forehead.

Meanwhile, Asalamalakim is going through motions with Maggie's hand. Maggie's hand is as limp as a fish, and probably as cold, despite the sweat, and she keeps trying to pull it back. It looks like Asalamalakim wants to shake hands but wants to do it fancy. Or maybe he don't know how people shake hands. Anyhow, he soon gives up on Maggie.

170 "Well," I say. "Dee."

"No, Mama," she says. "Not 'Dee,' Wangero Leewanika Kemanjo!"

"What happened to 'Dee'?" I wanted to know.

"She's dead," Wangero said. "I couldn't bear it any longer, being named after the people who **oppress** me."

---

3. **Asalamalakim:** Asalaam aleikum (ä·sə·läm′ ä·lä′kŏŏm′), greeting used by Muslims meaning "peace to you."

**CHARACTER**

In lines 146–149, circle the greetings Dee and her boyfriend use when they arrive. What do their words reveal about them?

_____

_____

**VOCABULARY**

**cowering** (kou′ər·iŋ) v. used as *adj.*: drawing back or huddling in fear.

**oppress** (ə·pres′) v.: persecute; keep down by unjust use of power.

*Oppress* is from a Latin word meaning "to press or push against." Related words include *suppress* and *repress*.

**INFER**

In lines 164–169, Mama refers to Dee's friend as *Asalamalakim*, the Muslim greeting he had used. Why does she use this word instead of asking what his name is?

_____

_____

**INFER**

Re-read lines 170–175. Who are the people who "oppress" Dee?

_____

_____

INFER

A Model A was a Ford car produced in the late 1920s. What do the actions of Dee (Wangero) and her friend reveal about their attitudes toward Mama?

_____

_____

_____

CHARACTER

In lines 193–199, what does the **dialogue** between Mama and Dee (Wangero) suggest about Mama?

_____

_____

_____

_____

_____

_____

IDENTIFY

Pause at line 211. What does Mama say that shows you she is not as old-fashioned as her visitors think?

_____

_____

_____

_____

"You know as well as me you was named after your aunt Dicie," I said. Dicie is my sister. She named Dee. We called her "Big Dee" after Dee was born.

"But who was *she* named after?" asked Wangero.

180 "I guess after Grandma Dee," I said.

"And who was she named after?" asked Wangero.

"Her mother," I said, and saw Wangero was getting tired. "That's about as far back as I can trace it," I said. Though, in fact, I probably could have carried it back beyond the Civil War through the branches.

"Well," said Asalamalakim, "there you are."

"Uhnnnh," I heard Maggie say.

"There I was not," I said, "before 'Dicie' cropped up in our family, so why should I try to trace it that far back?"

190 He just stood there grinning, looking down on me like somebody inspecting a Model A car. Every once in a while he and Wangero sent eye signals over my head.

"How do you pronounce this name?" I asked.

"You don't have to call me by it if you don't want to," said Wangero.

"Why shouldn't I?" I asked. "If that's what you want us to call you, we'll call you."

"I know it might sound awkward at first," said Wangero.

"I'll get used to it," I said. "Ream it out again."

200 Well, soon we got the name out of the way. Asalamalakim had a name twice as long and three times as hard. After I tripped over it two or three times, he told me to just call him Hakim-a-barber. I wanted to ask him was he a barber, but I didn't really think he was, so I didn't ask.

"You must belong to those beef-cattle peoples down the road," I said. They said "Asalamalakim" when they met you, too, but they didn't shake hands. Always too busy: feeding the cattle, fixing the fences, putting up salt-lick shelters, throwing down hay. When the white folks poisoned some of the herd, the men

210 stayed up all night with rifles in their hands. I walked a mile and a half just to see the sight.

Hakim-a-barber said, "I accept some of their **doctrines,** but farming and raising cattle is not my style." (They didn't tell me, and I didn't ask, whether Wangero—Dee—had really gone and married him.)

We sat down to eat and right away he said he didn't eat collards, and pork was unclean. Wangero, though, went on through the chitlins and corn bread, the greens, and everything else. She talked a blue streak over the sweet potatoes. Everything
220 delighted her. Even the fact that we still used the benches her daddy made for the table when we couldn't afford to buy chairs.

"Oh, Mama!" she cried. Then turned to Hakim-a-barber. "I never knew how lovely these benches are. You can feel the rump prints," she said, running her hands underneath her and along the bench. Then she gave a sigh, and her hand closed over Grandma Dee's butter dish. "That's it!" she said. "I knew there was something I wanted to ask you if I could have." She jumped up from the table and went over in the corner where the churn stood, the milk in it clabber[4] by now. She looked at the churn
230 and looked at it.

"This churn top is what I need," she said. "Didn't Uncle Buddy whittle it out of a tree you all used to have?"

"Yes," I said.

"Uh huh," she said happily. "And I want the dasher,[5] too."

"Uncle Buddy whittle that, too?" asked the barber.

Dee (Wangero) looked up at me.

"Aunt Dee's first husband whittled the dash," said Maggie so low you almost couldn't hear her. "His name was Henry, but they called him Stash."

240 "Maggie's brain is like an elephant's," Wangero said, laughing. "I can use the churn top as a centerpiece for the alcove table," she said, sliding a plate over the churn, "and I'll think of something artistic to do with the dasher."

---

4. **clabber** (klab′ər) *n:* thickened or curdled sour milk.
5. **dasher** *n:* pole that stirs the milk in a churn.

Everyday Use **61**

VOCABULARY

**doctrines** (däk′trinz) *n.:* principles; teachings; beliefs.

IDENTIFY

According to Mama, Dee never liked her home before. How has Dee's attitude changed (lines 219–230)?

_____

_____

_____

_____

_____

_____

_____

CHARACTER

Re-read lines 237–239. What do Maggie's words reveal about her?

_____

_____

_____

_____

_____

_____

_____

_____

VOCABULARY

**rifling** (rī'flin) *v.* used as *n.:* searching thoroughly or in a rough manner.

INFER

Re-read lines 265–269. Who has slammed the kitchen door? Why has she done this?

_____

_____

_____

_____

_____

_____

_____

_____

_____

_____

_____

_____

_____

_____

_____

_____

_____

_____

_____

_____

When she finished wrapping the dasher, the handle stuck out. I took it for a moment in my hands. You didn't even have to look close to see where hands pushing the dasher up and down to make butter had left a kind of sink in the wood. In fact, there were a lot of small sinks; you could see where thumbs and fingers had sunk into the wood. It was beautiful light-yellow wood, from a tree that grew in the yard where Big Dee and Stash had lived.

After dinner Dee (Wangero) went to the trunk at the foot of my bed and started **rifling** through it. Maggie hung back in the kitchen over the dishpan. Out came Wangero with two quilts. They had been pieced by Grandma Dee, and then Big Dee and me had hung them on the quilt frames on the front porch and quilted them. One was in the Lone Star pattern. The other was Walk Around the Mountain. In both of them were scraps of dresses Grandma Dee had worn fifty and more years ago. Bits and pieces of Grandpa Jarrell's paisley shirts. And one teeny faded blue piece, about the size of a penny matchbox, that was from Great Grandpa Ezra's uniform that he wore in the Civil War.

"Mama," Wangero said sweet as a bird. "Can I have these old quilts?"

I heard something fall in the kitchen, and a minute later the kitchen door slammed.

"Why don't you take one or two of the others?" I asked. "These old things was just done by me and Big Dee from some tops your grandma pieced before she died."

"No," said Wangero. "I don't want those. They are stitched around the borders by machine."

"That'll make them last better," I said.

"That's not the point," said Wangero. "These are all pieces of dresses Grandma used to wear. She did all this stitching by hand. Imagine!" She held the quilts securely in her arms, stroking them.

"Some of the pieces, like those lavender ones, come from old clothes her mother handed down to her," I said, moving up

to touch the quilts. Dee (Wangero) moved back just enough so that I couldn't reach the quilts. They already belonged to her.

"Imagine!" she breathed again, clutching them closely to her bosom.

"The truth is," I said, "I promised to give them quilts to Maggie, for when she marries John Thomas."

She gasped like a bee had stung her.

"Maggie can't appreciate these quilts!" she said. "She'd probably be backward enough to put them to everyday use."

"I reckon she would," I said. "God knows I been saving 'em for long enough with nobody using 'em. I hope she will!"

I didn't want to bring up how I had offered Dee (Wangero) a

**CHARACTER**

Circle the reason Mama says Dee cannot have the quilts (lines 283–284).

**COMPARE & CONTRAST**

Re-read lines 283–287. Circle what Dee says Maggie would do with the quilts. Read on to line 302, and underline what Dee would do with them. What does this difference between the sisters' attitudes reveal?

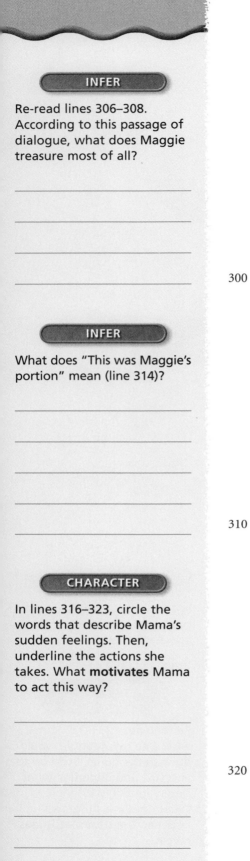

**INFER**

Re-read lines 306–308. According to this passage of dialogue, what does Maggie treasure most of all?

_____

_____

_____

_____

**INFER**

What does "This was Maggie's portion" mean (line 314)?

_____

_____

_____

_____

_____

**CHARACTER**

In lines 316–323, circle the words that describe Mama's sudden feelings. Then, underline the actions she takes. What **motivates** Mama to act this way?

_____

_____

_____

_____

_____

_____

quilt when she went away to college. Then she had told me they were old-fashioned, out of style.

"But they're *priceless!*" she was saying now, furiously; for she has a temper. "Maggie would put them on the bed and in five years they'd be in rags. Less than that!"

"She can always make some more," I said. "Maggie knows how to quilt."

Dee (Wangero) looked at me with hatred. "You just will not understand. The point is *these* quilts, these quilts!"

300 "Well," I said, stumped. "What would *you* do with them?"

"Hang them," she said. As if that was the only thing you *could* do with quilts.

Maggie by now was standing in the door. I could almost hear the sound her feet made as they scraped over each other.

"She can have them, Mama," she said, like somebody used to never winning anything or having anything reserved for her. "I can 'member Grandma Dee without the quilts."

I looked at her hard. She had filled her bottom lip with checkerberry snuff, and it gave her face a kind of dopey, hang-
310 dog look. It was Grandma Dee and Big Dee who taught her how to quilt herself. She stood there with her scarred hands hidden in the folds of her skirt. She looked at her sister with something like fear, but she wasn't mad at her. This was Maggie's portion. This was the way she knew God to work.

When I looked at her like that, something hit me in the top of my head and ran down to the soles of my feet. Just like when I'm in church and the spirit of God touches me and I get happy and shout. I did something I never had done before: hugged Maggie to me, then dragged her on into the room,
320 snatched the quilts out of Miss Wangero's hands, and dumped them into Maggie's lap. Maggie just sat there on my bed with her mouth open.

"Take one or two of the others," I said to Dee.

But she turned without a word and went out to Hakim-a-barber.

"You just don't understand," she said, as Maggie and I came out to the car.

"What don't I understand?" I wanted to know.

"Your heritage," she said. And then she turned to Maggie, kissed her, and said, "You ought to try to make something of yourself, too, Maggie. It's really a new day for us. But from the way you and Mama still live, you'd never know it."

She put on some sunglasses that hid everything above the tip of her nose and her chin.

Maggie smiled, maybe at the sunglasses. But a real smile, not scared. After we watched the car dust settle, I asked Maggie to bring me a dip of snuff. And then the two of us sat there just enjoying, until it was time to go in the house and go to bed.

330

**INTERPRET**

Dee says that Mama doesn't understand her "heritage"— their cultural traditions and past. What is surprising and even unfair about this remark?

**CHARACTER**

How do Dee's harsh words in lines 330–333 help bring Maggie and Mama closer at the end of the story?

# Everyday Use

**Character Boxes**    The chart that follows will help you make inferences about the characters in this story. The inferences will be based in part on what the characters say and do. Fill in the blank spaces with details from the story. (Some have been filled in for you.) Then, write your inferences in the last box of each row.

## Mama

| What She Says About Herself or to Others | What She Does | My Inferences |
|---|---|---|
| "I never had an education myself." (line 90) | "I can work outside all day." (lines 34–35) | |

## Maggie

| What She Says About Herself or to Others | What She Does | My Inferences |
|---|---|---|
| | "Maggie attempts to make a dash for the house, in her shuffling way. . . ." (lines 123–124) | |

## Dee (Wangero)

| What She Says About Herself or to Others | What She Does | My Inferences |
|---|---|---|
| "Maggie can't appreciate these quilts!" (line 286) | | |

# Standards Review

**TestPractice**   **Everyday Use**

Improve your test-taking skills by completing the sample test item. Then, check your answer, and read the explanation in the right-hand column.

| Sample Test Item | Explanation of the Correct Answer |
|---|---|
| Which of the following words or phrases would Mama *not* use to describe herself?<br><br>**A** hardworking<br>**B** good at killing animals<br>**C** fat<br>**D** light-skinned | The correct answer is *D*.<br><br>Mama says that she can work outside all day *(A)*; that she can kill a hog *(B)*; and that her fat keeps her warm *(C)*. She also says that Dee would want her to be the color of an "uncooked barley pancake," or light-skinned. |

**DIRECTIONS:** Circle the letter of each correct response.

1. Mama remembers Dee's behavior during the fire with—

   **A** gratitude

   **B** fear

   **C** anger

   **D** fondness

2. What can you infer about Mama from these words of hers?

   *"[Dee] used to read to us without pity, forcing words, lies, other folks' habits, whole lives upon us two . . ."*

   **F** She is proud of Dee.

   **G** She appreciates Dee's efforts.

   **H** She hates reading.

   **J** She resents Dee's attitude.

3. What **character trait** of Maggie's is evident in the passage below?

   *"'She can have them, Mama,' she said, like somebody used to never winning anything."*

   **A** She is defiant.

   **B** She accepts defeat easily.

   **C** She is easily irritated.

   **D** She is sulky.

4. At the end of the story, Maggie no longer seems—

   **F** happy

   **G** content

   **H** fearful

   **J** critical

**Reading Standard 3.4** Determine characters' traits by what the characters say about themselves in narration, dialogue, dramatic monologue, and soliloquy.

# Standards Review

## TestPractice   Everyday Use

### Context Clues

**DIRECTIONS:** Circle the letter of the context clue that helps define the boldface word.

**Reading Standard 1.3 (Grade 8 Review)** Use word meanings within the appropriate context, and show ability to verify those meanings by definition, restatement, example, comparison, or contrast.

1. The TV host laughed at my **witty** tongue; then he broke for a commercial.

   A  TV host        C  broke

   B  laughed        D  commercial

2. During the fire, her face had a look of **concentration,** or close attention.

   F  fire           H  look

   G  face           J  close attention

3. When Dee and Jimmy were **courting,** they sometimes double-dated with their friends.

   A  Dee            C  double-dated

   B  Jimmy          D  friends

4. Dee held the quilts **securely** in her arms, her hands tightly gripping the soft edges of the blanket.

   F  in her arms    H  soft edges

   G  tightly gripping  J  the blanket

### Vocabulary in Context

**DIRECTIONS:** Complete the passage by filling in each blank with the correct word from the box. Not all words will be used.

**Word Box**

sidle

furtive

cowering

oppress

doctrines

rifling

I saw my brother sneaking out of my room, his (1) _____ movements slow and silent. When he saw me the poor kid was flinching, practically (2) _____ under my gaze. "I was just looking at your CDs," he told me. At least he admitted he had been (3) _____ through my music collection. Although I was annoyed, I decided not to (4) _____ him with any "big-brother" lecture.

**Before You Go On...**

Check your Standards Mastery at the back of this book.

# Mary by Katherine Mansfield

Relationships between people, especially brothers and sisters, can be complex. Conflicting feelings of love, jealousy, admiration, and protectiveness can confuse us. In "Mary," you'll meet a pair of sisters who are very different, but also very close.

## LITERARY FOCUS: CHARACTER

Characters in stories, just like people in real life, form **relationships** with others. These relationships are important to the story, and often they can explain a character's **motivation**—the reasons he or she takes certain actions. A relationship between two friends may disintegrate, causing a terrible **conflict**. A relationship between two brothers may be so strong that one will give up his life for the other.

- As you read this story, pay close attention to how Kass describes her relationship with her sister, Mary.
- Look for Kass's **motivations**—the reasons she takes the actions she does. How does her relationship with her sister explain her actions?

## READING SKILLS: IDENTIFYING CAUSE AND EFFECT

Many of our actions in real life have cause-and-effect relationships. Look at the following example:

| Cause ⟶ | Effect | Cause ⟶ | Effect |
|---|---|---|---|
| The alarm rings. | You wake up. | You are hungry. | You make breakfast. |

Cause-and-effect relationships exist in stories, too. When you read a story, note the actions the characters take and why they take them. Note the effects of the characters' actions. Understanding cause and effect is essential to understanding plot structure and motivation.

**Reading Standard 1.3** Identify Greek, Roman, and Norse mythology and use the knowledge to understand the origin and meaning of new words (e.g., the word *narcissistic* drawn from the myth of Narcissus and Echo).

**Reading Standard 3.3** Analyze interactions between main and subordinate characters in a literary text (e.g., internal and external conflicts, motivations, relationships, influences), and explain the way those interactions affect the plot.

## VOCABULARY DEVELOPMENT

### PREVIEW SELECTION VOCABULARY

The following words appear in the story. Become familiar with these words before you read.

**ignominiously** (ig′nə·min′ē·əs·lē) *adv.:* shamefully; dishonorably.

*I behaved **ignominiously** when I revealed your secret.*

**contempt** (kən·tempt′) *n.:* scorn; attitude of someone who looks down on another.

*The girls felt **contempt** for Kass because she had acted foolishly.*

**doleful** (dōl′fəl) *adj.:* sad.

*Mr. England tried to comfort Kass, who looked **doleful**.*

**irreverent** (i·rev′ər·ənt) *adj.:* rude; disrespectful.

*Singing that religious song at a party would be **irreverent**.*

### WORD ORIGINS

Many words and names in English come from Greek, Roman, and Norse **mythology**—tales about gods and goddesses who were thought to control nature and human life. The word *heroic,* for example (in line 26 of "Mary"), comes from Greek mythology and means "a man of great strength and courage who is favored by the gods." In English, five of the names of the week come from the old myths:

| Day of the Week | Origin |
| --- | --- |
| Tuesday | from Tiu's day; Tiu was the Norse god of war. |
| Wednesday | from Wodin's day; Wodin was the chief Norse god. |
| Thursday | from Thor's day; Thor was the Norse god of Thunder. |
| Friday | from Frigg's day; Frigg was the Norse goddess of marriage and motherhood. |
| Saturday | from Saturn's day; Saturn was the Roman god of farming. |

# Mary

## Katherine Mansfield

On poetry afternoons Grandmother let Mary and me wear Mrs. Gardner's white hemstitched pinafores because we had nothing to do with ink or pencil.[1]

Triumphant and feeling unspeakably beautiful, we would fly along the road, swinging our kits and half chanting, half singing our new piece. I always knew my poetry, but Mary, who was a year and a half older, never knew hers. In fact, lessons of any sort worried her soul and body. She could never distinguish between "m" and "n."

10     "Now, Kass—turmip," she would say, wrinkling her nose, "t-o-u-r-*m*-i-p, isn't it?"

Also in words like "celery" or "gallery" she invariably said "cerely" and "garrely."

I was a strong, fat little child who burst my buttons and shot out of my skirts to Grandmother's entire satisfaction, but Mary was a "weed." She had a continual little cough. "Poor old Mary's bark," as Father called it.

Every spare moment of her time seemed to be occupied in journeying with Mother to the pantry and being forced to take

20     something out of a spoon—cod-liver oil, Easton's syrup, malt extract. And though she had her nose held and a piece of barley sugar after, these sorties, I am sure, told on her spirits.

"I can't bear lessons," she would say woefully. "I'm all tired in my elbows and my feet."

And yet, when she was well she was elfishly gay and bright—danced like a fairy and sang like a bird. And heroic! She would hold a rooster by the legs while Pat chopped his head off. She loved boys, and played with a fine sense of honor and

---

**1.** This story is set in New Zealand around 1900. In school in those days, children practiced handwriting using pens and ink.

Notes _____

_____

_____

_____

_____

_____

_____

_____

_____

**CHARACTER RELATIONSHIPS**

Pause at line 9. Circle how Kass says the sisters are different.

**COMPARE & CONTRAST**

In lines 14–16, Kass reveals more about how she and Mary differ. Circle the descriptions of the two girls.

**WORD STUDY**

In this context, *sorties* (line 22) means "trips." *Sortie* often means "a quick military action."

**CHARACTER RELATIONSHIPS**

Re-read lines 25–34. Underline the sentences that explain how Kass protects Mary. What does Kass love most about Mary?

_____

_____

_____

_____

_____

_____

_____

_____

**INFER**

Pause at line 34. What details in the story so far suggest that it is set many years ago?

_____

_____

_____

_____

_____

_____

_____

purity. In fact, I think she loved everybody; and I, who did not,
30    worshiped her. I suffered untold agonies when the girls laughed
at her in class, and when she answered wrongly I put up my
hand and cried, "Please, Teacher, she means something quite
different." Then I would turn to Mary and say, "You meant
'island' and not 'peninsula,' didn't you, dear?"

"Of course," she would say—"how very silly!"

But on poetry afternoons I could be of no help at all. The
class was divided into two and ranged on both sides of the
room. Two of us drew lots as to which side must begin, and
when the first half had each in turn said their piece, they left the

40　room while Teacher and the remaining ones voted for the best reciter. Time and again I was top of my side, and time and again Mary was bottom. To stand before all those girls and Teacher, knowing my piece, loving it so much that I *went* in the knees and shivered all over, was joy; but she would stand twisting "Mrs. Gardner's white linen stitched," blundering and finally breaking down **ignominiously.** There came a day when we had learned the whole of Thomas Hood's "I remember, I remember," and Teacher offered a prize for the best girl on each side. The prize for our side was a green-plush bracket[2] with a yellow china

50　frog stuck on it. All the morning these treasures had stood on Teacher's table; all through playtime and the dinner hour we had talked of nothing else. It was agreed that it was bound to fall to me. I saw pictures of myself carrying it home to Grandmother— I saw it hanging on her wall—never doubting for one moment that she would think it the most desirable ornament in life. But as we ran to afternoon school, Mary's memory seemed weaker than ever before, and suddenly she stopped on the road.

"Kass," she said, "think what a s'prise if I got it after all; I believe Mother would go mad with joy. I know I should. But

60　then—I'm so stupid, I know."

She sighed, and we ran on. Oh, from that moment I longed that the prize might fall to Mary. I said the "piece" to her three times over as we ran up the last hill and across the playground. Sides were chosen. She and I, as our names began with "B," were the first to begin. And alas! that she was older, her turn was before mine.

The first verse went splendidly. I prayed viciously for another miracle.

"Oh please, God, dear, do be nice!—If you won't—"

70　The Almighty slumbered. Mary broke down. I saw her standing there all alone, her pale little freckled face flushed, her mouth quivering, and the thin fingers twisting and twisting at the unfortunate pinafore frill. She was helped, in a critical

---

2.　**bracket:** wall shelf held up by brackets, or braces.

**INFER**

Pause at line 46. Once again, Kass describes the differences between the sisters' abilities. How might Mary feel about coming in last all the time?

_____

_____

_____

_____

**VOCABULARY**

**ignominiously** (ig′nə·min′ē·əs·lē) *adv.*: shamefully; dishonorably.

**CHARACTER RELATIONSHIPS**

Underline what Mary suddenly wishes for (line 58). Circle what Kass wishes for (lines 61–62).

**WORD STUDY**

Kass says that she "prayed *viciously*" for Mary's success (line 67). *Viciously* (vish′əs·lē) usually means "spitefully," but it can also mean "forcefully." When might someone pray "viciously"?

_____

_____

_____

_____

_____

**IDENTIFY
CAUSE & EFFECT**

Pause at line 83. Underline
the sentence that tells why
the girls clapped and why
Mary looks at Kass with
pride and love.

**IDENTIFY
CAUSE & EFFECT**

Pause at line 85. What has
Kass done, and why?

_____

_____

_____

_____

**IDENTIFY**

Re-read lines 87–98. Underline the words indicating
that Kass's feelings are
beginning to change.

**WORD STUDY**

In this context *expostulations*
(ek·späs′chə·lā′shənz), line
105, means "prayers."

*Deity* (line 105) is from *deus,*
the Latin word meaning
"god."

**IDENTIFY
CAUSE & EFFECT**

Why does Kass need to pray
in order to keep from crying
(lines 104–105)?

_____

_____

condition, to the very end. I saw Teacher's face smiling at me
suddenly—the cold, shivering feeling came over me—and then
I saw the house and "the little window where the sun came
peeping in at morn."[3]

When it was over, the girls clapped, and the look of pride
and love on Mary's face decided me.

80     "Kass has got it; there's no good trying now," was the spirit
on the rest of my side. Finally they left the room. I waited until
the moment the door was shut. Then I went over to Teacher and
whispered:

"If I've got it, put Mary's name. Don't tell anybody, and
don't let the others tell her—oh, *please.*"

I shot out the last word at her, and Teacher looked astounded.

She shook her head at me in a way I could not understand.
I ran out and joined the others. They were gathered in the
passage, twittering like birds. Only Mary stood apart, clearing

90 her throat and trying to hum a little tune. I knew she would cry
if I talked to her, so I paid no attention. I felt I would like to run
out of school and never come back again. Trying not to be sorry
for what I had done, trying not to think of that heavenly green
bracket, which seemed big and beautiful enough now to give
Queen Victoria—and longing for the voting to be over kept me
busy. At last the door opened, and we trooped in. Teacher stood
by the table. The girls were radiant. I shut my mouth hard and
looked down at my slippers.

"The first prize," said Teacher, "is awarded to Mary

100 Beetham." A great burst of clapping; but above it all I heard
Mary's little cry of joy. For a moment I could not look up; but
when I did, and saw her walking to the desk, so happy, so confi-
dent, so utterly unsuspecting, when I saw her going back to her
place with that green-plush bracket in her hands, it needed all
my wildest expostulations with the Deity to keep back my tears.
The rest of the afternoon passed like a dream; but when school
broke up, Mary was the heroine of the hour. Boys and girls

---

3.   **"the little window . . . at morn":** lines from the poem by Thomas
    Hood which each girl was reciting.

followed her—held the prize in their "own hands"—and all looked at me with pitying **contempt,** especially those who were

110    in on the secret and knew what I had done.

On the way home we passed the Karori bus going home from town full of businessmen. The driver gave us a lift, and we bundled in. We knew all the people.

"I've won a prize for po'try!" cried Mary, in a high, excited voice.

"Good old Mary!" they chorused.

Again she was the center of admiring popularity.

"Well, Kass, you needn't look so **doleful,**" said Mr. England, laughing at me, "you aren't clever enough to win everything."

120    "I know," I answered, wishing I were dead and buried.

I did not go into the house when we reached home, but wandered down to the loft and watched Pat mixing the chicken food.

But the bell rang at last, and with slow steps I crept up to the nursery.

Mother and Grandmother were there with two callers. Alice had come up from the kitchen; Vera was sitting with her arms round Mary's neck.

"Well, that's wonderful, Mary," Mother was saying. "Such a

130    lovely prize, too. Now, you see what you really can do, darling."

"That will be nice for you to show your little girls when you grow up," said Grandmother.

Slowly I slipped into my chair.

"Well, Kass, you don't look very pleased," cried one of the tactful callers.

Mother looked at me severely.

"Don't say you are going to be a sulky child about your sister," she said.

Even Mary's bright little face clouded.

140    "You are glad, aren't you?" she questioned.

**VOCABULARY**

**contempt** (kən·tempt′) *n.:* scorn; attitude of someone who looks down on another.

Why might the students who knew about Kass's gift to Mary feel "pitying contempt" for Kass?

_____

_____

_____

**VOCABULARY**

**doleful** (dōl′fəl) *adj.:* sad.

**INFER**

Re-read what Mother and Grandmother say to Mary (lines 129–132). How do you think their words make Kass feel?

_____

_____

_____

_____

**WORD STUDY**

*Tactful* (takt′fəl) (line 135) means "skilled at dealing with people." Does the caller really seem tactful, or is Kass using the word ironically? Explain.

_____

_____

_____

**irreverent** (i·rev′ər·ənt) *adj.:*
rude; disrespectful.

**IDENTIFY
CAUSE & EFFECT**

Pause at line 163. Underline
what Kass plans to do. What
**motivates** Kass to make that
decision?

_____

_____

_____

_____

**FLUENCY**

Read the boxed passage
aloud three times. Work on
improving your speed
and the smoothness of your
delivery with each read.

**IDENTIFY
CAUSE & EFFECT**

What has Kass decided at
the end of the story? What
motivates her?

_____

_____

_____

_____

_____

"I'm frightfully glad," I said, holding on to the handle of
my mug, and seeing all too plainly the glance of understanding
that passed between the grownups.

We had the yellow frog for tea, we had the green-plush
bracket for the entire evening when Father came home, and
even when Mary and I had been sent to bed she sang a little
song made out of her own head:

> I got a yellow frog for a prize,
> An' it had china eyes.

150  But she tried to fit this to the tune of "Sun of My Soul,"
which Grandmother thought a little **irreverent,** and stopped.

Mary's bed was in the opposite corner of the room. I lay
with my head pressed into the pillow. Then the tears came.
I pulled the clothes over my head. The sacrifice was too great.
I stuffed a corner of the sheet into my mouth to stop me from
shouting out the truth. Nobody loved me, nobody understood
me, and they loved Mary without the frog, and now that she
had it I decided they loved me less.

A long time seemed to pass. I got hot and stuffy, and came
160  up to breathe. And the Devil entered into my soul. I decided to
tell Mary the truth. From that moment I was happy and light
again, but I felt savage. I sat up—then got out of bed. The
linoleum was very cold. I crossed over to the other corner.

The moon shone through the window straight on to Mary's
bed. She lay on her side, one hand against her cheek, soundly
sleeping. Her little plait of hair stood straight up from her head;
it was tied with a piece of pink wool. Very white was her small
face, and the funny freckles I could see even in this light; she had
thrown off half the bedclothes; one button of her nightdress was
170  undone, showing her flannel chest protector.

I stood there for one moment, on one leg, watching her
asleep. I looked at the green-plush bracket already hung on the
wall above her head, at that perfect yellow frog with china eyes,
and then again at Mary, who stirred and flung out one arm
across the bed.

Suddenly I stooped and kissed her.

# Mary

**Character-Relationship Chart**    Characters in stories have reasons for the actions they take. Sometimes those reasons are based on the characters' relationships with other story characters. Fill in the following chart to track how Kass's actions stem from her relationship with Mary.

| Description of Kass | Description of Mary |
|---|---|
|  |  |

| Description of Kass and Mary's Relationship |
|---|
|  |

| Kass's Actions in Story | Why Kass Takes Those Actions (her motivation) |
|---|---|
| Kass asks Teacher to give the prize to Mary. |  |
| Kass plans to tell Mary that she didn't win the prize after all. |  |
| Kass decides not to tell Mary, after all. |  |

# Standards Review

## TestPractice   Mary

Improve your test-taking skills by completing the sample test item below.
Then, check your answer and read the explanation to the right.

| Sample Test Item | Explanation of the Correct Answer |
|---|---|
| Kass gives us the impression that Mary is *not*—<br><br>**A** often sick<br><br>**B** loving<br><br>**C** cheerful<br><br>**D** good at school | The answer is *D*.<br><br>We know that Mary is *not* good at school. *A* is not correct because Mary coughs and takes medicines; *B* is not correct because Kass says that Mary loves everybody; *C* is not correct because Mary is cheerful when well. |

**DIRECTIONS:** Circle the letter of the correct answer.

**Reading Standard 3.3**
Analyze interactions between main and subordinate characters in a literary text (e.g., internal and external conflicts, motivations, relationships, influences), and explain the way those interactions affect the plot.

1. Which sentence describes some of Mary's **character traits**?

   **A** "I pulled the clothes over my head."

   **B** "When she was well she was elfishly gay and bright."

   **C** " 'If I've got it, put Mary's name.' "

   **D** "Mary lay on her side, one hand against her cheek, soundly sleeping."

2. When Kass asks Teacher to give Mary the prize, Teacher is—

   **F** annoyed

   **G** grateful

   **H** overjoyed

   **J** surprised

3. Why does Kass let Mary have the prize?

   **A** She hopes Mary will be less annoying.

   **B** Mary asks her to.

   **C** She loves Mary and feels sorry for her.

   **D** She is tired of always winning.

4. Which word best describes the **relationship** between the sisters?

   **F** loving

   **G** unfriendly

   **H** bitter

   **J** foolish

# Standards Review

VOCABULARY DEVELOPMENT

 **Mary**

## WORD ORIGINS

Many words and names in English come from Greek, Roman, and Norse mythology—tales about the gods and goddesses who were thought to control nature and human life. For instance, the month of March is named for Mars, the Roman god of war.

**Reading Standard 1.3** Identify Greek, Roman, and Norse mythology and use the knowledge to understand the origin and meaning of new words (e.g., the word *narcissistic* drawn from the myth of Narcissus and Echo).

**DIRECTIONS:** The left-hand column lists some of the days of the week. For each day, choose the name of the god in the right-hand column that the name comes from. Write the letter of the answer in the blank.

1. _____ Wednesday     **a.** Saturn, Roman god of farming

2. _____ Thursday     **b.** Thor, Norse god of thunder

3. _____ Saturday     **c.** Wodin, chief Norse god

## Vocabulary in Context

**DIRECTIONS:** Complete the paragraph below by writing a word from the box in the correct numbered blank.

**Word Box**

contempt

ignominiously

doleful

irreverent

Susannah had a part in a comedy, but you might think the play was a tragedy. Although she was dressed in a cheerful costume, she looked very (1) _____ . She tried to cross the stage gracefully but instead tripped (2) _____ over the scenery. I felt anger and (3) _____ for audience members who laughed at her. Their rude and (4) _____ manner made me want to stop the show. Then, I noticed the audience was laughing *with* Susannah, not *at* her. Susannah got the most applause at the curtain call.

 **Before You Go On . . .**

Check your Standards Mastery at the back of this book.

# Narrator and Voice

# Academic Vocabulary for Chapter 3

These are the terms you should know
as you read and analyze the stories in this chapter.

---

**Narrator** The storyteller, the voice telling you the story.

**Point of View** The vantage point, or perspective, from which a writer tells a story. There are three main points of view: **omniscient** (äm·nish′ənt), **first person,** and **third person limited.** *Omniscient* means "all-knowing."

- In the **omniscient point of view,** the narrator knows everything that is going on in the story, including the characters' thoughts and feelings. This type of narrator rarely plays a direct role in the story.

- In the **first-person point of view,** one of the characters tells the story, using the personal pronoun *I.* We know only what this person knows and see only what this person sees. Some first-person narrators are **credible,** or **reliable**—we can believe what they tell us. Other first-person narrators are not credible—we can't necessarily believe what they say because they may not be telling the truth.

- In the **third-person limited point of view,** the narrator tells the story from the vantage point of only one character. The narrator reveals the thoughts and feelings of this character, and events are limited to what this character experiences and observes.

● ● ●

**Voice** A term in literature that refers to a writer's special use of language in a story, including diction and tone.

- **Diction** is the kinds of words a writer chooses. Diction can be formal, informal, poetic, plain, full of slang, and so on. Diction has a powerful effect on the **tone** of a piece of writing.

- **Tone** is the attitude a writer takes toward an audience, a subject, or a character. Tone is conveyed through a writer's choice of words and details. The tone can be humorous, sad, or friendly, for example.

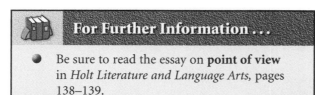

**For Further Information . . .**

- Be sure to read the essay on **point of view** in *Holt Literature and Language Arts,* pages 138–139.

**Reading Standard 1.1**
Identify and use the literal and figurative meanings of words and understand word derivations.

**Reading Standard 1.3 (Grade 8 Review)**
Use word meanings within the appropriate context and show ability to verify those meanings by definition, restatement, example, comparison, or contrast.

**Reading Standard 3.4 (Grade 8 Review)**
Analyze the relevance of the setting (e.g., place, time, customs) to the mood, tone, and meaning of the text.

**Reading Standard 3.9**
Explain how voice, persona, and the choice of a narrator affect characterization and the tone, plot, and credibility of a text.

# By the Waters of Babylon by Stephen Vincent Benét

The title of this fantasy is taken from Psalm 137 in the Bible. The psalm tells of the Israelites' great sorrow over the destruction of their Temple in Jerusalem (Zion) and their enslavement in Babylon. The psalm opens

> By the waters of Babylon,
> there we sat down and wept,
> when we remembered Zion.

Stephen Vincent Benét wrote this story partly as a cautionary tale, or a story meant to serve as a warning. As you read, be alert to what Benét is warning about. You should know that the story was written in 1937, before the invention of nuclear weapons.

## LITERARY FOCUS: FIRST-PERSON POINT OF VIEW AND SETTING

- John, a young man, narrates the story from his **first-person point of view.** We see the world and experience events as John does.
- Because he is a first-person narrator, John can tell us only what he knows and experiences. As you read, think about whether John is a **credible,** or believable, narrator. Is what he tells you totally accurate?
- **Setting**—the place and time of the story—is at the heart of "By the Waters of Babylon." The first location of the story—the land of the Hill People—may make you think of a Native American legend. The story's second major location—the Place of the Gods—is actually a famous city in the United States. Look for clues that help you identify the city and that reveal what has happened there.

**Reading Standard 3.4 (Grade 8 Review)** Analyze the relevance of the setting (e.g., place, time, customs) to the mood, tone, and meaning of the text.

**Reading Standard 3.9** Explain how voice, persona, and the choice of a narrator affect characterization and the tone, plot, and credibility of a text.

## READING SKILLS: DRAWING CONCLUSIONS

A **conclusion** is a judgment that you draw, or come to, after you have considered all the evidence. The conclusions you draw when you read a story are based on details you are given about the plot, the characters, and the setting. As you read this fantasy story, you will have to draw conclusions about many things. You'll have to decide, for example, where the narrator lives and when he lives. You will also have to decide just where this boy goes on his journey. The evidence is there; you have to read carefully and draw on your own experience to find the answers.

The narrator describes each of the places and things listed on the chart below. Based on just what is written there, fill in what you think each place or thing is. After you have read all the details in the story, you'll probably draw different conclusions.

| Detail | What It Might Be |
|---|---|
| Place of the Gods | |
| Great Burning | |
| Ou-dis-sun | |
| Statue of the man named ASHING | |
| Temple with stars on the ceiling | |
| Cooking place with no wood | |

# By the Waters of Babylon

## Stephen Vincent Benét

In the first paragraph, circle the rules and laws that the narrator describes. Then underline the word *forbidden* each time it is used.

The north and the west and the south are good hunting ground, but it is forbidden to go east. It is forbidden to go to any of the Dead Places except to search for metal, and then he who touches the metal must be a priest or the son of a priest. Afterward, both the man and the metal must be purified. These are the rules and the laws; they are well made. It is forbidden to cross the great river and look upon the place that was the Place of the Gods—this is most strictly forbidden. We do not even say its name though we know its name. It is there that spirits live, and demons—it is there that there are the ashes of the Great

Burning. These things are forbidden—they have been forbidden since the beginning of time.

My father is a priest; I am the son of a priest. I have been in the Dead Places near us, with my father—at first, I was afraid. When my father went into the house to search for the metal, I stood by the door and my heart felt small and weak. It was a dead man's house, a spirit house. It did not have the smell of man, though there were old bones in a corner. But it is not fitting that a priest's son should show fear. I looked at the
20 bones in the shadow and kept my voice still.

Then my father came out with the metal—a good, strong piece. He looked at me with both eyes but I had not run away. He gave me the metal to hold—I took it and did not die. So he knew that I was truly his son and would be a priest in my time. That was when I was very young—nevertheless, my brothers would not have done it, though they are good hunters. After that, they gave me the good piece of meat and the warm corner by the fire. My father watched over me—he was glad that I should be a priest. But when I boasted or wept without a reason,
30 he punished me more strictly than my brothers. That was right.

After a time, I myself was allowed to go into the dead houses and search for metal. So I learned the ways of those houses—and if I saw bones, I was no longer afraid. The bones are light and old—sometimes they will fall into dust if you touch them. But that is a great sin.

I was taught the chants and the spells—I was taught how to stop blood from a wound and many secrets. A priest must know many secrets—that was what my father said. If the hunters think we do all things by chants and spells, they may believe so—it
40 does not hurt them. I was taught how to read in the old books and how to make the old writings—that was hard and took a long time. My knowledge made me happy—it was like a fire in my heart. Most of all, I liked to hear of the Old Days and the stories of the gods. I asked myself many questions that I could not answer, but it was good to ask them. At night, I would lie

INFER

Pause at line 12. What do the rules and laws suggest about the narrator's society?

_____

_____

_____

_____

POINT OF VIEW

Circle the words in lines 13–20 that tell you the story is written from the **first-person point of view**. Who is the narrator?

_____

_____

_____

IDENTIFY

In lines 21–24, underline what the boy concludes when he holds the metal and does not die.

INFER

Re-read lines 36–42, and underline details describing how the boy prepared to be a priest. What can you infer, or guess, about the boy from the way he feels about knowledge?

_____

_____

**PREDICT**

Writers use **foreshadowing** to hint at events that will happen later in the story. In lines 61–62, underline what the boy sees in the smoke. What places do you think he will visit later on?

_____

_____

_____

_____

_____

_____

_____

_____

**INTERPRET**

What does the father mean when he says the boy's dream may "eat him up" (line 74)?

_____

_____

_____

_____

_____

_____

_____

_____

_____

_____

_____

awake and listen to the wind—it seemed to me that it was the voice of the gods as they flew through the air.

We are not ignorant like the Forest People—our women spin wool on the wheel, our priests wear a white robe. We do

50 not eat grubs from the tree, we have not forgotten the old writings, although they are hard to understand. Nevertheless, my knowledge and my lack of knowledge burned in me—I wished to know more. When I was a man at last, I came to my father and said, "It is time for me to go on my journey. Give me your leave."

He looked at me for a long time, stroking his beard, then he said at last, "Yes. It is time." That night, in the house of the priesthood, I asked for and received purification. My body hurt but my spirit was a cool stone. It was my father himself who questioned me about my dreams.

60 He bade me look into the smoke of the fire and see—I saw and told what I saw. It was what I have always seen—a river, and, beyond it, a great Dead Place and in it the gods walking. I have always thought about that. His eyes were stern when I told him— he was no longer my father but a priest. He said, "This is a strong dream."

"It is mine," I said, while the smoke waved and my head felt light. They were singing the Star song in the outer chamber and it was like the buzzing of bees in my head.

He asked me how the gods were dressed and I told him

70 how they were dressed. We know how they were dressed from the book, but I saw them as if they were before me. When I had finished, he threw the sticks three times and studied them as they fell.

"This is a very strong dream," he said. "It may eat you up."

"I am not afraid," I said and looked at him with both eyes. My voice sounded thin in my ears but that was because of the smoke.

He touched me on the breast and the forehead. He gave me the bow and the three arrows.

80    "Take them," he said. "It is forbidden to travel east. It is
forbidden to cross the river. It is forbidden to go to the Place
of the Gods. All these things are forbidden."

"All these things are forbidden," I said, but it was my voice
that spoke and not my spirit. He looked at me again.

"My son," he said. "Once I had young dreams. If your
dreams do not eat you up, you may be a great priest. If they eat
you, you are still my son. Now go on your journey."

I went fasting, as is the law. My body hurt but not my
heart. When the dawn came, I was out of sight of the village.
90    I prayed and purified myself, waiting for a sign. The sign was
an eagle. It flew east.

Sometimes signs are sent by bad spirits. I waited again on
the flat rock, fasting, taking no food. I was very still—I could
feel the sky above me and the earth beneath. I waited till the
sun was beginning to sink. Then three deer passed in the valley,
going east—they did not wind[1] me or see me. There was a white
fawn with them—a very great sign.

I followed them, at a distance, waiting for what would
happen. My heart was troubled about going east, yet I knew that
100    I must go. My head hummed with my fasting—I did not even
see the panther spring upon the white fawn. But, before I knew
it, the bow was in my hand. I shouted and the panther lifted his
head from the fawn. It is not easy to kill a panther with one arrow
but the arrow went through his eye and into his brain. He died
as he tried to spring—he rolled over, tearing at the ground. Then
I knew I was meant to go east—I knew that was my journey.
When the night came, I made my fire and roasted meat.

It is eight suns' journey to the east and a man passes by
many Dead Places. The Forest People are afraid of them but
110    I am not. Once I made my fire on the edge of a Dead Place at
night and, next morning, in the dead house, I found a good
knife, little rusted. That was small to what came afterward but it
made my heart feel big. Always when I looked for game, it was

---

1.  **wind** (wind) *v.:* detect the scent of.

**PREDICT**

Circle the forbidden things in lines 80–82. Do you think the boy will obey the rules? Why or why not?

_____

_____

_____

_____

_____

_____

_____

**CONFLICT**

An **internal conflict** takes place in a character's mind between opposing ideas or feelings. What is the narrator's internal conflict (lines 80–106)? Underline the signs that convince him to journey east.

_____

_____

_____

_____

_____

_____

_____

_____

*Ou-dis-sun* (line 125) is your first clue to where the Place of the Gods is. Can you tell by sounding it out? Don't worry if you don't yet recognize it. There will be more clues throughout the story.

_____

_____

_____

_____

_____

In lines 143–145, underline the narrator's reason for going on. What three words would you use to describe him?

_____

_____

_____

_____

_____

_____

_____

in front of my arrow, and twice I passed hunting parties of the Forest People without their knowing. So I knew my magic was strong and my journey clean, in spite of the law.

Toward the setting of the eighth sun, I came to the banks of the great river. It was half a day's journey after I had left the god-road—we do not use the god-roads now, for they are falling

120 apart into great blocks of stone, and the forest is safer going. A long way off, I had seen the water through trees but the trees were thick. At last, I came out upon an open place at the top of a cliff. There was the great river below, like a giant in the sun. It is very long, very wide. It could eat all the streams we know and still be thirsty. Its name is Ou-dis-sun, the Sacred, the Long. No man of my tribe had seen it, not even my father, the priest. It was magic and I prayed.

Then I raised my eyes and looked south. It was there, the Place of the Gods.

130 How can I tell what it was like—you do not know. It was there, in the red light, and they were too big to be houses. It was there with the red light upon it, mighty and ruined. I knew that in another moment the gods would see me. I covered my eyes with my hands and crept back into the forest.

Surely, that was enough to do, and live. Surely it was enough to spend the night upon the cliff. The Forest People themselves do not come near. Yet, all through the night, I knew that I should have to cross the river and walk in the places of the gods, although the gods ate me up. My magic did not help me at all

140 and yet there was a fire in my bowels, a fire in my mind. When the sun rose, I thought, "My journey has been clean. Now I will go home from my journey." But, even as I thought so, I knew I could not. If I went to the Place of the Gods, I would surely die, but, if I did not go, I could never be at peace with my spirit again. It is better to lose one's life than one's spirit, if one is a priest and the son of a priest.

Nevertheless, as I made the raft, the tears ran out of my eyes. The Forest People could have killed me without fight, if

they had come upon me then, but they did not come. When the
150  raft was made, I said the sayings for the dead and painted myself
for death. My heart was cold as a frog and my knees like water,
but the burning in my mind would not let me have peace. As I
pushed the raft from the shore, I began my death song—I had
the right. It was a fine song.

> "I am John, son of John," I sang. "My people
>     are the Hill People. They are the men.
> I go into the Dead Places but I am not slain.
> I take the metal from the Dead Places but
>     I am not blasted.
160  I travel upon the god-roads and am not
>     afraid. E-yah! I have killed the panther,
>     I have killed the fawn!
> E-yah! I have come to the great river. No
>     man has come there before.
> It is forbidden to go east, but I have gone,
>     forbidden to go on the great river, but
>     I am there.
> Open your hearts, you spirits, and hear my
>     song. Now I go to the Place of the Gods,
170      I shall not return.
> My body is painted for death and my limbs
>     weak, but my heart is big as I go to the
>     Place of the Gods!"

All the same, when I came to the Place of the Gods, I was afraid,
afraid. The current of the great river is very strong—it gripped
my raft with its hands. That was magic, for the river itself is
wide and calm. I could feel evil spirits about me, in the bright
morning; I could feel their breath on my neck as I was swept
down the stream. Never have I been so much alone—I tried to
180  think of my knowledge, but it was a squirrel's heap of winter nuts.
There was no strength in my knowledge anymore and I felt

**WORD STUDY**

Underline the **similes**—
comparisons using *like* or *as*—
that describe the narrator's
fear (line 151).

**IDENTIFY**

What important fact do you
learn in the first line of the
narrator's song (line 155)?

_____

_____

_____

_____

_____

_____

_____

_____

_____

_____

_____

_____

_____

_____

**FLUENCY**

Practice reading the song
aloud at least twice. Use
a tone of voice that the
narrator might have used,
and remember that he
described this song as his
"death song."

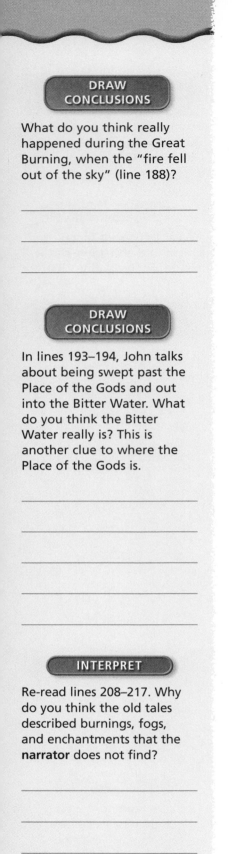

**DRAW CONCLUSIONS**

What do you think really happened during the Great Burning, when the "fire fell out of the sky" (line 188)?

_____

_____

_____

**DRAW CONCLUSIONS**

In lines 193–194, John talks about being swept past the Place of the Gods and out into the Bitter Water. What do you think the Bitter Water really is? This is another clue to where the Place of the Gods is.

_____

_____

_____

_____

_____

**INTERPRET**

Re-read lines 208–217. Why do you think the old tales described burnings, fogs, and enchantments that the **narrator** does not find?

_____

_____

_____

_____

_____

_____

small and naked as a new-hatched bird—alone upon the great river, the servant of the gods.

Yet, after a while, my eyes were opened and I saw. I saw both banks of the river—I saw that once there had been god-roads across it, though now they were broken and fallen like broken vines. Very great they were, and wonderful and broken—broken in the time of the Great Burning when the fire fell out of the sky. And always the current took me nearer to the Place of the Gods, 190 and the huge ruins rose before my eyes.

I do not know the customs of rivers—we are the People of the Hills. I tried to guide my raft with the pole but it spun around. I thought the river meant to take me past the Place of the Gods and out into the Bitter Water of the legends. I grew angry then—my heart felt strong. I said aloud, "I am a priest and the son of a priest!" The gods heard me—they showed me how to paddle with the pole on one side of the raft. The current changed itself—I drew near to the Place of the Gods.

When I was very near, my raft struck and turned over. I can 200 swim in our lakes—I swam to the shore. There was a great spike of rusted metal sticking out into the river—I hauled myself up upon it and sat there, panting. I had saved my bow and two arrows and the knife I found in the Dead Place but that was all. My raft went whirling downstream toward the Bitter Water. I looked after it, and thought if it had trod me under, at least I would be safely dead. Nevertheless, when I had dried my bow-string and restrung it, I walked forward to the Place of the Gods.

It felt like ground underfoot; it did not burn me. It is not true what some of the tales say, that the ground there burns 210 forever, for I have been there. Here and there were the marks and stains of the Great Burning, on the ruins, that is true. But they were old marks and old stains. It is not true either, what some of our priests say, that it is an island covered with fogs and enchantments. It is not. It is a great Dead Place—greater than any Dead Place we know. Everywhere in it there are god-roads, though most are cracked and broken. Everywhere there are the ruins of the high towers of the gods.

How shall I tell what I saw? I went carefully, my strung bow in my hand, my skin ready for danger. There should have been the wailings of spirits and the shrieks of demons, but there were not. It was very silent and sunny where I had landed—the wind and the rain and the birds that drop seeds had done their work—the grass grew in the cracks of the broken stone. It is a fair island—no wonder the gods built there. If I had come there, a god, I also would have built.

How shall I tell what I saw? The towers are not all broken— here and there one still stands, like a great tree in a forest, and the birds nest high. But the towers themselves look blind, for the gods are gone. I saw a fish-hawk, catching fish in the river. I saw a little dance of white butterflies over a great heap of broken stones and columns. I went there and looked about me—there was a carved stone with cut-letters, broken in half. I can read letters but I could not understand these. They said UBTREAS. There was also the shattered image of a man or a god. It had been made of white stone and he wore his hair tied back like a woman's. His name was ASHING, as I read on the cracked half of a stone. I thought it wise to pray to ASHING, though I do not know that god.

How shall I tell what I saw? There was no smell of man left, on stone or metal. Nor were there many trees in that wilderness of stone. There are many pigeons, nesting and dropping in the towers—the gods must have loved them, or, perhaps, they used them for sacrifices. There are wild cats that roam the god-roads, green-eyed, unafraid of man. At night they wail like demons but they are not demons. The wild dogs are more dangerous, for they hunt in a pack, but them I did not meet till later. Everywhere there are the carved stones, carved with magical numbers or words.

I went north—I did not try to hide myself. When a god or a demon saw me, then I would die, but meanwhile I was no

SETTING

Underline details in lines 221–238 that help you visualize the **setting** of the Place of the Gods.

_____

_____

_____

_____

_____

_____

_____

DRAW CONCLUSIONS

What do you think UBTREAS and ASHING once meant (lines 233 and 236)?

_____

_____

_____

_____

_____

_____

_____

_____

_____

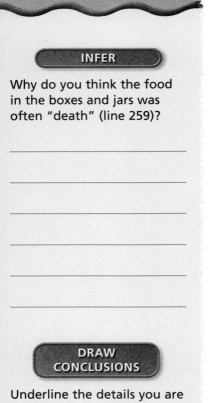

**INFER**

Why do you think the food in the boxes and jars was often "death" (line 259)?

_____

_____

_____

_____

_____

_____

**DRAW CONCLUSIONS**

Underline the details you are given about the great temple in midcity (lines 262–266). What could this be?

_____

_____

_____

_____

_____

_____

_____

_____

_____

_____

_____

_____

_____

_____

longer afraid. My hunger for knowledge burned in me—there was so much that I could not understand. After a while, I knew that my belly was hungry. I could have hunted for my meat, but I did not hunt. It is known that the gods did not hunt as we do—they got their food from enchanted boxes and jars. Sometimes these are still found in the Dead Places—once, when I was a child and foolish, I opened such a jar and tasted it and found the food sweet. But my father found out and punished me for it strictly, for, often, that food is death. Now, though,

260    I had long gone past what was forbidden, and I entered the likeliest towers, looking for the food of the gods.

     I found it at last in the ruins of a great temple in the midcity. A mighty temple it must have been, for the roof was painted like the sky at night with its stars—that much I could see, though the colors were faint and dim. It went down into great caves and tunnels—perhaps they kept their slaves there. But when I started to climb down, I heard the squeaking of rats, so I did not go—rats are unclean, and there must have been many

tribes of them, from the squeaking. But near there, I found food,
270 in the heart of a ruin, behind a door that still opened. I ate only
the fruits from the jars—they had a very sweet taste. There was
drink, too, in bottles of glass—the drink of the gods was strong
and made my head swim. After I had eaten and drunk, I slept on
the top of a stone, my bow at my side.

When I woke, the sun was low. Looking down from where
I lay, I saw a dog sitting on his haunches. His tongue was hanging
out of his mouth; he looked as if he were laughing. He was a big
dog, with a gray-brown coat, as big as a wolf. I sprang up and
shouted at him but he did not move—he just sat there as if he
280 were laughing. I did not like that. When I reached for a stone
to throw, he moved swiftly out of the way of the stone. He was
not afraid of me; he looked at me as if I were meat. No doubt
I could have killed him with an arrow, but I did not know if
there were others. Moreover, night was falling.

I looked about me—not far away there was a great, broken
god-road, leading north. The towers were high enough, but not
so high, and while many of the dead houses were wrecked, there
were some that stood. I went toward this god-road, keeping to
the heights of the ruins, while the dog followed. When I had
290 reached the god-road, I saw that there were others behind him.
If I had slept later, they would have come upon me asleep and
torn out my throat. As it was, they were sure enough of me; they
did not hurry. When I went into the dead house, they kept watch
at the entrance—doubtless they thought they would have a fine
hunt. But a dog cannot open a door and I knew, from the books,
that the gods did not like to live on the ground but on high.

I had just found a door I could open when the dogs
decided to rush. Ha! They were surprised when I shut the door
in their faces—it was a good door, of strong metal. I could hear
300 their foolish baying beyond it but I did not stop to answer them.
I was in darkness—I found stairs and climbed. There were many
stairs, turning around till my head was dizzy. At the top was
another door—I found the knob and opened it. I was in a long

CONFLICT

What **external conflict** does John face in lines 285–299?

_____
_____
_____
_____
_____
_____
_____
_____
_____

IDENTIFY
CAUSE & EFFECT

What prevents the dogs from killing John? Underline the details in lines 291–299 that support your answer.

_____
_____
_____
_____
_____
_____
_____
_____

**DRAW CONCLUSIONS**

John is in a tall building with a lot of stairs. What do you think the door with no handle (lines 303–305) leads to?

_____

_____

_____

_____

**SETTING**

In lines 317–328, John finds himself in a place of "great riches." Underline the things he sees.

**INFER**

Circle the everyday items John finds in lines 329–334. Why do they seem like "magic" to him?

_____

_____

_____

_____

_____

_____

_____

_____

_____

small chamber—on one side of it was a bronze door that could not be opened, for it had no handle. Perhaps there was a magic word to open it but I did not have the word. I turned to the door in the opposite side of the wall. The lock of it was broken and I opened it and went in.

Within, there was a place of great riches. The god who lived there must have been a powerful god. The first room was a small anteroom—I waited there for some time, telling the spirits of the place that I came in peace and not as a robber. When it seemed to me that they had had time to hear me, I went on. Ah, what riches! Few, even, of the windows had been broken—it was all as it had been. The great windows that looked over the city had not been broken at all though they were dusty and streaked with many years. There were coverings on the floors, the colors not greatly faded, and the chairs were soft and deep. There were pictures upon the walls, very strange, very wonderful— I remember one of a bunch of flowers in a jar—if you came close to it, you could see nothing but bits of color, but if you stood away from it, the flowers might have been picked yesterday. It made my heart feel strange to look at this picture—and to look at the figure of a bird, in some hard clay, on a table and see it so like our birds. Everywhere there were books and writings, many in tongues that I could not read. The god who lived there must have been a wise god and full of knowledge. I felt I had right there, as I sought knowledge also.

Nevertheless, it was strange. There was a washing-place but no water—perhaps the gods washed in air. There was a cooking-place but no wood, and though there was a machine to cook food, there was no place to put fire in it. Nor were there candles or lamps—there were things that looked like lamps but they had neither oil nor wick. All these things were magic, but I touched them and lived—the magic had gone out of them. Let me tell one thing to show. In the washing-place, a thing said "Hot" but it was not hot to the touch—another thing said "Cold" but it was not cold. This must have been a strong magic but the magic was gone. I do not understand—they had ways—I wish that I knew.

340     It was close and dry and dusty in their house of the gods. I have said the magic was gone but that is not true—it had gone from the magic things but it had not gone from the place. I felt the spirits about me, weighing upon me. Nor had I ever slept in a Dead Place before—and yet, tonight, I must sleep there. When I thought of it, my tongue felt dry in my throat, in spite of my wish for knowledge. Almost I would have gone down again and faced the dogs, but I did not.

I had not gone through all the rooms when the darkness fell. When it fell, I went back to the big room looking over
350     the city and made fire. There was a place to make fire and a box with wood in it, though I do not think they cooked there. I wrapped myself in a floor-covering and slept in front of the fire—I was very tired.

Now I tell what is very strong magic. I woke in the midst of the night. When I woke, the fire had gone out and I was cold. It seemed to me that all around me there were whisperings and voices. I closed my eyes to shut them out. Some will say that I slept again, but I do not think that I slept. I could feel the spirits drawing my spirit out of my body as a fish is drawn on a line.

360     Why should I lie about it? I am a priest and the son of a priest. If there are spirits, as they say, in the small Dead Places near us, what spirits must there not be in that great Place of the Gods? And would not they wish to speak? After such long years? I know that I felt myself drawn as a fish is drawn on a line. I had stepped out of my body—I could see my body asleep in front of the cold fire, but it was not I. I was drawn to look out upon the city of the gods.

It should have been dark, for it was night, but it was not dark. Everywhere there were lights—lines of light—circles and
370     blurs of light—ten thousand torches would not have been the same. The sky itself was alight—you could barely see the stars

WORD STUDY

During the night, John has a vision. What **simile** does he use in line 359 to describe his spirit?

In lines 377–394, underline at least six things that John notices about the way the gods lived in the past. How do you think he was able to "see" these things?

_____

_____

_____

_____

_____

_____

_____

_____

_____

_____

_____

_____

_____

_____

_____

_____

_____

_____

_____

_____

for the glow in the sky. I thought to myself, "This is strong magic," and trembled. There was a roaring in my ears like the rushing of rivers. Then my eyes grew used to the light and my ears to the sound. I knew that I was seeing the city as it had been when the gods were alive.

That was a sight indeed—yes, that was a sight: I could not have seen it in the body—my body would have died. Everywhere went the gods, on foot and in chariots—there were gods beyond
380 number and counting and their chariots blocked the streets. They had turned night to day for their pleasure—they did not sleep with the sun. The noise of their coming and going was the noise of many waters. It was magic what they could do—it was magic what they did.

I looked out of another window—the great vines of their bridges were mended and the god-roads went east and west. Restless, restless were the gods, and always in motion! They burrowed tunnels under rivers—they flew in the air. With unbelievable tools they did giant works—no part of the earth
390 was safe from them, for, if they wished for a thing, they summoned it from the other side of the world. And always, as they labored and rested, as they feasted and made love, there was a drum in their ears—the pulse of the giant city, beating and beating like a man's heart.

Were they happy? What is happiness to the gods? They were great, they were mighty, they were wonderful and terrible. As I looked upon them and their magic, I felt like a child—but a little more, it seemed to me, and they would pull down the moon from the sky. I saw them with wisdom beyond wisdom
400 and knowledge beyond knowledge. And yet not all they did was well done—even I could see that—and yet their wisdom could not but grow until all was peace.

Then I saw their fate come upon them and that was terrible past speech. It came upon them as they walked the streets of their city. I have been in the fights with the Forest People—I have seen men die. But this was not like that. When gods war

410    with gods, they use weapons we do not know. It was fire falling
out of the sky and a mist that poisoned. It was the time of the
Great Burning and the Destruction. They ran about like ants in
the streets of their city—poor gods, poor gods! Then the towers
began to fall. A few escaped—yes, a few. The legends tell it. But,
even after the city had become a Dead Place, for many years the
poison was still in the ground. I saw it happen, I saw the last of
them die. It was darkness over the broken city and I wept.

All this, I saw. I saw it as I have told it, though not in the
body. When I woke in the morning, I was hungry, but I did
not think first of my hunger, for my heart was perplexed and
confused. I knew the reason for the Dead Places but I did not
see why it had happened. It seemed to me it should not have
420    happened, with all the magic they had. I went through the
house looking for an answer. There was so much in the house
I could not understand—and yet I am a priest and the son of
a priest. It was like being on one side of the great river, at night,
with no light to show the way.

Then I saw the dead god. He was sitting in his chair, by
the window, in a room I had not entered before and, for the first
moment, I thought that he was alive. Then I saw the skin on the
back of his hand—it was like dry leather. The room was shut,
hot and dry—no doubt that had kept him as he was. At first
430    I was afraid to approach him—then the fear left me. He was
sitting looking out over the city—he was dressed in the clothes
of the gods. His age was neither young nor old—I could not
tell his age. But there was wisdom in his face and great sadness.
You could see that he would have not run away. He had sat at
his window, watching his city die—then he himself had died.
But it is better to lose one's life than one's spirit—and you could
see from the face that his spirit had not been lost. I knew that,
if I touched him, he would fall into dust—and yet, there was
something unconquered in the face.

DRAW CONCLUSIONS

What do you think the fire
that fell from the sky and
the poison mist (lines
407–408) might be?

_____

_____

_____

_____

_____

INTERPRET

Pause at line 424. What can't
John understand about the
gods, who seemed to have
so much wisdom and power?

_____

_____

_____

_____

_____

_____

INFER

Why does John think he
should be able to understand
these mysteries (lines
421–423)?

_____

_____

_____

_____

**IDENTIFY**

What "great knowledge" does John discover in the morning (lines 440–443)?

_____

_____

_____

_____

_____

_____

_____

_____

**INTERPRET**

What does John mean when he says that in the old days "they ate knowledge too fast" (line 460)?

_____

_____

_____

_____

_____

_____

**IDENTIFY**

In lines 465–469, underline what John plans to do when he is chief priest. Circle the name of the Place of the Gods.

440       That is all of my story, for then I knew he was a man—I knew then that they had been men, neither gods nor demons. It is a great knowledge, hard to tell and believe. They were men—they went a dark road, but they were men. I had no fear after that—I had no fear going home, though twice I fought off the dogs and I was hunted for two days by the Forest People. When I saw my father again, I prayed and was purified. He touched my lips and my breast, he said, "You went away a boy. You come back a man and a priest." I said, "Father, they were men! I have been in the Place of the Gods and seen it! Now slay me, if it is

450    the law—but still I know they were men."

      He looked at me out of both eyes. He said, "The law is not always the same shape—you have done what you have done. I could not have done it in my time, but you come after me. Tell!"

      I told and he listened. After that, I wished to tell all the people but he showed me otherwise. He said, "Truth is a hard deer to hunt. If you eat too much truth at once, you may die of the truth. It was not idly that our fathers forbade the Dead Places." He was right—it is better the truth should come little by little. I have learned that, being a priest. Perhaps, in the old days,

460    they ate knowledge too fast.

      Nevertheless, we make a beginning. It is not for the metal alone we go to the Dead Places now—there are the books and the writings. They are hard to learn. And the magic tools are broken—but we can look at them and wonder. At least, we make a beginning. And, when I am chief priest we shall go beyond the great river. We shall go to the Place of the Gods—the place newyork—not one man but a company. We shall look for the images of the gods and find the god ASHING and the others—the gods Lincoln and Biltmore[2] and Moses.[3] But they

470    were men who built the city, not gods or demons. They were men. I remember the dead man's face. They were men who were here before us. We must build again.

---

2.   **Biltmore:** a New York City hotel.
3.   **Moses:** Robert Moses (1888–1981): New York City public official who oversaw many large construction projects, such as bridges and public buildings.

# By the Waters of Babylon

**Conclusions Chart** "By the Waters of Babylon" is told from the **point of view** of a narrator, John, who goes on a journey of discovery. Until John completes his journey of discovery, his descriptions of places and events are incomplete or **unreliable.**

**Draw conclusions** about what the narrator sees in "By the Waters of Babylon." Fill in the chart by writing what you think he is describing.

| What the Narrator Names | My Conclusions About What the Narrator Is Describing |
|---|---|
| Dead Places | |
| Place of the Gods | |
| Great Burning | |
| Old Days | |
| Ou-dis-sun | |
| ASHING | |
| Temple with stars on the ceiling | |

# Standards Review

## TestPractice    By the Waters of Babylon

Sharpen your test-taking skills by completing the sample test item. Then, check your answer against the explanation in the right-hand column.

| Sample Test Item | Explanation of the Correct Answer |
|---|---|
| Which statement best describes the narrator's **voice**?<br><br>A  It is self-pitying.<br><br>B  It is courageous and intelligent.<br><br>C  It is shallow and lazy.<br><br>D  It is considerate and loving. | The correct answer is *B*.<br><br>*A* is incorrect because the writer never portrays John as feeling sorry for himself. Nothing that John does or says supports answer *C*. Although some of John's actions at the beginning of the story support the answer *D*, *B* is the best answer. |

**DIRECTIONS:** Circle the letter of each correct response.

**Reading Standard 3.9** Explain how voice, persona, and the choice of a narrator affect characterization and the tone, plot, and credibility of a text.

1. From what **point of view** is the story told?

   A  first person

   B  second person

   C  third-person limited

   D  omniscient

2. The **narrator** of the story is—

   F  a god

   G  a young man

   H  an old priest

   J  a dead man

3. Which word best describes what the **narrator** wants?

   A  love

   B  friends

   C  knowledge

   D  power

4. John learns that the inhabitants of the Place of the Gods—

   F  knew little more than the Hill People

   G  reestablished their community a few miles from their ruined city

   H  were killed by packs of wild dogs

   J  were actually people

5. The Place of the Gods was once called—

   A  New York

   B  Boston

   C  San Francisco

   D  Los Angeles

# Standards Review

## By the Waters of Babylon

### Suffixes: Clues to Word Meanings

Sometimes you can figure out the meaning of an unfamiliar word if you analyze the meaning of its parts. The more suffixes you know, the more words you'll be able to figure out. A **suffix** is a word part added to the end of a word or root. Increase your knowledge of suffixes by adding at least two more words to each of the example boxes in the chart below.

| Suffixes | Meanings | Examples |
|---|---|---|
| –able, –ible | "able; likely" | capable, flexible |
| –ance, –ence | "act; condition; fact" | patience, evidence |
| –er, –or | "one who does" | baker, director |
| –ic | "dealing with; caused by; showing" | classic, choleric, workaholic |
| –ion, –tion | "action; result; state" | union, fusion, selection |
| –ous | "marked by; given to" | religious, furious |
| –y | "quality; action" | jealousy, inquiry |

**Before You Go On . . .**

Check your Standards Mastery at the back of this book.

# Calling Home by Tim O'Brien

Two of the worst things a young soldier has to face in war are fear and homesickness. In "Calling Home," which is set during the Vietnam War, you will learn what happens when four soldiers have a chance to call home.

## LITERARY FOCUS: POINT OF VIEW AND SETTING

This story is told from the **third-person limited point of view.** The narrator, who does not appear in the story, zooms in on one character: Paul Berlin. The narrator describes what Paul sees, thinks, and feels. The other characters—Oscar, Eddie, Doc, and the young Pfc—are described only as Paul sees them, so we do not learn about their inner thoughts or feelings.

- While reading "Calling Home," pause every so often to think about Paul's world—what he thinks and what he sees.

The **setting**—the time, place, and customs of a story—in "Calling Home" is Vietnam during the Vietnam War. A second setting, however, is described in the story as Paul Berlin remembers his parents' home.

- As you read, think about the importance of both these settings to the message of "Calling Home."

## READING SKILLS: MAKING INFERENCES

Often writers do not state what they mean directly. In order to understand what is being said, the reader has to make **inferences,** or guesses based on evidence. You make inferences about a story based on evidence in the text and based on your own experiences and prior knowledge. What inferences can you make already, based just on the title of this story?

Keep track of the inferences you make as you read by filling in a chart like this one.

| Story Detail | My Inference |
|---|---|
| | |
| | |

**Reading Standard 1.3 (Grade 8 Review)** Use word meanings within the appropriate context and show ability to verify those meanings by definition, restatement, example, comparison, or contrast.

**Reading Standard 3.4 (Grade 8 Review)** Analyze the relevance of the setting (e.g., place, time, customs) to the mood, tone, and meaning of the text.

**Reading Standard 3.9** Explain how voice, persona, and the choice of a narrator affect characterization and the tone, plot, and credibility of a text.

## VOCABULARY DEVELOPMENT

### PREVIEW SELECTION VOCABULARY

The following words appear in the story that follows. Become familiar with these words before you begin reading.

**correlate** (kôr′ə·lāt) *v.:* bring one thing into relationship with another.

*Before they left the base, the troops would* **correlate** *their watches.*

**console** (kän′sōl′) *n.:* instrument panel used to operate electronic or other type of system.

*The soldiers sat at the* **console** *and got ready to place their calls.*

**pensive** (pen′siv) *adj.:* thoughtful.

*The young men became* **pensive** *after talking to their families.*

### CONTEXT CLUES: JARGON

**Jargon** is the special vocabulary used by people engaged in a particular activity or occupation. Jargon can include newly created words, existing words that are given new meanings, or abbreviations of words. You may be familiar with computer jargon such as *reboot, Web,* and *cookie.* The jargon in this story includes words that U.S. soldiers in Vietnam developed to describe the world around them.

Some of the jargon is explained for you in footnotes. For other words, you will find **context clues,** or hints in the surrounding words and sentences, that will help you figure out their meanings. There are different types of context clues, as shown below. In the examples given, the unfamiliar word is in bold type and the context clue is underlined.

- DEFINITION OR SYNONYM: The weary **grunts,** or <u>foot soldiers,</u> marched into camp.

- RESTATEMENT: Their **platoon** was made up of the most battle-weary <u>company squads.</u>

- CONTRAST: <u>Instead of rushing into action</u> when he heard the planes overhead, the commander became **pensive.**

# CALLING HOME

## Tim O'Brien

The word *bush* in line 1 is **jargon** for "forest, woods, or jungle." The phrase *stand down* (line 2) means "rest from fighting."

Circle the positive aspects of Chu Lai (lines 3–7). Underline the negatives.

In August, after two months in the bush, the platoon returned to Chu Lai for a week's stand down.

They swam, played mini-golf in the sand, and wrote letters and slept late in the mornings. At night there were floor shows. There was singing and dancing, and afterward there was homesickness. It was neither a good time nor a bad time. The war was all around them.

On the final day, Oscar and Eddie and Doc and Paul Berlin hiked down to the 42nd Commo Detachment. Recently the
10    outfit had installed a radio-telephone hookup with the States.

"It's called MARS," said a young Pfc[1] at the reception desk. "Stands for Military Air Radio System." He was a friendly, deeply tanned red-head without freckles. On each wrist was a gold watch, and the boy kept glancing at them as if to **correlate** time. He seemed a little nervous.

While they waited to place their calls, the Pfc explained how the system worked. A series of radio relays fed the signal across the Pacific to a telephone exchange in downtown Honolulu, where it was sent by regular undersea cable to San

20 Francisco and from there to any telephone in America. "Real wizardry," the boy said. "Depends a lot on the weather, but, wow, sometimes it's like talkin' to the guy next door. You'd swear you was there in the same room."

They waited nearly an hour. Relay problems, the Pfc explained. He grinned and gestured at Oscar's boots. "You guys are legs, I guess. Grunts."

"I guess so," Oscar said.

The boy nodded solemnly. He started to say something but then shook his head. "Legs," he murmured.

30 Eddie's call went through first.

The Pfc led him into a small, sound-proofed booth and had him sit behind a **console** equipped with speakers and a microphone and two pairs of headsets. Paul Berlin watched through a plastic window. For a time nothing happened. Then a red light blinked on and the Pfc handed Eddie one of the headsets. Eddie began rocking in his chair. He held the microphone with one hand, squeezing it, leaning slightly forward. It was hard to see his eyes.

He was in the booth a long time. When he came out his face

40 was bright red. He sat beside Oscar. He yawned, then immediately covered his eyes, rubbed them, then stretched and blinked.

"Geez," he said softly.

Then he laughed. It was a strange, scratchy laugh. He cleared his throat and smiled and kept blinking.

"Geez," he said.

---

1. **Pfc:** Private First Class.

**correlate** (kôr′ə·lāt) v.: bring one thing into relationship with another.

What two times might the Pfc be correlating?

_____

_____

_____

_____

**console** (kän′sōl′) n.: instrument panel used to operate an electronic or other type of system. As a verb, *console* (kən·sōl′) means "make someone feel better."

WORD STUDY

"Grunts" are infantrymen, or foot soldiers. Underline context clues in lines 25–26 that help reveal the meaning of the term.

FLUENCY

Read the boxed passage aloud at least twice. Build speed and smooth out your delivery with each read.

_____

_____

_____

_____

_____

_____

_____

Pause at line 50. When Eddie comes out from the booth, how do you think he is feeling?

What do you think Eddie means by "Graves Registration" (line 55)? Circle the context clue that helps you figure it out.

"What—"

Eddie giggled. "It was . . . You shoulda heard her. 'Who?' she goes. Like that—'*Who*?' Just like that."

He took out a handkerchief, blew his nose, shook his head.

50  His eyes were shiny.

"Just like that—'Who?' 'Eddie,' I say, and Ma says, 'Eddie who?' and I say, 'Who do you think Eddie?' She almost passes out. Almost falls down or something. She gets this call from Nam and thinks maybe I been shot. 'Where you at?' she says, like maybe I'm calling from Graves Registration, or something, and—"

"That's great," Doc said. "That's really great, man."

"Yeah. It's—"

"Really great."

60  Eddie shook his head violently, as though trying to clear stopped-up ears. He was quiet a time. Then he laughed.

"Honest, you had to hear it. 'Who?' she keeps saying. *'Who?'* Real clear. Like in the next . . . And Petie! He's in high school now—you believe that? My brother. Can't even call him Petie no more. 'Pete,' he says. Real deep voice, just like that guy on Lawrence Welk—'Pete, not Petie,' he goes. You believe that?"

"Hey, it's terrific," Doc said. "It really is."

"And clear? Man! Just like—I could hear Ma's cuckoo clock, that clear."

70 "Technology."

"Yeah," Eddie grinned. "Real technology. It's . . . I say, 'Hey Ma,' and what's she say? 'Who's this?' Real scared-soundin', you know? Man, I coulda just—"

"It's great, Eddie."

Doc was next, and then Oscar. Both of them came out looking a little funny, not quite choked up but trying hard not to be. Very quiet at first, then laughing, then talking fast, then turning quiet again. It made Paul Berlin feel warm to watch them. Even Oscar seemed happy.

80 "Technology," Doc said. "You can't beat technology."

"My old man, all he could say was 'Over.' Nothin' else. 'Weather's fine,' he'd say, 'over.' " Oscar wagged his head. His father had been an R.T.O.[2] in Italy. "You believe that? All he says is 'Over,' and 'Roger that.' Crazy."

They would turn **pensive**. Then one of them would chuckle or grin.

"Pirates are out of it this year. Not a prayer, Petie says."

"I bleed."

"Yeah, but Petie—he goes nuts over the Pirates. It's all he
90 knows. Thinks we're over here fightin' the Russians. The Pirates, that's *all* he knows."

"Crazy," Oscar said. He kept wagging his head. "Over 'n' out."

It made Paul Berlin feel good. Like buddies; he felt close to all of them. When they laughed, he laughed.

---

2. **R.T.O.:** radio-telephone operator.

Notes

_____
_____
_____
_____
_____
_____
_____
_____

**COMPARE & CONTRAST**

Pause at line 79. Are the reactions of Doc and Oscar similar to or different from Eddie's reaction?

_____
_____
_____
_____

**VOCABULARY**

**pensive** (pen'siv) *adj.:* thoughtful.

**POINT OF VIEW**

This story is told from the **third-person limited** point of view. Circle the name of the character that the narrator focuses on in the story.

**INFER**

Re-read lines 97–100. Why does the Pfc tell Paul to "ease up"?

_____

_____

_____

_____

_____

_____

_____

**SETTING**

Circle details in lines 101–121 that help you visualize the **setting** of Paul's home.

**IDENTIFY CAUSE & EFFECT**

Re-read lines 127–135. Why doesn't Paul want to tell his parents about his fear or about anything bad? Circle the detail that tells you.

_____

_____

_____

_____

_____

_____

_____

Then the Pfc tapped him on the shoulder.

He felt giddy. Everything inside the booth was painted white. Sitting down, he grinned and squeezed his fingers together. He saw Doc wave at him through the plastic window.

100     "Ease up," the Pfc said. "Pretend it's a local call."

The boy helped him with the headset. There was a crisp clicking sound, then a long electric hum like a vacuum cleaner running in another room. He remembered . . . his mother always used the old Hoover on Saturdays. The smell of carpets, a fine, powdery dust rising in the yellow window light. An uncluttered house. Things in their places.

He felt himself smiling. He pressed the headset tight. What day was it? Sunday, he hoped. His father liked to putz on Sundays. Putzing, he called it, which meant tinkering and
110     dreaming and touching things with his hands, fixing them or building them or tearing them down, studying things. Putzing . . . He hoped it was Sunday. What would they be doing? What month was it? He pictured the telephone. It was there in the kitchen, to the left of the sink. It was black. Black because his father hated pastels on his telephones. . . . He imagined the ring. He remembered it clearly, how it sounded both in the kitchen and in the basement, where his father had rigged up an extra bell, much louder-sounding in the cement. He pictured the basement. He pictured the living room and den and kitchen.
120     Pink formica on the counters and speckled pink-and-white walls. His father . . .

The Pfc touched his arm. "Speak real clear," he said. "And after each time you talk you got to say, 'Over,' it's in the regs, and the same for your loved ones. Got it?"

Paul Berlin nodded. Immediately the headphones buzzed with a different sort of sound.

He tried to think of something meaningful and cheerful to say. Nothing forced: easy and natural, but still loving. Maybe start by saying he was getting along. Tell them things weren't
130     really so bad. Then ask how his father's business was. Don't let

on about being afraid. Don't make them worry—that was Doc Peret's advice. Make it sound like a vacation, talk about the swell beaches, tell them how you're getting this spectacular tan. Tell them—tell them you're getting skin cancer from all the sun, a Miami holiday. That was Doc's advice. Tell them . . . The Pfc swiveled the microphone so that it faced him. The boy checked his two wristwatches, smiled, whispered something. The kitchen, Paul Berlin thought. He could see it now. The old walnut dining table that his mother had inherited from an aunt in Minnesota.

140 And the big white stove, the refrigerator, stainless steel cabinets over the sink, the black telephone, the windows looking out on Mrs. Stone's immaculate back yard. She was something, that Mrs. Stone. Yes, that was something to ask his father about: Was the old lady still out there in winter, using her broom to sweep away the snow, even in blizzards, sweeping and sweeping, and in the autumn was she still sweeping leaves from her yard, and in summer was she sweeping away the dandelion fuzz? Sure! He'd get his father to talk about her. Something fun and cheerful. The time old Mrs. Stone was out there in the rain, sweeping the

150 water off her lawn as fast as it fell, all day long, sweeping it out to the gutter and then sweeping it up the street, but how the street was at a slight angle so that the rain water kept flowing back down on her, and, Lord, how Mrs. Stone was out there until midnight, ankle-deep, trying to beat gravity with her broom. Lord, his father always said, shaking his head. Neighbors. That was one thing to talk about. And . . . and he'd ask his mother if she'd stopped smoking. There was a joke about that. She'd say, "Sure, I've stopped four times this week," which was a line she'd picked up on TV or someplace. Or she'd say, "No, but

160 at least I'm not smoking tulips anymore, just Luckies." They'd laugh. He wouldn't let on how afraid he was; he wouldn't mention Billy Boy Watkins or Frenchie Tucker or what happened to Bernie Lynn and the others who were gone.

Yes, they'd laugh, and afterward, near the end of the conversation, maybe then he'd tell them he loved them. He couldn't

SETTING

Circle details in lines 138–142 that help you visualize the kitchen in Paul's parents' home.

ANALYZE

Using details on this page, tell how you think Paul feels about his parents and his home.

_____

_____

_____

_____

_____

_____

_____

_____

INFER

Pause at line 163. What do you think happened to Billy Boy Watkins, Frenchie Tucker, and Bernie Lynn?

_____

_____

_____

## IDENTIFY

Pause at line 167. What does Paul want to say to his parents that he's never said before?

_____

_____

_____

_____

_____

## IDENTIFY

The narrator doesn't state directly what happened with Paul's phone call. Circle the details in lines 178–185 that tell you that no one answered.

## INFER

How do you think Paul feels at the end of the story?

_____

_____

_____

_____

_____

_____

_____

_____

_____

_____

_____

remember ever telling them that, except at the bottom of letters, but this time maybe . . . The line buzzed again, then clicked, then there was the digital pause that always comes as a connection is completed, and then he heard the first ring. He recognized it.

170    Hollow, washed out by distance, but it was still the old ring. He'd heard it ten thousand times. He listened to the ring as he would listen to family voices, his father's voice and his mother's voice, older now and changed by what time does to voices, but still the same voices. He stopped thinking of things to say. He concentrated on the ringing. He saw the black phone, heard it ringing and ringing. The Pfc held up a thumb but Paul Berlin barely noticed; he was smiling at the sound of the ringing.

"Tough luck," Doc said afterward.

Oscar and Eddie clapped him on the back, and the Pfc
180    shrugged and said it happened sometimes.

"What can you do?" Oscar said. "The world, it don't stop turning."

"Yeah."

"Who knows? Maybe they was out takin' a drive, or something. Buying groceries. The world don't stop."

# Calling Home

**Setting Graphics**     Show how you visualize the two **settings** described in this story. In the tent on the top, draw the setting in Vietnam. In the house on the bottom, draw Paul's home as he remembers it. Base your drawings on details in the story, and include as many details as you can. If you really dislike drawing, you can use the two spaces to describe the settings instead.

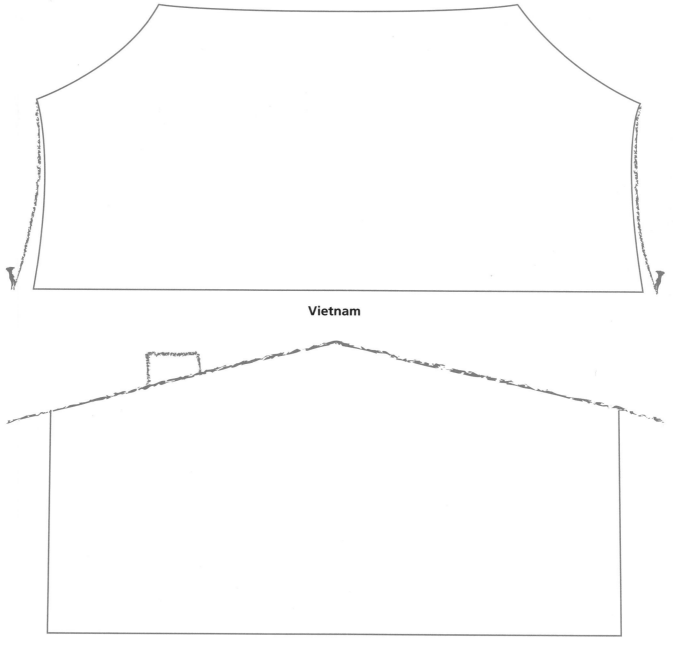

**Vietnam**

**Paul's Home**

# Standards Review

**TestPractice** Calling Home

Complete the sample test item below. Then, check your answer, and read the explanation that appears in the right-hand column.

| Sample Test Item | Explanation of the Correct Answer |
|---|---|
| The narrator describes the thoughts and feelings of—<br><br>A  Paul<br><br>B  Eddie<br><br>C  Doc<br><br>D  the Pfc | *A*, Paul, is the answer.<br><br>Although all the other characters appear in the story, the reader does not learn of their thoughts and feelings. |

**DIRECTIONS:** Circle the letter of each correct response.

**Reading Standard 3.4 (Grade 8 Review)** Analyze the relevance of the setting (e.g., place, time, customs) to the mood, tone, and meaning of the text.

**Reading Standard 3.9** Explain how voice, persona, and the choice of a narrator affect characterization and the tone, plot, and credibility of a text.

1. The action of this story takes place in which **setting**?
   A  Honolulu
   B  San Francisco
   C  Vietnam
   D  Mars

2. Which of the following might you **infer** from reading this story?
   F  The soldiers can't wait to get back to fighting.
   G  Their families mean a lot to these soldiers.
   H  There are people in the U.S. protesting the war.
   J  Many people die in wars.

3. After calling home, Eddie, Oscar, and Doc had all the following reactions *except*—
   A  happiness
   B  embarrassment
   C  amazement
   D  anger

4. Why does Paul smile while he is waiting for his call to go through?
   F  He learns that his little brother has grown up.
   G  He recognizes the ring of his family's telephone.
   H  He realizes you can't sweep away a rainstorm.
   J  His friend Doc has made a funny face.

# Standards Review

**TestPractice** : **Calling Home**

## Context Clues: Jargon

**DIRECTIONS:** Use **context clues** to determine the meaning of the boldface word in each of the following sentences. Circle the letter of each correct response.

1. He glanced at the soldier's worn-out boots and said, "You guys must be **legs.**"

   **A** footmen     **C** hikers

   **B** foot soldiers     **D** relay racers

2. The Pfc explained the rules for making a call: "You have to say, 'Over,' after each time you talk; it's in the **regs.**"

   **F** rags to riches     **H** requirements

   **G** reputations     **J** regulations

3. The **platoon** has a week's rest before they have to return to the fighting.

   **A** military unit     **C** play group

   **B** martial arts group     **D** spaceship

4. The **grunts** walked through the jungle for three weeks without encountering any enemy soldiers.

   **F** boars     **H** foot soldiers

   **G** elephants     **J** salesmen

## Vocabulary in Context

**DIRECTIONS:** Complete the paragraph below by writing a word from the word box to fit in each numbered blank.

### Word Box

correlate

console

pensive

The commander sat staring at the screen on the

(1) _____ in front of him. He was

(2) _____, searching his brain, trying to figure it all out.

What did the new information mean? He did not know how to

(3) _____ the new data with what was already known

about life on planet Xenia. Would it be safe to continue the mission?

**Before You Go On . . .**

Check your Standards Mastery at the back of this book.

# Comparing Themes

# Academic Vocabulary for Chapter 4

These are the terms you should know
as you read and analyze the selections in this chapter.

**Generalization** A statement that conveys a general truth, based on several specific details. A statement about a story's theme is a kind of generalization.

**Genres** The different forms of literature, such as stories, novels, plays, essays, and poems.

**Theme** A truth about life and human nature that gives meaning to a story. Different readers may discover different themes in a story, based on their own attitudes and backgrounds. The meaning of a story comes from both the writer and the reader.

**Universal themes** Themes that appear in the literature of all cultures, in all historical periods.

● ● ●

**Conflict** A struggle between two forces. Usually conflict results when a character wants something badly but encounters obstacles in trying to get it. An **external conflict** takes place between two characters, between a character and a group, or between a character and an animal or a force in nature. An **internal conflict** is a struggle that takes place within a character's mind or heart.

**Main character** The character who drives the action in a story. How the main character changes during the story provides clues to the story's theme.

**Motivation** The reason a character behaves in a certain way.

> ### 📚 For Further Information…
>
> Be sure to read these essays in *Holt Literature and Language Arts:*
> - **Theme,** pages 230–231
> - **Comparing Universal Themes,** page 232
> - **Comparing a Theme Across Genres,** page 255

**Reading Standard 1.1** Identify and use the literal and figurative meanings of words and understand word derivations.

**Reading Standard 1.1 (Grade 8 Review)** Analyze idioms, analogies, metaphors, and similes to infer the literal and figurative meanings of phrases.

**Reading Standard 1.2** Distinguish between the denotative and connotative meanings of words and interpret the connotative power of words.

**Reading Standard 3.2** Compare and contrast the presentation of a similar theme or topic across genres to explain how the selection of genre shapes the theme or topic.

**Reading Standard 3.5** Compare works that express a universal theme and provide evidence to support the ideas expressed in each work.

# Catch the Moon by Judith Ortiz Cofer
# The Secret Heart by Robert P. Tristram Coffin

In "Catch the Moon" you will look into the troubled heart of Luis Cintrón—a young man who sometimes behaves in ways that he himself doesn't really understand. As you read about his past and present experiences, look for ways he changes his outlook toward life—especially after he meets the beautiful Naomi. Then, read a poem about a secret heart and how it changes a boy's understanding of his father. Think about each selection's message about life and human nature as you read.

## LITERARY FOCUS: THEME AND CHARACTER

One way to identify the **theme** of a literary work—its underlying truth about life—is to pay close attention to its **main character.** The experiences of a story's main character may help you pinpoint the story's major themes. A main character will often change in an important way during the course of a story or come to a new realization about life. This change or realization is often linked to the story's theme.

- As you read "Catch the Moon," observe how Luis, the **main character,** handles his conflicts.
- Look for details that show how and why Luis changes his attitude toward life. These details may help you identify the story's **theme.**
- As you read "The Secret Heart," think about its title. The title of a work often hints at its theme.

## READING SKILLS: MAKING GENERALIZATIONS

When you make a **generalization,** you look at evidence and make a broad statement about what it tells you. Someone who says "All stories contain conflicts" is making a generalization based on his or her experience with many stories.

To make a generalization about a story's theme, you have to—
- think about the main events and conflicts in the story
- recognize what the characters have learned by the end of the story
- relate the story to your own experiences

**Reading Standard 1.1**
Identify and use the literal and figurative meanings of words and understand word derivations.

**Reading Standard 3.5**
Compare works that express a universal theme and provide evidence to support the ideas expressed in each work.

## VOCABULARY DEVELOPMENT

### PREVIEW SELECTION VOCABULARY

The following words appear in "Catch the Moon." Get to know these words before you begin reading.

**harassing** (har′əs·iŋ) *v.* used as *n.:* bothering; troubling.

*The gang got into trouble for **harassing** local authorities.*

**dismantled** (dis·mant′′ld) *v.:* took apart.

*After he **dismantled** the car, the mechanic put the parts in a specially marked place.*

**vintage** (vin′tij) *adj.:* dating from a time long past.

*The **vintage** car has not lost the style it had once been famous for.*

**ebony** (eb′ə·nē) *adj.:* dark or black.

*In the sun her **ebony** hair was as shiny as a blackbird's feathers.*

**sarcastic** (sär·kas′tik) *adj.:* mocking; taunting.

*To his father, Luis's unfriendly remarks and **sarcastic** tone sounded disrespectful.*

**relics** (rel′iks) *n.:* objects or things from the past that may have special meaning or associations, sometimes religious ones.

*Since her death, her possessions had become **relics**—objects that helped his father keep her memory alive.*

### FIGURATIVE LANGUAGE: IDIOMS, SIMILES, AND METAPHORS

Words and phrases describing one thing in terms of another, very different thing are called **figurative language**. Figurative language is not meant to be taken literally. Here are three common types of figurative language:

- An **idiom** is an expression peculiar to a particular language, one that cannot be understood from the literal, or dictionary, definitions of its words. For example, "I'm working my hands to the bone" is an expression that means "I'm working extra hard."
- A **simile** uses the word *like, as, than,* or *resembles* to compare two unlike things.
- A **metaphor** compares two unlike things by saying that something *is* something else. It omits the word *like, as, than,* or *resembles.* For example, in the story the pile of hubcaps Luis sits on is called a "silver mountain."

As you read "Catch the Moon," watch for the figurative language that Judith Ortiz Cofer uses in her story.

# CATCH THE MOON

## Judith Ortiz Cofer

**CHARACTER**

The main character of the story is revealed right away. Circle his name.

**CHARACTER**

Underline the sentence in lines 1–7 that gives Luis's **motivation,** or reason, for breaking into the woman's house. Then, circle the sentence that tells what Luis thinks of the woman. What do his actions and feelings suggest about Luis?

_____

_____

_____

_____

_____

_____

**INFER**

Re-read lines 8–19. How does Luis feel about his job?

_____

_____

_____

_____

_____

_____

Luis Cintrón sits on top of a six-foot pile of hubcaps and watches his father walk away into the steel jungle of his car junkyard. Released into his old man's custody[1] after six months in juvenile hall—for breaking and entering—and he didn't even take anything. He did it on a dare. But the old lady with the million cats was a light sleeper, and good with her aluminum cane. He has a scar on his head to prove it.

Now Luis is wondering whether he should have stayed in and done his full time. Jorge Cintrón of Jorge Cintrón & Son,
10 Auto Parts and Salvage, has decided that Luis should wash and polish every hubcap in the yard. The hill he is sitting on is only the latest couple of hundred wheel covers that have come in. Luis grunts and stands up on top of his silver mountain. He yells at no one, "Someday, son, all this will be yours," and sweeps his arms like the Pope blessing a crowd over the piles of car sandwiches and mounds of metal parts that cover this acre of land outside the city. He is the "Son" of Jorge Cintrón & Son, and so far his father has had more than one reason to wish it was plain Jorge Cintrón on the sign.

20 Luis has been getting in trouble since he started high school two years ago, mainly because of the "social group" he organized—a bunch of guys who were into **harassing** the local authorities. Their thing was taking something to the limit on a dare or, better still, doing something dangerous, like breaking into a house, not to steal, just to prove that they could do it. This was Luis's specialty, coming up with very complicated

---

1. **custody** *n.:* term describing the legal responsibility of one person for another.

Notes

_____
_____
_____
_____
_____
_____
_____
_____
_____
_____
_____

plans, like military strategies, and assigning the "jobs" to guys who wanted to join the Tiburones.

30    *Tiburón* means "shark," and Luis had gotten the name from watching an old movie about a Puerto Rican gang called the Sharks with his father. Luis thought it was one of the dumbest films he had ever seen. Everybody sang their lines, and the guys all pointed their toes and leaped in the air when they were supposed to be slaughtering each other. But he liked their name, the Sharks, so he made it Spanish and had it air-painted on his black T-shirt with a killer shark under it, jaws opened wide and dripping with blood. It didn't take long for other guys in the barrio[2] to ask about it.

40        Man, had they had a good time. The girls were interested too. Luis outsmarted everybody by calling his organization a social club and registering it at Central High. That meant they were legal, even let out of last-period class on Fridays for their "club" meetings. It was just this year, after a couple of botched

<hr />

2.  **barrio** (bär′ē·ō) *n.:* in the United States, a Spanish-speaking neighborhood.

---

**VOCABULARY**

**harassing** (har′əs·iŋ) *v.* used as *n.:* bothering; troubling.

**WORD STUDY**

In Spanish, unlike in English, each vowel is pronounced, making a syllable. *Tiburones* (line 28), meaning "sharks," is pronounced (tē·bʉ·rōō′nēs).

**CLARIFY**

Pause at line 34. The movie is *West Side Story* (1961), the film version of the 1956 Broadway musical based on Shakespeare's *Romeo and Juliet.*

_____

_____

_____

_____

_____

_____

_____

_____

_____

_____

_____

_____

_____

_____

**FLUENCY**

Read the boxed passage aloud two times. Be sure you practice how to pronounce unfamiliar words before you begin.

**IDENTIFY CAUSE & EFFECT**

Underline the important past event that is revealed in lines 67–73. Circle how that event affected Luis's father.

jobs, that the teachers had started getting suspicious. The first one to go wrong was when he sent Kenny Matoa to *borrow* some "souvenirs" out of Anita Robles's locker. He got caught. It seems that Matoa had been reading Anita's diary and didn't hear her coming down the hall. Anita was supposed to be in the gym at that time but had copped out with the usual female excuse of

50    cramps. You could hear her screams all the way to Market Street.

She told the principal all she knew about the Tiburones, and Luis had to talk fast to convince old Mr. Williams that the club did put on cultural activities such as the Save the Animals talent show. What Mr. Williams didn't know was that the animal that was being "saved" with the ticket sales was Luis's pet boa, which needed quite a few live mice to stay healthy and happy. They kept E. S. (which stood for "Endangered Species") in Luis's room, but she belonged to the club and it was the members' responsibility to raise the money to feed their mascot.[3] So last

60    year they had sponsored their first annual Save the Animals talent show, and it had been a great success. The Tiburones had come dressed as Latino Elvises and did a grand finale to "All Shook Up" that made the audience go wild. Mr. Williams had smiled while Luis talked, maybe remembering how the math teacher, Mrs. Laguna, had dragged him out in the aisle to rock-and-roll with her. Luis had gotten out of that one, but barely.

His father was a problem, too. He objected to the T-shirt logo, calling it disgusting and vulgar. Mr. Cintrón prided himself on his own neat, elegant style of dressing after work, and on his

70    manners and large vocabulary, which he picked up by taking correspondence courses[4] in just about everything. Luis thought it was just his way of staying busy since Luis's mother had died, almost three years ago, of cancer. He had never gotten over it.

All this was going through Luis's head as he slid down the hill of hubcaps. The tub full of soapy water, the can of polish,

---

3.  **mascot** *n.:* person, animal, or thing kept by a group or team as its symbol or for good luck.
4.  **correspondence courses** *n.:* courses of study conducted through the mail.

and the bag of rags had been neatly placed in front of a makeshift table made from two car seats and a piece of plywood. Luis heard a car drive up and someone honk their horn. His father emerged from inside a new red Mustang that had been
80 totaled. He usually **dismantled** every small feature by hand before sending the vehicle into the *cementerio,*[5] as he called the lot. Luis watched as the most beautiful girl he had ever seen climbed out of a **vintage** white Volkswagen Bug. She stood in the sunlight in her white sundress waiting for his father, while Luis stared. She was like a smooth wood carving. Her skin was mahogany, almost black, and her arms and legs were long and thin, but curved in places so that she did not look bony and hard—more like a ballerina. And her **ebony** hair was braided close to her head. Luis let his breath out, feeling a little dizzy.
90 He had forgotten to breathe. Both the girl and his father heard him. Mr. Cintrón waved him over.

"Luis, the señorita here has lost a wheel cover. Her car is twenty-five years old, so it will not be an easy match. Come look on this side."

Luis tossed a wrench he'd been holding into a toolbox like he was annoyed, just to make a point about slave labor. Then he followed his father, who knelt on the gravel and began to point out every detail of the hubcap. Luis was hardly listening. He watched the girl take a piece of paper from her handbag.
100 "Señor Cintrón, I have drawn the hubcap for you, since I will have to leave soon. My home address and telephone number are here, and also my parents' office number." She handed the paper to Mr. Cintrón, who nodded.

"Sí, señorita, very good. This will help my son look for it. Perhaps there is one in that stack there." He pointed to the pile of caps that Luis was supposed to wash and polish. "Yes, I'm almost certain that there is a match there. Of course, I do not know if it's near the top or the bottom. You will give us a few days, yes?"

---

5. **cementerio** (se·men·te′rē·ō) *n.*: Spanish for "cemetery."

### VOCABULARY

**dismantled** (dis·mant″ld) *v.*: took apart.

**vintage** (vin′tij) *adj.*: dating from a time long past.

**ebony** (eb′ə·nē) *adj.*: dark or black.

### WORD STUDY

In line 85, underline the **simile**. What two things are being compared?

_____

_____

_____

_____

_____

_____

### INFER

Underline the words in lines 89–91 that describe Luis's reaction to the girl. What does his response suggest about his feelings?

_____

_____

### WORD STUDY

*Señorita* (se′nyð·rē′tä), in line 92, means "miss" or "young woman" in Spanish. *Señor* (se·nyðr′), in line 100, means "Mr." or "sir" in Spanish.

### CHARACTER

Underline the words in lines 114–122 that describe how Naomi responds when she notices how sad Mr. Cintrón becomes. What can you **infer**, or guess, about Naomi from her actions?

_____

_____

### WORD STUDY

*Adiós* (a′dē·ōs′), in line 120, is Spanish for "goodbye." *Adiós* is from two Latin words: *ad,* meaning "to," and *deus,* meaning "God." (*Goodbye* is a shortened form of "God be with you.")

### CHARACTER

How did Luis react to his mother's death? Underline the passage in lines 127–133 that supports your answer.

_____

_____

### WORD STUDY

An **idiom** is an expression that cannot be understood from the dictionary definitions of the words. Underline the idiom in lines 140–143. What does the idiom mean?

_____

_____

_____

110     Luis just stared at his father like he was crazy. But he didn't say anything because the girl was smiling at him with a funny expression on her face. Maybe she thought he had X-ray eyes like Superman, or maybe she was mocking him.

    "Please call me Naomi, Señor Cintrón. You know my mother. She is the director of the funeral home. . . ." Mr. Cintrón seemed surprised at first; he prided himself on having a great memory. Then his friendly expression changed to one of sadness as he recalled the day of his wife's burial. Naomi did not finish her sentence. She reached over and placed her hand on Mr.

120  Cintrón's arm for a moment. Then she said "Adiós" softly, and got in her shiny white car. She waved to them as she left, and her gold bracelets flashing in the sun nearly blinded Luis.

    Mr. Cintrón shook his head. "How about that," he said as if to himself. "They are the Dominican owners of Ramirez Funeral Home." And, with a sigh, "She seems like such a nice young woman. Reminds me of your mother when she was her age."

    Hearing the funeral parlor's name, Luis remembered too. The day his mother died, he had been in her room at the hospital while his father had gone for coffee. The alarm had

130  gone off on her monitor and nurses had come running in, pushing him outside. After that, all he recalled was the anger that had made him punch a hole in his bedroom wall. And afterward he had refused to talk to anyone at the funeral. Strange, he did see a black girl there who didn't try like the others to talk to him, but actually ignored him as she escorted family members to the viewing room and brought flowers in. Could it be that the skinny girl in a frilly white dress had been Naomi? She didn't act like she had recognized him today, though. Or maybe she thought that he was a jerk.

140     Luis grabbed the drawing from his father. The old man looked like he wanted to walk down memory lane. But Luis was in no mood to listen to the old stories about his falling in love on a tropical island. The world they'd lived in before he was born wasn't his world. No beaches and palm trees here.

Only junk as far as he could see. He climbed back up his hill and studied Naomi's sketch. It had obviously been done very carefully. It was signed "Naomi Ramirez" in the lower right-hand corner. He memorized the telephone number.

150         Luis washed hubcaps all day until his hands were red and raw, but he did not come across the small silver bowl that would fit the VW. After work he took a few practice Frisbee shots across the yard before showing his father what he had accomplished: rows and rows of shiny rings drying in the sun. His father nodded and showed him the bump on his temple where one of Luis's flying saucers had gotten him. "Practice makes perfect, you know. Next time you'll probably decapitate[6] me." Luis heard him struggle with the word *decapitate,* which Mr. Cintrón pronounced in syllables. Showing off his big vocabulary again, Luis thought. He looked closely at the bump, though. He felt bad about it.

---

6. **decapitate** (dē·kap′ə·tāt′) *v.:* cut off the head of.

160 "They look good, hijo,[7]" Mr. Cintrón made a sweeping gesture with his arms over the yard. "You know, all this will have to be classified. My dream is to have all the parts divided by year, make of car, and condition. Maybe now that you are here to help me, this will happen."

"Pop . . ." Luis put his hand on his father's shoulder. They were the same height and build, about five foot six and muscular. "The judge said six months of free labor for you, not life, okay?" Mr. Cintrón nodded, looking distracted. It was then that Luis suddenly noticed how gray his hair had turned—it used to 170 be shiny black like his own—and that there were deep lines in his face. His father had turned into an old man and he hadn't even noticed.

"Son, you must follow the judge's instructions. Like she said, next time you get in trouble, she's going to treat you like an adult, and I think you know what that means. Hard time, no breaks."

"Yeah, yeah. That's what I'm doing, right? Working my hands to the bone instead of enjoying my summer. But listen, she didn't put me under house arrest, right? I'm going out 180 tonight."

"Home by ten. She did say something about a curfew, Luis." Mr. Cintrón had stopped smiling and was looking upset. It had always been hard for them to talk more than a minute or two before his father got offended at something Luis said, or at his **sarcastic** tone. He was always doing something wrong.

Luis threw the rag down on the table and went to sit in his father's ancient Buick, which was in mint condition. They drove home in silence.

After sitting down at the kitchen table with his father to 190 eat a pizza they had picked up on the way home, Luis asked to borrow the car. He didn't get an answer then, just a look that meant "Don't bother me right now."

---

7. **hijo** (ē′hō) *n.*: Spanish for "son."

Before bringing up the subject again, Luis put some ice cubes in a Baggie and handed it to Mr. Cintrón, who had made the little bump on his head worse by rubbing it. It had GUILTY written on it, Luis thought.

"Gracias, hijo." His father placed the bag on the bump and made a face as the ice touched his skin.

They ate in silence for a few minutes more; then Luis
200    decided to ask about the car again.

"I really need some fresh air, Pop. Can I borrow the car for a couple of hours?"

"You don't get enough fresh air at the yard? We're lucky that we don't have to sit in a smelly old factory all day. You know that?"

"Yeah, Pop. We're real lucky." Luis always felt irritated that his father was so grateful to own a junkyard, but he held his anger back and just waited to see if he'd get the keys without having to get in an argument.

210    "Where are you going?"

"For a ride. Not going anywhere. Just out for a while. Is that okay?"

His father didn't answer, just handed him a set of keys, as shiny as the day they were manufactured. His father polished everything that could be polished: doorknobs, coins, keys, spoons, knives, and forks, like he was King Midas counting his silver and gold. Luis thought his father must be really lonely to polish utensils only he used anymore. They had been picked out by his wife, though, so they were like **relics.** Nothing she had
220    ever owned could be thrown away. Only now the dishes, forks, and spoons were not used to eat the yellow rice and red beans, the fried chicken, or the mouth-watering sweet plantains that his mother had cooked for them. They were just kept in the cabinets that his father had turned into a museum for her. Mr. Cintrón could cook as well as his wife, but he didn't have the heart to do it anymore. Luis thought that maybe if they ate together once

**WORD STUDY**

Circle the **idiom** that Luis uses (lines 195–196). What does the idiom mean?

_____

_____

_____

_____


**WORD STUDY**

*Gracias* (grä′sē·äs′), in line 197, means "thank you." It has the same origin as the English word *gracious*.


**PREDICT**

In lines 210–212, Luis won't tell his father where he plans to go. Where do you predict he will go?

_____

_____

_____


**CHARACTER**

In lines 213–218, Luis comes to another important realization about his father. Locate and underline it.


**VOCABULARY**

**relics** (rel′iks) *n.:* objects or things from the past that may have special meaning or associations, sometimes religious ones.

_____

_____

_____

_____

_____

_____

_____

INFER

Pause at line 244. Why does Luis drive to the Ramirez Funeral Home?

_____

_____

_____

INTERPRET

Circle the **simile** in lines 246–248 that describes the tree at the time of Mrs. Cintrón's funeral. Underline the words that tell what the tree looks like now. What might the change in the tree suggest about how Luis might change?

_____

_____

_____

in a while things might get better between them, but he always had something to do around dinnertime and ended up at a hamburger joint. Tonight was the first time in months they had

230　sat down at the table together.

Luis took the keys. "Thanks," he said, walking out to take his shower. His father kept looking at him with those sad, patient eyes. "Okay. I'll be back by ten, and keep the ice on that egg," Luis said without looking back.

He had just meant to ride around his old barrio, see if any of the Tiburones were hanging out at El Building, where most of them lived. It wasn't far from the single-family home his father had bought when the business starting paying off: a house that his mother lived in for three months before she took up residence

240　at St. Joseph's Hospital. She never came home again. These days Luis wished he still lived in that tiny apartment where there was always something to do, somebody to talk to.

Instead Luis found himself parked in front of the last place his mother had gone to: Ramirez Funeral Home. In the front yard was a huge oak tree that Luis remembered having climbed during the funeral to get away from people. The tree looked different now, not like a skeleton as it had then, but green with leaves. The branches reached to the second floor of the house, where the family lived.

250　For a while Luis sat in the car allowing the memories to flood back into his brain. He remembered his mother before the illness changed her. She had not been beautiful, as his father told everyone; she had been a sweet lady, not pretty but not ugly. To him, she had been the person who always told him that she was proud of him and loved him. She did that every night when she came to his bedroom door to say goodnight. As a joke he would sometimes ask her, "Proud of what? I haven't done anything." And she'd always say, "I'm just proud that you are my son." She wasn't perfect or anything. She had bad days when nothing he

260　did could make her smile, especially after she got sick. But he never heard her say anything negative about anyone. She always blamed *el destino,* fate, for what went wrong. He missed her. He missed her so much. Suddenly a flood of tears that had been building up for almost three years started pouring from his eyes. Luis sat in his father's car, with his head on the steering wheel, and cried, "Mami, I miss you."

When he finally looked up, he saw that he was being watched. Sitting at a large window with a pad and a pencil on her lap was Naomi. At first Luis felt angry and embarrassed, but she wasn't laughing at him. Then she told him with her dark eyes that it was okay to come closer. He walked to the window, and she held up the sketch pad on which she had drawn him, not crying like a baby, but sitting on top of a mountain of silver disks, holding one up over his head. He had to smile.

The plate-glass window was locked. It had a security bolt on it. An alarm system, he figured, so nobody would steal the princess. He asked her if he could come in. It was soundproof too. He mouthed the words slowly for her to read his lips. She wrote on the pad, "I can't let you in. My mother is not home tonight." So they looked at each other and talked through the window for a little while. Then Luis got an idea. He signed to her that he'd be back, and drove to the junkyard.

Luis climbed up on his mountain of hubcaps. For hours he sorted the wheel covers by make, size, and condition, stopping only to call his father and tell him where he was and what he was doing. The old man did not ask him for explanations, and Luis was grateful for that. By lamppost light, Luis worked and worked, beginning to understand a little why his father kept busy all the time. Doing something that had a beginning, a middle, and an end did something to your head. It was like the satisfaction Luis got out of planning "adventures" for his Tiburones, but there was another element involved here that had nothing to do with showing off for others. This was a treasure hunt. And he knew what he was looking for.

Finally, when it seemed that it was a hopeless search, when it was almost midnight and Luis's hands were cut and bruised

**CHARACTER**

In line 266, underline the words Luis is finally able to express. Why is it important for Luis to be aware of these feelings?

_____

_____

_____

_____

_____

**IDENTIFY**

Pause at line 274. What does Naomi do to make Luis smile?

_____

_____

_____

_____

_____

**CLARIFY**

Who is the "princess" Luis refers to in line 277?

_____

_____

**CHARACTER**

Why is Luis finding such satisfaction in his "treasure hunt" (line 294)?

_____

_____

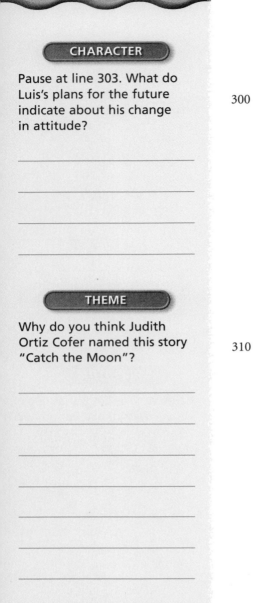

**CHARACTER**

Pause at line 303. What do Luis's plans for the future indicate about his change in attitude?

_____

_____

_____

_____

**THEME**

Why do you think Judith Ortiz Cofer named this story "Catch the Moon"?

_____

_____

_____

_____

_____

_____

_____

**THEME**

Re-read the sidenotes labeled **character**. Think about how Luis changes. Then, make a generalization in which you state the story's theme.

_____

_____

_____

_____

_____

from his work, he found it. It was the perfect match for Naomi's drawing, the moon-shaped wheel cover for her car, Cinderella's shoe. Luis jumped off the small mound of disks left under him

300  and shouted, "Yes!" He looked around and saw neat stacks of hubcaps that he would wash the next day. He would build a display wall for his father. People would be able to come into the yard and point to whatever they wanted.

Luis washed the VW hubcap and polished it until he could see himself in it. He used it as a mirror as he washed his face and combed his hair. Then he drove to the Ramirez Funeral Home. It was almost pitch-black, since it was a moonless night. As quietly as possible, Luis put some gravel in his pocket and climbed the oak tree to the second floor. He knew he was in

310  front of Naomi's window—he could see her shadow through the curtains. She was at a table, apparently writing or drawing, maybe waiting for him. Luis hung the silver disk carefully on a branch near the window, then threw the gravel at the glass. Naomi ran to the window and drew the curtains aside while Luis held on to the thick branch and waited to give her the first good thing he had given anyone in a long time.

# The Secret Heart

## Robert P. Tristram Coffin

Across the years he could recall
His father one way best of all.

In the stillest hour of night
The boy awakened to a light.

5　Half in dreams, he saw his sire
With his great hands full of fire.

The man had struck a match to see
If his son slept peacefully.

He held his palms each side the spark
10　His love had kindled in the dark.

His two hands were curved apart
In the semblance° of a heart.

He wore, it seemed to his small son,
A bare heart on his hidden one,

15　A heart that gave out such a glow
No son awake could bear to know.

It showed a look upon a face
Too tender for the day to trace.

One instant, it lit all about,
20　And then the secret heart went out.

But it shone long enough for one
To know that hands held up the sun.

---

° **semblance:** form.

"The Secret Heart" from *The Collected Poems of Robert P. Tristram Coffin.* Copyright 1935 by Macmillan Publishing Company; copyright renewed © 1963 by Margaret Coffin Halvosa. Reprinted by permission of **Simon & Schuster Inc.** Electronic format by permission of **June Coffin.**

**IDENTIFY**

Pause at line 6. Whom does the son see one night?

_____

**IDENTIFY CAUSE & EFFECT**

Why has the father come into his son's room (lines 7–8)?

_____

_____

**INTERPRET**

What does the son come to understand about his father (lines 13–18)?

_____

_____

**THEME**

Re-read the poem. What is its **theme,** or truth about human life?

_____

_____

_____

_____

# Catch the Moon; The Secret Heart

**Universal themes**—broad statements or observations about life—occur again and again in literature. Each time a theme is explored, it takes on new life as new characters facing new situations wrestle with age-old concerns.

**Comparison Chart**     Fill in the comparison chart below to compare the texts of "Catch the Moon" and "The Secret Heart." Then, review your completed chart and identify the theme the two selections share. Write the shared theme below the chart.

| | "Catch the Moon" | "The Secret Heart" |
|---|---|---|
| **Main Character(s)/Speaker** | | |
| **Conflict (what happens)** | | |
| **What the character/speaker learns or discovers** | | |
| **Theme(s)** | | |

**Statement of theme:** _____

_____

_____

_____

# Standards Review

LITERATURE

**TestPractice**   Catch the Moon; The Secret Heart

Complete the sample test item below. Then, read the explanation at the right.

| Sample Test Item | Explanation of the Correct Answer |
|---|---|
| In "Catch the Moon," Luis understands that his father stays active because he wants to—<br><br>A  avoid wasting time<br><br>B  pass on a thriving business to Luis<br><br>C  forget about the death of his wife<br><br>D  find a new wife | The correct answer is *C*.<br><br>*A* is not correct because the father never mentions time. *B* is not correct: Mr. Cintrón knows Luis doesn't want to own a junkyard. *D* is not correct because the father still mourns his dead wife. |

**DIRECTIONS:** Circle the letter of the best response.

1. In "Catch the Moon," Luis is working for his father because he—

   A  can make lots of money at the junkyard

   B  has been ordered to by a judge

   C  feels sorry for his overworked father

   D  wants to find a girlfriend

2. Luis probably planned his activities with the Tiburones to—

   F  get a part in a movie

   G  make some money on the side

   H  annoy his father

   J  forget his unhappiness

3. In "The Secret Heart," the boy realizes that his father is—

   A  about to go on a long journey

   B  walking in his sleep

   C  showing how much he loves him

   D  trying to relight a fire

4. Which sentence best expresses a **theme** the story and poem share?

   F  Small actions often reveal deep feelings.

   G  Hidden love is no love at all.

   H  Anger brings sympathy and love.

   J  Hearts sometimes get broken.

**Reading Standard** 3.5 Compare works that express a universal theme and provide evidence to support the ideas expressed in each work.

# Standards Review

**TestPractice**  **Catch the Moon; The Secret Heart**

## Figurative Language

**Reading Standard 1.1**
Identify and use the literal and figurative meanings of words and understand word derivations.

**DIRECTIONS:** Circle the letter of the best response.

1. "Working my hands to the bone" is an example of—
   A  a theme
   B  a simile
   C  literal language
   D  an idiom

2. In the phrase "steel jungle of his car junkyard," "steel jungle" is—
   F  a gang fight
   G  a metaphor
   H  a simile
   J  a nickname

3. Luis tells Mr. Cintrón to "keep the ice on that egg." "Egg" is used as a **metaphor** for—
   A  breakfast
   B  a cold drink
   C  the bump on his father's head
   D  a big head

4. The sentence "He didn't have the heart to do it anymore" contains—
   F  a theme          H  personification
   G  a simile         J  an idiom

## Vocabulary in Context

**DIRECTIONS:** Complete the paragraph below by writing words from the box in the blanks. Use each word only once.

**Word Box**

harassing
dismantled
vintage
ebony
sarcastic
relics

Those (1) _____ cars of yours must be fifty years old! Do they run, or do you keep them as (2) _____ in that auto museum you call a garage? The (3) _____ ones look as black as the deepest night. You probably think I'm (4) _____ you with my (5) _____, unwanted comments. Not really; I'd be sorry if you (6) _____ and sold off your palace of vehicles.

**Before You Go On . . .**

Check your Standards Mastery at the back of this book.

# An Hour with Abuelo by Judith Ortiz Cofer
# Grandma Ling by Amy Ling

Just what can you learn from grandparents? In the short story "An Hour with Abuelo," Arturo thinks he is doing his grandfather a favor by visiting him, but he learns something surprising about this supposed good deed. In Amy Ling's poem "Grandma Ling," the speaker tells of the surprising discoveries she makes when she meets her grandmother for the very first time. As you read, think about each selection's message about life or human nature.

## LITERARY FOCUS: THEME AND GENRE

The **theme** of a work of literature is the truth it expresses about our world and the people who live in it. Themes are important to all forms of literature, and similar themes can be found in different **genres**—in stories, poems, novels, plays, and nonfiction. In a story or a poem, a writer usually does not state the theme directly. It's up to you to read between the lines to find the theme.

You may discover the theme of a story by understanding how its main character changes during the story. To uncover a poem's theme, you may need to pay close attention to imagery, figurative language, and mood.

- To help you find the theme of "An Hour with Abuelo," look for what Arturo learns about himself and other people as he performs his good deed.
- As you read Amy Ling's "Grandma Ling," pay attention to the feelings and insights the speaker shares with you.

## READING SKILLS: COMPARING AND CONTRASTING

When you **compare** two works of literature, you look for ways they are alike. When you **contrast** two works of literature, you look for differences between them.

To compare and contrast two works of literature of two different genres, start by identifying each genre. Then, consider the following as you read each selection:

- What the narrator or speaker tells you
- What the main characters come to realize
- Meanings conveyed by settings and descriptions
- The narrator or speaker's problem and how it is resolved

**Reading Standard 1.2** Distinguish between the denotative and connotative meanings of words and interpret the connotative power of words.

**Reading Standard 3.2** Compare and contrast the presentation of a similar theme or topic across genres to explain how the selection of genre shapes the theme or topic.

## VOCABULARY DEVELOPMENT

### PREVIEW SELECTION VOCABULARY

The following words appear in the selections you're about to read. Get to know these words before you begin reading.

**embroidered** (em·broi′dərd) *v.* used as *adj.*: ornamented with needlework.

*The shirt was beautiful, **embroidered** with his mother's needlework.*

**ammunition** (am′yōō·nish′ən) *n.* used as *adj.*: having to do with weapons or military supplies.

*The **ammunition** box was locked and marked with a danger sign.*

**sturdy** (stʉr′dē) *adj.*: strong; firm.

*Her **sturdy** legs were planted firmly on the ground.*

### CONNOTATIONS

The **connotations** of a word are the meanings, associations, or emotions it suggests. Connotations are different from **denotations,** which are strict dictionary definitions.

In "An Hour with Abuelo," the narrator calls the place where his grandfather lives a "nursing home" and an "old people's home." Think about the connotations, or emotional overtones, of these phrases. Do you respond to the two phrases in the same way you react to the phrase *retirement home* or *leisure town*? Often connotations show shades of meaning or intensity. On a scale of 1 to 3 (3 being the most positive), rank the three phrases below in terms of their "intensity."

\_\_\_ nursing home        \_\_\_ old people's home        \_\_\_ retirement home

As you read the following selections, keep track of words or phrases that have strong connotations. List them in a chart like this one. In the column on the right, use the symbol "+" if you think the word or phrase has a positive connotation. Use "−" if the connotation seems negative.

| Word or Phrase | Connotation | + or − |
|---|---|---|
|  |  |  |
|  |  |  |

# An Hour with Abuelo

## Judith Ortiz Cofer

Notes

"Just one hour, *una hora*,[1] is all I'm asking of you, son." My
grandfather is in a nursing home in Brooklyn, and my mother
wants me to spend some time with him, since the doctors say
that he doesn't have too long to go now. I don't have much time
left of my summer vacation, and there's a stack of books next to
my bed I've got to read if I'm going to get into the AP English
class I want. I'm going stupid in some of my classes, and Mr.
Williams, the principal at Central, said that if I passed some
reading tests, he'd let me move up.

**WORD STUDY**

In the first sentence, circle
the context clue that restates
the Spanish phrase *una hora*.

**IDENTIFY**

Re-read lines 1–9. Underline
the sentence that tells what
the narrator is being asked
to do. What would he prefer
to do?

_____

_____

_____

_____

---

1.  *una hora* (o͞o′nä ō′rä): Spanish for "one hour."

Circle the name of the nursing home (line 21). What is the **connotation** of this phrase?

_____

_____

_____

_____

_____

_____

Pause at line 25. How does the narrator feel about his visit to Abuelo?

_____

_____

_____

Re-read lines 35–38. What does the narrator ask Abuelo? What is surprising about Abuelo's answer?

_____

_____

_____

_____

_____

_____

_____

10     Besides, I hate the place, the old people's home, especially the way it smells like industrial-strength ammonia and other stuff I won't mention, since it turns my stomach. And really the abuelo[2] always has a lot of relatives visiting him, so I've gotten out of going out there except at Christmas, when a whole van-load of grandchildren are herded over there to give him gifts and a hug. We all make it quick and spend the rest of the time in the recreation area, where they play checkers and stuff with some of the old people's games, and I catch up on back issues of *Modern Maturity.* I'm not picky, I'll read almost anything.

20     Anyway, after my mother nags me for about a week, I let her drive me to Golden Years. She drops me off in front. She wants me to go in alone and have a "good time" talking to Abuelo. I tell her to be back in one hour or I'll take the bus back to Paterson. She squeezes my hand and says, *"Gracias, hijo,"*[3] in a choked-up voice like I'm doing her a big favor.

    I get depressed the minute I walk into the place. They line up the old people in wheelchairs in the hallway as if they were about to be raced to the finish line by orderlies who don't even look at them when they push them here and there. I walk fast

30 to room 10, Abuelo's "suite." He is sitting up in his bed writing with a pencil in one of those old-fashioned black hardback notebooks. It has the outline of the island of Puerto Rico on it. I slide into the hard vinyl chair by his bed. He sort of smiles and the lines on his face get deeper, but he doesn't say anything. Since I'm supposed to talk to him, I say, "What are you doing, Abuelo, writing the story of your life?"

    It's supposed to be a joke, but he answers, "Sí, how did you know, Arturo?"

    His name is Arturo too. I was named after him. I don't

40 really know my grandfather. His children, including my mother, came to New York and New Jersey (where I was born) and he stayed on the Island until my grandmother died. Then he got

---

2.   **abuelo** (äb·wä′lō): Spanish for "grandfather."
3.   *Gracias, hijo* (grä′sē·äs′ ē′hō): Spanish for "Thank you, son."

sick, and since nobody could leave their jobs to take care of him, they brought him to this nursing home in Brooklyn. I see him a couple of times a year, but he's always surrounded by his sons and daughters. My mother tells me that Don Arturo[4] had once been a teacher back in Puerto Rico, but had lost his job after the war. Then he became a farmer. She's always saying in a sad voice, "*Ay, bendito!*[5] What a waste of a fine mind." Then she usually shrugs

50 her shoulders and says, "*Así es la vida.*" That's the way life is. It sometimes makes me mad that the adults I know just accept whatever crap is thrown at them because "that's the way things are." Not for me. I go after what I want.

Anyway, Abuelo is looking at me like he was trying to see inside my head, but he doesn't say anything. Since I like stories, I decide I may as well ask him if he'll read me what he wrote.

I look at my watch: I've already used up twenty minutes of the hour I promised my mother.

Abuelo starts talking in his slow way. He speaks what my

60 mother calls book English. He taught himself from a dictionary, and his words sound stiff, like he's sounding them out in his head before he says them. With his children he speaks Spanish, and that funny book English with us grandchildren. I'm surprised that he's still so sharp, because his body is shrinking like a crumpled-up brown paper sack with some bones in it. But I can see from looking into his eyes that the light is still on in there.

"It is a short story, Arturo. The story of my life. It will not take very much time to read it."

"I have time, Abuelo." I'm a little embarrassed that he saw

70 me looking at my watch.

"Yes, hijo. You have spoken the truth. La verdad. You have much time."

Abuelo reads: "'I loved words from the beginning of my life. In the *campo*[6] where I was born one of seven sons, there were few books. My mother read them to us over and over: the

---

4. **Don:** "Don" is a title of respect, like "Mr."
5. *bendito* (ben·dē′tō): Spanish for "bless him."
6. *campo* (käm′pō): Spanish for "country."

---

**IDENTIFY CAUSE & EFFECT**

How did Abuelo end up in a nursing home (lines 39–44)? Circle the details that reveal the causes.

**WORD STUDY**

Circle the context clue in line 50 that restates the Spanish sentence "Así es la vida."

**COMPARE & CONTRAST**

Pause at line 53. What is the mother's view of life? How does it differ from Arturo's?

_____

_____

_____

_____

_____

**WORD STUDY**

In lines 64–66, underline the **simile** that Arturo uses to describe his grandfather's body. Then, circle the **idiom** that the boy uses to describe Abuelo's mental ability. What is the boy learning about his grandfather?

_____

_____

_____

_____

IDENTIFY

Pause at line 83. According to Abuelo, who encouraged him to read? In what way are grandfather and grandson alike?

_____

_____

_____

IDENTIFY
CAUSE & EFFECT

Re-read lines 84–88. Why did Abuelo leave his family to go live in Mayagüez?

_____

_____

_____

_____

VOCABULARY

**embroidered** (em·broi′dərd) *v.* used as *adj.:* ornamented with needlework.

INTERPRET

Why did Abuelo feel like "a rich man" (lines 99–103)?

_____

_____

_____

_____

_____

Bible, the stories of Spanish conquistadors[7] and of pirates that she had read as a child and brought with her from the city of Mayagüez;[8] that was before she married my father, a coffee bean farmer; and she taught us words from the newspaper that a boy

80 on a horse brought every week to her. She taught each of us how to write on a slate with chalks that she ordered by mail every year. We used those chalks until they were so small that you lost them between your fingers.

"'I always wanted to be a writer and a teacher. With my heart and soul I knew that I wanted to be around books all of my life. And so against the wishes of my father, who wanted all his sons to help him on the land, she sent me to high school in Mayagüez. For four years I boarded with a couple she knew. I paid my rent in labor, and I ate vegetables I grew myself. I wore

90 my clothes until they were thin as parchment. But I graduated at the top of my class! My whole family came to see me that day. My mother brought me a beautiful *guayabera*, a white shirt made of the finest cotton and **embroidered** by her own hands. I was a happy young man.

"'In those days you could teach in a country school with a high school diploma. So I went back to my mountain village and got a job teaching all grades in a little classroom built by the parents of my students.

"'I had books sent to me by the government. I felt like a

100 rich man although the pay was very small. I had books. All the books I wanted! I taught my students how to read poetry and plays, and how to write them. We made up songs and put on shows for the parents. It was a beautiful time for me.

"'Then the war came, and the American President said that all Puerto Rican men would be drafted. I wrote to our governor and explained that I was the only teacher in the mountain village. I told him that the children would go back to the fields and grow up ignorant if I could not teach them their letters.

---

7.  **conquistadors** (kän·kēs′tə·dörz′): any of the Spanish conquerors of Mexico, Peru, or other parts of America in the 16th century.
8.  **Mayagüez** (mä′yä·gwes′): port city in western Puerto Rico.

I said that I thought I was a better teacher than a soldier. The
110 governor did not answer my letter. I went into the U.S. Army.

"'I told my sergeant that I could be a teacher in the army.
I could teach all the farm boys their letters so that they could
read the instructions on the **ammunition** boxes and not blow
themselves up. The sergeant said I was too smart for my own
good, and gave me a job cleaning latrines. He said to me there
is reading material for you there, scholar. Read the writing on
the walls. I spent the war mopping floors and cleaning toilets.

"'When I came back to the Island, things had changed.
You had to have a college degree to teach school, even the lower
120 grades. My parents were sick, two of my brothers had been killed
in the war, the others had stayed in Nueva York. I was the only
one left to help the old people. I became a farmer. I married a
good woman who gave me many good children. I taught them
all how to read and write before they started school.'"

Abuelo then puts the notebook down on his lap and closes
his eyes.

"*Así es la vida* is the title of my book," he says in a whisper,
almost to himself. Maybe he's forgotten that I'm there.

For a long time he doesn't say anything else. I think that he's
130 sleeping, but then I see that he's watching me through half-closed
lids, maybe waiting for my opinion of his writing. I'm trying to
think of something nice to say. I liked it and all, but not the title.
And I think that he could've been a teacher if he had wanted to
bad enough. Nobody is going to stop me from doing what I want
with my life. I'm not going to let la vida get in my way. I want
to discuss this with him, but the words are not coming into my
head in Spanish just yet. I'm about to ask him why he didn't
keep fighting to make his dream come true, when an old lady
in hot-pink running shoes sort of appears at the door.

140 She is wearing a pink jogging outfit too. The world's oldest
marathoner, I say to myself. She calls out to my grandfather in
a flirty voice, "Yoo-hoo, Arturo, remember what day this is? It's

---

**IDENTIFY CAUSE & EFFECT**

Re-read lines 104–110. What happened that destroyed Abuelo's teaching career? Locate and underline the cause.

**VOCABULARY**

ammunition (am'yoo·ni'shən) n.: used as *adj.*: having to do with weapons or military supplies.

**IDENTIFY CAUSE & EFFECT**

Why wasn't Abuelo able to resume teaching after the war (lines 118–122)? Underline the causes.

**FLUENCY**

Read the boxed passage aloud two times. On your second read, improve your reading rate and the smoothness of your delivery. *Nueva*, meaning "new," is pronounced (noo·ā'və).

**COMPARE & CONTRAST**

Re-read lines 127–139. How does Arturo's outlook on life differ from Abuelo's and his mother's?

_____

_____

_____

_____

## CHARACTER

Pause at line 156. How has Arturo's attitude toward the visit changed from the beginning of the story?

_____

_____

_____

_____

_____

_____

## THEME

Re-read the sidenotes to the story, and pay close attention to changes in Arturo's thoughts and feelings. What **theme,** or message about human nature, do they suggest?

_____

_____

_____

_____

_____

_____

_____

_____

_____

_____

_____

poetry-reading day in the rec room! You promised us you'd read your new one today."

I see my abuelo perking up almost immediately. He points to his wheelchair, which is hanging like a huge metal bat in the open closet. He makes it obvious that he wants me to get it. I put it together, and with Ms. Pink Running Shoes's help, we get him in it. Then he says in a strong deep voice I hardly recognize,

150   "Arturo, get that notebook from the table, please."

I hand him another map-of-the-Island notebook—this one is red. On it in big letters it says, POEMAS DE ARTURO.

I start to push him toward the rec room, but he shakes his finger at me.

"Arturo, look at your watch now. I believe your time is over." He gives me a wicked smile.

Then with her pushing the wheelchair—maybe a little too fast—they roll down the hall. He is already reading from his notebook, and she's making bird noises. I look at my watch and

160   the hour _is_ up, to the minute. I can't help but think that my abuelo has been timing _me_. It cracks me up. I walk slowly down the hall toward the exit sign. I want my mother to have to wait a little. I don't want her to think that I'm in a hurry or anything.

# Grandma Ling

## Amy Ling

If you dig that hole deep enough,
you'll reach China, they used to tell me,
a child in a back yard in Pennsylvania.
Not strong enough to dig that hole,

5   I waited twenty years,
then sailed back, half way around the world.

---

**IDENTIFY**

Pause at line 6. What do you learn about the speaker as a child? Circle the details that tell you.

**IDENTIFY**

Re-read lines 5–6. For how many years has the speaker waited? What has she done? Underline the details that tell you.

**IDENTIFY**

Where does the speaker first meet Grandma (line 7)?

_____

_____

**VOCABULARY**

**sturdy** (stʉr′dē) *adj.:* strong; firm.

**INTERPRET**

Pause at line 16. Why does the speaker describe her grandmother's appearance as "my five foot height" and "my image"? What does she mean by "acted on by fifty years"?

_____

_____

_____

_____

**THEME**

How does the speaker communicate with her grandmother? What realization has she come to about her grandmother?

_____

_____

_____

_____

_____

_____

In Taiwan I first met Grandma.

Before she came to view, I heard

her slippered feet softly measure

10    the tatami° floor with even step;

the aqua paper-covered door slid open

and there I faced

my five foot height, **sturdy** legs and feet,

square forehead, high cheeks and wide-set eyes;

15    my image stood before me,

acted on by fifty years.


She smiled, stretched her arms

to take to heart the eldest daughter

of her youngest son a quarter century away.

20    She spoke a tongue I knew no word of,

and I was sad I could not understand,

but I could hug her.

---

°    **tatami** (tə·tä′mē): floor mat woven of rice straw.

# An Hour with Abuelo; Grandma Ling

To make a statement about life through the clothes you wear, you pay attention to the fabrics, colors, and accessories you choose. To make the same statement about life in a song, you would pay careful attention to words or lyrics, melody, and rhythm. Writers make statements about life all the time, and they give careful thought to how they will convey those ideas, or themes.

- Writers of **short stories** will typically convey theme through a story's main character, the conflicts he or she faces, what that character learns, and how he or she changes.

- In **poems,** the theme may be revealed by repetition of key words, by vivid imagery, or even by insights directly shared by the poem's speaker.

**Theme/Genre Chart**    Fill in the following chart to understand how choice of genre affects the theme of a work. First, fill in the top two rows, identifying the genre and theme of each selection. Then, fill in the rest of the chart with details from each piece that helped to convey theme.

| "An Hour with Abuelo" | | "Grandma Ling" | |
|---|---|---|---|
| Theme | | Theme | |
| Genre | | Genre | |
| Characters | | Speaker/ Characters | |
| Conflict/Plot | | Topic | |
| Character's Discovery | | Images | |

# Standards Review

LITERATURE

TestPractice

## An Hour with Abuelo; Grandma Ling

Complete the sample test item below. The box at the right explains why three of these choices are not correct.

| Sample Test Item | Explanation of the Correct Answer |
|---|---|
| In "An Hour with Abuelo," one subject that does not come up between Arturo and his grandfather is— <br><br> A time <br><br> B doing what you want <br><br> C writing <br><br> D Abuelo's nursing care | The correct answer is *D*. <br><br> Arturo tells us about the nursing home but doesn't discuss it with his grandfather. The two characters discuss the topics in *A, B,* and *C,* all of which are important to the story. |

**DIRECTIONS:** Answer the following questions by circling the letter of the best response.

**Reading Standard 3.2**
Compare and contrast the presentation of a similar theme or topic across genres to explain how the selection of genre shapes the theme or topic.

1. Arturo's attitude toward visiting Abuelo changes when the boy—

    A realizes that he has something to learn from his grandfather

    B accepts his mother's attitude toward life

    C doesn't think his grandfather cares about him

    D realizes that his grandfather is very ill

2. The speaker in "Grandma Ling"—

    F is scared to meet her grandmother

    G dislikes being Taiwanese

    H is impatient with her grandmother

    J discovers she looks like her grandmother

3. "An Hour with Abuelo" and "Grandma Ling" have—

    A the same setting

    B similar themes

    C the same writer

    D similar plots

4. Which of the following **themes** applies to both selections?

    F Grandparents and grandchildren share a special bond.

    G Life goes on.

    H It's not good to be impatient.

    J Difficulty can always be overcome.

# Standards Review

 **An Hour with Abuelo; Grandma Ling**

## Connotations

**DIRECTIONS:** Read each sentence carefully. Decide whether each boldface word has a positive or a negative connotation. Put a check next to the answer.

1. The boy thought of his grandfather as **doddering.**

   _____ Positive          _____ Negative

2. The nursing home was filled with the **stench** of ammonia.

   _____ Positive          _____ Negative

3. The **cuisine** at the nursing home was simple yet delicious.

   _____ Positive          _____ Negative

4. As the grandfather spoke, his eyes **twinkled** with intelligence and humor.

   _____ Positive          _____ Negative

**Reading Standard 1.2** Distinguish between the denotative and connotative meanings of words and interpret the connotative power of words.

## Vocabulary in Context

**DIRECTIONS:** Complete the paragraph below by writing a word from the box that best fits in each blank.

| Word Box |
| :---: |
| embroidered |
| ammunition |
| sturdy |

Various kinds of wartime supplies, including

(1) _____ boxes, lay long forgotten in the shed. Rifles, helmets, and binoculars sat on a shelf next to rows of

(2) _____ boots, meant to last through marches of hundreds and hundreds of miles. Oddly enough, hanging by the shed's door was an (3) _____ robe that may have once belonged to a priest or minister. It was a garment of beauty and hope amid the sameness of dull gray and green.

✔ **Before You Go On . . .**
Check your Standards Mastery at the back of this book.

# Irony and Ambiguity

# Academic Vocabulary for Chapter 5

These are the terms you should know
as you read and analyze the selections in this chapter.

———————

**Irony** The difference between what we expect to happen and what actually
happens. There are three main types of irony:

- **Verbal irony** occurs when someone *says* one thing but *means*
  the opposite.

  Example: "Thanks for your support," said the basketball player
  to the coach when he was cut from the team.

- In **situational irony,** an event is not just surprising but is the
  *opposite* of what we had expected.

  Example: A thief is hired to guard the palace treasures.

- **Dramatic irony** takes place when we know what is going to
  happen to the character but the character does not know.

  Example: *We* know, but Ron does *not* know, that when he flicks on
  his computer, a horrible virus will begin destroying its hard drive.

●  ●  ●

**Ambiguity** A quality that allows readers to interpret a story or other work in
more than one way. Ambiguity is not something that can be cleared up
by careful interpretation. Sometimes, writers deliberately make stories
ambiguous to reinforce the idea that life itself is often ambiguous and
can be interpreted in more than one way.

**Reading Standard 1.1**
Identify and use the literal and figurative meanings of words and understand word derivations.

**Reading Standard 1.3 (Grade 8 Review)**
Use word meanings within the appropriate context and show ability to verify those meanings by definition, restatement, example, comparison, or contrast.

**Reading Standard 3.8**
Interpret and evaluate the impact of ambiguities, subtleties, contradictions, ironies, and incongruities in a text.

> ### For Further Information ...
>
> - Be sure to read the essay on **irony** and
>   **ambiguity** in *Holt Literature and
>   Language Arts*, pages 314–315.

# Lamb to the Slaughter by Roald Dahl

The wife loves her husband and eagerly waits for him to come home from work each day at 5:00 P.M. The house is clean and well run. The husband is a reliable man and a respected police officer. What on earth could possibly go wrong? Read on to find out.

## LITERARY FOCUS: TWO KINDS OF IRONY

"Lamb to the Slaughter" contains two kinds of irony. The use of irony upsets our expectations of how the story will turn out, yet it leaves a memorable impression. **Situational irony** occurs when an event in a story turns out to be the exact opposite of what the reader had expected. In **dramatic irony** the reader knows something important that one or more of the characters don't know.

- Look for the story events that lead to **situational irony**. Ask yourself: "Which story events are expected? Which are unexpected?"
- As the story progresses, you are "in on" information that some story characters are not. Look to see how this situation creates **dramatic irony**.

## READING SKILLS: MAKING PREDICTIONS

You probably make predictions all the time: You may predict which team will win a sports event, or you might predict that your friend Jeff will ask Lily to the prom. Making predictions about life is fun, and doing so keeps you involved in what's going on around you. The same holds true when you make predictions about stories you read—you become involved with the characters and their experiences as you try to predict what they will do next.

Make predictions as you read "Lamb to the Slaughter." Fill out a chart like this one to help you keep track of your predictions. The first row has been filled in as an example.

| Detail from Story | Prediction |
|---|---|
| Mary is happily waiting for her husband to come home. | He will be happy to see her, too. |
| | |
| | |

**Reading Standard 1.3 (Grade 8 Review)** Use word meanings within the appropriate context and show ability to verify those meanings by definition, restatement, example, comparison, or contrast.

**Reading Standard 3.8** Interpret and evaluate the impact of ambiguities, subtleties, contradictions, ironies, and incongruities in a text.

## VOCABULARY DEVELOPMENT

### PREVIEW SELECTION VOCABULARY

Get to know the following words before you begin reading "Lamb to the Slaughter."

**anxiety** (aŋ·zī′ə·tē) *n.:* state of being worried or uneasy; stress.

*Although the news filled her with* **anxiety,** *she smiled calmly.*

**placid** (plas′id) *adj.:* calm; tranquil.

*Her* **placid** *look showed how peaceful she felt.*

**luxuriate** (lug·zhŏŏr′ē·āt′) *v.* (used with *in*): take great pleasure.

*She would* **luxuriate** *in the feeling of closeness to her husband.*

**administered** (ad·min′is·tərd) *v.* used as *adj.:* given; applied.

**Administered** *with great force, the blow knocked the man over.*

**premises** (prem′is·iz) *n.:* house or building and its surrounding property.

*Did the police find clues in the house or anywhere else on the* **premises***?*

**consoling** (kən·sōl′iŋ) *v.* used as *adj.:* comforting.

*The officer tried to comfort her, but Mary did not find his words* **consoling.**

**hospitality** (häs′pi·tal′ə·tē) *n.:* friendly, caring treatment of guests.

*In a show of* **hospitality,** *Mary invited the police officers for dinner.*

### CONTEXT CLUES

When you come across an unfamiliar word, look for clues in the **context**—the words, phrases, and sentences surrounding the word. Context clues may provide a definition, a restatement, an example, a comparison, or a contrast that helps you figure out the meaning of the unfamiliar word. In the examples below, the *italicized* context clues help you figure out the meaning of the **boldface** words.

DEFINITION: Her **instinct,** or *automatic response,* is to run away.

RESTATEMENT: She knows what the **penalty** is and will accept her *punishment.*

EXAMPLE: Her action might bring **relief**—*for example, it would end the anger she felt.*

COMPARISON: Ice cubes **clinking** in a glass *sound like pencils tapping on a table.*

CONTRAST: Although she looks **tranquil,** she *doesn't feel peaceful.*

# Lamb to the Slaughter

## Roald Dahl

**IDENTIFY**

Re-read lines 1–15. What is Mary doing? How would you describe her mood?

_____

_____

_____

_____

_____

_____

_____

_____

_____

The room was warm and clean, the curtains drawn, the two table lamps alight—hers and the one by the empty chair opposite. On the sideboard behind her, two tall glasses, soda water, whisky. Fresh ice cubes in the Thermos bucket.

Mary Maloney was waiting for her husband to come home from work.

Now and again she would glance up at the clock, but without **anxiety,** merely to please herself with the thought that each minute gone by made it nearer the time when he could come.
10 There was a slow smiling air about her, and about everything she did. The drop of the head as she bent over her sewing was curiously tranquil. Her skin—for this was her sixth month with child—had acquired a wonderful translucent[1] quality, the mouth was soft, and the eyes, with their new **placid** look, seemed larger, darker than before.

When the clock said ten minutes to five, she began to listen, and a few moments later, punctually as always, she heard the tires on the gravel outside, and the car door slamming, the footsteps passing the window, the key turning in the lock. She laid
20 aside her sewing, stood up, and went forward to kiss him as he came in.

"Hullo, darling," she said.

"Hullo," he answered.

She took his coat and hung it in the closet. Then she walked over and made the drinks, a strongish one for him, a weak one for herself; and soon she was back again in her chair

**VOCABULARY**

**anxiety** (aŋ·zī′ə·tē) *n.:* state of being worried or uneasy; stress.

**placid** (plas′id) *adj.:* calm; tranquil.

*Placid* is from the Latin *placere,* meaning "to calm or soothe." *Tranquil* (line 12) is a **synonym,** or word with the same meaning.

---

1.  **translucent** (trans·lōō′sənt) *adj.:* glowing; clear.

with the sewing, and he in the other, opposite, holding the tall glass with both his hands, rocking it so the ice cubes tinkled against the side.

30    For her, this was always a blissful time of day. She knew he didn't want to speak much until the first drink was finished, and she, on her side, was content to sit quietly, enjoying his company after the long hours alone in the house. She loved to **luxuriate** in the presence of this man, and to feel—almost as a sunbather feels the sun—that warm male glow that came out of him to her when they were alone together. She loved him for the way he sat loosely in a chair, for the way he came in a door, or moved slowly across the room with long strides. She loved the intent, far look in his eyes when they rested on her, the funny shape of the mouth, and especially the way he remained silent about his

40    tiredness, sitting still with himself until the whisky had taken some of it away.

"Tired, darling?"

"Yes," he said. "I'm tired." And as he spoke, he did an unusual thing. He lifted his glass and drained it in one swallow although there was still half of it, at least half of it left. She wasn't really watching him, but she knew what he had done because she heard the ice cubes falling back against the bottom of the empty glass when he lowered his arm. He paused a

50    moment, leaning forward in the chair, then he got up and went slowly over to fetch himself another.

"I'll get it!" she cried, jumping up.

"Sit down," he said.

When he came back, she noticed that the new drink was dark amber with the quantity of whisky in it.

"Darling, shall I get your slippers?"

"No."

She watched him as he began to sip the dark yellow drink, and she could see little oily swirls in the liquid because it was

60    so strong.

**INFER**

Pause at line 29. From her actions, would you think this was an ordinary day for Mary?

_____

_____

_____

**VOCABULARY**

**luxuriate** (lug·zhoor'ē·āt') _v._ (used with _in_): take great pleasure.

**FLUENCY**

Read the boxed passage aloud two times. Improve the speed and smoothness of your delivery with your second read.

**PREDICT**

Pause at line 51. Underline the "unusual thing" that Mary's husband does. Make a **prediction** about the change in his behavior—how might this change affect Mary?

_____

_____

_____

_____

_____

_____

## IRONY

Re-read lines 61–77, and underline each of the husband's responses to Mary. In what way is this situation ironic?

_____

_____

_____

_____

_____

_____

_____

_____

_____

_____

## PREDICT

Pause at line 93. What do you predict the husband will tell Mary?

_____

_____

_____

_____

_____

_____

_____

_____

"I think it's a shame," she said, "that when a policeman gets to be as senior as you, they keep him walking about on his feet all day long."

He didn't answer, so she bent her head again and went on with her sewing; but each time he lifted the drink to his lips, she heard the ice cubes clinking against the side of the glass.

"Darling," she said. "Would you like me to get you some cheese? I haven't made any supper because it's Thursday."

"No," he said.

70 "If you're too tired to eat out," she went on, "it's still not too late. There's plenty of meat and stuff in the freezer, and you can have it right here and not even move out of the chair."

Her eyes waited on him for an answer, a smile, a little nod, but he made no sign.

"Anyway," she went on, "I'll get you some cheese and crackers first."

"I don't want it," he said.

She moved uneasily in her chair, the large eyes still watching his face. "But you *must* have supper. I can easily do it here.

80 I'd like to do it. We can have lamb chops. Or pork. Anything you want. Everything's in the freezer."

"Forget it," he said.

"But, darling, you *must* eat! I'll fix it anyway, and then you can have it or not, as you like."

She stood up and placed her sewing on the table by the lamp.

"Sit down," he said. "Just for a minute, sit down."

It wasn't till then that she began to get frightened.

"Go on," he said. "Sit down."

She lowered herself back slowly into the chair, watching

90 him all the time with those large, bewildered eyes. He had finished the second drink and was staring down into the glass, frowning.

"Listen," he said. "I've got something to tell you."

"What is it, darling? What's the matter?"

He had now become absolutely motionless, and he kept his head down so that the light from the lamp beside him fell across the upper part of his face, leaving the chin and mouth in shadow. She noticed there was a little muscle moving near the corner of his left eye.

100     "This is going to be a bit of a shock to you, I'm afraid," he said. "But I've thought about it a good deal and I've decided the

Notes _____

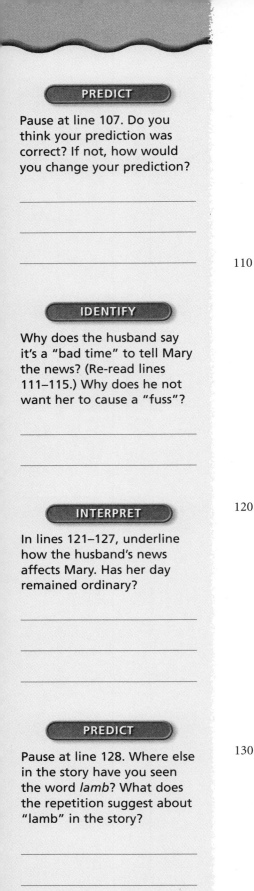

only thing to do is tell you right away. I hope you won't blame me too much."

And he told her. It didn't take long, four or five minutes at most, and she sat very still through it all, watching him with a kind of dazed horror as he went further and further away from her with each word.

"So there it is," he added. "And I know it's kind of a bad time to be telling you, but there simply wasn't any other way. Of
110   course I'll give you money and see you're looked after. But there needn't really be any fuss. I hope not anyway. It wouldn't be very good for my job."

Her first instinct was not to believe any of it, to reject it all. It occurred to her that perhaps he hadn't even spoken, that she herself had imagined the whole thing. Maybe, if she went about her business and acted as though she hadn't been listening, then later, when she sort of woke up again, she might find none of it had ever happened.

"I'll get the supper," she managed to whisper, and this time
120   he didn't stop her.

When she walked across the room she couldn't feel her feet touching the floor. She couldn't feel anything at all—except a slight nausea and a desire to vomit. Everything was automatic now—down the steps to the cellar, the light switch, the deep freeze, the hand inside the cabinet taking hold of the first object it met. She lifted it out, and looked at it. It was wrapped in paper, so she took off the paper and looked at it again.

A leg of lamb.

All right then, they would have lamb for supper. She carried
130   it upstairs, holding the thin bone-end of it with both her hands, and as she went through the living room, she saw him standing over by the window with his back to her, and she stopped.

"For God's sake," he said, hearing her, but not turning round. "Don't make supper for me. I'm going out."

At that point, Mary Maloney simply walked up behind him and without any pause she swung the big frozen leg of lamb high in the air and brought it down as hard as she could on the back of his head.

She might just as well have hit him with a steel club.

She stepped back a pace, waiting, and the funny thing was that he remained standing there for at least four or five seconds, gently swaying. Then he crashed to the carpet.

The violence of the crash, the noise, the small table over-turning, helped bring her out of the shock. She came out slowly, feeling cold and surprised, and she stood for a while blinking at the body, still holding the ridiculous piece of meat tight with both hands.

All right, she told herself. So I've killed him.

It was extraordinary, now, how clear her mind became all of a sudden. She began thinking very fast. As the wife of a detective, she knew quite well what the penalty would be. That was fine. It made no difference to her. In fact, it would be a relief. On the other hand, what about the child? What were the laws about murderers with unborn children? Did they kill them both—mother and child? Or did they wait until the tenth month? What did they do?

Mary Maloney didn't know. And she certainly wasn't prepared to take the chance.

She carried the meat into the kitchen, placed it in a pan, turned the oven on high, and shoved it inside. Then she washed her hands and ran upstairs to the bedroom. She sat down before the mirror, tidied her face, touched up her lips and face. She tried a smile. It came out rather peculiar. She tried again.

"Hullo Sam," she said brightly, aloud.

The voice sounded peculiar too.

"I want some potatoes please, Sam. Yes, and I think a can of peas."

That was better. Both the smile and the voice were coming out better now. She rehearsed it several times more. Then she ran downstairs, took her coat, went out the back door, down the garden, into the street.

IRONY

Re-read lines 135–139. What does Mary do to her husband? How does her behavior create **situational irony**?

_____

_____

_____

_____

_____

PREDICT

Pause at line 147. What will Mary do next, now that she's come out of her state of shock?

_____

_____

_____

IRONY

Underline the words in lines 159–163 that tell you what Mary does with the lamb after using it as a weapon. In what way does her behavior create **situational irony**?

_____

_____

_____

_____

_____

_____

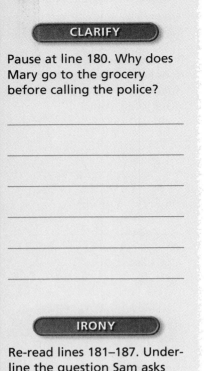

**CLARIFY**

Pause at line 180. Why does Mary go to the grocery before calling the police?

_____

_____

_____

_____

_____

_____

**IRONY**

Re-read lines 181–187. Underline the question Sam asks that creates **dramatic irony**. What important information does Sam *not* know?

_____

_____

_____

_____

**IRONY**

What is ironic about the "thank-yous" that Sam and Mary exchange in lines 200–202?

_____

_____

_____

_____

_____

It wasn't six o'clock yet and the lights were still on in the grocery shop.

"Hullo Sam," she said brightly, smiling at the man behind the counter.

"Why, good evening, Mrs. Maloney. How're *you*?"

"I want some potatoes please, Sam. Yes, and I think a can of peas."

180 The man turned and reached up behind him on the shelf for the peas.

"Patrick's decided he's tired and doesn't want to eat out tonight," she told him. "We usually go out Thursday, you know, and now he's caught me without any vegetables in the house."

"Then how about meat, Mrs. Maloney?"

"No, I've got meat, thanks. I got a nice leg of lamb, from the freezer."

"Oh."

"I don't much like cooking it frozen, Sam, but I'm taking a chance on it this time. You think it'll be all right?"

190 "Personally," the grocer said, "I don't believe it makes any difference. You want these Idaho potatoes?"

"Oh yes, that'll be fine. Two of those."

"Anything else?" The grocer cocked his head on one side, looking at her pleasantly. "How about afterwards? What you going to give him for afterwards?"

"Well—what would you suggest, Sam?"

The man glanced around his shop. "How about a nice big slice of cheesecake? I know he likes that."

"Perfect," she said. "He loves it."

200 And when it was all wrapped and she had paid, she put on her brightest smile and said, "Thank you, Sam. Good night."

"Good night, Mrs. Maloney. And thank *you*."

And now, she told herself as she hurried back, all she was doing now, she was returning home to her husband and he was waiting for his supper; and she must cook it good, and make it as tasty as possible because the poor man was tired; and if, when she entered the house, she happened to find anything unusual, or tragic, or terrible, then naturally it would be a shock and she'd become frantic with grief and horror. Mind you, she wasn't *expecting* to find anything. She was just going home with the vegetables. Mrs. Patrick Maloney going home with the vegetables on Thursday evening to cook supper for her husband.

That's the way, she told herself. Do everything right and natural. Keep things absolutely natural and there'll be no need for any acting at all.

Therefore, when she entered the kitchen by the back door, she was humming a little tune to herself and smiling.

"Patrick!" she called. "How are you, darling?"

She put the parcel down on the table and went through into the living room; and when she saw him lying there on the floor with his legs doubled up and one arm twisted back underneath his body, it really was rather a shock. All the old love and longing for him welled up inside her, and she ran over to him, knelt down beside him, and began to cry her heart out. It was easy. No acting was necessary.

A few minutes later she got up and went to the phone. She knew the number of the police station, and when the man at the other end answered, she cried to him, "Quick! Come quick! Patrick's dead!"

"Who's speaking?"

"Mrs. Maloney. Mrs. Patrick Maloney."

"You mean Patrick Maloney's dead?"

"I think so," she sobbed. "He's lying on the floor and I think he's dead."

"Be right over," the man said.

The car came very quickly, and when she opened the front door, two policemen walked in. She knew them both—she knew nearly all the men at that precinct—and she fell right into Jack Noonan's arms, weeping hysterically. He put her gently into a chair, then went over to join the other one, who was called O'Malley, kneeling by the body.

**PREDICT**

In lines 219–225, it becomes clear that Mary really did love her husband. What do you predict she will do now?

_____

_____

_____

_____

_____

_____

_____

_____

_____

_____

_____

_____

_____

**WORD STUDY**

*Precinct* (line 238) means "division of a city for law enforcement purposes." In common usage, *precinct* also refers to the actual building that police officers work out of. Locate and circle context clues that help you figure out the meaning of *precinct*.

"Is he dead?" she cried.

"I'm afraid he is. What happened?"

Briefly, she told her story about going out to the grocer and coming back to find him on the floor. While she was talking, crying and talking, Noonan discovered a small patch of congealed[2] blood on the dead man's head. He showed it to O'Malley who got up at once and hurried to the phone.

---

2. **congealed** (kən·jēld′) *v.* used as *adj.:* thickened; made solid.

Soon, other men began to come into the house. First a
doctor, then two detectives, one of whom she knew by name.
Later, a police photographer arrived and took pictures, and a
man who knew about fingerprints. There was a great deal of
whispering and muttering beside the corpse, and the detectives
kept asking her a lot of questions. But they always treated her
kindly. She told her story again, this time right from the beginning, when Patrick had come in, and she was sewing, and he was
tired, so tired he hadn't wanted to go out for supper. She told
how she'd put the meat in the oven—"it's there now, cooking"—
and how she'd slipped out to the grocer for vegetables, and come
back to find him lying on the floor.

"Which grocer?" one of the detectives asked.

She told him, and he turned and whispered something to
the other detective who immediately went outside into the street.

In fifteen minutes he was back with a page of notes, and
there was more whispering, and through her sobbing she heard
a few of the whispered phrases—". . . acted quite normal . . . very
cheerful . . . wanted to give him a good supper . . . peas . . .
cheesecake . . . impossible that she . . ."

After a while, the photographer and the doctor departed and
two other men came in and took the corpse away on a stretcher.
Then the fingerprint man went away. The two detectives
remained, and so did the two policemen. They were exceptionally
nice to her, and Jack Noonan asked if she wouldn't rather go
somewhere else, to her sister's house perhaps, or to his own wife
who would take care of her and put her up for the night.

No, she said. She didn't feel she could move even a yard at
the moment. Would they mind awfully if she stayed just where
she was until she felt better? She didn't feel too good at the
moment, she really didn't.

Then hadn't she better lie down on the bed? Jack Noonan
asked.

No, she said. She'd like to stay right where she was, in this
chair. A little later perhaps, when she felt better, she would move.

250

260

270

280

INFER

Re-read lines 255–263. Where
did the detective go?

_____

_____

_____

_____

_____

_____

_____

_____

_____

INFER

In lines 276–283, Mary tells
the officers she doesn't feel
well enough to go anywhere.
What might be the *real*
reason she wants to stay?

_____

_____

_____

_____

_____

_____

So they left her there while they went about their business, searching the house. Occasionally one of the detectives asked her another question. Sometimes Jack Noonan spoke to her gently as he passed by. Her husband, he told her, had been killed by a blow on the back of the head **administered** with a heavy blunt instrument, almost certainly a large piece of metal. They were

290    looking for the weapon. The murderer may have taken it with him, but on the other hand he may've thrown it away or hidden it somewhere on the **premises.**

"It's the old story," he said. "Get the weapon, and you've got the man."

Later, one of the detectives came up and sat beside her. Did she know, he asked, of anything in the house that could've been used as the weapon? Would she mind having a look around to see if anything was missing—a very big spanner,[3] for example, or a heavy metal vase.

300    They didn't have any heavy metal vases, she said.

"Or a big spanner?"

She didn't think they had a big spanner. But there might be some things like that in the garage.

The search went on. She knew that there were other policemen in the garden all around the house. She could hear their footsteps on the gravel outside, and sometimes she saw the flash of a torch through a chink in the curtains. It began to get late, nearly nine she noticed by the clock on the mantel. The four men searching the rooms seemed to be growing weary, a trifle

310    exasperated.

"Jack," she said, the next time Sergeant Noonan went by. "Would you mind giving me a drink?"

"Sure I'll give you a drink. You mean this whisky?"

"Yes, please. But just a small one. It might make me feel better."

He handed her the glass.

---

**3.**   **spanner** *n.:* British English for "wrench."

"Why don't you have one yourself," she said. "You must be awfully tired. Please do. You've been very good to me."

"Well," he answered. "It's not strictly allowed, but I might take just a drop to keep me going."

One by one the others came in and were persuaded to take a little nip of whisky. They stood around rather awkwardly with the drinks in their hands, uncomfortable in her presence, trying to say **consoling** things to her. Sergeant Noonan wandered into the kitchen, came out quickly and said, "Look, Mrs. Maloney. You know that oven of yours is still on, and the meat still inside."

"Oh *dear* me!" she cried. "So it is!"

"I better turn it off for you, hadn't I?"

"Will you do that, Jack. Thank you so much."

When the sergeant returned the second time, she looked at him with her large, dark, tearful eyes. "Jack Noonan," she said.

"Yes?"

"Would you do me a small favor—you and these others?"

"We can try, Mrs. Maloney."

"Well," she said. "Here you all are, and good friends of dear Patrick's too, and helping to catch the man who killed him. You must be terrible hungry by now because it's long past your supper time, and I know Patrick would never forgive me, God bless his soul, if I allowed you to remain in his house without offering you decent **hospitality.** Why don't you eat up that lamb that's in the oven? It'll be cooked just right by now."

"Wouldn't dream of it," Sergeant Noonan said.

"Please," she begged. "Please eat it. Personally I couldn't touch a thing, certainly not what's been in the house when he was here. But it's all right for you. It'd be a favor to me if you'd eat it up. Then you can go on with your work again afterwards."

There was a good deal of hesitating among the four policemen, but they were clearly hungry, and in the end they were persuaded to go into the kitchen and help themselves. The woman stayed where she was, listening to them through the open door,

320

330

340

350

**VOCABULARY**

**consoling** (kən·sōl′iŋ) *v.* used as *adj.*: comforting.

**INFER**

Pause at line 327. Has Mary *really* forgotten that the meat is in the oven? Explain.

_____

_____

_____

_____

_____

**VOCABULARY**

**hospitality** (häs′pi·tal′ə·tē) *n.*: friendly, caring treatment of guests.

**IRONY**

Pause at line 346. Mary says the police would do her "a favor" by eating the lamb. Why is this an example of **dramatic irony**?

_____

_____

_____

_____

_____

_____

_____

_____

_____

_____

_____

_____

_____

_____

_____

_____

_____

_____

PREDICT

What do you think will happen to Mary?

_____

_____

_____

_____

_____

_____

_____

_____

and she could hear them speaking among themselves, their voices thick and sloppy because their mouths were full of meat.

"Have some more, Charlie?"

"No. Better not finish it."

"She _wants_ us to finish it. She said so. Be doing her a favor."

"Okay then. Give me some more."

"That's the hell of a big club the guy must've used to hit poor Patrick," one of them was saying. "The doc says his skull was smashed all to pieces just like from a sledgehammer."

360    "That's why it ought to be easy to find."

"Exactly what I say."

"Whoever done it, they're not going to be carrying a thing like that around with them longer than they need."

One of them belched.

"Personally, I think it's right here on the premises."

"Probably right under our very noses. What you think, Jack?"

And in the other room, Mary Maloney began to giggle.

# Lamb to the Slaughter

**Irony Chart**    The contrast between expectations and reality is referred to as **irony. Situational irony** occurs when events are the *opposite* of what we expected. **Dramatic irony** occurs when readers know something important that a character doesn't know. To help you appreciate the irony in "Lamb to the Slaughter," fill in the blanks in this chart.

| Story Passage | How Passage Creates Irony |
|---|---|
| "At that point, Mary Maloney simply walked up behind him and without any pause she swung the big frozen leg of lamb high in the air and brought it down as hard as she could on the back of his head." (lines 135–138) | • Mary's actions before this point in the story: <br><br> • Mary's actions now: <br><br> • What actions you expected: <br><br> • What Mary actually does: |
| " 'Have some more, Charlie?' " <br> " 'No. Better not finish it.' " <br> " 'She *wants* us to finish it. She said so. Be doing her a favor.' " (lines 353–355) | • Why the police think Mary wants them to finish the lamb: <br><br> • Why she really wants the police to finish the lamb: <br><br> • What is ironic about the police eating the lamb: |

# Standards Review

TestPractice **Lamb to the Slaughter**

Improve your test-taking skills by completing the sample test item below. Then, read the explanation that appears in the right-hand column.

| Sample Test Item | Explanation of the Correct Answer |
|---|---|
| From your knowledge of the events in "Lamb to the Slaughter," which of the following is an example of **irony**?<br><br>**A** Mary is a devoted wife.<br><br>**B** Patrick is a police officer.<br><br>**C** The grocer asks Mary whether she needs meat.<br><br>**D** The investigators know both Mary and Patrick. | The correct answer is C.<br><br>Irony takes place when there is a difference between what we expect to happen and what actually happens. The grocer thinks that Mary is shopping for dinner and may need meat. The truth is that Mary has just killed her husband with meat from her freezer. *A, B,* and *D* are statements of fact that do not suggest a difference between an expectation and a reality. |

**DIRECTIONS:** Circle the letter of each correct response.

**Reading Standard 3.8**
Interpret and evaluate the impact of ambiguities, subtleties, contradictions, ironies, and incongruities in a text.

1. Which of the following shows **situational irony**?

   **A** Calm, loving Mary violently kills her husband.

   **B** The police officer goes to the grocer's.

   **C** Patrick is a police officer.

   **D** The doctor says that Patrick's skull was smashed.

2. Why does Mary go shopping for groceries?

   **F** Her husband wants dinner at home.

   **G** She needs fresh air.

   **H** She needs an alibi, or excuse.

   **J** She wants to confess to Sam.

3. It is an **irony** that the grieving widow is also the—

   **A** murderer

   **B** victim

   **C** grocer

   **D** investigating officer

4. **Dramatic irony** takes place when Mary tells the police that—

   **F** she would like a drink

   **G** they would do her a favor by eating the lamb

   **H** she feels too ill to leave

   **J** she went grocery shopping

# Standards Review

## Lamb to the Slaughter

### Context Clues

**DIRECTIONS:** Use context clues to figure out the meaning of the boldface word. Circle the letter next to the correct definition.

1. With an **intent** look, he observed her closely and thoughtfully.

   A attentive     C careless

   B angry     D sleepy

2. After he told her the awful news, her face had a look of **dazed** horror.

   F careful     H insulted

   G new     J shocked

3. The situation was **extraordinary**—nothing prepared Mary for Patrick's news.

   A ordinary     C difficult

   B shocking     D unclear

4. Was Patrick's death **tragic** for Mary, or was she happy about it?

   F helpful     H sad

   G happy     J exciting

**Reading Standard 1.3 (Grade 8 Review)** Use word meanings within the appropriate context and show ability to verify those meanings by definition, restatement, example, comparison, or contrast.

### Vocabulary in Context

**DIRECTIONS:** Complete the passage by writing words from the box in the spaces provided. Not all words will be used.

**Word Box**

anxiety

placid

luxuriate

administered

premises

consoling

hospitality

My grandmother, who died last month, usually had a (1) _____, calm look. She wouldn't let (2) _____ about family problems trouble her. She often gave parties and was famous for her (3) _____. She invited family and friends to (4) _____ in the warmth of her home. We would walk around the (5) _____, from the front porch to the shed way in back. When I felt sad, I would go to the garden, because Grandma's flowers were always (6) _____ to me.

**Before You Go On . . .**

Check your Standards Mastery at the back of this book.

# The Listeners by Walter de la Mare

Why would a horseman ride to a house in the middle of the night, demanding entry? What promise is he keeping? Why does no one come to the door? Is anyone listening? If so, who? The answers to these questions may (or may *not*) be found in "The Listeners," a famous poem by Walter de la Mare.

## LITERARY FOCUS: AMBIGUITY

When a story or poem offers more than one meaning or interpretation, it is ambiguous, or shows **ambiguity.** Works that contain ambiguity are thought-provoking because there is no single correct interpretation. Instead, you are left to think and rethink story events, characters' actions, and the meanings you extract from them.

- As you read "The Listeners," you may be left with more questions than answers. How, in your view, should the poem be interpreted?

## READING SKILLS: MAKING INFERENCES

In literary works containing ambiguity, you, the reader, are not told every-thing; in fact, you may not be told much of *anything.* Instead, it is up to you to make inferences, or educated guesses, about what is happening and why. Making inferences about an ambiguous work won't lead you to one correct answer, because one doesn't exist. By making inferences, however, you become an active participant in the literary work's ongoing debate or puzzle.

To make an inference about a character or an event:

- Identify all the details you can find that describe the character or the event.
- Think about how that character or event is like or unlike people or situations you've encountered in your own life, perhaps even in other stories.
- Make a careful guess about the kind of person you are meeting in the story or about the significance of the events in the story.
- Revise your inferences as the story goes on. Often in stories, as in life itself, we are surprised by people or by situations.

**Reading Standard 1.1**
Identify and use the literal and figurative meanings of words and understand word derivations.

**Reading Standard 3.8**
Interpret and evaluate the impact of ambiguities, subtleties, contradictions, ironies, and incongruities in a text.

## VOCABULARY DEVELOPMENT

### AFFIXES

An **affix** is a word part that is added to a base word or root and changes its meaning. Affixes that come *before* a base word are called **prefixes.** Affixes that come *after* a base word are called **suffixes.** Learning about prefixes and suffixes will help you understand and use a wider variety of words.

The following words are from "The Listeners." Notice how the suffix changes the meaning of the base word:

fern + y = "full of ferns"
strange + ness = "quality of being strange"
soft + ly = "in a way that is soft"

The following chart lists common affixes, their meanings, and examples.

| Prefix (Meaning) | Word with Affix |
|---|---|
| *re–* (again) | revisit |
| *ir–* (not) | irregular |
| *dis–* (without) | disbelief |
| *sub–* (under) | subway |
| *mis–* (badly or incorrectly) | misspoke |

| Suffix (Meaning) | Word with Affix |
|---|---|
| *–less* (without) | faultless |
| *–ness* (state or quality of being) | quietness |
| *–able* (capable of) | likable |
| *–ly* (in a manner or direction) | clearly |
| *–ive* (have the nature or quality of) | supportive |

# The Listeners

## Walter de la Mare

**INTERPRET**

Who is the main character (line 1)?

_____

_____

"Is there anybody there?" said the Traveler,
    Knocking on the moonlit door;
And his horse in the silence champed the grasses
    Of the forest's ferny floor;
5  And a bird flew up out of the turret,[1]
    Above the Traveler's head:
And he smote[2] upon the door again a second time;
    "Is there anybody there?" he said.

**CLARIFY**

Re-read lines 1–12. What is the Traveler doing? What response does he get?

_____

_____

_____

But no one descended to the Traveler;
10    No head from the leaf-fringed sill
Leaned over and looked into his gray eyes,
    Where he stood perplexed and still.
But only a host of phantom listeners
    That dwelt in the lone house then
15  Stood listening in the quiet of the moonlight
    To that voice from the world of men:
Stood thronging[3] the faint moonbeams on the dark stair
    That goes down to the empty hall.
Hearkening[4] in an air stirred and shaken
20    By the lonely Traveler's call.

**AMBIGUITY**

Who do you think the "phantom listeners" and the "world of men" might be (lines 13–16)?

_____

_____

_____

_____

And he felt in his heart their strangeness,
    Their stillness answering his cry,
While his horse moved, cropping the dark turf,
    'Neath the starred and leafy sky;
25  For he suddenly smote on the door, even
    Louder, and lifted his head—

**FLUENCY**

Read the boxed passage aloud several times. Note punctuation marks that signal pauses and full stops. Improve your speed and your interpretation with each reading.

---

1. **turret:** small tower.
2. **smote:** struck; here, knocked loudly.
3. **thronging:** crowding; filling.
4. **hearkening** (här′kən·iŋ): listening.

"Tell them I came, and no one answered,

    That I kept my word," he said.

Never the least stir made the listeners,

30      Though every word he spake

Fell echoing through the shadowiness of the still house

    From the one man left awake:

Aye, they heard his foot upon the stirrup,

    And the sound of iron on stone,

35  And how the silence surged softly backward,

    When the plunging hoofs were gone.

**AMBIGUITY**

Why do you think no one answers?

_____

_____

_____

_____

## OWN THE POEM

# The Listeners

**Ambiguity Chart**    "The Listeners" has plenty of **ambiguity.** The details are vivid but not clearly explained. It's up to you to decide what they mean. For help interpreting the story's details, answer the questions in the chart below.

| Details Showing Ambiguity | What Details May Mean |
|---|---|
| " 'Is there anybody there?' he said. / But no one descended to the Traveler. . . ." (lines 8–9) | |
| "But only a host of phantom listeners / That dwelt in the lone house then / Stood listening in the quiet of the moonlight. . . ." (lines 13–15) | |
| "And he felt in his heart their strangeness, / Their stillness answering his cry. . . ." (lines 21–22) | |
| " 'Tell them I came, and no one answered, / That I kept my word,' he said. . . ." (lines 27–28) | |

**TestPractice** : **The Listeners**

Improve your test-taking skills by completing the sample test item below. Then, read the explanation in the right-hand column.

| Sample Test Item | Explanation of the Correct Answer |
|---|---|
| Which of the following describes the poem's **setting**?<br><br>**A** a forest<br><br>**B** a turret<br><br>**C** a prison<br><br>**D** an inn | *A* is the correct answer; line 4 describes a "forest's ferny floor." *B* is incorrect; a turret is mentioned in the poem, but no action takes place there. No prisons or inns are mentioned, therefore *C* and *D* are incorrect. |

**DIRECTIONS:** Circle the letter of each correct response.

**Reading Standard 3.8**
Interpret and evaluate the impact of ambiguities, subtleties, contradictions, ironies, and incongruities in a text.

1. What is the Traveler doing at the beginning of the poem?

    **A** He is asking for a chance to be heard.

    **B** He is fleeing from an enemy.

    **C** He is trying to find shelter for the night.

    **D** He is knocking on the door of a home.

2. Why is the Traveler "perplexed and still" (line 12)?

    **F** He has lost his way in the forest.

    **G** The listeners have confused him.

    **H** He has suffered a head injury.

    **J** No one is answering his knock.

3. What makes the "phantom listeners" an **ambiguous** element in the poem?

    **A** They are in the poem's title.

    **B** It is never clearly stated who they are.

    **C** They frighten the Traveler by their silence.

    **D** They are really birds in the turret.

4. Which of the following statements is true about "The Listeners"?

    **F** In the last line, you find out what the poem means.

    **G** The writer doesn't know what the poem means.

    **H** There are several ways to interpret the meaning of the poem.

    **J** The poem does not have a mysterious feeling.

# Standards Review

 **The Listeners**

## Matching Affixes

**DIRECTIONS:** The left column contains a list of affixes. For each affix, find the item in the right column that gives its type (prefix *or* suffix) and meaning. Write the letter of that item on the blank.

1. _____ –able

2. _____ –less

3. _____ ir–

4. _____ dis–

5. _____ sub–

a. prefix meaning "not"

b. prefix meaning "under"

c. suffix meaning "without"

d. suffix meaning "capable of"

e. prefix meaning "without"

**Reading Standard 1.1** Identify and use the literal and figurative meanings of words and understand word derivations.

## Using Affixes

**DIRECTIONS:** Write the affix from the box to complete each item.

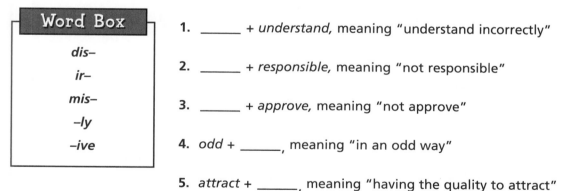

**Word Box**

dis–

ir–

mis–

–ly

–ive

1. _____ + *understand,* meaning "understand incorrectly"

2. _____ + *responsible,* meaning "not responsible"

3. _____ + *approve,* meaning "not approve"

4. *odd* + _____, meaning "in an odd way"

5. *attract* + _____, meaning "having the quality to attract"

**Before You Go On...**

Check your Standards Mastery at the back of this book.

# Symbolism and Allegory

# Academic Vocabulary for Chapter 6

These are the terms you should know
as you read and analyze the selections in this chapter.

_____

**Symbol** An object, a setting, an animal, or a person that functions as itself and as something more than itself, usually something abstract.

**Figurative language** Language that describes one thing in terms of another and is not meant to be understood on a literal level. Common figures of speech include similes, metaphors, and personification.

**Theme** An idea or insight about life or human nature revealed in a work of literature.

● ● ●

**Allegory** A work of literature in which characters and places stand for abstract qualities, usually virtues and vices. Sometimes the characters and places in an allegory have names that describe what they symbolize, such as a character called Mr. Mean and a place called Sea of Troubles.

**Fable** An allegory in which animal characters who usually symbolize vices and virtues act out a story in order to teach a practical lesson about how to succeed in life.

**Parable** An allegory in the form of a brief story, set in the everyday world, told to teach a lesson about ethics or morality.

**Reading Standard 1.1** Identify and use the literal and figurative meanings of words and understand word derivations.

**Reading Standard 1.3 (Grade 8 Review)** Use word meanings within the appropriate context and show ability to verify those meanings by definition, restatement, example, comparison, or contrast.

**Reading Standard 3.7** Recognize and understand the significance of various literary devices, including figurative language, imagery, allegory, and symbolism, and explain their appeal.

> **📚 For Further Information . . .**
>
> ● Be sure to read the essay on **symbolism and allegory** in *Holt Literature and Language Arts*, pages 398–399.

# Through the Tunnel by Doris Lessing

In stories and even in real life, tunnels are often seen as symbols of a passage from one place or stage of life to another. Adolescents must go through a tunnel and survive its threats and terrors before they can be considered adults. As you read this story, think about what the dangerous underwater tunnel means to Jerry, the story's main character.

## LITERARY FOCUS: SYMBOLIC MEANING

A **symbol** is something—a person, a place, an object, or an event—that stands both for itself and for something beyond itself. For example, cars are a means of transportation, but in a story a car may also symbolize independence, freedom, maturity, responsibility—or even death.

- "Through the Tunnel" contains several **symbols.** As you read, decide which people, places, or things could be symbols for something else.
- When you have finished reading, think about why those symbols were chosen to be part of the story and what meanings those symbols create.

## READING SKILLS: RE-READING AND READING FOR DETAILS

Successful readers read, and re-read, and re-read some more. They know that it's nearly impossible to come to a full understanding of any piece of literature in a single reading. There are many good reasons for re-reading. You may re-read to—

- refresh your memory about characters and events
- clear up any misunderstandings or confusion
- deepen your understanding about a story's symbols or theme

After you read "Through the Tunnel," think of questions you have about the story. Then re-read, looking for answers to your questions.

**Reading Standard 1.1**
Identify and use the literal and figurative meanings of words and understand word derivations.

**Reading Standard 1.3 (Grade 8 Review)**
Use word meanings within the appropriate context and show ability to verify those meanings by definition, restatement, example, comparison, or contrast.

**Reading Standard 3.7**
Recognize and understand the significance of various literary devices, including figurative language, imagery, allegory, and symbolism, and explain their appeal.

## VOCABULARY DEVELOPMENT

### PREVIEW SELECTION VOCABULARY

The following words appear in the story you're about to read. You may want to become familiar with them before you begin reading.

**contrition** (kən·trish′ən) *n.:* regret or a sense of guilt at having done wrong.

*Jerry felt **contrition** whenever he seemed to disappoint his mother.*

**supplication** (sup′lə·kā′shən) *n.:* humble appeal or request.

*Jerry smiled in **supplication:** He was silently appealing to the other boys to let him join them.*

**defiant** (dē·fī′ənt) *adj.:* challenging authority.

*Jerry, who was usually obedient, became **defiant** in demanding what he wanted from his mother.*

**inquisitive** (in·kwiz′ə·tiv) *adj.:* questioning; curious.

*His mother was **inquisitive** about Jerry's odd request.*

**minute** (mī·nōōt′) *adj.:* small; tiny.

*Jerry swam through a school of millions of **minute,** tiny fish.*

**incredulous** (in·krej′oo·ləs) *adj.:* disbelieving; skeptical.

*Jerry was **incredulous:** He could not believe that the big boys could stay under the water for so long.*

### ANALOGIES: MATCHING RELATIONSHIPS

In a **word analogy,** the words in the first pair relate to each other in the same way as the words in a second pair. In word analogies, many different types of relationships are possible. For example:

MINUTE : TINY :: huge : gigantic

In this analogy, both pairs of word are synonyms. The first two words are synonyms meaning "very small." The second two words are synonyms meaning "very large." The following chart shows some of the most common relationships in word analogies.

| Analogy Relationship | Example |
|---|---|
| synonyms | HAPPY : JOYOUS :: pretty : attractive |
| antonyms | START : STOP :: old : young |
| part to whole | TOE : FOOT :: sleeve : jacket |
| object to function | SCISSORS : CUT :: towel : dry |
| degree | TIRED : EXHAUSTED :: hungry : starving |

# THROUGH THE TUNNEL

## Doris Lessing

### IDENTIFY

Pause at line 9. Underline the words that tell you how long the boy and his mother have been on vacation. Circle the words that tell you they have been there before.

### VOCABULARY

contrition (kən·trish′ən) n.: regret or a sense of guilt at having done wrong.

### INFER

Pause at line 25. Why do you think Jerry wants to go to the wild bay instead of the beach he is used to?

Going to the shore on the first morning of the vacation, the young English boy stopped at a turning of the path and looked down at a wild and rocky bay and then over to the crowded beach he knew so well from other years. His mother walked on in front of him, carrying a bright striped bag in one hand. Her other arm, swinging loose, was very white in the sun. The boy watched that white naked arm and turned his eyes, which had a frown behind them, toward the bay and back again to his mother. When she felt he was not with her, she swung around.

10 "Oh, there you are, Jerry!" she said. She looked impatient, then smiled. "Why, darling, would you rather not come with me? Would you rather—" She frowned, conscientiously worrying over what amusements he might secretly be longing for, which she had been too busy or too careless to imagine. He was very familiar with that anxious, apologetic smile. **Contrition** sent him running after her. And yet, as he ran, he looked back over his shoulder at the wild bay; and all morning, as he played on the safe beach, he was thinking of it.

Next morning, when it was time for the routine of swim-
20 ming and sunbathing, his mother said, "Are you tired of the usual beach, Jerry? Would you like to go somewhere else?"

"Oh, no!" he said quickly, smiling at her out of that unfailing impulse of contrition—a sort of chivalry.[1] Yet, walking down the path with her, he blurted out, "I'd like to go and have a look at those rocks down there."

She gave the idea her attention. It was a wild-looking place, and there was no one there, but she said, "Of course, Jerry. When you've had enough, come to the big beach. Or just go

---

1.  **chivalry** (shiv′əl·rē) n.: here, an act of gentlemanly politeness.

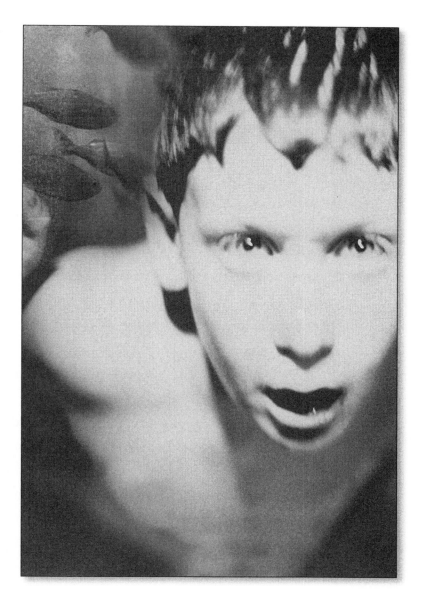

straight back to the villa, if you like." She walked away, that bare
arm, now slightly reddened from yesterday's sun, swinging.
And he almost ran after her again, feeling it unbearable that
she should go by herself, but he did not.

She was thinking, Of course he's old enough to be safe
without me. Have I been keeping him too close? He mustn't
feel he ought to be with me. I must be careful.

He was an only child, eleven years old. She was a widow.
She was determined to be neither possessive nor lacking in
devotion. She went worrying off to her beach.

**INTERPRET**

Pause at line 38. What kind
of relationship do you think
Jerry and his mother have?

RE-READING

Re-read lines 39–54.
Underline details that hint
at possible danger for Jerry.

INFER

Pause at line 68. Why do you
think Jerry wants to be with
the other boys so badly?

_____

_____

_____

_____

_____

_____

_____

_____

_____

_____

_____

_____

_____

_____

_____

_____

VOCABULARY

**supplication** (sup′lə·kā′shən)
*n.:* humble appeal or request.

40 As for Jerry, once he saw that his mother had gained her beach, he began the steep descent to the bay. From where he was, high up among red-brown rocks, it was a scoop of moving bluish green fringed with white. As he went lower, he saw that it spread among small promontories and inlets of rough, sharp rock, and the crisping, lapping surface showed stains of purple and darker blue. Finally, as he ran sliding and scraping down the last few yards, he saw an edge of white surf and the shallow, luminous movement of water over white sand and, beyond that, a solid, heavy blue.

He ran straight into the water and began swimming. 50 He was a good swimmer. He went out fast over the gleaming sand, over a middle region where rocks lay like discolored monsters under the surface, and then he was in the real sea— a warm sea where irregular cold currents from the deep water shocked his limbs.

When he was so far out that he could look back not only on the little bay but past the promontory that was between it and the big beach, he floated on the buoyant surface and looked for his mother. There she was, a speck of yellow under an umbrella that looked like a slice of orange peel. He swam back to shore, 60 relieved at being sure she was there, but all at once very lonely.

On the edge of a small cape that marked the side of the bay away from the promontory was a loose scatter of rocks. Above them, some boys were stripping off their clothes. They came running, naked, down to the rocks. The English boy swam toward them but kept his distance at a stone's throw. They were of that coast; all of them were burned smooth dark brown and speaking a language he did not understand. To be with them, of them, was a craving that filled his whole body. He swam a little closer; they turned and watched him with narrowed, alert dark 70 eyes. Then one smiled and waved. It was enough. In a minute, he had swum in and was on the rocks beside them, smiling with a desperate, nervous **supplication.** They shouted cheerful greetings at him; and then, as he preserved his nervous, uncomprehending smile, they understood that he was a foreigner strayed from his own beach, and they proceeded to forget him. But he was happy. He was with them.

They began diving again and again from a high point into a well of blue sea between rough, pointed rocks. After they had dived and come up, they swam around, hauled themselves up,

80 and waited their turn to dive again. They were big boys—men, to Jerry. He dived, and they watched him; and when he swam around to take his place, they made way for him. He felt he was accepted and he dived again, carefully, proud of himself.

Soon the biggest of the boys poised himself, shot down into the water, and did not come up. The others stood about, watching. Jerry, after waiting for the sleek brown head to appear, let out a yell of warning; they looked at him idly and turned their eyes back toward the water. After a long time, the boy came up on the other side of a big dark rock, letting the air out of his

90 lungs in a sputtering gasp and a shout of triumph. Immediately the rest of them dived in. One moment, the morning seemed full of chattering boys; the next, the air and the surface of the water were empty. But through the heavy blue, dark shapes could be seen moving and groping.

Jerry dived, shot past the school of underwater swimmers, saw a black wall of rock looming at him, touched it, and bobbed up at once to the surface, where the wall was a low barrier he could see across. There was no one visible; under him, in the water, the dim shapes of the swimmers had disappeared. Then

100 one and then another of the boys came up on the far side of the barrier of rock, and he understood that they had swum through some gap or hole in it. He plunged down again. He could see nothing through the stinging salt water but the blank rock. When he came up, the boys were all on the diving rock, preparing to attempt the feat again. And now, in a panic of failure, he yelled up, in English, "Look at me! Look!" and he began splashing and kicking in the water like a foolish dog.

INTERPRET

Pause at line 83. Why does Jerry feel proud of himself?

_____

_____

_____

_____

_____

_____

_____

_____

_____

_____

_____

_____

_____

_____

_____

_____

_____

_____

RE-READING

Re-read lines 84–107. Underline details that explain what the big boys are doing.

**COMPARE & CONTRAST**

Pause at line 115. How do Jerry's efforts to gain the attention of the big boys differ from his behavior when he won their approval?

_____

_____

_____

_____

_____

_____

_____

**IDENTIFY CAUSE & EFFECT**

Why is Jerry counting (lines 120–130)?

_____

_____

_____

_____

_____

_____

_____

**IDENTIFY CAUSE & EFFECT**

Why is Jerry crying (lines 131–136)? Underline the cause.

They looked down gravely, frowning. He knew the frown. At moments of failure, when he clowned to claim his mother's attention, it was with just this grave, embarrassed inspection that she rewarded him. Through his hot shame, feeling the pleading grin on his face like a scar that he could never remove, he looked up at the group of big brown boys on the rock and shouted, _"Bonjour! Merci! Au revoir! Monsieur, monsieur!"_[2] while he hooked his fingers round his ears and waggled them.

Water surged into his mouth; he choked, sank, came up. The rock, lately weighted with boys, seemed to rear up out of the water as their weight was removed. They were flying down past him now, into the water; the air was full of falling bodies. Then the rock was empty in the hot sunlight. He counted one, two, three . . .

At fifty, he was terrified. They must all be drowning beneath him, in the watery caves of the rock! At a hundred, he stared around him at the empty hillside, wondering if he should yell for help. He counted faster, faster, to hurry them up, to bring them to the surface quickly, to drown them quickly—anything rather than the terror of counting on and on into the blue emptiness of the morning. And then, at a hundred and sixty, the water beyond the rock was full of boys blowing like brown whales. They swam back to the shore without a look at him.

He climbed back to the diving rock and sat down, feeling the hot roughness of it under his thighs. The boys were gathering up their bits of clothing and running off along the shore to another promontory. They were leaving to get away from him. He cried openly, fists in his eyes. There was no one to see him, and he cried himself out.

It seemed to him that a long time had passed, and he swam out to where he could see his mother. Yes, she was still there, a yellow spot under an orange umbrella. He swam back to the big rock, climbed up, and dived into the blue pool among the

---

2. _**Bonjour! Merci! Au revoir! Monsieur, monsieur!:**_ French for "Hello! Thank you! Goodbye! Mister, mister!"—probably the only French words Jerry knows.

fanged and angry boulders. Down he went, until he touched the wall of rock again. But the salt was so painful in his eyes that he could not see.

He came to the surface, swam to shore, and went back to the villa to wait for his mother. Soon she walked slowly up the path, swinging her striped bag, the flushed, naked arm dangling beside her. "I want some swimming goggles," he panted, **defiant** and beseeching.

150 She gave him a patient, **inquisitive** look as she said casually, "Well, of course, darling."

But now, now, now! He must have them this minute, and no other time. He nagged and pestered until she went with him to a shop. As soon as she had bought the goggles, he grabbed them from her hand as if she were going to claim them for herself, and was off, running down the steep path to the bay.

Jerry swam out to the big barrier rock, adjusted the goggles, and dived. The impact of the water broke the rubber-enclosed vacuum, and the goggles came loose. He understood that he must swim down to the base of the rock from the surface of the 160 water. He fixed the goggles tight and firm, filled his lungs, and floated, face down, on the water. Now he could see. It was as if he had eyes of a different kind—fish eyes that showed everything clear and delicate and wavering in the bright water.

Under him, six or seven feet down, was a floor of perfectly clean, shining white sand, rippled firm and hard by the tides. Two grayish shapes steered there, like long, rounded pieces of wood or slate. They were fish. He saw them nose toward each other, poise motionless, make a dart forward, swerve off, and come around again. It was like a water dance. A few inches 170 above them the water sparkled as if sequins were dropping through it. Fish again—myriads of **minute** fish, the length of his fingernail—were drifting through the water, and in a moment he could feel the innumerable tiny touches of them against his limbs. It was like swimming in flaked silver. The great rock the big boys had swum through rose sheer out of the

**IDENTIFY CAUSE & EFFECT**

Pause at line 148. Circle the detail that explains why Jerry wants his mother to buy him goggles.

**VOCABULARY**

**defiant** (dē·fī′ənt) adj.: challenging authority.

**inquisitive** (in·kwiz′ə·tiv) adj.: questioning; curious.

**minute** (mī·nōōt′) adj.: small; tiny.

What other meaning does *minute* have? How is it pronounced when it is used in that sense?

_____

_____

_____

_____

_____

_____

_____

_____

**RE-READING**

Re-read lines 164–177. Underline the **imagery** that helps you visualize the underwater scene.

**INFER**

Pause at line 183. Why was Jerry so anxious to find the hole in the rock?

white sand—black, tufted lightly with greenish weed. He could see no gap in it. He swam down to its base.

Again and again he rose, took a big chestful of air, and went down. Again and again he groped over the surface of the 180 rock, feeling it, almost hugging it in the desperate need to find the entrance. And then, once, while he was clinging to the black wall, his knees came up and he shot his feet out forward and they met no obstacle. He had found the hole.

He gained the surface, clambered about the stones that littered the barrier rock until he found a big one, and with this in his arms, let himself down over the side of the rock. He dropped, with the weight, straight to the sandy floor. Clinging tight to the anchor of stone, he lay on his side and looked in

under the dark shelf at the place where his feet had gone. He
could see the hole. It was an irregular, dark gap; but he could
not see deep into it. He let go of his anchor, clung with his
hands to the edges of the hole, and tried to push himself in.

He got his head in, found his shoulders jammed, moved
them in sidewise, and was inside as far as his wrist. He could
see nothing ahead. Something soft and clammy touched his
mouth; he saw a dark frond[3] moving against the grayish rock,
and panic filled him. He thought of octopuses, of clinging
weed. He pushed himself out backward and caught a glimpse,
as he retreated, of a harmless tentacle of seaweed drifting in
the mouth of the tunnel. But it was enough. He reached the
sunlight, swam to shore, and lay on the diving rock. He looked
down into the blue well of water. He knew he must find his way
through that cave, or hole, or tunnel, and out the other side.

First, he thought, he must learn to control his breathing.
He let himself down into the water with another big stone in
his arms, so that he could lie effortlessly on the bottom of the
sea. He counted. One, two, three. He counted steadily. He could
hear the movement of blood in his chest. Fifty-one, fifty-two. . . .
His chest was hurting. He let go of the rock and went up into
the air. He saw that the sun was low. He rushed to the villa and
found his mother at her supper. She said only, "Did you enjoy
yourself?" and he said, "Yes."

All night the boy dreamed of the water-filled cave in the
rock, and as soon as breakfast was over, he went to the bay.

That night, his nose bled badly. For hours he had been
underwater, learning to hold his breath, and now he felt weak
and dizzy. His mother said, "I shouldn't overdo things, darling,
if I were you."

That day and the next, Jerry exercised his lungs as if everything, the whole of his life, all that he would become, depended
upon it. Again his nose bled at night, and his mother insisted on
his coming with her the next day. It was a torment to him to

3. **frond** (fränd) *n.:* large leaf or leaflike part of seaweed.

CLARIFY

What is Jerry doing in lines
184–192?

IDENTIFY

In lines 200–203, we learn
about Jerry's ultimate goal.
Find it and underline it.

INFER

Why do you think Jerry
doesn't reveal his plans to
his mother (lines 210–212)?

_____

_____

_____

_____

**incredulous** (in·krej′oo·ləs) *adj.:* disbelieving; skeptical.

Pause at line 244. Why do you think swimming through the tunnel is "necessary" for Jerry?

_____

_____

_____

_____

_____

Pause at line 257. What decision must Jerry make?

_____

_____

_____

_____

waste a day of his careful self-training, but he stayed with her on that other beach, which now seemed a place for small children, a place where his mother might lie safe in the sun. It was not his beach.

He did not ask for permission, on the following day, to go to his beach. He went, before his mother could consider the complicated rights and wrongs of the matter. A day's rest, he
230 discovered, had improved his count by ten. The big boys had made the passage while he counted a hundred and sixty. He had been counting fast, in his fright. Probably now, if he tried, he could get through that long tunnel, but he was not going to try yet. A curious, most unchildlike persistence, a controlled impatience, made him wait. In the meantime, he lay underwater on the white sand, littered now by stones he had brought down from the upper air, and studied the entrance to the tunnel. He knew every jut and corner of it, as far as it was possible to see. It was as if he already felt its sharpness about his shoulders.

240 He sat by the clock in the villa, when his mother was not near, and checked his time. He was **incredulous** and then proud to find he could hold his breath without strain for two minutes. The words "two minutes," authorized by the clock, brought close the adventure that was so necessary to him.

In another four days, his mother said casually one morning, they must go home. On the day before they left, he would do it. He would do it if it killed him, he said defiantly to himself. But two days before they were to leave—a day of triumph when he increased his count by fifteen—his nose bled so badly that he
250 turned dizzy and had to lie limply over the big rock like a bit of seaweed, watching the thick red blood flow onto the rock and trickle slowly down to the sea. He was frightened. Supposing he turned dizzy in the tunnel? Supposing he died there, trapped? Supposing—his head went around, in the hot sun, and he almost gave up. He thought he would return to the house and lie down, and next summer, perhaps, when he had another year's growth in him—then he would go through the hole.

But even after he had made the decision, or thought he had, he found himself sitting up on the rock and looking down into 260 the water; and he knew that now, this moment, when his nose had only just stopped bleeding, when his head was still sore and throbbing—this was the moment when he would try. If he did not do it now, he never would. He was trembling with fear that he would not go; and he was trembling with horror at the long, long tunnel under the rock, under the sea. Even in the open sunlight, the barrier rock seemed very wide and very heavy; tons of rock pressed down on where he would go. If he died there, he would lie until one day—perhaps not before next year—those big boys would swim into it and find it blocked.

270 He put on his goggles, fitted them tight, tested the vacuum. His hands were shaking. Then he chose the biggest stone he could carry and slipped over the edge of the rock until half of him was in the cool enclosing water and half in the hot sun. He looked up once at the empty sky, filled his lungs once, twice, and then sank fast to the bottom with the stone. He let it go and began to count. He took the edges of the hole in his hands and drew himself into it, wriggling his shoulders in sidewise as he remembered he must, kicking himself along with his feet.

Soon he was clear inside. He was in a small rock-bound 280 hole filled with yellowish-gray water. The water was pushing him up against the roof. The roof was sharp and pained his back. He pulled himself along with his hands—fast, fast—and used his legs as levers. His head knocked against something; a sharp pain dizzied him. Fifty, fifty-one, fifty-two . . . He was without light, and the water seemed to press upon him with the weight of rock. Seventy-one, seventy-two . . . There was no strain on his lungs. He felt like an inflated balloon, his lungs were so light and easy, but his head was pulsing.

He was being continually pressed against the sharp roof, 290 which felt slimy as well as sharp. Again he thought of octopuses, and wondered if the tunnel might be filled with weed that could tangle him. He gave himself a panicky, convulsive kick forward,

RE-READING

Re-read lines 258–269, and underline the passages that describe Jerry's **inner conflict**.

IDENTIFY

At line 270, Jerry has solved his inner conflict by making a decision. Jerry now faces an **external conflict**. What, now, poses a challenge to Jerry?

_____

_____

_____

_____

_____

_____

_____

FLUENCY

Read the boxed passage aloud two times. Focus on conveying meaning the first time you read. On your second reading, use the tone of your voice and your rate of delivery to bring the scene to life.

IDENTIFY

Re-read lines 279–304. The big boys made it through the tunnel in a count of one hundred and sixty. Underline places where the writer uses Jerry's counting to build **suspense**.

**INFER**

Pause at line 308. Why might Jerry be stuck counting past one hundred and fifteen?

_____

_____

_____

_____

_____

_____

_____

_____

_____

_____

_____

_____

_____

_____

_____

_____

**RE-READING**

Re-read lines 309–318. Circle details that describe what's happening to Jerry.

**IDENTIFY CAUSE & EFFECT**

In lines 319–326, underline the effects of Jerry's swim through the tunnel.

ducked his head, and swam. His feet and hands moved freely, as if in open water. The hole must have widened out. He thought he must be swimming fast, and he was frightened of banging his head if the tunnel narrowed.

300 A hundred, a hundred and one . . . The water paled. Victory filled him. His lungs were beginning to hurt. A few more strokes and he would be out. He was counting wildly; he said a hundred and fifteen and then, a long time later, a hundred and fifteen again. The water was a clear jewel-green all around him. Then he saw, above his head, a crack running up through the rock. Sunlight was falling through it, showing the clean, dark rock of the tunnel, a single mussel[4] shell, and darkness ahead.

He was at the end of what he could do. He looked up at the crack as if it were filled with air and not water, as if he could put his mouth to it to draw in air. A hundred and fifteen, he heard himself say inside his head—but he had said that long ago. He must go on into the blackness ahead, or he would drown. His

310 head was swelling, his lungs cracking. A hundred and fifteen, a hundred and fifteen, pounded through his head, and he feebly clutched at rocks in the dark, pulling himself forward, leaving the brief space of sunlit water behind. He felt he was dying. He was no longer quite conscious. He struggled on in the darkness between lapses into unconsciousness. An immense, swelling pain filled his head, and then the darkness cracked with an explosion of green light. His hands, groping forward, met nothing; and his feet, kicking back, propelled him out into the open sea.

He drifted to the surface, his face turned up to the air. He

320 was gasping like a fish. He felt he would sink now and drown; he could not swim the few feet back to the rock. Then he was clutching it and pulling himself up onto it. He lay face down, gasping. He could see nothing but a red-veined, clotted dark. His eyes must have burst, he thought; they were full of blood.

---

4. **mussel** _n._: shellfish, similar to a clam or an oyster, that attaches itself to rocks.

He tore off his goggles and a gout[5] of blood went into the sea. His nose was bleeding, and the blood had filled the goggles.

He scooped up handfuls of water from the cool, salty sea, to splash on his face, and did not know whether it was blood or salt water he tasted. After a time, his heart quieted, his eyes cleared, and he sat up. He could see the local boys diving and playing half a mile away. He did not want them. He wanted nothing but to get back home and lie down.

In a short while, Jerry swam to shore and climbed slowly up the path to the villa. He flung himself on his bed and slept, waking at the sound of feet on the path outside. His mother was coming back. He rushed to the bathroom, thinking she must not see his face with bloodstains, or tearstains, on it. He came out of the bathroom and met her as she walked into the villa, smiling, her eyes lighting up.

"Have a nice morning?" she asked, laying her hand on his warm brown shoulder a moment.

"Oh, yes, thank you," he said.

"You look a bit pale." And then, sharp and anxious, "How did you bang your head?"

"Oh, just banged it," he told her.

She looked at him closely. He was strained; his eyes were glazed-looking. She was worried. And then she said to herself, Oh, don't fuss! Nothing can happen. He can swim like a fish.

They sat down to lunch together.

"Mummy," he said, "I can stay underwater for two minutes—three minutes, at least." It came bursting out of him.

"Can you, darling?" she said. "Well, I shouldn't overdo it. I don't think you ought to swim anymore today."

She was ready for a battle of wills, but he gave in at once. It was no longer of the least importance to go to the bay.

INFER

Pause at line 332. Why doesn't Jerry care about the local boys anymore?

_____

_____

_____

_____

INFER

Pause at line 351. Why might Jerry have decided to share this information with his mother?

_____

_____

_____

_____

_____

INTERPRET

Re-read the story's final paragraph. In your own words, explain why Jerry no longer wants to go to the bay.

_____

_____

_____

_____

_____

_____

330

340

350

5. **gout** (gout) *n.:* large glob.

# Through the Tunnel

**Symbol Chart**  "Through the Tunnel" contains a number of **symbols**—people, places, and things that stand for themselves but also for something else. The chart below lists some passages from the story. In the right-hand column, identify the symbol in each, and write what you think it means. Then, use the lines at the bottom to write your own interpretation of the story's symbolic meaning.

| Passage from Story | Symbol/Meaning |
|---|---|
| "It was a torment to him to waste a day of his careful self-training, but he stayed with her on that other beach, which now seemed a place for small children, a place where his mother might lie safe in the sun." (lines 222–225) | |
| "And yet, as he ran, he looked back over his shoulder at the wild bay; and all morning, as he played on the safe beach, he was thinking of it." (lines 16–18) | |
| "After they had dived and come up, they swam around, hauled themselves up, and waited their turn to dive again. They were big boys—men, to Jerry." (lines 78–81) | |
| "He could see the hole. It was an irregular, dark gap; but he could not see deep into it. . . . He knew he must find his way through that cave, or hole, or tunnel, and out the other side." (lines 189–191, 202–203) | |

**Symbolic Meaning of the Story**

_____

_____

_____

# Standards Review

 **Through the Tunnel**

Complete the sample test item below. The box at the right explains why three of these choices are not correct.

| Sample Test Item | Explanation of the Correct Answer |
|---|---|
| Who or what is Jerry in **conflict** with?<br><br>**A** a shark<br>**B** the big boys<br>**C** the tunnel<br>**D** the beach patrol | The correct answer is C.<br><br>Jerry doesn't meet a shark (*A*); Jerry wants to do what the big boys do, but he does not do battle with them (*B*); there is no beach patrol in the story (*D*). |

**DIRECTIONS:** Circle the letter of each correct answer.

**1.** Which word *best* describes Jerry's journey through the tunnel?

  **A** interesting

  **B** relaxing

  **C** boring

  **D** frightening

**2.** In their relationship with each other, Jerry and his mother are both—

  **F** considerate

  **G** inconsiderate

  **H** unconcerned

  **J** overconcerned

**3.** The sharp rocks and seaweed in the tunnel may **symbolize**—

  **A** the trials of life

  **B** yucky, slimy stuff

  **C** his mother's hold on Jerry

  **D** the dislike of the older boys

**4.** Which sentence best expresses the **symbolic meaning** of the story?

  **F** Children have to rebel against their parents to grow up.

  **G** Mothers and sons can never understand each other.

  **H** The journey to adulthood can be hazardous and frightening.

  **J** Life is nasty, brutish, and short.

**Reading Standard 3.7** Recognize and understand the significance of various literary devices, including figurative language, imagery, allegory, and symbolism, and explain their appeal.

# Standards Review

**TestPractice  Through the Tunnel**

## Word Analogies

**DIRECTIONS:** Circle the letter of the best completion of each word analogy.

**Reading Standard 1.1**
Identify and use the literal and figurative meanings of words and understand word derivations.

1. DEFIANT : RESPECTFUL ::
   - **A** mean : kind
   - **B** able : capable
   - **C** angry : furious
   - **D** pretty : sunset

2. INQUISITIVE : CURIOUS ::
   - **F** hungry : satisfied
   - **G** fast : running
   - **H** happy : joyous
   - **J** impulsive : thoughtful

3. CONTRITION : REMORSE ::
   - **A** petunia : flower
   - **B** saxophone : band
   - **C** sorrow : sadness
   - **D** worry : wisdom

4. INCREDULOUS : SKEPTICAL ::
   - **F** alert : sleepy
   - **G** funny : hilarious
   - **H** monstrous : elegant
   - **J** eating : drinking

## Vocabulary in Context

**DIRECTIONS:** Complete the paragraph below by writing a word from the word box in the correct numbered blank.

**Word Box**

- contrition
- supplication
- defiant
- inquisitive
- minute
- incredulous

Despite weeks of begging and (1) _____, Jesse couldn't get permission to use the canoe alone. But he was feeling (2) _____, so he got a paddle and climbed in anyway. Jesse was (3) _____ and wanted to explore the island in the middle of the lake. Jesse was almost there, when he leaned over to watch millions of tiny, (4) _____ fish. Suddenly, he was (5) _____. He was filled with disbelief because he found himself in the water. He had to be rescued by his parents. After that, Jesse felt (6) _____ for disobeying the rules.

**Before You Go On . . .**
Check your Standards Mastery at the back of this book.

# Animal Farm *based on the novel* by George Orwell

In 1917, revolutionaries in Russia overthrew the emperor, Czar Nicholas II, and established a new Communist government. This government promised that all people would be equal and would share equally in labor and its rewards. In 1945, British writer George Orwell published *Animal Farm* (the novel on which this screenplay is based). In the novel, Orwell expresses his disgust with the way the ideals of Communism were mocked after the dictator Joseph Stalin came to power. In Orwell's story, the characters who set up a supposedly "classless" society are animals; humans play a role in the story, too.

## LITERARY FOCUS: ALLEGORY

An **allegory** is a story in which characters and places stand for abstract qualities: slyness, goodness, humility, hope, meanness, cleverness, and so on. Allegories are intended to be read on two levels: On one level is the literal story, telling us who does what to whom. On another level is the story's symbolic meaning, the issues that the story is really about.

- Writers sometimes clue readers into the vices or virtues the characters represent by giving them names that indicate their traits. As you read *Animal Farm,* decide what the characters' names **symbolize.**
- First, read the story for its basic meaning—and enjoy it! Then, re-read the story and think about its broader allegorical meaning.

## READING SKILLS: IDENTIFYING RELATIONSHIPS

We don't exist in a vacuum. We interact with other people—at home, in school, at work, even on public transportation. Our relationships with people affect our lives profoundly. Most stories are about relationships. Analyzing these relationships—trying to understand a character's behavior and motivations—can help us understand our own relationships in life.

- As you read, look for characters who have control or influence over other characters.
- Take note of alliances—friendships between characters that benefit the people involved.
- Look for characters who dislike each other and the reasons for their feelings.
- Look for characters who take control—who want power.

**Reading Standard 1.3 (Grade 8 Review)** Use word meanings within the appropriate context and show ability to verify those meanings by definition, restatement, example, comparison, or contrast.

**Reading Standard 3.7** Recognize and understand the significance of various literary devices, including figurative language, imagery, allegory, and symbolism, and explain their appeal.

## VOCABULARY DEVELOPMENT

### PREVIEW SELECTION VOCABULARY

Get to know the following words before you begin reading *Animal Farm*.

**dilapidated** (di·lap′i·dā′tid) *adj.:* broken-down; shabby.

> The **dilapidated** farm was littered with broken tractors and rusted tools.

**laborious** (lə·bôr′ē·əs) *adj.:* involving or calling for hard work.

> The animals had a **laborious** life under their demanding owner.

**squalor** (skwäl′ər) *n.:* filth; misery; wretchedness.

> The animals lived in **squalor,** with no comforts.

**compatriots** (kəm·pā′trē·əts) *n.:* people from the same country; fellow workers.

> The animals felt that they were **compatriots** in a new society. They were working together to throw off their oppressors.

**prophesied** (präf′ə·sīd) *v.:* predicted; foretold.

> The perfect state that was **prophesied** for the future did not come about.

**conspicuously** (kən·spik′yoō·əs·lē) *adv.:* obviously; in a manner that attracts attention.

> The other animals stared at the pigs who were **conspicuously** walking on their hind legs.

**tactics** (tak′tiks) *n.:* methods used to gain an end.

> The leader used dishonest **tactics** to win the struggle.

**decree** (di·krē′) *v.:* order.

> One of the first acts of the new government by the animals was to **decree** that all animals are equal.

### CONTEXT CLUES

You can often figure out the meaning of an unfamiliar word from its context—the words surrounding the unfamiliar word. For example, what words in the following passage help you define *sabotaging*?

> My friends, I have learned that the archcriminal Snowball is **sabotaging** this farm and our glorious windmill. He has upset our milk pails. He has trodden our seedbeds. This is the reason for our shortage of food.

The context clues "criminal," "upset our milk pails," and "trodden our seedbeds" help you figure out that *sabotaging* means "deliberately destroying."

Use these tips to help you find context clues:
- Look for a synonym, definition, or restatement. Writers sometimes include definitions of difficult words right in the sentence.
- Look for examples that reveal the meaning of the unfamiliar word.
- Look for antonyms, or words that contrast the unfamiliar word with a word or phrase that you already know.

# ANIMAL FARM

## based on the novel by George Orwell

**CHARACTERS**

- **Mr. Pilkington,** a wealthy farmer
- **Mrs. Pilkington,** his wife
- **Older Pilkington boy,** age 9
- **Younger Pilkington boy,** age 7
- **Farmer Jones,** a drunken lout
- **Dennis,** his field hand
- **Boxer,** a work horse
- **Mollie,** a show horse
- **Snowball,** a nice pig

- **Squealer,** a devious pig
- **Napoleon,**[1] an ambitious pig
- **Old Major,** a wise pig
- **Jessie,** the sheepdog
- **Muriel,** the goat
- **Rat,** a selfish rat
- **Workers and miscellaneous bad guys, chickens, sheep, and so on**
- **Narrator**

*The English countryside. Sometime during the mid-20th century.*

**Narrator.** A carriage rolls briskly past fields and small stands of trees, until it arrives at a rundown, neglected farm. The carriage passes under a **dilapidated** gate, where a faded sign reads MANOR FARM. Inside the carriage, Mr. and Mrs. Pilkington are outfitted in tasteless splendor. Two boys, ages 7 and 9, ride in back. The older boy aims a slingshot at three pigs in a pen. A pig squeals in pain. Mr. Pilkington and the boys laugh.

**Mrs. Pilkington.** Now, boys. Not too much.

10 **Younger Boy.** I want to try it! Let me!

**Mrs. Pilkington.** You really shouldn't do that.

**Pilkington.** Oh, leave the boys alone. They're just having a bit of fun.

**Older Boy.** Yeah, we're only playing, Ma.

---

1. **Napoleon.** Name taken from Napoleon Bonaparte, French military leader and emperor of France from 1804 to 1815. He conquered most of Europe and is considered the first modern dictator.

> **ALLEGORY**
>
> The character list directly describes the personality traits of some of the animals. Circle at least one vice (bad quality) and underline at least one virtue (good quality).

> **VOCABULARY**
>
> **dilapidated** (di·lap′i·dā′tid) *adj.:* broken-down; shabby.

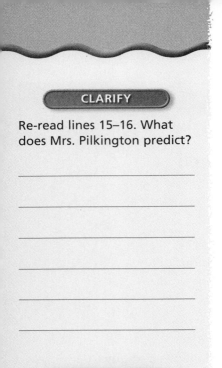

**CLARIFY**

Re-read lines 15–16. What does Mrs. Pilkington predict?

_____

_____

_____

_____

_____

**IDENTIFY RELATIONSHIPS**

Pause at line 30. What is the relationship between Jones and Pilkington?

_____

_____

_____

_____

**INFER**

Re-read lines 34–47. Why do you think Farmer Jones beats Boxer?

_____

_____

_____

_____

_____

**Mrs. Pilkington.** Not very nice play. One day those pigs might play that way with you.

**Pilkington.** What a load of rubbish. Look, there's that fool Jones, drunk as a skunk again.

**Mrs. Pilkington.** Why, Mr. Jones! Whatever have you done to

20     your field?

**Jones** (*He looks up from his plow. He has driven it in zigzags all over the field.*). What's that? Oh! Mr. (*hiccups*) . . . Mrs. Pilkington, yes, well I'm working hard, working hard, you see.

**Pilkington.** Very interesting way of plowing, Jones. Rather . . . experimental?

**Jones.** Mr. Pilkington, sir. About the money I owe you . . . I'm afraid I need a bit more time.

**Pilkington.** Why Mr. Jones, I didn't come to talk about my loan. We just stopped by for a visit, didn't we, missus? Didn't we,

30     boys? (*The boys aim at* JONES's *sheep.*)

**Mrs. Pilkington.** Yes, yes, of course we did, didn't we, boys . . . BOYS!

**Sheep** (*taking a hit*). BAAAAAA!

**Jones.** I'm desperate, Mr. Pilkington. The bank is on to me. I don't know what to do.

**Pilkington.** You can sign your farm over to me. Then your worries will be over.

**Jones.** I can't do that. This place has been in my family for generations.

40     **Pilkington.** Yes. Pity no one ever learned how to farm it. Good day, Jones. And good luck with the bank. Giddap, horse. (*The boys aim at* JONES.)

**Jones.** Mr. Pilkington! Mr. Pilkington, wait—OW! (*The rock strikes home. In a fury,* JONES *turns on* BOXER, *the plow horse.*) This is all your fault! Look what you did to that field, you worthless piece of dog meat! You're going to the glue factory! (*He whips* BOXER *mercilessly.* JESSIE, *a collie, turns to her sheep.*)

**Jessie.** Something must be done. Tell the others! Spread the word! Meeting tonight in the barn.

**50**  **MANOR FARM BARN. THAT EVENING.**

**Narrator.** The farm animals assemble. Three pigs—Napoleon, Snowball, and Squealer—call the meeting to order.

**Snowball.** Animals! Hear me! The wisest of us all has words to say which must now be heard!

**Napoleon.** Animals! Hear me! These words came to Old Major in a vision, and must now be spoken! (*A rustle of straw, and* OLD MAJOR, *a huge and very wrinkled retired show pig, enters.*)

**Old Major.** My friends, I have had a long life, and before I leave this world, it is my duty to pass on to you such as I understand

**60**  of the nature of our lives. Here it is: Animalkind is born to a short, miserable, **laborious** existence . . . then slaughtered with hideous cruelty.

**All Animals.** True, true!

**Old Major.** And who is responsible for our suffering? Man! Man is our enemy. Remove man and the cause of our hunger and overwork is abolished forever. Remove man and the fruits of our labor will be our own. Remove man, and overnight we will become free and equal!

**All Animals.** Free and equal!

**70**  **Boxer.** Hey, Jessie. Does free mean no harnesses?

**Jessie.** I don't know. Sounds too good to be true, if you ask me.

**Rat.** No humans means no **squalor.** How am I supposed to live without squalor?

**Mollie.** If there are no humans, who will brush my mane? Who will braid it with ribbons?

**Muriel.** You shouldn't care about looking pretty for humans.

**Mollie.** But I like looking pretty for humans.

**Muriel.** That's the stupidest thing I ever heard.

**Old Major.** Stop! Please! Fighting with each other is the nature

**80**  of man, and we cannot stoop to his level. After all, we are animals! We must never, ever act like man in any way. No animal can ever live in a house! Or smoke tobacco! Or drink alcohol! Wear clothes! Sleep in a bed! Kill his own kind! Use their filthy money or do

**ALLEGORY**

Pause at line 52, and underline the names of the three leaders of the meeting. What qualities do you think these animals will represent, based on their names?

_____

_____

_____

_____

**PREDICT**

Pause at line 68. Do you think that removing man will make the animals "free and equal"? Why or why not?

_____

_____

_____

**VOCABULARY**

**laborious** (lə·bôr′ē·əs) *adj.:* involving or calling for hard work.

**squalor** (skwäl′ər) *n.:* filth; misery; wretchedness.

**IDENTIFY**

Circle Mollie's concerns in lines 74–75. What vice does Mollie have?

_____

_____

**ALLEGORY**

Re-read Old Major's speech (lines 79–85). What trait do you think he represents?

_____
_____
_____
_____
_____
_____

**VOCABULARY**

**compatriots** (kəm·pā′trē·əts) *n.:* people from the same country; fellow workers.

business with them! Among us animals there must be unity! All animals are friends! All humans are enemies!

**All Animals.** Four legs good! Two legs bad! Four legs good! Two legs bad! (*To* JONES, *the animals' cheering sounds like mad bleatings. He rushes into the barn with his shotgun.*)

**Jones.** Here, what's all that noise? Must be foxes! I'll give 'em

90     what-for! (*He trips, falls. The gun goes off; a bullet ricochets. Panicked, animals and* JONES *race in all directions. The bullet hits* OLD MAJOR. *He collapses and dies. The barn is suddenly quiet.* JONES *stumbles to the door.*) There. That'll teach 'em. Dumb animals. (*He exits. The animals grieve over* OLD MAJOR.)

**Snowball. Compatriots,** Old Major left us with words that can free us from our oppressors. This spot where Old Major has fallen for the cause will be a shrine. No animal can ever tread on it.

**Napoleon.** Friends, we must always remember that Old Major
100 died for every one of us. Now we have a duty to him—and that
duty is, Revolution!

## THE BARN. A FEW WEEKS LATER.

**Narrator.** Jones and his field hand, Dennis, spend a whole day at
the pub instead of doing their chores. As night falls, the animals
are desperately hungry.

**Boxer.** We're all starving. No one's been fed all day.

**Squealer.** Not yesterday, either.

**Jessie.** The sheep are crying. The cows are in pain. They need
to be milked.

110 **Muriel.** Look there! Headlights! That's Jones's truck, all right.

**Mollie.** Good! He'll feed us now! (JONES *parks the truck. He and*
DENNIS *emerge with a full bottle of whiskey.*)

**Jones.** Come on, Dennis. What do you say we watch that football match on the tele?

**Dennis.** Sure, but—what about the animals? They ain't been
fed all day.

**Jones.** Animals? Let 'em rot!

**Narrator.** The flickering blue glow of a TV set can be seen from
the barn. Boxer walks to the grain bin. With one powerful kick,
120 he demolishes the door. The animals tear open sacks, eating their
fill. The hubbub in the barn alerts Jones and Dennis, who fly out
of the house armed with whips and the shotgun.

**Jones.** What are you animals on about, eh? Think you can do
what you please? I'll show you!

**Snowball.** Animals, unite! Remember Old Major!

**Napoleon.** Animals, seize the day! Revolution is at hand!

**Narrator.** Boxer leads the charge with Snowball close behind.
Napoleon and Squealer, fearful in the fray, hide in the hay.
Jones and Dennis are fiercely butted, kicked, and pecked.
130 They run for the truck and escape. Napoleon and Squealer move
to the front; no one realizes they were missing during the action.

**IDENTIFY**

Pause at line 101. What have
the animals decided to do?

_____

_____

_____

**IDENTIFY RELATIONSHIPS**

Pause at line 117. What is the
relationship between Jones
and the animals?

_____

_____

_____

_____

_____

**IDENTIFY CAUSE & EFFECT**

Pause at line 122. What is
the immediate cause of the
animals' revolt?

_____

_____

_____

_____

Pause at line 140. Which animals lead the battle? Who takes credit for the victory?

_____

_____

_____

_____

_____

_____

_____

What does Napoleon's comment "under his breath" (line 138) tell you about his relationship with Squealer?

_____

_____

_____

_____

_____

_____

_____

_____

**Napoleon.** Victory is ours!

**Snowball.** Let's hear it for Boxer, the bravest of us all. An Animal Hero First Class! (*cheers*)

**Boxer.** There was none braver than Snowball!

**Sheep.** Snowball! Snowball! Snowball!

**Napoleon** (*cutting off the sheep*). My friends, we are all heroes. (*Under his breath*) Squealer!

**Squealer** (*starts the chant*). Napoleon! Napoleon! Napoleon!

140    **All Animals.** Napoleon! Napoleon!


**MANOR FARM. THE NEXT DAY.**

**Narrator.** It is Day One of the new regime. Snowball paints the sign above the gate.

**Muriel.** Looks nice. What does it say?

**Snowball.** That is the farm's new name. Since the farm belongs to us now, what words do you think I painted?

**Boxer.** Us Farm?

**Snowball.** No, dear Boxer. Animal Farm.

**Jessie.** Animal Farm! It's perfect.

150    **Muriel.** If you pigs can write, does that mean you can read now, too?

**Snowball.** Yes! We can read, we can write, we can paint signs, we can do anything! We can take care of everything all by ourselves!

**Jessie.** Youch. I could use a little care myself right now.

**Boxer.** Jessie! What's wrong?

**Jessie.** I hate to say it, but I think my time has come.

**Boxer.** No, no, Jessie! You can't die! We've only just begun to live!

**Jessie.** I'm not dying, Boxer, I'm having puppies.

**Boxer.** Puppies? Puppies! Gracious, puppies. Quick! Somebody

160    do something! What do we do?

**Snowball.** Steady now, Boxer. Let's get Jessie into the barn. The harness room is nice and snug.

## THE FARMHOUSE.

**Narrator.** While Jessie gives birth, Napoleon leads the rest of the animals to the farmhouse.

**Napoleon.** My friends, with my leadership, we have driven out humankind just as Old Major **prophesied**! And now, we will inspect the fruits of our victorious battle. Mollie, the door.

**Mollie.** The door? Are you sure it's OK?

170 **Napoleon.** The door, Mollie. (*She kicks the front door off its hinges.*) Animals, follow me. (*Leading a tour of the house*) Animals, pay attention. This is the way humans lived—steeping themselves in luxury while we lived in squalor. Look! A horsehair chair. Animals had to die for humans to sit in comfort. And there! A bed, filled with feathers, plucked from animals. And here, the kitchen, the room of unspeakable butchery, the source of all evil. (*He opens the refrigerator door. The light comes on; they see it is full of meat. Animals run, screaming.*)

## OUTSIDE THE BARN.

180 **Narrator.** It is Day Two of the new regime. Snowball has painted a manifesto[2] on the outside of the barn. Animals gather to look and listen. Napoleon and Squealer are **conspicuously** absent.

> **Snowball.** The principles of Animalism can be summed up in Seven Commandments. One: Whatever goes upon two legs is an enemy. Two: Whatever goes upon four legs or has wings is a friend. Three: No animal shall wear clothes. Four: No animal shall sleep in a bed. Five: No animal shall drink alcohol. Six: No animal may kill another animal. And, most important, Seven: All animals are equal. Here's to animal equality!

190 **All Animals.** Animals are equal! (*meanwhile, on the other side of the barn*)

---

2. **manifesto** (ma′nə·fes′tō) *n.:* a public announcement of plans and intentions. Here the model is the *Communist Manifesto*, a pamphlet written in 1848 by Karl Marx and Friedrich Engels, summarizing the theory of and program for communism.

**VOCABULARY**

**prophesied** (präf′ə·sīd) *v.:* predicted; foretold.

**INFER**

Pause at line 178. Why do the animals run screaming?

_____

_____

_____

_____

_____

_____

_____

_____

_____

_____

_____

**VOCABULARY**

**conspicuously** (kən·spik′yōō·əs·lē) *adv.:* obviously; in a manner that attracts attention.

**FLUENCY**

Read the boxed passage aloud two times. Note that the speech is divided into seven principles. Decide, on your second read, how you will convey these principles.

**INTERPRET**

Pause at line 197. Which of the Seven Commandments of Animalism has Napoleon just broken?

_____

_____

_____

**IDENTIFY RELATIONSHIPS**

What is the relationship between Boxer and Napoleon (lines 201–203)?

_____

_____

_____

_____

_____

**PREDICT**

Pause at line 208. What do you think Napoleon wants Jessie's puppies for?

_____

_____

_____

_____

_____

_____

_____

**Napoleon.** Repeat after me. Napoleon is my leader.

**Squealer.** Napoleon is my leader.

**Napoleon.** I swear to serve Napoleon before all others.

**Squealer.** I swear to serve Napoleon before all others.

**Napoleon.** Rise up and take your new position as Captain of the Animal Guard![3]

**TWO MONTHS LATER.**

**Narrator.** The animals toil in the fields, pulling stones, harvest-
200   ing crops, fighting exhaustion as Napoleon supervises.

**Napoleon.** Only eleven bales of hay today. We need more effort!

**Boxer** (_straining with his load_). I will work harder for Napoleon and the Revolution.

**Napoleon** (_quietly_). Squealer, are those puppies weaned yet?

**Squealer.** Nearly sir, but not quite.

**Napoleon.** Bother. I'm tired of waiting. We've got milk enough to feed them. Take them away from Jessie today. Give her some kind of explanation, I don't care what. I want those puppies.

**THE LOCAL PUB.**

210   **Narrator.** Pilkington finds Jones snoring, head down on a table.

**Pilkington.** I knew I'd find you with your neck in a bottle. (_He bangs his fist on the table._ JONES _wakes with a start._)

**Jones.** Help! They're after me! They're pecking me eyes out!

**Pilkington.** Finished in a fortnight, you said. Well, guess what, Mr. Jones. It's two months and the animals are still running your farm. We have to do something! But first—we need to know what goes on over there.

**Jones.** Send in a spy, then. Somebody what can eavesdrop on 'em.

**Pilkington.** Hmmm . . . perhaps you aren't quite as stupid as
220   you look, Jones.

---

3. **Animal Guard:** Term adapted from Red Guard, armed workers who took part in the Russian Revolution of 1917.

### ANIMAL FARM.

**Narrator.** Jessie races about the barnyard until she finds Napoleon and Squealer.

**Jessie.** Napoleon, please! I beg you.

**Napoleon.** I've told you, Jessie. You cannot see your puppies yet.

**Jessie.** But why?

**Squealer.** You should be grateful for the special education we are giving them. Surely you don't want to disadvantage your own puppies.

230 **Jessie.** No, but—

**Napoleon.** Good! Well, a leader's work is never done. We must be off, Squealer. (*They exit,* BOXER *comes in bone tired after another day of hard labor.*)

**Boxer.** Jessie! What's wrong?

**Jessie.** Napoleon won't let me see my puppies.

**Boxer.** Where are the puppies?

**Jessie.** I don't know . . . Boxer, the pigs always tell us how to think . . . what to do . . .

**Boxer.** We must have leaders, Jessie.

240 **Jessie.** But what if they are wrong?

**Boxer.** Napoleon is never wrong, Jessie. You know that.


### ANIMAL FARM BARN.

**Narrator.** Snowball has carefully studied books on agriculture and architecture, and has drawn up plans to build a windmill. Napoleon calls a meeting on the matter.

**Napoleon.** My friends, surely you can see that building a windmill is a waste of time and labor.

**All Animals.** That's right!

**Snowball.** It's not a waste of time! Once it is built, the windmill

250 will ease our labor!

**All Animals.** That's right!

ANALYZE

In lines 235–240, Jessie voices misgivings about the pigs. What is her concern?

_____

_____

_____

_____

_____

_____

_____

_____

_____

COMPARE & CONTRAST

In lines 249–254, Snowball and Napoleon disagree about what needs to be done. What does each want to do?

_____

_____

_____

_____

_____

_____

_____

_____

**INTERPRET**

Pause at line 267. Why does Napoleon drive Snowball away and label him a traitor?

_____

_____

_____

_____

**IDENTIFY RELATIONSHIPS**

Pause at line 272. What is the relationship of the Animal Guard to Napoleon and to the other animals?

_____

_____

_____

_____

_____

**ANALYZE**

What do you learn about Squealer in his defense of Napoleon (lines 273–277)?

_____

_____

_____

_____

**VOCABULARY**

**tactics** (tak'tiks) _n.:_ methods used to gain an end.

**Napoleon.** All of our efforts must be directed at feeding ourselves, arming ourselves, securing our borders, and defending animalism!

**All Animals.** That's right!

**Snowball.** Animals, think of the benefits. So much labor will be saved that we may only need to work three days a week. Now, all those in favor . . .

**All Animals.** AYE.

260 **Napoleon** (_with an evil look at_ SNOWBALL). Fine. Squealer . . . send in the Animal Guard. (_The barking of dogs is heard. A motley group of mongrels fierce as wolves bound in._)

**Jessie.** Puppies? Are these my little ones? (_The dogs howl and snap their jaws, ready for action._)

**Napoleon.** Animal Guard, attack! Get Snowball. (SNOWBALL _runs for the back exit. The dogs howl and run after him._) Snowball is a traitor! He has been in league with Jones!

**Boxer.** No! It can't be! Snowball was a brave fighter in the Revolution!

270 **Napoleon.** My friends, bravery is not enough. Loyalty is more important. Snowball is a traitor and a criminal. And what I say is always true. Is that understood?

**Squealer.** You see how clever Napoleon is! Of course he's not against the windmill. In fact, the windmill was his idea! Snowball stole it! So Napoleon opposed the windmill just to show Snowball for the traitor he is! **Tactics,** friends. That's why Napoleon is a great leader! Listen!

**Napoleon.** Animals. We must now move to the next stage of our Revolution. There will be no more meetings to waste everyone's

280 time. From now on, a special committee of pigs will decide on all aspects of running this farm. (_Uproar from the animals. The_ ANIMAL GUARD _growls fiercely. The animals fall silent._) Now . . . let me tell you about my plan for the windmill . . .

## PILKINGTON'S HOUSE.

**Narrator.** Pilkington has "bugged" Animal Farm, and now listens to radio transmissions from the farmhouse and barn. He discovers that the pigs have learned to read and write. Mr. and Mrs. Pilkington, with Jones at their side, now listen to Napoleon's last speech.

290 **Pilkington.** Windmill, eh. Well, if these animals can talk and think, they can do business.

**Jones.** You can't do business with . . . with animals!

**Pilkington.** Why not? I did business with you.

**Mrs. Pilkington.** Isn't it immoral, dear?

**Pilkington.** It's business.

**Jones.** It's my farm!

**Pilkington.** Not anymore, it's not.

**ALLEGORY**

Re-read lines 290–297. What group of people and what trait does Pilkington represent?

Notes

**INTERPRET**

Pause at line 307. What do Boxer's actions tell you about his **character**?

_____

_____

_____

_____

_____

**INTERPRET**

Pause at line 313. What do Squealer's and Napoleon's actions reveal about them?

_____

_____

_____

_____

_____

_____

_____

**IDENTIFY**

What two Animal Commandments is Napoleon violating now (lines 318–328)?

_____

_____

_____

_____

_____

### ANIMAL FARM. WEEKS LATER.

**Narrator.** The animals work, day in, day out, on the windmill,

300 always supervised by Napoleon with the ferocious Animal Guard at his side. One night, Jessie can't sleep. She leaves the barnyard to gaze at the windmill. Boxer is on his own, still pulling heavy timbers up the hill.

**Jessie.** Boxer, you will overstrain yourself.

**Boxer.** I must work harder for Napoleon and the Revolution.

**Jessie.** Boxer, please! Come to the barn and rest. (*But* BOXER *plods on. Just then,* JESSIE *sees a light come on in the farmhouse. Curious, she peeks through a window.* NAPOLEON *and* SQUEALER *sit in chairs.* SQUEALER *reads with a pair of broken glasses.*

310 NAPOLEON *watches television. Suddenly, the* GUARD *surrounds* JESSIE, *barking.*) Puppies! Stop that right now! I'm your mother! (SQUEALER *hears the commotion and races out.*)

**Squealer.** Jessie! This area is out of bounds! Go back to the barn!

### THE FARMHOUSE. LATER THAT NIGHT.

**Narrator.** A truck drives quietly into the barnyard. Pilkington gets out and enters the farmhouse. There, a secret meeting takes place between Pilkington, Napoleon, and Squealer.

**Napoleon.** I need money to finish the windmill.

**Pilkington.** Well, I'm sure our new arrangement will prove very

320 profitable, my dear boy.

**Napoleon.** Dear boy? (*He turns to* SQUEALER *and laughs.*) Dear boy!

**Squealer.** Dear boy! Ha! Dear boy!

**Pilkington.** You know you can trust me, don't you? (*He produces a cigar;* NAPOLEON *sniffs the tobacco.*) Jones is your enemy. I am your friend. I even brought you a little present. (*He produces a bottle of whiskey;* NAPOLEON *grins.*) A little token of my gratitude.

**Napoleon.** Why, thank you, dear boy. (*They laugh.*)

**Pilkington.** Now—to business. There's a shortage of hay in the
market at the moment. It's fetching a very good price. If I could
have a wagonload or two, say . . . tomorrow?

**ANIMAL FARM BARN.**

**Narrator.** The next morning, in the barn, Jessie secretly meets
with other animals.

**Jessie.** Listen! There is something I must tell you all. It's the pigs.
They're living in the farmhouse. They're wearing clothes. And
they're sleeping in the beds!

**All Animals.** No!

**Muriel.** But the commandment says no animal shall sleep in a—
oh! (SQUEALER *enters, smiling.*)

**Squealer.** My friends, I'm so glad that you are all here so that I
may explain. As you know, we the pigs are the brains of the
farm. You don't want your glorious leaders to live in a sty, do
you? Of course not. You don't want your glorious leaders to
sleep on a cold floor, do you? Of course not.

**Jessie.** But the commandment, Squealer! You can't ignore the
commandment.

**Squealer.** What commandment? There never was any commandment against beds. Go on. Read it. (*The animals look up at the
wall. The commandment has been altered; the paint is still wet.*)

**Jessie.** "No animal shall sleep in a bed . . . with sheets."

**Squealer.** You see! It's a commandment against sheets, not beds.
And we certainly don't sleep in sheets. Not at all.

**Boxer.** There, you see, Jessie. Napoleon is always right.

**Squealer.** Exactly. Your glorious leader is working ever harder to
further the Revolution. Napoleon! Napoleon!

**All Animals.** Napoleon! Napoleon! (NAPOLEON *appears, with
the* GUARD.)

**Napoleon.** Friends! Today marks the beginning of a new direction
for us. Animal Farm cannot exist in isolation. To improve our

330

340

350

360

Notes

_____
_____
_____
_____
_____
_____
_____
_____
_____
_____
_____
_____

**IDENTIFY**

Pause at line 351. How
has Squealer altered the
commandment against
sleeping in beds?

_____
_____
_____
_____
_____
_____
_____

**INTERPRET**

Re-read Boxer's statements in lines 364–365, and think about his past behavior. What vice might you say Boxer stands for?

_____

_____

_____

_____

_____

**COMPARE & CONTRAST**

Re-read lines 379–387. How are Dennis's and Pilkington's attitudes different?

_____

_____

_____

_____

_____

_____

_____

_____

_____

_____

_____

_____

quality of life, to feed ourselves, and to complete our glorious windmill, we need to do business with the outside world.

**Muriel.** Old Major said we must never do business!

**Boxer.** Shh! We must listen to Napoleon. Napoleon never makes mistakes.

**Napoleon.** That is correct. And, as your leader, I am willing to shoulder the heavy burden of business myself, for the good of the Revolution. Long live Animal Farm!

**All Animals.** Long live Animal Farm! (PILKINGTON *appears. The*
370     *animals fall immediately into stunned silence.*)

**Pilkington.** Good afternoon . . . animals.


**THE LOCAL PUB.**

**Narrator.** Pilkington is entertaining farmers and field hands in the local pub. Dennis, Jones's former field hand, listens grimly as the others laugh.

**Pilkington.** Yesterday, I sold the animals a bunch of rusty equipment I've been trying to get rid of. They couldn't wait to buy it. Now they don't know what to do with it.

**Dennis.** Some of them animals is starving, Mr. Pilkington.

380     **Pilkington.** They look well enough to me.

**Dennis.** Maybe you can't see straight for all the money you've been making. Them dirty rotten pigs is selling you all the food while the other animals starve.

**Pilkington.** If the pigs like to do business with me, why should I refuse? Animal Farm is a thousand times more successful now than Jones's farm ever was. It's not my fault if they pour their profits into that silly windmill.


**ANIMAL FARM.**

**Narrator.** The windmill stands half-built. Exhausted from their
390     work, the animals search in every trough and food bin. Everything is empty.

**Boxer.** Where is the food?

**Jessie.** I don't think there is any.

**Muriel.** I'm so hungry.

**Rat.** You? Look at me. I'm dying over here!

**Squealer.** Make way for the glorious leader! Make way!

(NAPOLEON *struts through the barn wearing two shiny medals.*)
Our valiant leader Animal Hero First Class and Animal Hero
Second Class will now speak.

400 **Napoleon.** My friends, I have learned that the archcriminal
Snowball is sabotaging this farm and our glorious windmill.
He has upset our milk pails. He has trodden our seedbeds.
This is the reason for our shortage of food. It is clear that this
traitor must have had help from the inside.

**Squealer.** Now then, let's have it: Which of you is in the league
with our sworn enemy? (*Animals look at each other in fear.*) Well,
as Captain of the Animal Guard, I promise we will find you.

**Napoleon.** Because of this sabotage, hens must now surrender
their eggs for sale.

410 **Chickens.** You can't take our eggs! It's murder!

**Napoleon.** You hens should welcome this sacrifice as your
special contribution to animalism!

**Chickens.** No! Never!

**Squealer.** Chickens, do you dare defy our glorious leader?

**Chickens.** We will smash our eggs before we give them to you!
(*They fly up to the rafters.*)

**Napoleon.** All hens are now criminals! No hen will be fed! Any
animal seen giving food to a hen will be punished by death!
Any friend of the enemy is an enemy! Death to our enemies!

420 **THE BARNYARD.**

**Narrator.** The animals huddle together, staring at a cage where
two ducks, a sheep, the rat, and several chickens are imprisoned.
Napoleon wears a judge's wig. Squealer, the prosecutor, also
wears a wig. There is no defense attorney.

**ANALYZE**

Pause at line 404. Who does
Napoleon say is responsible
for the food shortage? Circle
that information. Do you
think Napoleon is telling the
truth? Explain.

_____

_____

_____

_____

_____

_____

_____

**INTERPRET**

Re-read Napoleon's command
in lines 417–419. What type of
government have Napoleon
and Squealer imposed on
Animal Farm?

_____

_____

_____

_____

**PREDICT**

Pause at line 424. What
does the lack of a defense
attorney tell you about the
trial that is to be held?

_____

_____

## CONNECT

Re-read what Jessie says in line 432. Why does she say that?

_____

_____

_____

_____

_____

_____

_____

_____

_____

## PREDICT

Pause at line 454. Based on this passage and what you have already read, what do you think will happen to Boxer?

_____

_____

_____

_____

_____

_____

_____

**Napoleon.** Order! (*bangs a gavel*) Order in the court!

**Squealer.** With efficiency and patriotism, the Animal Guard has rooted out the enemies of the farm, proving there is no place to hide and no escape from justice. These animals are hereby accused of crimes against animalism, and will now

430    be tried before our impartial leader.

**Napoleon.** Guilty! (*banging down the gavel*) The penalty is death!

**Jessie** (*softly*). No animal shall kill any other animal.

**Napoleon.** Silence! Take them away! (*The prisoners are led away by the* ANIMAL GUARD.) As for the rest of you—get back to work! Long live the Revolution! Long live the windmill!

### ANIMAL FARM.

**Narrator.** Exhausted and starving, most of the animals are too weak and sick to work. Boxer tries to carry on alone. One evening, as he tries to pull a load of stones up the hill to the

440    windmill, the cart overturns and he is seriously injured. The animals help him back to his stall in the barn.

**Boxer.** I can't breathe very well.

**Jessie.** Shh, lie still, Boxer.

**Boxer.** Perhaps . . . there are enough stones now . . . to finish the windmill. . . . Perhaps . . . I may now be allowed . . . to stop. . . .

**Jessie.** Oh, Boxer. If any animal deserves to rest, it's you. Try to drink some water now.

**Muriel.** We brought some food, too. (SQUEALER *enters;* MURIEL *hides the food.*)

450    **Squealer.** Any improvement?

**Jessie.** Oh, yes! He's getting better every day! See for yourself.

**Squealer.** Hmmm. Our leader has made arrangements to have his most loyal worker treated at an animal hospital. (*Sound of truck doors slamming. Two men in overalls enter.*)

**Boxer.** Thank you. Please, Squealer. Thank Napoleon for me.

**Squealer.** Oh, I will. Let's go, Boxer. Get up. (BOXER *tries to stand.*)

**Boxer.** Sorry . . . I can't . . . very weak. . . .

**First Worker.** Come on, you nag.

**Second Worker.** Just drag him up.

460     **First Worker.** I'll kick him up in a minute.

**Jessie.** Boxer! You must summon all your strength to get up. Please. For your friends. (BOXER *gathers the last of his herculean strength and stands. The animals cheer him, and walk him outside and up a ramp into a truck.*)

**All Animals.** Goodbye, Boxer!

**Jessie.** Get well soon, old friend. (*The engine of the truck roars to life. One of the* WORKERS *comes around to shut the two back doors. As the engine starts,* MURIEL *cries out in horror as she reads the painted lettering on the doors.*)

470     **Muriel.** No! No!

**Jessie.** Muriel! What is it?

**Muriel.** The words on the van! SLAUGHTERHOUSE. Oh, Jessie, we've been tricked. They're taking Boxer to the glue factory! Oh, please, we've got to stop them! (*The truck pulls away. The animals run alongside, shouting to* BOXER.)

**Jessie.** Boxer! Boxer, get out quick!

**Muriel.** It's a trick! Boxer, they're taking you to your death!

**Jessie.** Boxer! Boxer, kick your way out! Boxer! (*Suddenly, a tremendous drumming can be heard inside the truck.*) That's it,

480     Boxer! Fight! (*The drumming stops. The truck speeds away.*) Boxer . . . oh, Boxer . . . what have we done?


## THE FARMHOUSE.

**Narrator.** Napoleon and Pilkington watch the truck pull away.

**Pilkington.** Well, that's that. A very profitable afternoon. (*Counts out a stack of bills, hands a share to* NAPOLEON.) There's your share.

**Napoleon.** Buy me whiskey.

**Pilkington.** Whiskey is expensive.

490     **Napoleon.** I don't care. Use all the money.

**Pilkington.** Whatever you say, dear boy.

**IDENTIFY RELATIONSHIPS**

Pause at line 465. What is the relationship between Boxer and the other animals?

_____

_____

_____

_____

_____

_____

_____

**INTERPRET**

Horse parts are used to make glue. Why do you think Napoleon sends Boxer to the slaughterhouse (line 472)?

_____

_____

_____

_____

_____

_____

_____

_____

_____

**WORD STUDY**

A *crocodile tear* (line 494) is a false or insincere tear. What does this detail tell you about Squealer's speech?

## THE BARN. LATER THAT NIGHT.

**Squealer.** Animals, I have a solemn announcement to make. Our noble friend, Boxer, has died. I was there, at his bedside in the hospital. (*Wipes away a crocodile tear*) At the very last, he beckoned me close and whispered, "Forward, forward in the name of the Revolution. Long live Animal Farm! Long live our beloved Napoleon!" Those were Boxer's last words. (*He sniffles a little; then his tone turns nasty.*) I've heard terrible rumors. I've heard that some of you are saying the truck that took Boxer

500 away had the name of a slaughterhouse on it. How can you be so stupid? Surely you know our beloved leader better than that. So, no more rumors. Goodnight. (SQUEALER *exits, flanked by the* ANIMAL GUARD.)

**Jessie.** I could have saved him.

**Muriel.** Nobody can save any of us.

**Jessie.** I can. There's a place at the edge of the farm. We could hide there. I could have taken Boxer there . . . if only I'd known.

**Muriel.** Jessie, there are many animals who won't last much longer.

510 **Jessie.** You're right. We must save them. We must leave with as many animals as we can.

**Rat.** But—they'll kill us if they find out. They'll sic the Guard on us!

**Muriel.** Maybe, but we'll die just as surely if we stay.

**Jessie.** Gather the animals, as many as can walk. I'll do a little scouting and meet you back here.

## THE FARMHOUSE.

**Narrator.** Jessie slips over to the farmhouse and peeks through the window. She sees the Pilkingtons, and Napoleon, who snorts
520 up a trough of whiskey.

**Mrs. Pilkington.** May I compliment you on how you keep your animals in order?

**Napoleon.** Thank you.

**Pilkington.** You're an example to all farmers. After all, no animal ever suffered from working a little harder and eating a little less . . . present company excluded, of course. Another toast: to Animal Farm!

**Napoleon.** Not Animal Farm. I've decided we shall return to our proper name: Manor Farm.

530 **Pilkington.** To Manor Farm, then . . . and to our continued prosperity.

**Napoleon.** Absolutely, dear boy. (*They all laugh.*)

## MANOR FARM BARN.

**Narrator.** Jessie has returned to the animals, who are gathered beneath Snowball's commandments.

**IDENTIFY CAUSE & EFFECT**

Pause at line 516. Why do Jessie, Muriel, and Rat plan to leave Animal Farm?

_____

_____

_____

_____

**INTERPRET**

What is the significance of Napoleon's decision to call the farm by its original name (lines 528–529)?

_____

_____

_____

_____

**IDENTIFY RELATIONSHIPS**

Re-read lines 521–532. What is the relationship between Napoleon and the Pilkingtons?

_____

_____

_____

_____

## IDENTIFY RELATIONSHIPS

Pause at line 542. How has Jessie's relationship with the other animals changed?

_____

_____

_____

_____

_____

_____

_____

_____

## VOCABULARY

decree (di·krē′) v.: order.

## ALLEGORY

Pause to think over the story's events, from the animals' mistreatment, to the revolution, to the end of the revolution. What is the story's lesson?

_____

_____

_____

_____

_____

_____

_____

**Muriel.** Jessie! Thank God you're all right. Squealer was just here. Look! (MURIEL _points at the commandments, where new paint glistens in the moonlight._)

540 **Jessie** (_reading aloud_). "All animals are equal, but some animals are more equal than others."

**Muriel.** Time to leave . . . while we still have the chance.

**Jessie.** Follow me, and stay close.

## THE FARMHOUSE.

**Narrator.** As the animals pass the farmhouse, they can see the Pilkingtons, Squealer, and Napoleon parading about the living room, chanting, "Four legs good, two legs better!" Just like the Pilkingtons, Squealer and Napoleon prance on two legs. Suddenly Napoleon's voice echoes through the barnyard.

**Napoleon.** Animals! Never again will we be threatened by

550 enemies. I **decree** that from this time forward, this farm will devote itself to the making of weapons, the building of walls, the protection of ourselves and our way of life. The Revolution is over. All animals are now free!

# Animal Farm

**Allegory Chart**  *Animal Farm* is an **allegory:** Most of the characters stand for good and bad human traits, or virtues and vices. Match the characters listed below with the vices and virtues they represent. Then, in the space below, write the moral of the story.

| Character | Vice or Virtue |
|---|---|
| _____ **1.** Mr. Pilkington | **a.** vanity; foolishness |
| _____ **2.** Mr. Jones | **b.** deceitfulness |
| _____ **3.** Boxer | **c.** ambition; cruelty |
| _____ **4.** Mollie | **d.** greed; exploitation |
| _____ **5.** Old Major | **e.** loyalty; hard work |
| _____ **6.** Snowball | **f.** viciousness |
| _____ **7.** Napoleon | **g.** wisdom; idealism |
| _____ **8.** Squealer | **h.** weakness; drunkenness |
| _____ **9.** The dogs | **i.** truthfulness; expertise |

**Moral or Lesson of the Story:**

_____

_____

_____

_____

_____

_____

_____

_____

_____

_____

_____

# Standards Review

**TestPractice** Animal Farm

Complete the sample test item below. The box at the right explains why three of these choices are not correct.

| Sample Test Item | Explanation of the Correct Answer |
|---|---|
| In the play, Boxer **symbolizes** which virtues?<br><br>**A** wisdom and mercy<br>**B** hard work and loyalty<br>**C** humor and creativity<br>**D** ability and expertise | The correct answer is *B*.<br><br>Boxer works very hard and is loyal. *A*, *C*, and *D* are not correct because Boxer shows none of those qualities. |

**DIRECTIONS:** Circle the letter of each correct answer.

**Reading Standard 3.7**
Recognize and understand the significance of various literary devices, including figurative language, imagery, allegory, and symbolism, and explain their appeal.

1. Which of the following best describes what makes *Animal Farm* an **allegory**?

    **A** Animals talk like human beings.

    **B** It has a central conflict.

    **C** The characters stand for virtues and vices.

    **D** It contains dialogue, characters, a plot, and a setting.

2. Which animals seem to represent ordinary, decent citizens?

    **F** Jessie and Muriel

    **G** Boxer and Mollie

    **H** Napoleon and Squealer

    **J** Jessie's puppies

3. After Old Major's death, which character **symbolizes** positive leadership for the revolution?

    **A** Napoleon

    **B** Jessie

    **C** Snowball

    **D** Boxer

4. Which of the following best expresses the **moral** of *Animal Farm*?

    **F** People and pigs oppress other animals.

    **G** An idealistic system can easily be corrupted.

    **H** Animals are more honest than people.

    **J** There should be no rulers.

# Standards Review

**TestPractice**  Animal Farm

## Context Clues

**DIRECTIONS:** Circle the letter of the context clue that helps you define each boldface word.

1. Boxer did not seem to mind the **laborious** work, although the others could see that he was exhausted at the end of the day.

   **A** day          **C** exhausted

   **B** others       **D** mind

2. The roof of the **dilapidated** farmhouse had nearly collapsed.

   **F** nearly       **H** had

   **G** collapsed    **J** farmhouse

3. Away from the farm, Jessie and Muriel did not miss the **squalor** of the barn with its filthy stalls.

   **A** barn         **C** bossy

   **B** filthy       **D** labor

4. A new **decree** was sent out by Napoleon ordering animals to work in day and night shifts.

   **F** new          **H** ordering

   **G** sent         **J** work

**Reading Standard 1.3 (Grade 8 Review)** Use word meanings within the appropriate context and show ability to verify those meanings by definition, restatement, example, comparison, or contrast.

## Vocabulary in Context

**DIRECTIONS:** Complete the paragraph below by writing a word from the word box in the correct numbered blank. Not all words will be used.

### Word Box

dilapidated

laborious

squalor

compatriots

prophesied

conspicuously

tactics

decree

The leaders of the Russian Revolution (1) _____ that they would create an earthly paradise in which everyone would share in labor and its rewards. In order to bring about this paradise, however, (2) _____ effort and many sacrifices were required. The (3) _____ used to bring about change were harsh but effective. The leadership, however, was seen to be leading a (4) _____ more comfortable lifestyle than was available to the ordinary workers.

**Before You Go On . . .**

Check your Standards Mastery at the back of this book.

# Poetry

# Academic Vocabulary for Chapter 7

These are the terms you should know
as you read and analyze the selections in this chapter.

---

**Image** A description of anything we can see, hear, taste, touch, or smell. The image of a spaniel's floppy ears, for example, appeals to the senses of sight and touch.

**Imagery** Language that appeals to one or more of the senses and creates images, or pictures, in our minds.

• • •

**Figurative language** Language based on a comparison that is not literally true.

**Figures of speech** Language in which one thing is compared to something that seems to be entirely different. A figure of speech is never literally true, but a good one always suggests a powerful truth.

- A **simile** is a comparison containing the word *like* or *as:* "His eyes were like laser beams."
- A **metaphor** is a comparison without *like* or *as:* In a **direct metaphor** the two parts of the comparison are generally linked by a form of the verb *to be:* "The old man was a dinosaur." In an **implied metaphor** the comparison is suggested: "The leftover cereal had all the crunch of wet cardboard." An **extended metaphor** continues through several lines of a work.
- A special kind of metaphor, in which an object, animal, or idea is described as if it were a person, is called **personification:** "After the rain, the flowers hung their heads."

• • •

**Rhythm** A musical quality in poetry that comes from the alternation of stressed and unstressed sounds that make the voice rise and fall.

**Meter** A pattern of stressed and unstressed sounds. In the line "Your locks are like the snow" (*locks* here means "hair"), from a poem by Robert Burns, the pattern is unstressed-stressed. Meter is measured in **feet;** a **foot** is a unit of sound with at least one stressed syllable and usually one or more unstressed syllables.

**Free verse** Poetry that does not follow a regular, or steady, pattern of rhyme and meter.

• • •

*(continued on next page)*

**Reading Standard 3.1 (Grade 8 Review)** Determine and articulate the relationship between the purposes and characteristics of different forms of poetry (e.g., ballad, lyric, couplet, epic, elegy, ode, sonnet).

**Reading Standard 3.7** Recognize and understand the significance of various literary devices, including figurative language, imagery, allegory, and symbolism, and explain their appeal.

**Rhyme** The repetition of the accented (stressed) vowel sound and all remaining sounds in a word (*lime, time; mixture, fixture*).

- Most rhymes occur at the end of lines and are called **end rhymes.**
- Rhymes that occur within a line are called **internal rhymes**—for example, in this line by Alfred, Lord Tennyson: "The long light *shakes* across the *lakes.*"
- In **approximate rhyme** the repetition of sound is not exact (*now, know*).

**Alliteration** (ə·lit′ər·ā′shən) The repetition of consonant sounds in words that appear close together. The line by Tennyson above has alliteration: *long light* and *lakes.*

**Onomatopoeia** (än′ō·mat′ō·pē′ə) The use of words that sound like what they mean—for instance, the *buzzing* of bees and *croaking* of frogs.

---

### For Further Information . . .

Be sure to read these essays in *Holt Literature and Language Arts:*

- **Imagery,** pages 456–457.
- **Figurative Language,** pages 477–478.
- **The Sounds of Poetry,** pages 503–505.

# A Storm in the Mountains

by Aleksandr Solzhenitsyn

POEM

In "A Storm in the Mountains," the speaker and his friend are camping in the mountains at night when suddenly a violent storm erupts. In this prose poem—a mixture of poetry and nature essay—the writer examines the dangerous beauty of nature.

## LITERARY FOCUS: PROSE POEMS

A **prose poem** looks like a short essay. It's written in **prose**—in sentences and paragraphs—as you'd see in stories, essays, and articles. Prose poems, however, like other poems, contain striking **images,** or word pictures that appeal to one or more of the five senses: sight, touch, hearing, taste, and smell.

- "A Storm in the Mountains" is full of images, vivid descriptions of an unforgettable storm. Look for those images as you read, and let those images take you to the mountaintop along with the poem's speaker.
- When you have finished reading "A Storm in the Mountains," think of ways it is like a poem and ways it is like a brief essay.

**Reading Standard 3.1 (Grade 8 Review)** Determine and articulate the relationship between the purposes and characteristics of different forms of poetry (e.g., ballad, lyric, couplet, epic, elegy, ode, sonnet).

# A Storm in the Mountains

## Aleksandr Solzhenitsyn, *translated by* Michael Glenny

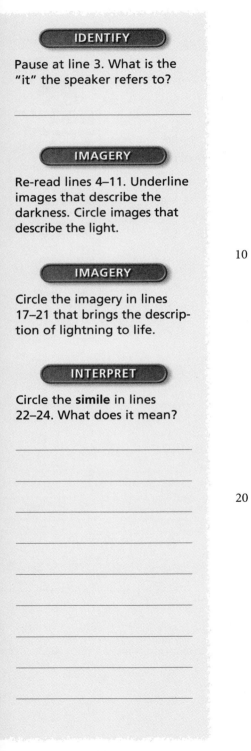

**IDENTIFY**

Pause at line 3. What is the "it" the speaker refers to?

_____

_____

**IMAGERY**

Re-read lines 4–11. Underline images that describe the darkness. Circle images that describe the light.

**IMAGERY**

Circle the imagery in lines 17–21 that brings the description of lightning to life.

**INTERPRET**

Circle the **simile** in lines 22–24. What does it mean?

_____

_____

_____

_____

_____

_____

_____

_____

It caught us one pitch-black night at the foot of the pass. We crawled out of our tents and ran for shelter as it came towards us over the ridge.

Everything was black—no peaks, no valleys, no horizon to be seen, only the searing flashes of lightning separating darkness from light, and the gigantic peaks of Belaya-Kaya and Djuguturlyuchat[1] looming up out of the night. The huge black pine trees around us seemed as high as the mountains themselves. For a split second we felt ourselves on terra firma;[2] then once more everything would be plunged into darkness and chaos.

The lightning moved on, brilliant light alternating with pitch blackness, flashing white, then pink, then violet, the mountains and pines always springing back in the same place, their hugeness filling us with awe; yet when they disappeared we could not believe that they had ever existed.

The voice of the thunder filled the gorge, drowning the ceaseless roar of the rivers. Like the arrows of Sabaoth,[3] the lightning flashes rained down on the peaks, then split up into serpentine streams as though bursting into spray against the rock face, or striking and then shattering like a living thing.

As for us, we forgot to be afraid of the lightning, the thunder, and the downpour, just as a droplet in the ocean has no fear of a hurricane. Insignificant yet grateful, we became part of this world—a primal world in creation before our eyes.

---

1. **Belaya-Kaya** (bye·lī′ə kī′ə) **and Djuguturlyuchat** (djoo·goo·toor·lyoo′chət): two mountains in Russia.
2. **terra firma** (ter′ə fur′mə): Latin expression meaning "solid ground."
3. **Sabaoth** (sab′ā·äth′): biblical term meaning "armies."

# A Storm in the Mountains

**Questionnaire**     For each question below, write at least one response. If you quote directly from the poem, use quotation marks. A response to the first question has been provided as an example.

1. Where is the speaker as the storm begins?

   He is at the foot of a mountain pass, at night, in a tent.
   _____

2. What is the storm like at first?

   _____

   _____

3. Why does the speaker feel he is on "terra firma" when lightning flashes?

   _____

   _____

4. How is the lightning described?

   _____

   _____

5. What sounds does the speaker hear?

   _____

   _____

6. What is the lightning compared to as it rains down on the peaks?

   _____

   _____

7. How does the storm change the speaker's ideas about people and nature?

   _____

   _____

# Standards Review

 **A Storm in the Mountains**

Sharpen your test-taking skills by completing the sample test item below. Then, read the explanation in the right-hand column.

| Sample Test Item | Explanation of the Correct Answer |
|---|---|
| Which of the following is *not* an **image**? <br><br> **A** serpentine streams <br><br> **B** voice of the thunder <br><br> **C** the ridge <br><br> **D** huge black pine trees | The correct answer is *C*. It names a thing; it is not a vivid description. <br><br> Items *A*, *B*, and *D* do name images— things you can take in through the senses. |

**DIRECTIONS:** Circle the letter of the correct response.

**Reading Standard 3.1 (Grade 8 Review)** Determine and articulate the relationship between the purposes and characteristics of different forms of poetry (e.g., ballad, lyric, couplet, epic, elegy, ode, sonnet).

1. What makes "A Storm in the Mountains" a **prose poem**?

   **A** It has rhyme.

   **B** It has powerful images.

   **C** It is in paragraph form.

   **D** The speaker reveals his thoughts.

2. The image in the line "ceaseless roar of the rivers" appeals mostly to which of the senses?

   **F** sight

   **G** hearing

   **H** taste

   **J** smell

3. To the speaker, the lightning flashes are like—

   **A** a colorless event

   **B** something not to be thankful for

   **C** a war fought with bows and arrows

   **D** the beginning of the world

4. The **imagery** in "A Storm in the Mountains" evokes a feeling of—

   **F** wonder

   **G** sorrow

   **H** silliness

   **J** hate

# Dreams by Langston Hughes; Ice by Mary Oliver

## BEFORE YOU READ

What is it that makes life worth living? Is it keeping dreams and hope alive, as suggested in a poem by Langston Hughes? Perhaps it is in keeping busy and remaining useful, as a poem by Mary Oliver suggests. Read on to learn of their ideas.

## LITERARY FOCUS: FIGURATIVE LANGUAGE

An important element of poetry is **figurative language**—language based on comparisons that are not literally true. Through figurative language, poets reveal truths in surprising, imaginative ways. Figures of speech are a type of figurative language: Through them, writers compare unlike things to uncover hidden similarities. **Metaphor** is a type of figurative language in which the comparisons are made without the use of words such as *like* or *as*.

• Look for the two striking metaphors in "Dreams." How do the metaphors help readers understand the importance of "dreams" in their lives?

• As you read "Ice," look for metaphors that help describe life and death.

## READING SKILLS: READING A POEM

When you read a poem, keep the following strategies in mind:

1. **Look for punctuation in the poem telling you where sentences begin and end.** Most poems—though not all of them—are written in full sentences.

2. **Do not make a full stop at the end of a line if there is no period, comma, colon, semicolon, or dash there.** If a line of poetry has no punctuation at its end, most poets expect us to read right on to the next line to complete the sense of the sentence.

3. **If a passage of a poem is difficult to understand, look for the subject, verb, and complement.** Try to decide what words the clauses and phrases modify.

4. **Be alert for comparisons—for figures of speech.** Try to visualize what the poet is describing for you.

5. **Read the poem aloud.** Poets are not likely to work in silence. The sound of a poem is very important.

6. **After you have read the poem, talk about it and read it again.** This time, the poem's meaning will change, slightly or dramatically. You'll see things in the poem you didn't see before.

7. **Read the poem a third time.** This time, the poem should become "yours."

**Reading Standard 3.7** Recognize and understand the significance of various literary devices, including figurative language, imagery, allegory, and symbolism, and explain their appeal.

# Dreams

## Langston Hughes

### WORD STUDY

*Fast,* in line 1, is used as an adverb meaning "firmly." Circle the context clue that helps you figure out the word's meaning.

### FIGURATIVE LANGUAGE

Underline the **metaphor** in the first stanza, and briefly explain what truth it reveals.

_____

_____

_____

_____

### FIGURATIVE LANGUAGE

Underline the **metaphor** in the poem's second stanza. (*Barren* means "lifeless or empty.") Then, briefly explain the metaphor.

_____

_____

_____

### FLUENCY

Read the poem aloud a few times. Try to convey the speaker's ideas by emphasizing important words and using a persuasive tone.

Hold fast to dreams
For if dreams die
Life is a broken-winged bird
That cannot fly.

5    Hold fast to dreams
For when dreams go
Life is a barren field
Frozen with snow.

# Ice

## Mary Oliver

My father spent his last winter
Making ice-grips for shoes

Out of strips of inner tube and scrap metal.
(A device which slips over the instep

5      And holds under the shoe
A section of roughened metal, it allows you to walk

Without fear of falling
Anywhere on ice or snow.) My father

Should not have been doing
10     All that close work

In the drafty workshop, but as though
He sensed travel at the edge of his mind,

He would not be stopped. My mother
Wore them, and my aunt, and my cousins.

15     He wrapped and mailed
A dozen pairs to me, in the easy snows

Of Massachusetts, and a dozen
To my sister, in California.

Later we learned how he'd given them away
20     To the neighbors, an old man

---

**IDENTIFY**

Pause at line 3. Who is the **speaker,** or the narrator, of the poem?

_____

_____

_____

**MONITOR YOUR READING**

In lines 4–8, circle the punctuation clues that signal that extra information is being provided.

**FIGURATIVE LANGUAGE**

Line 12 contains an **implied metaphor**—the comparison is suggested, not directly stated. What is the "travel" the father senses? Why is the subject "at the edge of his mind"?

_____

_____

_____

_____

_____

_____

**FIGURATIVE LANGUAGE**

Line 26 contains an **implied metaphor.** What does the metaphor compare death with?

_____

_____

**CLARIFY**

In lines 31–35, who is the "I" speaker? In line 36, who is the first "I" speaker, and who is the second "I" speaker?

_____

_____

_____

_____

_____

**INFER**

Why does the daughter tell her mother to save all the ice-grips (lines 41–42)?

_____

_____

_____

_____

_____

**FLUENCY**

Read lines 30–42 aloud two times. As you read, focus on making the meaning clear and distinguishing between the two "I"s.

Appearing with cold blue cheeks at every door.
No one refused him,

For plainly the giving was an asking,
A petition to be welcomed and useful—

25    Or maybe, who knows, the seed of a desire
Not to be sent alone out over the black ice.

Now the house seems neater: books,
Half-read, set back on the shelves;

Unfinished projects put away.

30    This spring

Mother writes to me: I am cleaning the workshop
And I have found

So many pairs of the ice-grips,
Cartons and suitcases stuffed full,

35    More than we can ever use.
What shall I do? And I see myself

Alone in that house with nothing
But darkly gleaming cliffs of ice, the sense

Of distant explosions,
40    Blindness as I look for my coat—

And I write back: Mother, please
Save everything.

# Dreams; Ice

**Elements of Poetry Chart** **Metaphors** are unusual comparisons; the writer compares two unlike things in order to uncover a truth. To better understand metaphors and how they work, fill in the following chart with details from "Dreams" and "Ice."

| Dreams |
|---|
| **1.** What two things is a life without dreams compared to? |
| _____ |
| _____ |
| **2.** The comparisons suggest that dreams are important in our lives because _____ |
| _____ |
| _____ |

| Ice |
|---|
| **3.** The father's thoughts of "travel" (line 12) are compared to his awareness of _____ |
| _____ |
| **4.** What metaphor for death do you find in lines 36–42? |
| _____ |
| **5.** What metaphor for panic do you find in lines 36–42? |
| _____ |

# Standards Review

**Test Practice**  **Dreams; Ice**

Practice your test-taking skills by completing the sample test item below. Then, read the explanation in the right column.

| Sample Test Item | Explanation of the Correct Answer |
|---|---|
| In Hughes's poem, the two **metaphors** suggest that dreams— <br><br> A  help us sleep <br><br> B  are a waste of time <br><br> C  give us something to work toward <br><br> D  are like broken wings | The correct answer is C. <br><br> *A* is incorrect because the dreams in the poem are hopes about the future, not dreams during sleep. *B* is incorrect because the poem says that dreams are important to our lives. *D* is not correct because the metaphor compares life *without* dreams to a bird with a broken wing. |

**DIRECTIONS:** Circle the letter of each correct response.

**Reading Standard 3.7**
Recognize and understand the significance of various literary devices, including figurative language, imagery, allegory, and symbolism, and explain their appeal.

1. In Hughes's poem, the **two metaphors** have to do with—

   A  a fast race

   B  the human mind

   C  city living

   D  nature that is hurt or lifeless

2. In "Ice," the father worries about—

   F  working too hard

   G  his approaching death

   H  asking the neighbors for help

   J  hurting his family

3. The father's desire to make the ice-grips represents his need to—

   A  remain useful

   B  walk on slippery snow

   C  skate on a pond

   D  fill the workshop with useless items

4. The daughter understands that some day she may—

   F  want to clean the workshop

   G  feel the way her father did

   H  borrow ice-grips from the neighbors

   J  answer her mother's letter

# "Out, Out—" by Robert Frost
# Spring is like a perhaps hand by E. E. Cummings
# Bailando by Pat Mora

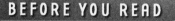

POEMS

## BEFORE YOU READ

Poets create sounds by choosing words and arranging them carefully. Experience a sampling of sounds and ideas by reading the following poems by Robert Frost, E. E. Cummings, and Pat Mora.

### LITERARY FOCUS: SOUND DEVICES

The tools of a poet are words. Through word choice and placement, poets can create a variety of sound effects. The use of sound effects helps poets create meaning and also helps make their ideas vivid and memorable. Following are types of sound devices you'll encounter when reading the three poems that follow.

| repetition | the use of repeated word parts, words, or phrases |
|---|---|
| rhyme | the repetition of the accented vowel sound and all the sounds following it in a word |
| end rhyme | rhyme in which the chiming sounds occur at the ends of lines |
| internal rhyme | rhyme in which the chiming sounds occur within lines |
| alliteration | the repetition of consonant sounds in words that are close together |
| onomatopoeia | the use of words that sound like what they mean (screech, hoot) |
| rhythm | pattern of stressed and unstressed syllables |

- In "Out, Out—" the poet Robert Frost tells a story and makes it vivid through the use of onomatopoeia.
- The rhymes in E. E. Cummings's "Spring is like a perhaps hand" create a playful, musical quality.
- The rhythmic quality of "Bailando" fits the subject: a woman who has enjoyed dancing for nearly ninety years.

**Reading Standard 3.7** Recognize and understand the significance of various literary devices, including figurative language, imagery, allegory, and symbolism, and explain their appeal.

# "Out, Out—"

## Robert Frost

**SOUNDS OF POETRY**

Find two examples of **onomatopoeia** in line 1, and circle them. Then, read on to line 9. Find and circle the two places these words are repeated.

**INTERPRET**

Re-read lines 10–14. What have you learned about the poem's speaker? What does he wish?

_____

_____

_____

_____

_____

_____

_____

**CLARIFY**

What is meant by "Neither refused the meeting," in line 18?

_____

_____

_____

_____

The buzz saw snarled and rattled in the yard
And made dust and dropped stove-length sticks of wood,
Sweet-scented stuff when the breeze drew across it.
And from there those that lifted eyes could count
5   Five mountain ranges one behind the other
Under the sunset far into Vermont.
And the saw snarled and rattled, snarled and rattled,
As it ran light, or had to bear a load.
And nothing happened: day was all but done.
10  Call it a day, I wish they might have said
To please the boy by giving him the half hour
That a boy counts so much when saved from work.
His sister stood beside them in her apron
To tell them "Supper." At the word, the saw,
15  As if to prove saws knew what supper meant,
Leaped out at the boy's hand, or seemed to leap—
He must have given the hand. However it was,
Neither refused the meeting. But the hand!
The boy's first outcry was a rueful laugh,
20  As he swung toward them holding up the hand,
Half in appeal, but half as if to keep
The life from spilling. Then the boy saw all—
Since he was old enough to know, big boy
Doing a man's work, though a child at heart—
25  He saw all spoiled. "Don't let him cut my hand off—
The doctor, when he comes. Don't let him, sister!"
So. But the hand was gone already.
The doctor put him in the dark of ether.°

---

° **ether** (ē′thər) *n.:* chemical compound used as an anesthetic.

**CLARIFY**

Re-read lines 19–26. What two things does the boy do after the accident?

_____

_____

_____

_____

**INTERPRET**

What does the speaker mean when he says "No more to build on there" in line 33?

_____

_____

_____

**IDENTIFY**

What do the boy's relatives do after his death (lines 33–34)?

_____

_____

_____

_____

**FLUENCY**

Read the poem aloud two times. Read once for meaning and once for sound effects.

He lay and puffed his lips out with his breath.

30 And then—the watcher at his pulse took fright.

No one believed. They listened at his heart.

Little—less—nothing!—and that ended it.

No more to build on there. And they, since they

Were not the one dead, turned to their affairs.

# spring is like a perhaps hand

## E. E. Cummings

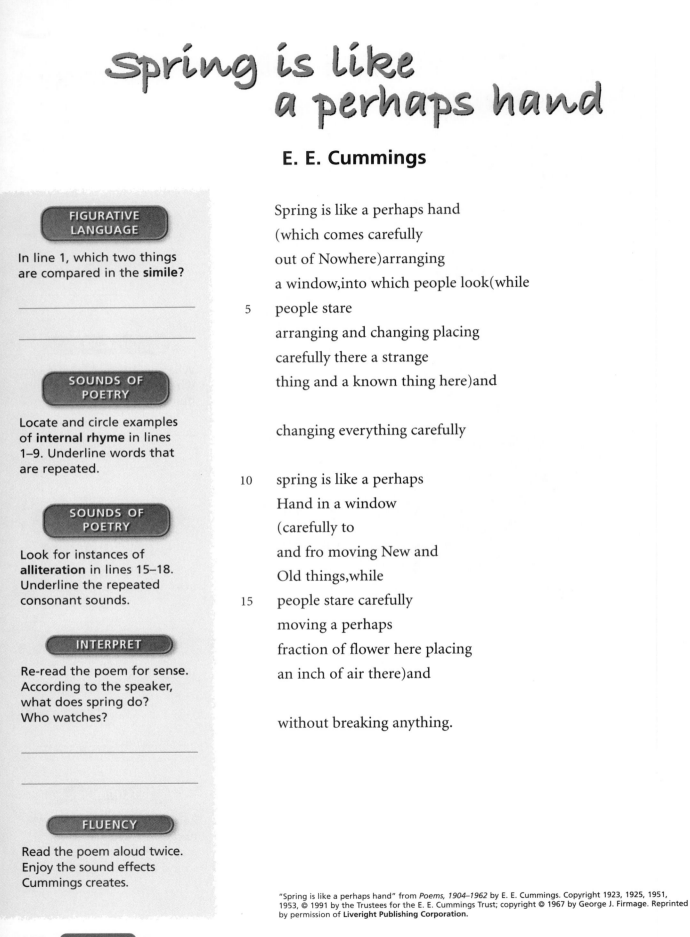

Spring is like a perhaps hand

(which comes carefully

out of Nowhere)arranging

a window,into which people look(while

5 people stare

arranging and changing placing

carefully there a strange

thing and a known thing here)and


changing everything carefully


10 spring is like a perhaps

Hand in a window

(carefully to

and fro moving New and

Old things,while

15 people stare carefully

moving a perhaps

fraction of flower here placing

an inch of air there)and


without breaking anything.

**FIGURATIVE LANGUAGE**

In line 1, which two things are compared in the **simile**?

_____

_____

**SOUNDS OF POETRY**

Locate and circle examples of **internal rhyme** in lines 1–9. Underline words that are repeated.

**SOUNDS OF POETRY**

Look for instances of **alliteration** in lines 15–18. Underline the repeated consonant sounds.

**INTERPRET**

Re-read the poem for sense. According to the speaker, what does spring do? Who watches?

_____

_____

**FLUENCY**

Read the poem aloud twice. Enjoy the sound effects Cummings creates.

# Bailando[1]

## Pat Mora

I will remember you dancing,
spinning round and round
a young girl in Mexico,
your long, black hair free in the wind,
5  spinning round and round
a young woman at village dances
your long, blue dress swaying
to the beat of *La Varsoviana*,[2]
smiling into the eyes of your partners,
10  years later smiling into my eyes
when I'd reach up to dance with you,
my dear aunt, who years later
danced with my children,
you, white-haired but still young
15  waltzing on your ninetieth birthday,
more beautiful than the orchid
pinned on your shoulder,
tottering now when you walk
but saying to me, *"Estoy bailando,"*[3]
20  and laughing.

---

**SOUNDS OF POETRY**

Pause at line 10. Underline words and phrases that are examples of **repetition**. What **rhythmic effect** does the repetition create?

_____

_____

_____

**INTERPRET**

Re-read the poem. In what ways has the speaker's aunt changed? In what way is she the same?

_____

_____

_____

_____

_____

_____

**FLUENCY**

Read the poem aloud two times. First, practice pronouncing the Spanish words and phrases if they are unfamiliar to you. As you read, allow your voice to convey the rhythms of the dance.

---

1.  *Bailando* (bī·län′dō): Spanish for "dancing."
2.  *La Varsoviana:* a popular folk dance tune.
3.  *"Estoy bailando":* Spanish for "I am dancing."

# "Out, Out—"; Spring is like a perhaps hand; Bailando

**Sound Devices Grid**     Poets use sounds in special ways to give their works a musical quality or to emphasize ideas. The chart below lists some of these sound devices. For each device listed, give an example from the poems you've just read.

| Sound Device | Example from Poem |
|---|---|
| repetition | |
| internal rhyme | |
| alliteration | |
| onomatopoeia | |

# Standards Review

## "Out, Out—"; Spring is like a perhaps hand; Bailando

Practice your test-taking skills by completing the sample test item below. Then, read the explanation in the right-hand column.

| Sample Test Item | Explanation of the Correct Answer |
|---|---|
| The title "Spring is like a perhaps hand" is an example of—<br><br>**A** metaphor<br>**B** end rhyme<br>**C** literal meaning<br>**D** simile | The correct answer is *D*.<br><br>*A* is incorrect—the comparison uses *like* and is not a metaphor. *B* is incorrect because there is only one line and no rhymes. *C* is not correct because figurative language is not meant to be taken literally. |

**DIRECTIONS:** Circle the letter of each correct answer.

1. Which of the following lines from "Out, Out—" contains **alliteration**?

   **A** "Five mountain ranges one behind the other . . ."

   **B** "Sweet-scented stuff when the breeze drew across it."

   **C** "Under the sunset far into Vermont."

   **D** ". . . But the hand was gone already."

2. Which kind of **rhyme** does the following passage from Cummings's poem contain?

   *people stare / arranging and changing placing*

   **F** end rhyme

   **G** approximate rhyme

   **H** no rhyme

   **J** internal rhyme

3. Which of the following statements is true of the poem "Bailando"?

   **A** It has end rhyme.

   **B** It contains repetition.

   **C** It is full of onomatopoeia.

   **D** It has a strict rhythmic pattern.

4. Which sentence best expresses the meaning of "Bailando"?

   **F** Life is as pointless as a village dance.

   **G** Elderly family members should not be dancing.

   **H** Dancing and poetry are not at all alike.

   **J** The aunt is full of life in old age, just as she was in her youth.

**Reading Standard 3.7** Recognize and understand the significance of various literary devices, including figurative language, imagery, allegory, and symbolism, and explain their appeal.

# Literary Criticism:
# Evaluating Style

# Academic Vocabulary for Chapter 8

These are the terms you should know
as you read and analyze the selections in this chapter.

_____

**Style**  The special way a writer uses language. A writer's style may be
described as plain, complex, ornate, simple, poetic, conversational,
formal, informal, and so on.

**Diction**  The words a writer chooses. Diction contributes to a writer's style.

**Sentence structure**  The way words are put together to form sentences.
Sentences may be long and complex, plain and direct, or short
and punchy. Some writers deliberately use sentence fragments for
certain effects.

● ● ●

**Figures of speech**  Expressions that are based on unusual comparisons
and are not literally true. Some writers avoid using figures of speech;
other writers use them all the time.

**Tone**  The attitude a writer takes toward the subject of a work, its
characters, or the audience.

**Mood**  The atmosphere or feeling a writer creates in a work.

**Theme**  The revelation or truth about human experience expressed in a story.

**Reading
Standard 1.1**
Identify and
use the literal
and figurative
meanings of
words and
understand
word
derivations.

**Reading
Standard 3.11**
Evaluate the
aesthetic
qualities of style,
including the
impact of
diction and
figurative
language on
tone, mood, and
theme, using
the terminology
of literary
criticism.
(Aesthetic
approach)

> **📚 For Further Information …**
>
> ● Be sure to read the essay on **evaluating style**
> in *Holt Literature and Language Arts*,
> pages 556–557.

# Geraldo No Last Name by Sandra Cisneros

Who is Geraldo? Why has he made such a difference to the girl who met him only briefly? How does this little sketch make *you* feel?

## LITERARY FOCUS: STYLE, DICTION, AND TONE

**Style** is a writer's individual way of expressing himself or herself. Just as people have different styles in dress and in speaking, they also have different styles in writing. Word choice and sentence length have an important effect on style. When you evaluate style, look also for how extensively the writer uses figurative language, dialogue, and description.

**Diction,** or word choice, is another element of style. Writers select words to help communicate their feelings and thoughts—and to create an overall effect. For example, if a writer uses the word *dough* instead of the word *money,* then we say the diction is informal and streetwise. If a writer changes the phrase "a charging elephant" to "a swiftly approaching pachyderm," the style changes from informal to formal.

Diction also has a strong effect on **tone,** the attitude a writer takes toward his or her characters, or toward life in general. Like a person's voice, the tone of a work can be playful, sarcastic, affectionate, or full of remorse. Adjusting a word or two can change tone; if a writer changes the phrase "an odor filled the room" to "a stink filled the room," the tone changes.

- Some writers, like Sandra Cisneros, have a very personal **style** that makes their work easily recognizable. As you read "Geraldo No Last Name," notice how Cisneros uses sentence structure (even fragments) to create her unique style.
- Also, pay close attention to Cisneros's **diction.** Is her diction formal or informal? What effect does Cisneros create by using Spanish words?
- Finally, think about Cisneros's attitude toward Geraldo, Marin, and their situation. What is her **tone** in this story?

## READING SKILLS: MONITORING YOUR READING

When you read, you almost "talk" with a text. By asking questions, you carry on a dialogue with the text. You can ask questions about a character's actions, motivations, or feelings. You can ask questions about plot, setting, and style. For example, you might ask, "Why does Cisneros use so many short sentences?" or "Why doesn't she give Geraldo a last name?" Then, read on to see if you can find the answers to your questions.

**Reading Standard 1.1**
Identify and use the literal and figurative meanings of words and understand word derivations.

**Reading Standard 3.11**
Evaluate the aesthetic qualities of style, including the impact of diction and figurative language on tone, mood, and theme, using the terminology of literary criticism. (Aesthetic approach)

## VOCABULARY DEVELOPMENT

### WORDS FROM SPANISH

Immigrants to the United States bring not only their food, music, and customs but their language as well. As a result, American English now includes many words from foreign languages. The chart below contains just a few examples of words from Spanish.

### Words from Spanish

| Word | Definition |
|---|---|
| adobe | sun-dried brick |
| barbecue | party or picnic at which meat is broiled |
| bonanza | source of great wealth |
| canyon | long, narrow valley between high cliffs |
| mustang | small wild or half-wild horse |
| patio | paved area next to a house |
| poncho | blanket-like cloak, with an opening in the middle for the head |
| ranch | large farm devoted to raising crops or livestock |
| rodeo | public exhibition of the skills of cowboys |

Sandra Cisneros uses many words from Spanish in "Geraldo No Last Name." For example, she uses the Spanish word *salsa* to describe a lively type of dance. How does this mixture of Spanish and English affect her style?

# Geraldo No Last Name

## Sandra Cisneros

*El Club* (1990) by Nick Quijano. Gouache on paper (22" x 30").

**IDENTIFY**

Pause at line 4. Underline what the girl remembers about Geraldo.

**MONITOR YOUR READING**

Pause at line 6. What has happened to Geraldo? Underline the answer to this question.

She met him at a dance. Pretty too, and young. Said he worked in a restaurant, but she can't remember which one. Geraldo. That's all. Green pants and Saturday shirt. Geraldo. That's what he told her.

And how was she to know she'd be the last one to see him alive. An accident, don't you know. Hit and run. Marin, she goes to all those dances. Uptown. Logan. Embassy. Palmer. Aragon. Fontana. The manor. She likes to dance. She knows

how to do cumbias and salsas and rancheras even. And he was
10  just someone she danced with. Somebody she met that night.
That's right.

That's the story. That's what she said again and again. Once
to the hospital people and twice to the police. No address. No
name. Nothing in his pockets. Ain't it a shame.

Only Marin can't explain why it mattered, the hours
and hours, for somebody she didn't even know. The hospital
emergency room. Nobody but an intern working all alone. And
maybe if the surgeon would've come, maybe if he hadn't lost so
much blood, if the surgeon had only come, they would know
20  who to notify and where.

But what difference does it make? He wasn't anything to
her. He wasn't her boyfriend or anything like that. Just another
brazer[1] who didn't speak English. Just another wetback.[2] You
know the kind. The ones who always look ashamed. And what
was she doing out at 3:00 A.M. anyway? Marin who was sent
home with her coat and some aspirin. How does she explain?

She met him at a dance. Geraldo in his shiny shirt and
green pants. Geraldo going to a dance.

What does it matter?

30  They never saw the kitchenettes. They never knew about the
two-room flats[3] and sleeping rooms he rented, the weekly money
orders sent home, the currency exchange. How could they?

His name was Geraldo. And his home is in another
country. The ones he left behind are far away, will wonder,
shrug, remember. Geraldo—he went north . . . we never heard
from him again.

**INFER**

Pause at line 20. Why is Marin so upset about Geraldo's death?

_____

_____

_____

_____

_____

**STYLE**

What effect does Cisneros create by using the word *brazer* and the slang word *wetback* in line 23?

_____

_____

_____

_____

_____

**IDENTIFY**

Pause at line 32. Underline the details you learn about Geraldo's life.

**FLUENCY**

Read the boxed passage aloud twice. In the second reading, try to express the narrator's tone.

---

1.  **brazer** (brā′zer) *n.:* Americanization of the Spanish word *bracero,*
    used in the United States to refer to a Mexican laborer allowed
    into the United States temporarily to work.
2.  **wetback** *n.:* offensive term for a Mexican laborer who illegally
    enters the United States, often by swimming or wading the
    Rio Grande.
3.  **flats** *n.:* apartments.

# Geraldo No Last Name

**Style Chart**    Use the chart below to record examples of Cisneros's style. Then, review your chart entries, and analyze Cisneros's style below the chart. Not all the elements of style listed here may be present in her story.

| Style Elements | Text Examples | Effect on Style |
|---|---|---|
| Word choices | | |
| Sentence structure | | |
| Use of figurative language | | |
| Tone | | |

**Analyze Style**    Select one or two of these adjectives to describe Cisneros's style: (1) plain, (2) conversational, (3) personal, (4) complex, (5) formal, (6) informal. Then, write two or three sentences telling which elements of style are key in creating this style. Quote directly from the story to support your answers.

_____

_____

_____

# Standards Review

TestPractice : **Geraldo No Last Name**

Complete the sample test item below. Then, read the explanation at right.

| Sample Test Item | Explanation of the Correct Answer |
|---|---|
| When applied to writing in general, the word **style** refers to— <br><br> **A** how the writer dresses <br><br> **B** a writer's attitude toward his or her subject matter <br><br> **C** the writer's special way of using words and punctuation <br><br> **D** a story's mood or atmosphere | The correct answer is *C*. <br><br> Style is a writer's unique way of using language to express his or her ideas. *A* is wrong because clothing does not apply to writing. *B* and *D* are wrong because although attitude and mood are elements of style, they are not an overall definition of style. |

**DIRECTIONS:** Circle the letter of each correct answer.

1. In "Geraldo No Last Name," Cisneros's **diction** is best described as—

   **A** formal

   **B** informal

   **C** technical

   **D** fancy

2. The use of fragments such as "An accident, don't you know. Hit and run."—

   **F** suggests the way the narrator thinks and speaks

   **G** shows how poor a writer Cisneros is

   **H** indicates that the narrator is a Spanish speaker

   **J** reveals the narrator's sorrow at Geraldo's death

3. You could most accurately identify the **tone** of "Geraldo No Last Name" as—

   **A** regretful

   **B** sarcastic

   **C** playful

   **D** awed

4. Cisneros's **tone** suggests that she—

   **F** dislikes illegal immigration

   **G** thinks that immigrants do not obey the rules

   **H** sympathizes with people like Geraldo

   **J** thinks people are generally fair

**Reading Standard 3.11**
Evaluate the aesthetic qualities of style, including the impact of diction and figurative language on tone, mood, and theme, using the terminology of literary criticism. (Aesthetic approach)

# Standards Review

**TestPractice**  **Geraldo No Last Name**

## Words from Spanish

**DIRECTIONS:** Circle the letter of the correct answer. Refer to the chart on page 239 if you need help.

**Reading Standard 1.1**
Identify and use the literal and figurative meanings of words and understand word derivations.

1. If Marin is buying a *poncho,* she is buying a—

   **A** ranch     **C** horse

   **B** cape      **D** deck

2. When a person receives a *bonanza,* they feel—

   **F** embarrassed and ashamed

   **G** surprised and happy

   **H** upset and confused

   **J** sick and injured

3. Which word *best* completes this sentence:

   *The guests sit on a _____ built from bricks and mortar.*

   **A** poncho

   **B** bonanza

   **C** rodeo

   **D** patio

## Vocabulary in Context

**DIRECTIONS:** Complete the paragraph below by writing a word from the word box to fit each numbered blank. Use each word only once. Refer to the chart on page 239 if you need help.

### Word Box

barbecue

mustang

ranch

rodeo

One of the featured events at the annual (1) _____ was cow-roping. Jack, who worked at the Lazy K (2) _____, was favored to win the contest. The horse Jack rode was very wild and unpredictable, almost like a (3) _____. About a minute and a half into the contest, Jack's own horse threw him! Back at the big tent, during the (4) _____, people ate their fill of hot dogs and hamburgers, all the while talking about Jack's bad luck.

**Before You Go On...**

Check your Standards Mastery at the back of this book.

# The Bridegroom by Alexander Pushkin

## BEFORE YOU READ

"The Bridegroom" is based on an old folk tale about a young woman who witnesses a terrible crime. She is silent about the crime—until she realizes she is to become the next victim.

### LITERARY FOCUS: STYLE AND MOOD

**Mood** is the atmosphere, or feeling, created in a piece of writing. Mood can be described as scary, romantic, depressing, comic, mysterious, and so on. Mood is usually created by word choice. In stories, mood can be affected by the story elements themselves: by events in the plot, the characters, the settings, and the story's theme, or revelation about life.

- "The Bridegroom" is a narrative poem—a poem that tells a story. Read it once for enjoyment and for basic comprehension.
- Then, re-read the poem. What mood does this strange story create?

### READING SKILLS: CAUSE AND EFFECT

A **plot** is a series of causes and their effects. One event causes something else to happen: It has an effect. That event causes another event to happen, and so on. As you read this narrative poem, watch for the **causes** of certain events. Watch for the **effects** of other events. For example, as the poem opens we learn that Natasha has been missing for three days. What do you later find out caused this event?

**Reading Standard 1.1**
Identify and use the literal and figurative meanings of words and understand word derivations.

**Reading Standard 3.11**
Evaluate the aesthetic qualities of style, including the impact of diction and figurative language on tone, mood, and theme, using the terminology of literary criticism. (Aesthetic approach)

## VOCABULARY DEVELOPMENT

### PREVIEW SELECTION VOCABULARY

The following words appear in the poem you're about to read. You may want to become familiar with them before you begin reading.

**foreboding** (fôr·bōd′iŋ) *n.:* a feeling that something bad will happen.

*Natasha is filled with* **foreboding** *at the prospect of marrying someone she mistrusts.*

**tumult** (tōo′mult) *n.:* noisy commotion.

*In all the* **tumult,** *Natasha shouted to be heard.*

**clamor** (klam′ər) *n.:* loud noise.

*When the excited men enter, their voices create a* **clamor.**

**blanches** (blanch′iz) *v.:* turns white; becomes pale.

*Natasha* **blanches** *at her father's commanding words.*

### PREFIXES AND SUFFIXES

A **prefix** is a letter or group of letters added to the beginning of a word to change its meaning. A **suffix** is a letter or group of letters added to the end of a word to change its meaning. Below are some examples.

| Word | Meaning | Prefix | Meaning | New Word | Meaning |
|------|---------|--------|---------|----------|---------|
| acquaint | meet | *re–* | again | reacquaint | meet again |
| expected | looked for | *un–* | not | unexpected | not looked for |
| nuptial | referring to a wedding | *pre–* | before | prenuptial | happening before a wedding |

| Word | Meaning | Suffix | Meaning | New Word | Meaning |
|------|---------|--------|---------|----------|---------|
| wonder | awe | *–ment* | state of being | wonderment | state of awe |
| rebel | resist | *–ion* | act of | rebellion | act of resisting |
| novel | new | *–ty* | quality | novelty | quality of being new |

In line 13 of the poem, you read that Natasha's cheeks regained their color. You can figure out the meaning of *regained* by looking at its prefix, *re–,* meaning "again." *Regained* means "gained again."

# THE BRIDEGROOM

## Alexander Pushkin, *translated* by D. M. Thomas

For three days Natasha,
The merchant's daughter,
Was missing. The third night,
She ran in, distraught.[1]

5 Her father and mother
Plied her with questions.
She did not hear them,
She could hardly breathe.

Stricken with **foreboding**
10 They pleaded, got angry,
But still she was silent;
At last they gave up.
Natasha's cheeks regained
Their rosy color.

15 And cheerfully again
She sat with her sisters.

Once at the shingle-gate[2]
She sat with her friends
—And a swift troika[3]
20 Flashed by before them;
A handsome young man
Stood driving the horses;
Snow and mud went flying,
Splashing the girls.

---

1. **distraught** (di·strôt′) *adj.:* extremely troubled.
2. **shingle-gate:** gate to the beach (a shingle is a pebbly beach).
3. **troika** (troi′kə) *n.:* Russian sleigh or carriage drawn by three horses.

"The Bridegroom" from *The Bronze Horseman and Other Poems* by Alexander Pushkin, translated by D. M. Thomas. Translation copyright © 1982 by D. M. Thomas. Reprinted by permission of **John Johnson Ltd.**

**IDENTIFY**

What important detail do you learn about Natasha in lines 1–3?

_____

_____

_____

_____

**STYLE**

Re-read lines 1–8. What **mood** is created by the words *missing, night, distraught,* and *hardly breathe*?

_____

_____

_____

_____

**VOCABULARY**

**foreboding** (fôr·bōd′in) *n.:* a feeling that something bad will happen.

**STYLE**

Sensory details help us imagine how something looks, sounds, feels, or tastes. Underline the sensory details in lines 17–24 that help you "see" and "hear" this incident.

**IDENTIFY
CAUSE & EFFECT**

Pause at line 32. Why do you
think Natasha is so afraid of
the handsome young man in
the carriage?

_____

_____

_____

_____

_____

_____

_____

_____

_____

25    He gazed as he flew past,

      And Natasha gazed.

      He flew on. Natasha froze.

      Headlong she ran home.

      "It was he! It was he!"

30    She cried. "I know it!

      I recognized him! Papa,

      Mama, save me from him!"


      Full of grief and fear,

      They shake their heads, sighing.

35    Her father says: "My child,

      Tell me everything.

      If someone has harmed you,

      Tell us . . . even a hint."

      She weeps again and

40    Her lips remain sealed.

The next morning, the old
Matchmaking woman
Unexpectedly calls and
Sings the girl's praises;
45    Says to the father: "You
Have the goods and I
A buyer for them:
A handsome young man.

"He bows low to no one,
50    He lives like a lord
With no debts nor worries;
He's rich and he's generous,
Says he will give his bride,
On their wedding-day,
55    A fox-fur coat, a pearl,
Gold rings, brocaded[4] dresses.

"Yesterday, out driving,
He saw your Natasha;
Shall we shake hands
60    And get her to church?"
The woman starts to eat
A pie, and talks in riddles,
While the poor girl
Does not know where to look.

65    "Agreed," says her father;
"Go in happiness
To the altar, Natasha;
It's dull for you here;
A swallow should not spend
70    All its time singing,
It's time for you to build
A nest for your children."

---

**4. brocaded** (brō·kād′əd) *adj.:* having a raised design woven into the fabric.

**IDENTIFY
CAUSE & EFFECT**

What has caused the matchmaker to call suddenly (lines 41–48)?

_____

_____

_____

_____

_____

_____

_____


**IDENTIFY**

Re-read lines 49–56. Underline the facts you learn about the young man in this stanza.

**INTERPRET**

In lines 69–72, Natasha's father compares her to a bird. What do her parents want her to do?

_____

_____

_____

_____

_____

_____

_____

_____

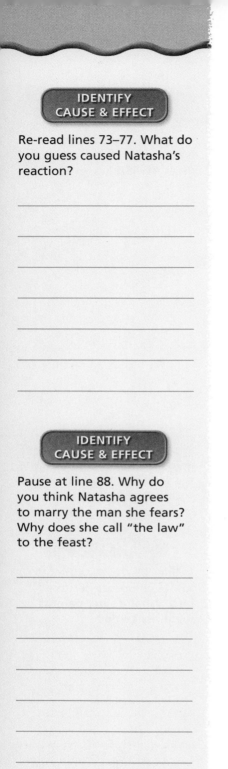

**IDENTIFY CAUSE & EFFECT**

Re-read lines 73–77. What do you guess caused Natasha's reaction?

_____

_____

_____

_____

_____

_____

**IDENTIFY CAUSE & EFFECT**

Pause at line 88. Why do you think Natasha agrees to marry the man she fears? Why does she call "the law" to the feast?

_____

_____

_____

_____

_____

_____

_____

_____

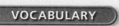

**VOCABULARY**

**tumult** (tōō′mult) *n.:* noisy commotion.

Natasha leaned against

The wall and tried

75    To speak—but found herself

Sobbing; she was shuddering

And laughing. The matchmaker

Poured out a cup of water,

Gave her some to drink,

80    Splashed some in her face.


Her parents are distressed.

Then Natasha recovered,

And calmly she said:

"Your will be done. Call

85    My bridegroom to the feast,

Bake loaves for the whole world,

Brew sweet mead[5] and call

The law to the feast."


"Of course, Natasha, angel!

90    You know we'd give our lives

To make you happy!"

They bake and they brew;

The worthy guests come,

The bride is led to the feast,

95    Her maids sing and weep;

Then horses and a sledge[6]


With the groom—and all sit.

The glasses ring and clatter,

The toasting-cup is passed


100    From hand to hand in **tumult,**

The guests are drunk.

---

5.    **mead** (mēd) *n.:* alcoholic drink made of fermented honey and water.
6.    **sledge** (slej) *n.:* sleigh.

BRIDEGROOM
"Friends, why is my fair bride
Sad, why is she not

105     Feasting and serving?"

The bride answers the groom:
"I will tell you why
As best I can. My soul
Knows the rest, day and night

110     I weep; an evil dream
Oppresses me." Her father
Says: "My dear child, tell us
What your dream is."

"I dreamed," she says, "that I

115     Went into a forest,
It was late and dark;
The moon was faintly
Shining behind a cloud;
I strayed from the path;

120     Nothing stirred except
The tops of the pine-trees.

"And suddenly, as if
I was awake, I saw
A hut. I approach the hut

125     And knock at the door
—Silence. A prayer on my lips
I open the door and enter.
A candle burns. All
Is silver and gold."

STYLE

Pause at line 129. What **mood** does Natasha create as she begins to tell her dream? Underline the words that create that mood.

FLUENCY

Read the boxed passage aloud twice. Remember, in poetry you should stop at the end of a line only if it ends with a mark of punctuation. On your second reading, raise and lower your voice at appropriate places to heighten the tension.

130   BRIDEGROOM
      "What is bad about that?
      It promises wealth."

      BRIDE
      "Wait, sir, I've not finished.
135   Silently I gazed
      On the silver and gold,
      The cloths, the rugs, the silks,
      From Novgorod,[7] and I
      Was lost in wonder.

140   "Then I heard a shout
      And a clatter of hoofs . . .

---

7.   **Novgorod:** city in the northwestern part of Russia.

Someone has driven up
To the porch. Quickly
I slammed the door and hid

145 Behind the stove. Now
I hear many voices . . .
Twelve young men come in,

"And with them is a girl,
Pure and beautiful.

150 They've taken no notice
Of the ikons,[8] they sit
To the table without
Praying or taking off
Their hats. At the head,

155 The eldest brother,
At his right, the youngest;
At his left, the girl.
Shouts, laughs, drunken **clamor** . . ."

BRIDEGROOM

160 "That betokens merriment."

BRIDE

"Wait, sir, I've not finished.
The drunken din goes on
And grows louder still.

165 Only the girl is sad.

"She sits silent, neither
Eating nor drinking;
But sheds tears in plenty;
The eldest brother

**VOCABULARY**

**clamor** (klam′ər) *n.:* loud noise. The word *din* in line 163 also means "loud noise."

**STYLE**

Line 160 contains two old-fashioned words that give this the flavor of an old fairy tale. *Betokens* is a verb meaning "indicates or shows." *Merriment* is a noun meaning "fun or joy."

_____

8. **ikons** (ī′känz) *n.:* images of Christ, the Virgin, and saints, used in the Eastern Orthodox Church (also spelled *icons*).

**IDENTIFY CAUSE & EFFECT**

Pause at line 181. Why does the crowd rise in silence?

_____

_____

_____

_____

_____

_____

_____

**VOCABULARY**

**blanches** (blanch'iz) _v._: turns white; becomes pale.

**IDENTIFY CAUSE & EFFECT**

What do we realize caused Natasha's disappearance earlier?

_____

_____

_____

_____

_____

_____

_____

_____

_____

170    Takes his knife and, whistling,
       Sharpens it; seizing her by
       The hair he kills her
       And cuts off her right hand."

       "Why," says the groom, "this
175    Is nonsense! Believe me,
       My love, your dream is not evil."
       She looks him in the eyes.
       "And from whose hand
       Does this ring come?"
180    The bride said. The whole throng
       Rose in the silence.

       With a clatter the ring
       Falls, and rolls along
       The floor. The groom **blanches,**
185    Trembles. Confusion . . .
       "Seize him!" the law commands.
       He's bound, judged, put to death.
       Natasha is famous!
       Our song at an end.

# The Bridegroom

**Mood Chart**    When you examine a story to describe its mood, you look at word choice as well as at the events of the story itself. Fill out the following chart with details from "The Bridegroom" that help establish its mood. In the bottom row of the chart, describe the overall mood of the narrative poem.

Remember that **mood** is the atmosphere created by a text. Mood is what you *feel* as you read a text. Mood can usually be described by a single adjective, such as *romantic, joyful, mysterious, horrifying, frightening, sinister, comic, positive, disgusting*, and so on.

| | Details from Text |
|---|---|
| **Word choice** | |
| **Story elements (characters, events, settings, climax, theme)** | |
| **Overall mood of the poem** | |

# Standards Review

## TestPractice : The Bridegroom

Complete the sample test item below. Then, read the explanation at right.

| Sample Test Item | Explanation of the Correct Answer |
|---|---|
| Which word best describes the **mood** set in the first stanza of the poem?<br><br>**A** joyful<br><br>**B** sorrowful<br><br>**C** mysterious<br><br>**D** humorous | The correct answer is *C*. We are immediately gripped by suspense, and wonder what happened to the girl. No details create joy (*A*) or sorrow (*B*) (since we do not know yet what has happened). Nothing is humorous (*D*) about the first stanza. |

**DIRECTIONS:** Circle the letter of each correct answer.

**Reading Standard 3.11**
Evaluate the aesthetic qualities of style, including the impact of diction and figurative language on tone, mood, and theme, using the terminology of literary criticism. (Aesthetic approach)

1. The matchmaker describes Natasha as "the goods" and her prospective husband as the "buyer." These word choices tell you that the matchmaker—

   **A** sees Natasha's marriage as a business deal

   **B** is trying to appeal to the father's sentimental side

   **C** is emphasizing the young man's wealth

   **D** is saying she wants a big fee

2. Which word best describes the **mood** at the wedding?

   **F** joyous     **H** tense

   **G** sad       **J** serious

3. The **climax** of a story is the moment when we discover what will resolve the hero's or heroine's problem: It is the most emotional moment of the plot. The climax of this story comes when—

   **A** Natasha comes home after being gone for three days

   **B** the rich man splashes mud on the girls

   **C** the bride asks where the ring came from

   **D** the bridegroom is arrested

4. The **style** of "The Bridegroom" is best described as—

   **F** scholarly

   **G** like a fairy tale

   **H** very formal

   **J** full of slang

# Standards Review

**Test Practice**    **The Bridegroom**

## Prefixes and Suffixes

**DIRECTIONS:** Circle the letter of the *best* meaning for each boldface word. Use your knowledge of prefixes and suffixes to help you.

**Reading Standard 1.1** Identify and use the literal and figurative meanings of words and understand word derivations.

1. Natasha's cheeks **regained** their rosy color.

   **A** got back        **C** climbed up

   **B** put on weight    **D** drained of

2. The matchmaker seemed **unconcerned** about Natasha's feelings.

   **F** without money

   **G** not worried

   **H** full of sympathy

   **J** worried again

3. Natasha knew she had to expose the man's **cruelty.**

   **A** brutal quality   **C** faults

   **B** being bad again   **D** ideas

4. The wedding guests looked on in **astonishment.**

   **F** lessening horror   **H** new concern

   **G** a state of surprise  **J** boredom

## Vocabulary in Context

**DIRECTIONS:** Complete the paragraph below by writing a word from the word box to fit each numbered blank. Use each word only once.

### Word Box

clamor

tumult

blanches

foreboding

As I entered the forest, I was suddenly filled with

(1) _____. The shrieks of the forest animals created a

(2) _____. A sudden shot in the nearby bushes sent

wildlife running for cover. In the (3) _____ that followed,

I could scarcely hear the footsteps coming up behind me. Just as a desert sun

(4) _____ bone to pure white, the presence behind me

drained my skin of all color.

**Before You Go On . . .**

Check your Standards Mastery at the back of this book.

# Chapter
# 9

# Literary Criticism: Biographical and Historical Approach

# Academic Vocabulary for Chapter 9

These are the terms you should know
as you read and analyze the stories in this chapter.

———————

**Biographical knowledge** Information about a writer's life that helps the reader understand the text.

**Biographical approach** The use of a writer's life experiences to help analyze and respond to a text. Writers often draw on their own backgrounds to create a piece of literature.

**Historical context** or **historical setting** The historical period that shapes a work of literature.

**Historical approach** The use of historical context to help analyze and respond to a work.

● ● ●

**Myths** Stories that are closely linked to a particular society and reflect its values and religious beliefs.

**Legends** Stories that are based on historical events and take on elements of fantasy as they are retold over the years.

**Reading Standard 1.2** Distinguish between the denotative and connotative meanings of words and interpret the connotative power of words.

**Reading Standard 1.3 (Grade 8 Review)** Use word meanings within the appropriate context and show ability to verify those meanings by definition, restatement, example, comparison, or contrast.

**Reading Standard 3.7 (Grade 8 Review)** Analyze a work of literature, showing how it reflects the heritage, traditions, attitudes, and beliefs of its author. (Biographical approach)

**Reading Standard 3.12** Analyze the way in which a work of literature is related to the themes and issues of its historical period. (Historical approach)

---

### For Further Information . . .

● Be sure to read the essay on **biography and history** in *Holt Literature and Language Arts*, pages 618–619.

# Where Have You Gone, Charming Billy?

by Tim O'Brien

You're in a foreign country with enemies all around and land mines underfoot. You don't even know your fellow soldiers. Imagine how Paul Berlin feels as he begins his tour of duty during the Vietnam War. Will his second day go better than his first? It may, if he can control his greatest fear—his fear of fear itself.

## LITERARY FOCUS: UNDERSTANDING HISTORICAL CONTEXT AND THE WRITER'S BACKGROUND

- **Historical context** is the time and place that shapes a piece of literature. As you read Tim O'Brien's story, keep in mind its historical context, the Vietnam War. This war was different from other wars the United States had fought. There were no front lines, or battlefields where opposing sides fought face to face. Instead, in Vietnam, soldiers hid in jungles and launched surprise attacks on opposing forces. As you read, look for **historical details** that give you insight into characters and events.

- Also look for details from the author's life. Tim O'Brien lived through the events he writes about: He is a veteran of the Vietnam War, which has served as a focus for almost all of his writing. O'Brien's feelings about the war are reflected through the **tone,** or attitude, he adopts and the themes he explores. To learn more about O'Brien's life, see page 628 of *Holt Literature and Language Arts.*

- **Theme** is an insight about life that a story reveals. As you read the story, consider how the writer's experiences may have shaped his attitudes about the Vietnam War.

## READING SKILLS: RECOGNIZING HISTORICAL DETAILS

"Where Have You Gone, Charming Billy?" contains details of the Vietnam War—for example, geographical details such as rice paddies and strategic details such as the soldiers' march to the sea. Look for other historical details as you read, and add them to a chart like the one below. The first row is filled in as a guide.

| Historical Details |
| --- |
| Soldiers march single file at night. |
|  |

**Reading Standard 1.2** Distinguish between the denotative and connotative meanings of words and interpret the connotative power of words.

**Reading Standard 3.7 (Grade 8 Review)** Analyze a work of literature, showing how it reflects the heritage, traditions, attitudes, and beliefs of its author. (Biographical approach)

**Reading Standard 3.12** Analyze the way in which a work of literature is related to the themes and issues of its historical period. (Historical approach)

## VOCABULARY DEVELOPMENT

### PREVIEW SELECTION VOCABULARY

Preview the following words from the story before you begin reading.

**stealth** (stelth) *n.:* secretiveness; sly behavior.

*Using **stealth** to conceal their movements, the soldiers prepared to ambush the enemy.*

**diffuse** (di·fyoōs′) *adj.:* spread out; unfocused.

*His thoughts were **diffuse,** drifting from one subject to another.*

**skirted** (skʉrt′id) *v.:* passed around rather than through. *Skirted* also means "missed narrowly; avoided."

*The soldier **skirted** the land mine by walking to the other side of the field.*

**agile** (aj′əl) *adj.:* lively; moving easily and quickly.

*He remembered the training exercises that had helped him become **agile.***

**inertia** (in·ʉr′shə) *n.:* tendency to remain either at rest or in motion.

*Overcome by **inertia,** Paul was unable to move from the spot.*

**valiantly** (val′yənt·lē) *adv.:* bravely.

*He wanted to act **valiantly,** but he felt like a coward.*

**consolation** (kän′sə·lā′shən) *n.:* act of comforting.

*Rather than provide **consolation,** the soldiers' kindness increased his misery.*

### WORD CHOICE AND CONNOTATION

**Word choice,** or **diction,** is a writer's choice of words. Writers use different types of words depending on their audience, their subject, and the effect they are trying to produce. Connotation is an important part of word choice. Several words may have the same **denotation,** or literal meaning. However, their **connotations,** or the emotional associations we have for these words, may vary greatly. For example, a *hungry* person wants to eat; a *ravenous* person desperately wants to eat. Thinking about a word's connotations is a big part of word choice. Word choice is an essential element of a writer's style and has a major effect on the **tone** of a piece of writing.

# Where Have You Gone, Charming Billy?

## Tim O'Brien

**HISTORICAL CONTEXT**

In lines 1–4, underline the word and details that help create a **historical context** for the story.

**VOCABULARY**

**stealth** (stelth) *n.*: secretiveness; sly behavior.

**INTERPRET**

Pause at line 12. Underline the four types of feelings the soldiers had. In this list, is O'Brien emphasizing the excitement of war or the stresses of war?

_____

_____

**INFER**

Circle the word repeated (in various forms) in lines 14–25. Why do you think O'Brien repeats this word so often?

_____

_____

_____

The platoon of twenty-six soldiers moved slowly in the dark, single file, not talking. One by one, like sheep in a dream, they passed through the hedgerow, crossed quietly over a meadow, and came down to the rice paddy.[1] There they stopped. Their leader knelt down, motioning with his hand, and one by one the other soldiers squatted in the shadows, vanishing in the primitive **stealth** of warfare. For a long time they did not move. Except for the sounds of their breathing, the twenty-six men were very quiet: some of them excited by the adventure, some of them

10 afraid, some of them exhausted from the long night march, some of them looking forward to reaching the sea, where they would be safe. At the rear of the column, Private First Class Paul Berlin lay quietly with his forehead resting on the black plastic stock of his rifle, his eyes closed. He was pretending he was not in the war, pretending he had not watched Billy Boy Watkins die of a heart attack that afternoon. He was pretending he was a boy again, camping with his father in the midnight summer along the Des Moines River.[2] In the dark, with his eyes pinched shut, he pretended. He pretended that when he opened his eyes,

20 his father would be there by the campfire and they would talk softly about whatever came to mind and then roll into their sleeping bags, and that later they'd wake up and it would be morning and there would not be a war, and that Billy Boy Watkins had not died of a heart attack that afternoon. He pretended he was not a soldier.

---

1. **rice paddy:** a flooded field for growing rice.
2. **Des Moines River:** a river in Des Moines, Iowa.

In the morning, when they reached the sea, it would be better. The hot afternoon would be over, he would bathe in the sea, and he would forget how frightened he had been on his first day at the war. The second day would not be so bad. He would learn.

30     There was a sound beside him, a movement, and then a breathed "Hey!"

He opened his eyes, shivering as if emerging from a deep nightmare.

"Hey!" a shadow whispered. "We're *moving*. Get up."

"Okay."

"You sleepin', or something?"

"No." He could not make out the soldier's face. With clumsy, concrete hands he clawed for his rifle, found it, found his helmet.

40     The soldier shadow grunted. "You got a lot to learn, buddy. I'd shoot you if I thought you was sleepin'. Let's go."

Private First Class Paul Berlin blinked.

Ahead of him, silhouetted against the sky, he saw the string of soldiers wading into the flat paddy, the black outline of their shoulders and packs and weapons. He was comfortable. He did not want to move. But he was afraid, for it was his first night at the war, so he hurried to catch up, stumbling once, scraping his knee, groping as though blind; his boots sank into the thick paddy water, and he smelled it all around him. He would tell his

50 mother how it smelled: mud and algae and cattle manure and chlorophyll;[3] decay, breeding mosquitoes and leeches as big as mice; the fecund[4] warmth of the paddy waters rising up to his cut knee. But he would not tell how frightened he had been.

Once they reached the sea, things would be better. They would have their rear guarded by three thousand miles of ocean, and they would swim and dive into the breakers and hunt crayfish and smell the salt, and they would be safe.

---

**3. chlorophyll** (klôr′ə·fil′) *n.:* green substance found in plant cells.
**4. fecund** (fē′kənd) *adj.:* fertile; producing abundantly.

**INFER**

Re-read lines 37–41. Underline what the soldier tells Paul. Why is the soldier so angry?

_____

_____

_____

_____

_____

_____

_____

_____

_____

_____

_____

_____

_____

_____

_____

_____

**HISTORICAL CONTEXT**

In lines 43–53, underline the details about Vietnam's geography that help establish the story's **historical context**.

WORD STUDY

In line 67, the narrator reveals that Billy Boy Watkins "got killed by a heart attack." If he had said "died of a heart attack" instead, how would the **connotation** differ?

VOCABULARY

**diffuse** (di·fyo͞os′) *adj.:* spread out; unfocused.

He followed the shadow of the man in front of him. It was a clear night. Already the Southern Cross[5] was out. And other stars he could not yet name—soon, he thought, he would learn their names. And puffy night clouds. There was not yet a moon. Wading through the paddy, his boots made sleepy, sloshing sounds, like a lullaby, and he tried not to think. Though he was afraid, he now knew that fear came in many degrees and types and peculiar categories, and he knew that his fear now was not so bad as it had been in the hot afternoon, when poor Billy Boy Watkins got killed by a heart attack. His fear now was **diffuse** and unformed: ghosts in the tree line, nighttime fears of a child, a boogeyman in the closet that his father would open to show empty, saying, "See? Nothing there, champ. Now you can sleep." In the afternoon it had been worse: The fear had been bundled and tight and he'd been on his hands and knees, crawling like an insect, an ant escaping a giant's footsteps, and thinking nothing, brain flopping like wet cement in a mixer, not thinking at all, watching while Billy Boy Watkins died.

60

70

---

5. **Southern Cross:** constellation, or group of stars, in the Southern Hemisphere.

Now, as he stepped out of the paddy onto a narrow dirt path, now the fear was mostly the fear of being so terribly afraid again.

He tried not to think.

There were tricks he'd learned to keep from thinking.

80  Counting: He counted his steps, concentrating on the numbers, pretending that the steps were dollar bills and that each step through the night made him richer and richer, so that soon he would become a wealthy man, and he kept counting and considered the ways he might spend the money after the war and what he would do. He would look his father in the eye and shrug and say, "It was pretty bad at first, but I learned a lot and I got used to it." Then he would tell his father the story of Billy Boy Watkins. But he would never let on how frightened he had been. "Not so bad," he would say instead, making his father feel proud.

90  Songs, another trick to stop from thinking: *Where have you gone, Billy Boy, Billy Boy, oh, where have you gone, charming Billy? I have gone to seek a wife, she's the joy of my life, but she's a young thing and cannot leave her mother,* and other songs that he sang in his thoughts as he walked toward the sea. And when he reached the sea, he would dig a deep hole in the sand and he would sleep like the high clouds and he would not be afraid anymore.

---

The moon came out. Pale and shrunken to the size of a dime.

The helmet was heavy on his head. In the morning he would adjust the leather binding. He would clean his rifle, too.

100  Even though he had been frightened to shoot it during the hot afternoon, he would carefully clean the breech and the muzzle and the ammunition so that next time he would be ready and not so afraid. In the morning, when they reached the sea, he would begin to make friends with some of the other soldiers. He would learn their names and laugh at their jokes. Then when the war was over, he would have war buddies, and he would write to them once in a while and exchange memories.

**CLARIFY**

Re-read lines 76–77. What is Paul most afraid of at this point?

_____

_____

_____

_____

_____

**IDENTIFY**

What two tricks of Paul's are described in lines 79–96? What is the purpose of the tricks?

_____

_____

_____

_____

_____

_____

_____

**FLUENCY**

Read the boxed passage aloud two times. Vary your tone of voice and your pacing to suggest both Paul's fear and his attempts to calm himself.

**VOCABULARY**

**skirted** (skʉrt′id) *v.:* passed around rather than through. *Skirted* also means "missed narrowly; avoided."

**HISTORICAL CONTEXT**

Re-read lines 121–130. Underline things O'Brien might have actually learned in training for the war. What did he *not* learn? Circle the passage that tells you.

**VOCABULARY**

**agile** (aj′əl) *adj.:* lively; moving easily and quickly.

**inertia** (in·ʉr′shə) *n.:* tendency to remain either at rest or in motion.

Walking, sleeping in his walking, he felt better. He watched the moon come higher.

110　Once they **skirted** a sleeping village. The smells again—straw, cattle, mildew. The men were quiet. On the far side of the village, buried in the dark smells, a dog barked. The column stopped until the barking died away; then they marched fast away from the village, through a graveyard filled with conical-shaped[6] burial mounds and tiny altars made of clay and stone. The graveyard had a perfumy smell. A nice place to spend the night, he thought. The mounds would make fine battlements,[7] and the smell was nice and the place was quiet. But they went on, passing through a hedgerow and across another paddy and east

120　toward the sea.

He walked carefully. He remembered what he'd been taught: Stay off the center of the path, for that was where the land mines and booby traps were planted, where stupid and lazy soldiers like to walk. Stay alert, he'd been taught. Better alert than inert.[8] **Ag-ile,** mo-bile, hos-tile. He wished he'd paid better attention to the training. He could not remember what they'd said about how to stop being afraid; they hadn't given any lessons in courage—not that he could remember—and they hadn't mentioned how Billy Boy Watkins would die of a heart

130　attack, his face turning pale and the veins popping out.

Private First Class Paul Berlin walked carefully.

Stretching ahead of him like dark beads on an invisible chain, the string of shadow soldiers whose names he did not yet know moved with the silence and slow grace of smoke. Now and again moonlight was reflected off a machine gun or a wristwatch. But mostly the soldiers were quiet and hidden and faraway-seeming in a peaceful night, strangers on a long street, and he felt quite separate from them, as if trailing behind like the caboose on a night train, pulled along by **inertia,** sleep-

140　walking, an afterthought to the war.

---

6.　conical- (kän′i·kəl) **shaped** *adj.:* shaped like a cone.
7.　**battlements** *n.:* fortifications from which to shoot.
8.　**inert** (in·ʉrt′) *adj.:* without movement; here, dead.

So he walked carefully, counting his steps. When he had counted to 3,485, the column stopped.

One by one the soldiers knelt or squatted down.

The grass along the path was wet. Private First Class Paul Berlin lay back and turned his head so that he could lick at the dew with his eyes closed, another trick to forget the war. He might have slept. "I *wasn't* afraid," he was screaming or dreaming, facing his father's stern eyes. "I wasn't afraid," he was saying. When he opened his eyes, a soldier was sitting beside him,

150 quietly chewing a stick of Doublemint gum.

"You sleepin' again?" the soldier whispered.

"No," said Private First Class Paul Berlin. "Hell, no."

The soldier grunted, chewing his gum. Then he twisted the cap off his canteen, took a swallow, and handed it through the dark.

"Take some," he whispered.

"Thanks."

"You're the new guy?"

"Yes." He did not want to admit it, being new to the war.

160 The soldier grunted and handed him a stick of gum. "Chew it quiet—OK? Don't blow no bubbles or nothing."

"Thanks. I won't." He could not make out the man's face in the shadows.

They sat still and Private First Class Paul Berlin chewed the gum until all the sugars were gone; then the soldier said, "Bad day today, buddy."

Private First Class Paul Berlin nodded wisely, but he did not speak.

"Don't think it's always so bad," the soldier whispered. "I

170 don't wanna scare you. You'll get used to it soon enough. . . . They been fighting wars a long time, and you get used to it."

"Yeah."

"You will."

COMPARE & CONTRAST

Re-read lines 149–161. How does the soldier's attitude toward Paul's sleeping differ from his attitude earlier (lines 30–41)? Why might the soldier's feelings have changed?

_____

_____

_____

_____

_____

_____

_____

_____

BIOGRAPHICAL CONTEXT

O'Brien's strong feelings about war are often expressed by the characters he creates. What idea about war do the soldier's words suggest (lines 169–171)?

_____

_____

_____

_____

_____

They were quiet awhile. And the night was quiet, no crickets or birds, and it was hard to imagine it was truly a war. He searched for the soldier's face but could not find it. It did not matter much. Even if he saw the fellow's face, he would not know the name; and even if he knew the name, it would not matter much.

180    "Haven't got the time?" the soldier whispered.

"No."

"Rats. . . . Don't matter, really. Goes faster if you don't know the time, anyhow."

"Sure."

"What's your name, buddy?"

"Paul."

"Nice to meet ya," he said, and in the dark beside the path, they shook hands. "Mine's Toby. Everybody calls me Buffalo, though." The soldier's hand was strangely warm and soft. But it

190    was a very big hand. "Sometimes they just call me Buff," he said.

And again they were quiet. They lay in the grass and waited. The moon was very high now and very bright, and they were waiting for cloud cover. The soldier suddenly snorted.

"What is it?"

"Nothin'," he said, but then he snorted again. "A bloody *heart attack!*" the soldier said. "Can't get over it—old Billy Boy croaking from a lousy heart attack. . . . A heart attack—can you believe it?"

The idea of it made Private First Class Paul Berlin smile.

200    He couldn't help it.

"Ever hear of such a thing?"

"Not till now," said Private First Class Paul Berlin, still smiling.

"Me neither," said the soldier in the dark. "Gawd, dying of a heart attack. Didn't know him, did you."

"No."

"Tough as nails."

"Yeah."

INTERPRET

Why is the idea of dying of a heart attack so grimly amusing (lines 194–212)?

"And what happens? A heart attack. Can you imagine it?"

210      "Yes," said Private First Class Paul Berlin. He wanted to laugh. "I can imagine it." And he imagined it clearly. He giggled—he couldn't help it. He imagined Billy's father opening the telegram: SORRY TO INFORM YOU THAT YOUR SON BILLY BOY WAS YESTERDAY SCARED TO DEATH IN ACTION IN THE REPUBLIC OF VIETNAM, **VALIANTLY** SUCCUMBING[9] TO A HEART ATTACK SUFFERED WHILE UNDER ENORMOUS STRESS, AND IT IS WITH GREATEST SYMPATHY THAT . . . He giggled again. He rolled onto his belly and pressed his face into his arms. His body was shaking with giggles.

220      The big soldier hissed at him to shut up, but he could not stop giggling and remembering the hot afternoon, and poor Billy Boy, and how they'd been drinking Coca-Cola from bright-red aluminum cans, and how they'd started on the day's march, and how a little while later poor Billy Boy stepped on the mine, and how it made a tiny little sound—*poof*—and how Billy Boy stood there with his mouth wide open, looking down at where his foot had been blown off, and how finally Billy Boy sat down very casually, not saying a word, with his foot lying behind him, most of it still in the boot.

230      He giggled louder—he could not stop. He bit his arm, trying to stifle it, but remembering: "War's over, Billy," the men had said in **consolation,** but Billy Boy got scared and started crying and said he was about to die. "Nonsense," the medic said, Doc Peret, but Billy Boy kept bawling, tightening up, his face going pale and transparent and his veins popping out. Scared stiff. Even when Doc Peret stuck him with morphine, Billy Boy kept crying.

     "Shut up!" the big soldier hissed, but Private First Class Paul Berlin could not stop. Giggling and remembering, he
240 covered his mouth. His eyes stung, remembering how it was when Billy Boy died of fright.

VOCABULARY

**valiantly** (val′yənt·lē) *adv.*: bravely.

HISTORICAL CONTEXT

In lines 224–229, underline the factual details describing a land mine accident.

VOCABULARY

**consolation** (kän′sə·lā′shən) *n.*: act of comforting.

INFER

Pause at line 241. Why can't Paul stop laughing?

---

**9. succumbing** *v.* used as *adj.* (used with *to*): here, dying from.

COMPARE &
CONTRAST

Re-read lines 245–248.
Underline the words telling
what caused Billy Boy's heart
attack. What "enemy" do
Billy Boy and Paul both do
battle with?

**COMPARE &
CONTRAST**

Re-read lines 245–248.
Underline the words telling
what caused Billy Boy's heart
attack. What "enemy" do
Billy Boy and Paul both do
battle with?

**HISTORICAL
CONTEXT**

Re-read lines 249–258.
Underline the details that tell
what happened to the dead
and wounded during the
Vietnam War.

"Shut up!"

But he could not stop giggling, the same way Billy Boy
could not stop bawling that afternoon.

Afterward Doc Peret had explained: "You see, Billy Boy
really died of a heart attack. He was scared he was gonna die—
so scared he had himself a heart attack—and that's what really
killed him. I seen it before."

So they wrapped Billy in a plastic poncho, his eyes still wide
250    open and scared stiff, and they carried him over the meadow to
a rice paddy, and then when the medevac helicopter[10] arrived,
they carried him through the paddy and put him aboard, and
the mortar rounds were falling everywhere, and the helicopter
pulled up, and Billy Boy came tumbling out, falling slowly and
then faster, and the paddy water sprayed up as if Billy Boy had
just executed a long and dangerous dive, as if trying to escape
Graves Registration, where he would be tagged and sent home
under a flag, dead of a heart attack.

"Shut up!" the soldier hissed, but Paul Berlin could not
260    stop giggling, remembering: scared to death.

Later they waded in after him, probing for Billy Boy with
their rifle butts, elegantly and delicately probing for Billy Boy

---

10. **medevac** (med′i·vak′) **helicopter:** helicopter used to evacuate
    wounded soldiers to hospitals and medical care.

in the stinking paddy, singing—some of them—*Where have you gone, Billy Boy, Billy Boy, oh, where have you gone, charming Billy?* Then they found him. Green and covered with algae, his eyes still wide open and scared stiff, dead of a heart attack suffered while—

"Shut up!" the soldier said loudly, shaking him.

But Private First Class Paul Berlin could not stop. The
270   giggles were caught in his throat, drowning him in his own laughter: scared to death like Billy Boy.

Giggling, lying on his back, he saw the moon move, or the clouds moving across the moon. Wounded in action, dead of fright. A fine war story. He would tell it to his father, how Billy Boy had been scared to death, never letting on . . . He could not stop.

The soldier smothered him. He tried to fight back, but he was weak from the giggles.

The moon was under the clouds and the column was moving.
280   The soldier helped him up. "You OK now, buddy?"

"Sure."

"What was so bloody funny?"

"Nothing."

"You can get killed, laughing that way."

"I know. I know that."

"You got to stay calm, buddy." The soldier handed him his rifle. "Half the battle, just staying calm. You'll get better at it," he said. "Come on, now."

He turned away and Private First Class Paul Berlin hurried
290   after him. He was still shivering.

He would do better once he reached the sea, he thought, still smiling a little. A funny war story that he would tell to his father, how Billy Boy Watkins was scared to death. A good joke. But even when he smelled salt and heard the sea, he could not stop being afraid.

**INFER**

Pause at line 276. Why is it important for Paul to conceal his fear?

_____

_____

_____

**HISTORICAL CONTEXT**

What does the soldier mean when he says that laughing can get you killed (line 284)?

_____

_____

_____

_____

_____

_____

**BIOGRAPHICAL CONTEXT**

Circle the description of Paul's feelings at the end of the story. What does the description suggest about O'Brien's experiences in the Vietnam War?

_____

_____

_____

_____

_____

# Where Have You Gone, Charming Billy?

**Historical Context Chart**    "Where Have You Gone, Charming Billy?" is filled with details about the Vietnam War. Re-read the story to collect information about wartime in Vietnam. Fill in the chart with your findings. Then, identify the **theme,** or insight, about war that the story conveys.

| Historical Context | Story Passages/Descriptions |
|---|---|
| **What you learn about the setting of Vietnam** | |
| **What you learn about the soldiers' training** | |
| **What you learn about wartime events and procedures** | |
| **What you learn about the soldiers' feelings** | |
| **The Story's Theme** | |
| | |

# Standards Review

## Where Have You Gone, Charming Billy?

Improve your test-taking skills by completing the sample test item below. Then, read the explanation in the right-hand column.

| Sample Test Item | Explanation of the Correct Answer |
|---|---|
| As the story opens, Paul is most upset by memories of— <br><br> **A** his parents <br> **B** his training in dealing with courage <br> **C** Billy Boy's death <br> **D** an old song | The correct answer is *C*. <br><br> Paul thinks about his parents but is not upset by them, so *A* is incorrect. He doesn't remember lessons on courage, so *B* is not correct. He sings an old song as he tries to forget Billy Boy's death, so *D* is not correct. |

**DIRECTIONS:** Circle the letter of each correct response.

1. Where is the story set?

    **A** Indiana

    **B** Vietnam

    **C** Europe

    **D** training camp

2. Paul's **internal conflict** is his difficulty in dealing with—

    **F** Toby

    **G** his fear

    **H** his desire to sleep

    **J** military rules

3. In what ways are Paul and Billy Boy alike?

    **A** They both like the outdoors.

    **B** They both come from Iowa.

    **C** They are both really tall.

    **D** Both are overcome with fear.

4. Which sentence *best* describes Tim O'Brien's attitude toward the Vietnam War, as expressed in "Where Have You Gone, Charming Billy?"

    **F** He shows compassion for the soldiers and their fears.

    **G** He supports the war.

    **H** He thinks soldiers should be friendlier to each other.

    **J** He thinks the Vietnamese people should surrender.

**Reading Standard 3.7 (Grade 8 Review)** Analyze a work of literature, showing how it reflects the heritage, traditions, attitudes, and beliefs of its author. (Biographical approach)

**Reading Standard 3.12** Analyze the way in which a work of literature is related to the themes and issues of its historical period. (Historical approach)

# Standards Review

 **Test Practice**

## Where Have You Gone, Charming Billy?

### Word Choice

**DIRECTIONS:** Write the word or phrase that has a more positive connotation to complete each sentence.

**Reading Standard 1.2** Distinguish between the denotative and connotative meanings of words and interpret the connotative power of words.

1. The soldier's face was _____. (gaunt / thin)

2. The sound of gunfire made Paul _____. (upset / hysterical)

3. The other soldier was _____ Paul for making noise. (unhappy with / furious with)

4. The young soldier's hands shook with _____. (terror / fear)

5. War is a _____ experience. (grueling / challenging)

### Vocabulary in Context

**DIRECTIONS:** Complete the paragraph by writing words from the box in the correct blanks. Not all words from the box will be used.

**Word Box**

stealth

diffuse

skirted

agile

inertia

valiantly

consolation

The soldiers were in a life-threatening situation. The enemy was close behind, and a rocky mountain loomed ahead. A young soldier (1) _____ volunteered to take on the dangerous mission of going first up the mountain, creating a path for the others. The soldier's (2) _____ body moved quickly up the rocks. At one point, his progress was blocked by a huge boulder, but he found a path and (3) _____ the large rock successfully. Although he was covered with cuts and bruises by the day's end, his (4) _____ came from leading his platoon to safety.

 **Before You Go On . . .**

Check your Standards Mastery at the back of this book.

# The Man to Send Rain Clouds by Leslie Marmon Silko

BEFORE YOU READ

In "The Man to Send Rain Clouds," a Pueblo Indian family and a Catholic priest join together to bury a loved one.

## LITERARY FOCUS: BIOGRAPHICAL APPROACH

Leslie Marmon Silko, whose background is Plains Indian, Mexican, and European, grew up in the Laguna Pueblo in New Mexico and attended Catholic school in Albuquerque. She has said of the Laguna Pueblo, "This place I am from is everything I am as a writer and a human being." As a child, Silko learned stories the Laguna Pueblos told about themselves and their land. These tales became the inspiration for Silko's stories.

- As you read, look for ways in which Silko's background affects her **tone**— her attitude toward the characters in "The Man to Send Rain Clouds."
- Also, take note of how the Pueblo Indians and the Catholic priest *interact.* What do those interactions reveal about relations between the two cultures?

## READING SKILLS: COMPARE AND CONTRAST

When you **compare** two things, you look for *similarities,* or ways the things are alike. When you **contrast** two things, you look for *differences* between them.

As you read "The Man to Send Rain Clouds," compare and contrast the customs and concerns of the Pueblos and Father Paul. You can keep a chart like this one to show similarities and differences. Some items have been filled in as a guide.

| Similarities | | Differences | |
| --- | --- | --- | --- |
| **Pueblos** | **Father Paul** | **Pueblos** | **Father Paul** |
| Concerned about Teofilo | Concerned about Teofilo | Sometimes go to Mass | Wants them to come to Mass every Sunday |
| | | | |
| | | | |

**Reading Standard 1.3 (Grade 8 Review)** Use word meanings within the appropriate context and show ability to verify those meanings by definition, restatement, example, comparison, or contrast.

**Reading Standard 3.7 (Grade 8 Review)** Analyze a work of literature, showing how it reflects the heritage, traditions, attitudes, and beliefs of its author. (Biographical approach)

SHORT STORY

## PREVIEW SELECTION VOCABULARY

The following words appear in "The Man to Send Rain Clouds." Get to know these words before you read the story.

**arroyo** (ə·roi′ō) *n.:* narrow, steep-sided ditch hollowed out by water and usually dry except after heavy rain.

*The now dry arroyo had been a long rushing river during the rainy season.*

**pueblo** (pweb′lō) *n.:* southwestern village. The word also refers to a multilevel stone or adobe dwelling made up of adjoining flat-roofed houses in the southwestern United States. When capitalized, *Pueblo* refers to a member of a group who lives in these family dwellings, such as the Laguna Pueblo.

*Indian families live in the pueblo, a large building in the village.*

**mesa** (mā′sə) *n.:* flat-topped hill, most common in the southwestern United States.

*The mesa looked like a table poking up from the flat desert.*

**adobe** (ə·dō′bē) *adj.:* built of sun-dried bricks. As a noun *adobe* means "sun-dried brick made of straw and clay" or "building made from sun-dried brick."

*Adobe bricks, made from clay and straw, are dried in the sun.*

## CONTEXT CLUES

Don't let unfamiliar words be a stumbling block to your reading progress. Look at a word's **context**—the words, phrases, and sentences that surround it—for clues to its meaning. In the examples below, the *italicized* context clues will help you figure out the meaning of the **boldface** words.

DEFINITION: His body looked **shriveled,** or *small and wrinkled.*

RESTATEMENT: Walking down the **bank,** Ken slid on the loose earth of the *low hill.*

EXAMPLE: We had **toiled** all summer to ensure a good harvest—*for instance, we watered the plants daily and used special screens to protect them* from the burning sun.

COMPARISON: *Like a small park surrounded by houses,* the **patio** was surrounded by the church walls.

CONTRAST: Some magazines are *printed on rough newsprint,* but **glossy** magazines *are not.*

# The Man to Send Rain Clouds

## Leslie Marmon Silko

They found him under a big cottonwood tree. His Levi jacket and pants were faded light blue so that he had been easy to find. The big cottonwood tree stood apart from a small grove of winterbare cottonwoods which grew in the wide, sandy **arroyo.** He had been dead for a day or more, and the sheep had wandered and scattered up and down the arroyo. Leon and his brother-in-law, Ken, gathered the sheep and left them in the pen at the sheep camp before they returned to the cottonwood tree. Leon waited under the tree while Ken drove the truck through the deep sand

10 to the edge of the arroyo. He squinted up at the sun and unzipped his jacket—it sure was hot for this time of year. But high and northwest the blue mountains were still in snow. Ken came sliding down the low, crumbling bank about fifty yards down, and he was bringing the red blanket.

Before they wrapped the old man, Leon took a piece of string out of his pocket and tied a small gray feather in the old man's long white hair. Ken gave him the paint. Across the brown wrinkled forehead he drew a streak of white and along the high cheekbones he drew a strip of blue paint. He paused and watched

20 Ken throw pinches of corn meal and pollen into the wind that fluttered the small gray feather. Then Leon painted with yellow under the old man's broad nose, and finally, when he had painted green across the chin, he smiled.

"Send us rain clouds, Grandfather." They laid the bundle in the back of the pickup and covered it with a heavy tarp before they started back to the **pueblo.**

They turned off the highway onto the sandy pueblo road. Not long after they passed the store and post office they saw

---

### VOCABULARY

**arroyo** (ə·rɔi′ō) *n.:* narrow, steep-sided ditch hollowed out by heavy rain.

**pueblo** (pweb′lō) *n.:* southwestern village.

### INFER

Re-read lines 15–23. Underline the things Leon and Ken do as they prepare the dead man for burial. Why might they be doing these things?

_____

_____

_____

### INFER

In line 24 we learn who the dead man is. Who is he, and why does Leon ask him to send rain clouds?

_____

_____

_____

_____

_____

_____

_____

_____

IDENTIFY

Re-read lines 28–32. Underline the name and title of the new character. Then, circle the name of the grandfather, revealed by the new character.

INFER

Pause at line 41. **Dramatic irony** occurs when the reader knows something that a character doesn't know. What important news about Teofilo does Father Paul *not* know? Why don't Ken and Leon tell him?

_____

_____

_____

_____

_____

_____

_____

_____

FLUENCY

Read the boxed passage aloud two times. On your first read, focus on conveying the basic meaning of the passage. The second time you read, use your tone of voice and reading speed to bring the scene to life for your listeners.

30   Father Paul's car coming toward them. When he recognized their faces, he slowed his car and waved for them to stop. The young priest rolled down the car window.

"Did you find old Teofilo?" he asked loudly.

Leon stopped the truck. "Good morning, Father. We were just out to the sheep camp. Everything is OK now."

"Thank God for that. Teofilo is a very old man. You really shouldn't allow him to stay at the sheep camp alone."

"No, he won't do that anymore now."

"Well, I'm glad you understand. I hope I'll be seeing you at Mass this week—we missed you last Sunday. See if you can get
40   old Teofilo to come with you." The priest smiled and waved at them as they drove away.

Louise and Teresa were waiting. The table was set for lunch, and the coffee was boiling on the black iron stove. Leon looked at Louise and then at Teresa.

"We found him under a cottonwood tree in the big arroyo near sheep camp. I guess he sat down to rest in the shade and never got up again." Leon walked toward the old man's bed. The red plaid shawl had been shaken and spread carefully over the bed, and a new brown flannel shirt and pair of stiff new Levi's
50   were arranged neatly beside the pillow. Louise held the screen door open while Leon and Ken carried in the red blanket. He looked small and shriveled, and after they dressed him in the new shirt and pants, he seemed more shrunken.

It was noontime now, because the church bells rang the Angelus.[1] They ate the beans with hot bread, and nobody said anything until after Teresa poured the coffee.

Ken stood up and put on his jacket. "I'll see about the gravediggers. Only the top layer of soil is frozen. I think it can be ready before dark."

60   Leon nodded his head and finished his coffee. After Ken had been gone for a while, the neighbors and clanspeople came

---

1.   **Angelus** (an'jə·ləs): in the Catholic tradition, a prayer recited at dawn, noon, and sunset, announced by the ringing of bells.

quietly to embrace Teofilo's family and to leave food on the table because the gravediggers would come to eat when they were finished.

The sky in the west was full of pale yellow light. Louise stood outside with her hands in the pockets of Leon's green army jacket that was too big for her. The funeral was over, and the old men had taken their candles and medicine bags and were gone. She waited until the body was laid into the pickup before

70 she said anything to Leon. She touched his arm, and he noticed that her hands were still dusty from the corn meal that she had sprinkled around the old man. When she spoke, Leon could not hear her.

"What did you say? I didn't hear you."

"I said that I had been thinking about something."

"About what?"

"About the priest sprinkling holy water for Grandpa. So he won't be thirsty."

**BIOGRAPHICAL CONTEXT**

Re-read lines 65–73. Underline details that reveal some of the traditions of Pueblo funerals. Then, in lines 77–78, circle a Catholic ritual Louise would like to have take place.

mesa (māʹsə) *n.:* flat-topped hill, most common in the southwestern United States.

*Mesa,* a Spanish word used in English, is from the Latin word for "table."

PREDICT

Pause at line 109. What do you think the priest's response to Leon's request for holy water will be?

_____

_____

_____

_____

_____

_____

_____

_____

_____

_____

_____

_____

_____

_____

Leon stared at the new moccasins that Teofilo had made for the
80  ceremonial dances in the summer. They were nearly hidden by the red blanket. It was getting colder, and the wind pushed gray dust down the narrow pueblo road. The sun was approaching the long **mesa** where it disappeared during the winter. Louise stood there shivering and watching his face. Then he zipped up his jacket and opened the truck door. "I'll see if he's there."

Ken stopped the pickup at the church, and Leon got out; and then Ken drove down the hill to the graveyard where people were waiting. Leon knocked at the old carved door with its symbols of the Lamb. While he waited he looked up at the twin bells
90  from the king of Spain with the last sunlight pouring around them in their tower.

The priest opened the door and smiled when he saw who it was. "Come in! What brings you here this evening?"

The priest walked toward the kitchen, and Leon stood with his cap in his hand, playing with the earflaps and examining the living room—the brown sofa, the green armchair, and the brass lamp that hung down from the ceiling by links of chain. The priest dragged a chair out of the kitchen and offered it to Leon.

"No thank you, Father. I only came to ask you if you would
100  bring your holy water to the graveyard."

The priest turned away from Leon and looked out the window at the patio full of shadows and the dining-room windows of the nuns' cloister across the patio. The curtains were heavy, and the light from within faintly penetrated; it was impossible to see the nuns inside eating supper. "Why didn't you tell me he was dead? I could have brought the Last Rites[2] anyway."

Leon smiled. "It wasn't necessary, Father."

The priest stared down at his scuffed brown loafers and the worn hem of his cassock. "For a Christian burial it was necessary."
110  His voice was distant, and Leon thought that his blue eyes looked tired.

---

2.  **Last Rites:** Catholic ceremony performed at the time of death.

"It's O.K., Father, we just want him to have plenty of water."

The priest sank down into the green chair and picked up a glossy missionary magazine. He turned the colored pages full of lepers and pagans[3] without looking at them.

"You know I can't do that, Leon. There should have been the Last Rites and a funeral Mass at the very least."

Leon put on his green cap and pulled the flaps down over his ears. "It's getting late, Father. I've got to go."

120 When Leon opened the door Father Paul stood up and said, "Wait." He left the room and came back wearing a long brown overcoat. He followed Leon out the door and across the dim churchyard to the **adobe** steps in front of the church. They both stooped to fit through the low adobe entrance. And when they started down the hill to the graveyard only half of the sun was visible above the mesa.

The priest approached the grave slowly, wondering how they had managed to dig into the frozen ground; and then he remembered that this was New Mexico, and saw the pile of cold 130 loose sand beside the hole. The people stood close to each other with little clouds of steam puffing from their faces. The priest looked at them and saw a pile of jackets, gloves, and scarves in the yellow, dry tumbleweeds that grew in the graveyard. He looked at the red blanket, not sure that Teofilo was so small, wondering if it wasn't some perverse Indian trick—something they did in March to ensure a good harvest—wondering if maybe old Teofilo was actually at sheep camp corralling the sheep for the night. But there he was, facing into a cold dry wind and squinting at the last sunlight, ready to bury a red 140 wool blanket while the faces of his parishioners were in shadow with the last warmth of the sun on their backs.

His fingers were stiff, and it took him a long time to twist the lid off the holy water. Drops of water fell on the red blanket

---

3. **lepers** (lep′ərz) **and pagans** (pā′gənz): People with leprosy, a skin disease, were once scorned, but religious groups have traditionally helped them. Here, *pagans* refers to people whom missionaries seek to convert.

COMPARE & CONTRAST

Re-read lines 107–117. What religious differences exist between Leon and the priest?

_____

_____

_____

_____

_____

VOCABULARY

adobe (ə·dō′bē) adj.: built of sun-dried bricks.

INFER

Pause at line 126. Why do you think Father Paul agrees to sprinkle holy water on Teofilo's grave?

_____

_____

_____

_____

IDENTIFY

In lines 134–141, underline the words revealing that Father Paul does not always trust the Pueblos.

Pause at line 151. What might Father Paul's task remind him of? (For one answer, see Louise's action in lines 70–72.)

_____

_____

_____

_____

_____

_____

_____

INTERPRET

How does the sprinkling of holy water on Teofilo's body provide a **resolution**, or ending, to the story?

_____

_____

_____

_____

_____

_____

_____

_____

_____

_____

_____

and soaked into dark icy spots. He sprinkled the grave and the water disappeared almost before it touched the dim, cold sand; it reminded him of something—he tried to remember what it was, because he thought if he could remember he might understand this. He sprinkled more water; he shook the container until it was empty, and the water fell through the light from sundown 150 like August rain that fell while the sun was still shining, almost evaporating before it touched the wilted squash flowers.

The wind pulled at the priest's brown Franciscan[4] robe and swirled away the corn meal and pollen that had been sprinkled on the blanket. They lowered the bundle into the ground, and they didn't bother to untie the stiff pieces of new rope that were tied around the ends of the blanket. The sun was gone, and over on the highway the eastbound lane was full of headlights. The priest walked away slowly. Leon watched him climb the hill, and when he had disappeared within the tall, thick walls, Leon 160 turned to look up at the high blue mountains in the deep snow that reflected a faint red light from the west. He felt good because it was finished, and he was happy about the sprinkling of the holy water; now the old man could send them big thunderclouds for sure.

---

4.  **Franciscan** (fran·sis′kən): referring to a Christian religious order, or group of holy men, founded by Saint Francis of Assisi, in Italy (1209).

# The Man to Send Rain Clouds

**Chart of Common Ground**     In the story, members of two cultures find common ground, something they can agree on. Use the graphic organizer below to show how, despite the differences between the two groups, they are able to share one ceremony. On the left-hand side of the chart, write in the Pueblo traditions from the story. On the right-hand side, fill in the Catholic traditions from the story. In the connecting "common ground," explain how the two groups come to share the burial ceremony. Then, state the story's **theme,** or insight, about shared traditions.

| Pueblo Traditions | Common Ground | Catholic Traditions |
|---|---|---|
|  |  |  |

| The Story's Theme |
|---|
|  |

# Standards Review

**TestPractice**  **The Man to Send Rain Clouds**

Improve your test-taking skills by completing the sample test item below. Then, read the explanation of the correct answer.

| Sample Test Item | Explanation of the Correct Answer |
|---|---|
| Because the writer grew up in the Laguna Pueblo, you might **infer** that the face painting of the dead— <br><br> A  is a Laguna Pueblo tradition <br><br> B  was invented by the writer <br><br> C  is a Catholic tradition <br><br> D  cannot be used by other societies | The correct answer is *A*. <br><br> *B* is not correct because many of the story details seem based on fact. *C* is not correct because if it were a Catholic tradition, the priest would have participated. *D* is not correct because face painting is used by other societies. |

**DIRECTIONS:** Circle the letter of each correct response.

**Reading Standard 3.7 (Grade 8 Review)**
Analyze a work of literature, showing how it reflects the heritage, traditions, attitudes, and beliefs of its author. (Biographical approach)

1. Father Paul is upset because the dead man's family—

   A  is unfriendly to him

   B  refuses to become Christian

   C  did not tell him that Teofilo died

   D  doesn't want holy water sprinkled on Teofilo

2. The story's **conflict** begins when the family asks the priest to—

   F  sprinkle holy water on the body

   G  perform Last Rites

   H  take part in the Pueblo ceremony

   J  stay away from the Pueblo community

3. The priest's decision to sprinkle holy water on Teofilo shows that—

   A  everyone should have the same religion

   B  people with different traditions can cooperate

   C  religions should be kept apart

   D  funerals are sad ceremonies

4. Why might water be so important to the Pueblos?

   F  They are a boating community.

   G  They need water for their crops.

   H  Water stands for a baptism.

   J  They have no running water in their homes.

# Standards Review

 **TestPractice** : **The Man to Send Rain Clouds**

## Context Clues

**DIRECTIONS:** Circle the letter of the word or phrase that best defines the boldface word. Use context clues to help you.

1. The sunlight **penetrated** the thin curtains covering the window and brightened the room.

   **A** hid       **C** tore

   **B** passed through    **D** covered

2. After Sunday's church service, the **parishioners** spoke to the priest.

   **F** people at a funeral

   **G** speakers

   **H** members of a church

   **J** priests

3. The girl put soft **moccasins** on her feet.

   **A** shoes      **C** pants

   **B** gloves     **D** glasses

4. Did you polish your **scuffed** shoes?

   **F** new-looking

   **G** worn-looking

   **H** formal

   **J** athletic

**Reading Standard 1.3 (Grade 8 Review)** Use word meanings within the appropriate context and show ability to verify those meanings by definition, restatement, example, comparison, or contrast.

## Vocabulary in Context

**DIRECTIONS:** Complete the paragraph below by writing words from the word box in the correct numbered blanks. Use each word only once.

| Word Box |
| --- |
| arroyo |
| pueblo |
| mesas |
| adobe |

Carlos grew up in a(n) (1) _____, a group of adjoining houses where many families in his village lived. Made of sun-dried bricks, the (2) _____ house had a flat roof. Carlos's village was located at the end of a(n) (3) _____, a long canyon that wound around the hills and the flat-topped (4) _____ that dotted the desert.

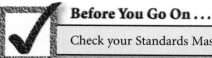
**Before You Go On . . .**
Check your Standards Mastery at the back of this book.

# Drama

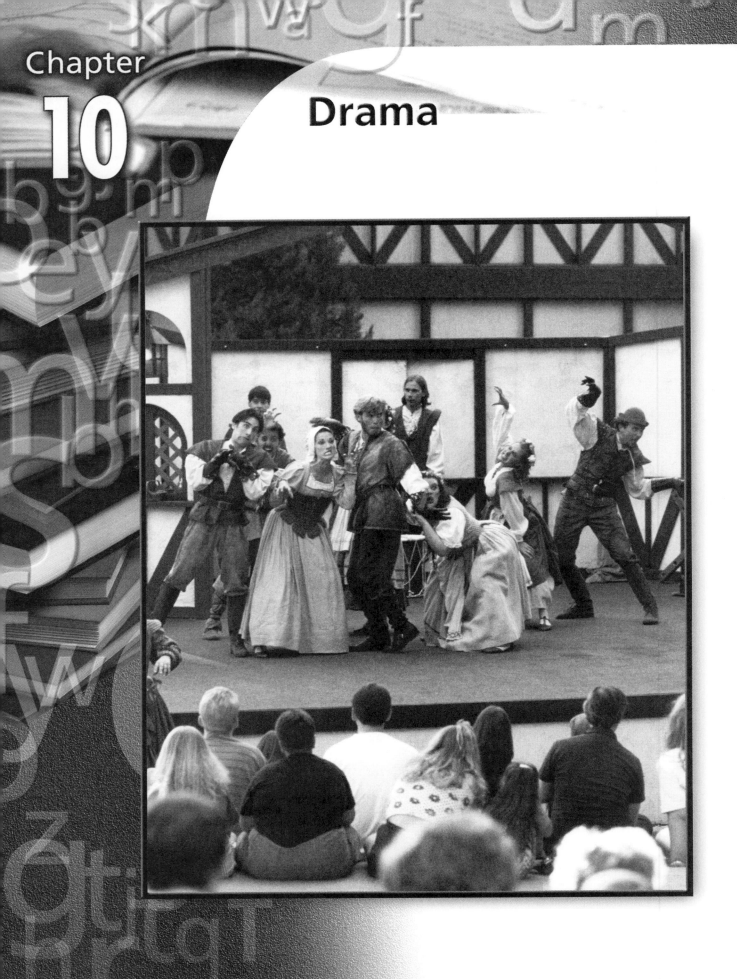

# Academic Vocabulary for Chapter 10

These are the terms you should know
as you read and analyze the plays in this chapter.

---

**Play** A story acted out live, using dialogue and action.

**Tragedy** A play that presents serious and important actions that end unhappily for the main character.

**Tragic hero** An admirable figure who has a personal failing that leads to his or her downfall.

**Tragic flaw** A failing that leads a character to make choices that result in tragedy.

**Comedy** A play that ends happily, in which the main character gets what he or she wants.

**Character foil** A character who contrasts dramatically with another character. A "foil" serves to highlight the qualities of the characters he or she is contrasted with.

● ● ●

**Dialogue** Conversations between characters in a play.

**Monologue** A long speech made by one character to one or more other characters onstage.

**Soliloquy** A speech made by a character who is alone onstage, speaking to himself or herself or to the audience.

**Aside** A short speech, delivered to the audience or to another character, that others onstage are not supposed to hear.

**Reading Standard 1.2** Distinguish between the denotative and connotative meanings of words and interpret the connotative power of words.

**Reading Standard 1.2 (Grade 8 Review)** Understand the most important points in the history of English language and use common word origins to determine the historical influences on English word meanings.

**Reading Standard 3.1** Articulate the relationship between the expressed purposes and the characteristics of different forms of dramatic literature (e.g., comedy, tragedy, drama, dramatic monologue).

**Reading Standard 3.10** Identify and describe the function of dialogue, scene designs, soliloquies, asides, and character foils in dramatic literature.

---

### For Further Information . . .

Be sure to read these essays in *Holt Literature and Language Arts:*

● **Drama: Forms and Stagecraft,** pages 720–723.
● **The Elizabethan Stage,** pages 745–749.
● **How to Read Shakespeare,** pages 752–753.

# The Tragedy of Julius Caesar

*from* **Act III, Scene 2** by William Shakespeare

**Reading Standard 1.2 (Grade 8 Review)** Understand the most important points in the history of English language and use common word origins to determine the historical influences on English word meanings.

**Reading Standard 3.1** Articulate the relationship between the expressed purposes and the characteristics of different forms of dramatic literature (e.g., comedy, tragedy, drama, dramatic monologue).

**Reading Standard 3.10** Identify and describe the function of dialogue, scene designs, soliloquies, asides, and character foils in dramatic literature.

## BEFORE YOU READ

Julius Caesar was a controversial leader—he was loved by many of his people and despised by many others, who believed he was assuming too much power. What kind of person is Caesar in Shakespeare's tragedy? Read the scene that follows, and decide whose side Shakespeare is on.

### LITERARY FOCUS: TRAGEDY

A **tragedy** tells of serious events in the life of its main character. Tragedies have been performed onstage for literally thousands of years. Most tragedies have these characteristics:

- The main character is often high-ranking or dignified.
- The main character, also called a tragic hero, has a **tragic flaw,** or a defect in his or her character or judgment.
- The main character usually dies, and the ending is unhappy.

### READING SKILLS: PARAPHRASING

Paraphrasing helps you better understand a text. When you **paraphrase,** you restate all of the writer's ideas in your own words. Below is a sample paraphrase of lines of Brutus's speech in Act III, Scene 2.

| Brutus's Lines | Sample Paraphrase |
|---|---|
| Then follow me, and give me audience, friends. / Cassius, go you into the other street / And part the numbers. / Those that will hear me speak, let 'em stay here; / Those that will follow Cassius, go with him; / And public reasons shall be renderèd / Of Caesar's death. | Follow me and listen to me, friends. Cassius, go into the other street so that we'll divide the audience between us. Whoever wants to hear my speech, stay here; whoever wants to hear Cassius, go with him. We'll tell the public the reasons for Caesar's death. |

**To paraphrase—**
- Read carefully, pausing at natural places such as commas and periods.
- Use context clues, footnotes, and a dictionary to help you reason out the meanings of unfamiliar words and phrases.
- Think about the text's meaning, sentence by sentence, line by line.
- Explain figures of speech in your own words.
- Put sentences in standard subject-verb-complement order.
- Write your paraphrase in prose, not poetry.

## VOCABULARY DEVELOPMENT

### WORD ORIGINS: ARCHAIC WORDS

**Archaic** words are words that are no longer commonly used. In Shakespeare's writings you will find unfamiliar words that have passed out of use altogether, as well as familiar words that have archaic meanings.

Footnotes are provided that explain the meanings of the archaic words, but if you preview these words from Act III, Scene 2, before you begin reading, your reading experience will be easier and more enjoyable.

| Words No Longer in Common Use | |
|---|---|
| **severally:** separately; individually | **thou:** you |
| **'twere:** it would be | **art:** are |
| **nay:** no | **methinks:** I think |
| **oft:** often | **'tis:** it is |
| **hath:** has | |

Words whose meanings have changed over time can be even more confusing. For example, when Brutus calls the Romans his "lovers," he means "friends." Here are some other words from Act III, Scene 2, whose meanings have changed since Shakespeare's day.

| Words Whose Meanings Have Changed | |
|---|---|
| **base:** low-born | **parts:** qualities |
| **rude:** rough and uncivilized | **save:** except |
| **enforced:** exaggerated | **mark:** observe; take notice of |

# THE TRAGEDY OF JULIUS CAESAR
## from ACT III, SCENE 2

### William Shakespeare

*The Tragedy of Julius Caesar* begins as Caesar, the ruler of the Roman Empire, returns to Rome after a victorious battle. As Caesar and his men pass, a fortune-teller calls out, warning Caesar of "the ides of March" (March 15th). Caesar dismisses the man as "a dreamer." In the meanwhile, Cassius and a group of Roman politicians have decided that Caesar has grown so powerful that he threatens the existence of the Republic. Cassius convinces Brutus, who is an honorable man and a loyal supporter of Caesar's, to join the conspiracy.

Despite warnings from his wife (who has had a dream foretelling his death), Caesar decides to go to the Senate on March 15th. Outside the Capitol the conspirators surround Caesar and stab him to death. When Mark Antony, Caesar's loyal supporter, hears of Caesar's death, he pretends to join sides with the conspirators and even shakes their bloody hands. Convinced by his seeming loyalty, Brutus grants Antony's request to take Caesar's body to the Forum and to give a speech praising and honoring him—as long as he does not condemn Brutus and the rest of the conspirators. Secretly, though, Antony vows to avenge Caesar's death by turning the Roman people against those who murdered Caesar.

**CLARIFY**

Pause at line 5. What are Cassius and Brutus doing?

_____

_____

_____

_____

_____

_____

### Scene 2. The Forum.

*Enter* BRUTUS *and goes into the pulpit, and* CASSIUS, *with the* PLEBEIANS.[1]

**Plebeians.**

    We will be satisfied! Let us be satisfied!

**Brutus.**

    Then follow me, and give me audience, friends.

    Cassius, go you into the other street

    And part the numbers.

5    Those that will hear me speak, let 'em stay here;

---

1.  **Plebeians:** the common people.

Those that will follow Cassius, go with him;

And public reasons shall be renderèd

Of Caesar's death.

**First Plebeian.**     I will hear Brutus speak.

**Second Plebeian.**

I will hear Cassius, and compare their reasons,

10    When severally we hear them renderèd.

[*Exit* CASSIUS, *with some of the* PLEBEIANS.]

**Third Plebeian.**

The noble Brutus is ascended. Silence!

**Brutus.** Be patient till the last.

Romans, countrymen, and lovers, hear me for my cause,

and be silent, that you may hear. Believe me for mine

15    honor, and have respect to mine honor, that you may

believe. Censure² me in your wisdom, and awake your

senses,³ that you may the better judge. If there be any in

this assembly, any dear friend of Caesar's, to him I say

that Brutus' love to Caesar was no less than his. If then

20    that friend demand why Brutus rose against Caesar, this

is my answer: Not that I loved Caesar less, but that I

loved Rome more. Had you rather Caesar were living,

and die all slaves, than that Caesar were dead, to live all

free men? As Caesar loved me, I weep for him; as he was

25    fortunate, I rejoice at it; as he was valiant, I honor him;

but, as he was ambitious, I slew him. There is tears, for

his love; joy, for his fortune; honor, for his valor; and

death, for his ambition. Who is here so base, that would

be a bondman?⁴ If any, speak; for him have I offended.

30    Who is here so rude,⁵ that would not be a Roman? If any,

speak; for him have I offended. Who is here so vile, that

---

2. **Censure:** judge.
3. **senses:** reasoning powers.
4. **bondman:** slave.
5. **rude:** rough and uncivilized.

**Notes** _____

_____

_____

_____

_____

_____

_____

_____

_____

_____

_____

**IDENTIFY**

Re-read lines 12–29 of Brutus's monologue. Underline the reasons he gives for killing Caesar.

**INTERPRET**

What is Brutus's main point in this speech (lines 19–31)?

_____

_____

_____

_____

_____

_____

_____

_____

_____

_____

_____

_____

_____

_____

_____

_____

IDENTIFY

Pause at line 52. How does the crowd react to Brutus's speech?

_____

_____

_____

_____

_____

_____

_____

_____

will not love his country? If any, speak; for him have I offended. I pause for a reply.

**All.** None, Brutus, none!

35   **Brutus.** Then none have I offended. I have done no more to Caesar than you shall do to Brutus. The question of his death is enrolled[6] in the Capitol; his glory not extenuated,[7] wherein he was worthy, nor his offenses enforced,[8] for which he suffered death.

[*Enter* MARK ANTONY, *with Caesar's body.*]

40       Here comes his body, mourned by Mark Antony, who, though he had no hand in his death, shall receive the benefit of his dying, a place in the commonwealth, as which of you shall not? With this I depart, that, as I slew my best lover for the good of Rome, I have the same

45       dagger for myself, when it shall please my country to need my death.

**All.** Live, Brutus! Live, live!

**First Plebeian.**

  Bring him with triumph home unto his house.

**Second Plebeian.**

  Give him a statue with his ancestors.

**Third Plebeian.**

  Let him be Caesar.

50   **Fourth Plebeian.**     Caesar's better parts[9]

  Shall be crowned in Brutus.

**First Plebeian.**

  We'll bring him to his house with shouts and clamors.

**Brutus.** My countrymen—

**Second Plebeian.**        Peace! Silence! Brutus speaks.

**First Plebeian.** Peace, ho!

---

6.   In other words, there is a record of the reasons he was killed.
7.   **extenuated:** lessened.
8.   **enforced:** exaggerated.
9.   **better parts:** better qualities.

**Brutus.**

55      Good countrymen, let me depart alone,

        And, for my sake, stay here with Antony.

        Do grace to Caesar's corpse, and grace his speech[10]

        Tending to Caesar's glories, which Mark Antony

        By our permission, is allowed to make.

60      I do entreat you, not a man depart,

        Save I alone, till Antony have spoke.              [*Exit.*]

**First Plebeian.**

        Stay, ho! And let us hear Mark Antony.

**Third Plebeian.**

        Let him go up into the public chair;[11]

        We'll hear him. Noble Antony, go up.

**Antony.**

65      For Brutus' sake, I am beholding to you.

**Fourth Plebeian.**

        What does he say of Brutus?

**Third Plebeian.**                    He says, for Brutus' sake,

        He finds himself beholding to us all.

**Fourth Plebeian.**

        'Twere best he speak no harm of Brutus here!

**First Plebeian.**

        This Caesar was a tyrant.

**Third Plebeian.**                    Nay, that's certain.

70      We are blest that Rome is rid of him.

**Second Plebeian.**

        Peace! Let us hear what Antony can say.

**Antony.**

        You gentle Romans—

**All.**                    Peace, ho! Let us hear him.

**INTERPRET**

Re-read lines 62–73. What do these lines of **dialogue** reveal about the scene and the feelings of the mob?

---

10. **grace his speech:** listen respectfully to Antony's funeral oration.
11. **public chair:** pulpit or rostrum.

Re-read lines 73–87 of Antony's speech, and circle the repeated phrases. Why does Mark Antony keep repeating these ideas? Does Antony really believe Brutus is honorable?

_____

_____

_____

_____

_____

_____

_____

_____

_____

FLUENCY

Read aloud the boxed passage of this famous speech two times. On your first reading, pay special attention to marks of punctuation. You should make a complete pause at a period, which indicates the end of a sentence. Pause briefly at commas and semi-colons. If a line has no mark of punctuation at its end, keep reading until the sentence and the thought are complete. For your second reading, decide how you will read Antony's repeated remarks to make his unspoken meaning clear.

**Antony.**

Friends, Romans, countrymen, lend me your ears;

I come to bury Caesar, not to praise him.

75 The evil that men do lives after them,

The good is oft interrèd with their bones;

So let it be with Caesar. The noble Brutus

Hath told you Caesar was ambitious.

If it were so, it was a grievous fault,

80 And grievously hath Caesar answered[12] it.

Here, under leave of Brutus and the rest

(For Brutus is an honorable man,

So are they all, all honorable men),

Come I to speak in Caesar's funeral.

85 He was my friend, faithful and just to me;

But Brutus says he was ambitious,

And Brutus is an honorable man.

He hath brought many captives home to Rome,

Whose ransoms did the general coffers[13] fill;

90 Did this in Caesar seem ambitious?

---

12. **answered:** paid the penalty for.
13. **general coffers:** public funds.

When that the poor have cried, Caesar hath wept;

Ambition should be made of sterner stuff.

Yet Brutus says he was ambitious;

And Brutus is an honorable man.

95     You all did see that on the Lupercal

I thrice presented him a kingly crown,

Which he did thrice refuse. Was this ambition?

Yet Brutus says he was ambitious;

And sure he is an honorable man.

100     I speak not to disprove what Brutus spoke,

But here I am to speak what I do know.

You all did love him once, not without cause;

What cause withholds you then to mourn for him?

O judgment, thou art fled to brutish beasts,

105     And men have lost their reason! Bear with me;

My heart is in the coffin there with Caesar,

And I must pause till it come back to me.

**First Plebeian.**

Methinks there is much reason in his sayings.

**Second Plebeian.**

If thou consider rightly of the matter,

Caesar has had great wrong.

110   **Third Plebeian.**           Has he, masters?

I fear there will a worse come in his place.

**Fourth Plebeian.**

Marked ye his words? He would not take the crown,

Therefore 'tis certain he was not ambitious.

**First Plebeian.**

If it be found so, some will dear abide it.[14]

**Second Plebeian.**

115     Poor soul, his eyes are red as fire with weeping.

**Third Plebeian.**

There's not a nobler man in Rome than Antony. . . .

✫ ✫ ✫ ✫ ✫ ✫ ✫ ✫

---

14. **dear abide it:** pay dearly for it.

INTERPRET

Re-read lines 105–107. What does Antony mean? What might he be doing as the focus of the scene shifts to the crowd?

_____

_____

_____

_____

_____

_____

_____

_____

ANALYZE

Re-read the **dialogue** in lines 108–116. How has the crowd's opinion changed?

_____

_____

_____

_____

_____

_____

_____

_____

_____

_____

_____

_____

# The Tragedy of Julius Caesar, *from* Act III, Scene 2

**Paraphrase Charts**    Read the original lines from *Julius Caesar* on the left. Use the space at the right to paraphrase those lines. Include all the details in your paraphrase; do not summarize.

| Original | Paraphrase |
|---|---|
| **Brutus:**<br>Be patient till the last. Romans, countrymen, and lovers, hear me for my cause, and be silent, that you may hear. Believe me for mine honor, and have respect to mine honor, that you may believe. Censure me in your wisdom, and awake your senses, that you may the better judge. If there be any in this assembly, any dear friend of Caesar's, to him I say that Brutus' love to Caesar was no less than his. If then that friend demand why Brutus rose against Caesar, this is my answer: Not that I loved Caesar less, but that I loved Rome more. . . . | |
| **Antony:**<br>Friends, Romans, countrymen, lend me<br>    your ears;<br>I come to bury Caesar, not to praise him.<br>The evil that men do lives after them,<br>The good is oft interrèd with their bones;<br>So let it be with Caesar. The noble Brutus<br>Hath told you Caesar was ambitious.<br>If it were so, it was a grievous fault,<br>And grievously hath Caesar answered it.<br>. . .<br>He was my friend, faithful and just to me;<br>But Brutus says he was ambitious,<br>And Brutus is an honorable man.<br>He hath brought many captives home<br>    to Rome,<br>Whose ransoms did the general coffers fill;<br>Did this in Caesar seem ambitious? | |

# Standards Review

TestPractice

## The Tragedy of Julius Caesar,
*from* **Act III, Scene 2**

Improve your test-taking skills by completing the sample test item below. Then, check your answer and read the explanation at right.

| Sample Test Item | Explanation of the Correct Answer |
|---|---|
| Which detail in Act III, Scene 2, is *not* characteristic of a **tragedy**?<br><br>**A** a main character who is dead<br><br>**B** a series of serious events<br><br>**C** wordplay and puns<br><br>**D** characters who are noble in status and bearing | The correct answer is *C*.<br><br>The main character in a tragedy usually comes to a bad end; therefore, *A* is not correct. *B*, too, is incorrect because tragedies involve serious events. Tragic heroes are often noble or respected characters. Therefore, *D* is not correct. |

**DIRECTIONS:** Circle the letter of the best response.

**1.** What is happening as Act III, Scene 2, begins?

  **A** Brutus is hiding from the crowds in the Forum.

  **B** Mark Antony is carrying Caesar's body.

  **C** Cassius and Brutus are fighting.

  **D** Cassius and Brutus are preparing to speak to the crowd.

**2.** Why does Brutus say he killed Caesar?

  **F** Caesar was too ill to rule.

  **G** Brutus wanted to rule Rome.

  **H** Caesar was a tyrant.

  **J** Brutus killed Caesar to save Antony.

**3.** The purpose of Mark Antony's speech is to—

  **A** calm the angry crowd

  **B** accuse Brutus of treachery

  **C** explain what happened to Caesar

  **D** apologize for Brutus's actions

**4.** What do you learn from the **dialogue** of the plebeians following Mark Antony's speech?

  **F** They think Brutus is a better speaker.

  **G** They are beginning to doubt Brutus's honor.

  **H** They wish to make Mark Antony ruler.

  **J** They are anxious to leave.

**Reading Standard 3.1** Articulate the relationship between the expressed purposes and the characteristics of different forms of dramatic literature (e.g., comedy, tragedy, drama, dramatic monologue).

**Reading Standard 3.10** Identify and describe the function of dialogue, scene designs, soliloquies, asides, and character foils in dramatic literature.

# Standards Review

**TestPractice**

## The Tragedy of Julius Caesar
*from* **Act III, Scene 2**

### Word Origins: Archaic Words

**Reading Standard 1.2 (Grade 8 Review)** Understand the most important points in the history of English language and use common word origins to determine the historical influences on English word meanings.

**DIRECTIONS:** Match each archaic word with its definition by writing the correct letter on the lines provided.

_____ **1.** art          **a.** often

_____ **2.** nay          **b.** yes

_____ **3.** thou         **c.** you

_____ **4.** yea          **d.** no

_____ **5.** oft          **e.** are

### Vocabulary in Context

**DIRECTIONS:** Have fun speaking like someone from Shakespeare's time. Complete the paragraph below by writing the correct archaic word from the word box in each numbered blank.

**Word Box**

severally

methinks

'tis

rude

enforced

parts

Our principal said, "Teachers and students, lend me your ears!

(1) _____ we must rejoice at the good work of our

basketball team. (2) _____ only fitting that we

praise the fine (3) _____ of the team members,

(4) _____ and together. No one within the gates of our

school is so (5) _____ as to dishonor our players. They are

deserving of praise, for descriptions of their skills are well earned and not

(6) _____ .

**Before You Go On . . .**

Check your Standards Mastery at the back of this book.

# The Governess by Neil Simon

In Russia, more than a hundred years ago, a meek servant is called before her employer. What happens between the two is the subject of a short story by the famous Russian writer Anton Chekhov (1860–1904). Modern playwright Neil Simon reworked Chekhov's story into *The Governess,* a short play that explores the timeless tensions between employee and employer, between those with different means—and with different natures. As you read *The Governess,* ask yourself what the Mistress's motivations might be for being so cruel to Julia.

## LITERARY FOCUS: COMEDY

A **comedy** is a story or play that usually tells about ordinary characters whose problems are happily resolved at the story's end.

- Note the problem in this play. While a tragedy focuses on serious events (the fall of a king, the end of an empire), comedy usually focuses on ordinary domestic events.
- This is a two-character play. Watch for ways in which the Mistress's and Julia's personalities and behavior make vivid contrasts.
- Comedy thrives on reversals—unexpected things happen.

As you read, think about how you expect Julia to react to the Mistress. Then, compare your expectations with how Julia actually reacts. Compare how you expect the Mistress to react to Julia with how she does react. What do these characters' reactions say about them? What do their responses tell you about the type of society Julia and the Mistress live in?

## READING SKILLS: MAKING INFERENCES

In the script of a play, you find out who is talking to whom, what the characters say to each other, and how and when the characters move, enter, and exit the stage. Despite all this information, there may be many things left unspecified in a script. It's up to you to make inferences, or logical guesses, to fill the gaps.

When questions about the characters or events arise—
- Think about the information given in the play.
- Recall people or situations from real life that are similar to these characters or events.
- Make educated guesses about the characters and events.

Check your guesses as you read. If any prove incorrect, make new inferences, and read on.

**Reading Standard 1.2** Distinguish between the denotative and connotative meanings of words and interpret the connotative power of words.

**Reading Standard 3.1** Articulate the relationship between the expressed purposes and the characteristics of different forms of dramatic literature (e.g., comedy, tragedy, drama, dramatic monologue).

**Reading Standard 3.10** Identify and describe the function of dialogue, scene designs, soliloquies, asides, and character foils in dramatic literature.

ONE-ACT PLAY

## PREVIEW SELECTION VOCABULARY

These words appear in *The Governess*. Get to know them before you begin reading.

**inferior** (in·fir′ē·ər) *adj.:* low or lower in order, status, rank, quality, or value.

*Because the governess felt **inferior**, she never complained about unfair working conditions.*

**discrepancies** (di·skrep′ən·sēz) *n.:* differences; inconsistencies; instances of lack of agreement.

*"There are **discrepancies** between the salary you believe you are owed and the salary I want to give you."*

**discharged** (dis·chärjd′) *v.:* fired; dismissed from employment.

*The Mistress **discharged** the maid for not performing her duties well.*

**guileless** (gīl′lis) *adj.:* without slyness or cunning.

*She is not a schemer; she is a gentle, **guileless** soul.*

## DENOTATION/CONNOTATION

A word's **denotation** is its dictionary definition. A word's **connotations** are all the emotions attached to it and all the associations it brings to mind. For example, the words *sweat* and *perspire* have the same meaning, but *sweat* has negative associations. *Perspire* is a more polite word.

Here are some more examples:

| Positive Connotations | Negative Connotations |
|---|---|
| assertive | bossy |
| delicate | frail |
| ornate | gaudy |
| mistake | error |
| curious | nosy |
| adventure | exploit |

# The Governess

## Neil Simon

**CHARACTERS**
- **Mistress**
- **Julia**

**Mistress.** Julia! (*Calls again*) Julia!

[*A young governess,* JULIA, *comes rushing in. She stops before the desk and curtsies.*]

**Julia.** (*Head down*) Yes, madame?

**Mistress.** Look at me, child. Pick your head up. I like to see your eyes when I speak to you.

**Julia.** (*Lifts her head up*) Yes, madame. (*But her head has a habit of slowly drifting down again*)

**Mistress.** And how are the children coming along with their
10   French lessons?

**Julia.** They're very bright children, madame.

**Mistress.** Eyes up . . . They're bright, you say. Well, why not? And mathematics? They're doing well in mathematics, I assume?

**Julia.** Yes, madame. Especially Vanya.

**Mistress.** Certainly. I knew it. I excelled in mathematics. He gets that from his mother, wouldn't you say?

**Julia.** Yes, madame.

**Mistress.** Head up . . . (*She lifts head up.*) That's it. Don't be
20   afraid to look people in the eyes, my dear. If you think of yourself as **inferior,** that's exactly how people will treat you.

**Julia.** Yes, ma'am.

**INFER**

What can you tell about Julia from the **stage directions** (lines 1–8)? Circle the stage direction that you feel says most about the character.

_____

_____

_____

_____

**INFER**

Pause at line 17. What can you infer about the Mistress's personality from what she has said about her children?

_____

_____

_____

**VOCABULARY**

**inferior** (in·fir′ē·ər) *adj.:* low or lower in order, status, rank, quality, or value.

VOCABULARY

**discrepancies**
(di·skrep′ən·sēz) *n.:* differences; inconsistencies; instances of lack of agreement.

INTERPRET

Re-read lines 50–57. According to the **stage directions,** what should Julia's voice suggest during this interchange?

_____

_____

_____

_____

_____

_____

_____

_____

_____

_____

_____

_____

**Mistress.** A quiet girl, aren't you? . . . Now then, let's settle our accounts. I imagine you must need money, although you never ask me for it yourself. Let's see now, we agreed on thirty rubles a month, did we not?

**Julia.** (*Surprised*) Forty, ma'am.

**Mistress.** No, no, thirty. I made a note of it. (*Points to the book*) I always pay my governess thirty . . . Who told you forty?

30 **Julia.** You did, ma'am. I spoke to no one else concerning money . . .

**Mistress.** Impossible. Maybe you *thought* you heard forty when I said thirty. If you kept your head up, that would never happen. Look at me again and I'll say it clearly. *Thirty rubles a month.*

**Julia.** If you say so, ma'am.

**Mistress.** Settled. Thirty a month it is . . . Now then, you've been here two months exactly.

**Julia.** Two months and five days.

**Mistress.** No, no. Exactly two months. I made a note of it. You
40 should keep books the way I do so there wouldn't be these **discrepancies.** So—we have two months at thirty rubles a month . . . comes to sixty rubles. Correct?

**Julia.** (*Curtsies*) Yes, ma'am. Thank you, ma'am.

**Mistress.** Subtract nine Sundays . . . We did agree to subtract Sundays, didn't we?

**Julia.** No, ma'am.

**Mistress.** Eyes! Eyes! . . . Certainly we did. I've always subtracted Sundays. I didn't bother making a note of it because I always do it. Don't you recall when I said we will subtract Sundays?

50 **Julia.** No, ma'am.

**Mistress.** Think.

**Julia.** (*Thinks*) No, ma'am.

**Mistress.** You weren't thinking. Your eyes were wandering. Look straight at my face and look hard . . . Do you remember now?

**Julia.** (*Softly*) Yes, ma'am.

**Mistress.** I didn't hear you, Julia.

**Julia.** (*Louder*) Yes, ma'am.

**Mistress.** Good. I was sure you'd remember . . . Plus three holidays. Correct?

60 **Julia.** Two, ma'am. Christmas and New Year's.

**Mistress.** And your birthday. That's three.

**Julia.** I worked on my birthday, ma'am.

**Mistress.** You did? There was no need to. My governesses never worked on their birthdays . . .

**Julia.** But I did work, ma'am.

**Mistress.** But that's not the question, Julia. We're discussing financial matters now. I will, however, only count two holidays if you insist . . . Do you insist?

**Julia.** I did work, ma'am.

70 **Mistress.** Then you *do* insist.

**Julia.** No, ma'am.

**Mistress.** Very well. That's three holidays, therefore we take off twelve rubles. Now then, four days little Kolya was sick, and there were no lessons.

**Julia.** But I gave lessons to Vanya.

**Mistress.** True. But I engaged you to teach two children, not one. Shall I pay you in full for doing only half the work?

**Julia.** No, ma'am.

**Mistress.** So we'll deduct it . . . Now, three days you had a

80 toothache and my husband gave you permission not to work after lunch. Correct?

**Julia.** After four. I worked until four.

**Mistress.** (*Looks in the book*) I have here: "Did not work after lunch." We have lunch at one and are finished at two, not at four, correct?

**Julia.** Yes, ma'am. But I—

**Mistress.** That's another seven rubles . . . Seven and twelve is nineteen . . . Subtract . . . that leaves . . . forty-one rubles . . . Correct?

90 **Julia.** Yes, ma'am. Thank you, ma'am.

**INTERPRET**

Pause at line 71. How does Julia act when challenged?

_____

_____

_____

_____

_____

_____

_____

**INFER**

Re-read lines 72–81. Underline the reasons the Mistress gives for deducting money from Julia's pay. What might be her motive, or reason, for being mean?

_____

_____

_____

_____

_____

_____

_____

_____

_____

**Mistress.** Now then, on January fourth you broke a teacup and saucer, is that true?

**Julia.** Just the saucer, ma'am.

**Mistress.** What good is a teacup without a saucer, eh? . . . That's two rubles. The saucer was an heirloom. It cost much more, but let it go. I'm used to taking losses.

**Julia.** Thank you, ma'am.

**Mistress.** Now then, January ninth, Kolya climbed a tree and tore his jacket.

100   **Julia.** I forbid him to do so, ma'am.

**Mistress.** But he didn't listen, did he? . . . Ten rubles . . . January fourteenth, Vanya's shoes were stolen . . .

**Julia.** But the maid, ma'am. You **discharged** her yourself.

**Mistress.** But you get paid good money to watch everything. I explained that in our first meeting. Perhaps you weren't listening. Were you listening that day, Julia, or was your head in the clouds?

**Julia.** Yes, ma'am.

**Mistress.** Yes, your head was in the clouds?

110   **Julia.** No, ma'am. I was listening.

**Mistress.** Good girl. So that means another five rubles off (*Looks in the book*) . . . Ah, yes . . . The sixteenth of January I gave you ten rubles.

**Julia.** You didn't.

**Mistress.** But I made a note of it. Why would I make a note of it if I didn't give it to you?

**Julia.** I don't know, ma'am.

**Mistress.** That's not a satisfactory answer, Julia . . . Why would I make a note of giving you ten rubles if I did not in fact give it

120      to you, eh? . . . No answer? . . . Then I must have given it to you, mustn't I?

**Julia.** Yes, ma'am. If you say so, ma'am.

**Mistress.** Well, certainly I say so. That's the point of this little talk. To clear these matters up. Take twenty-seven from forty-one, that leaves . . . fourteen, correct?

**Julia.** Yes, ma'am. (*She turns away, softly crying.*)

**Mistress.** What's this? Tears? Are you crying? Has something made you unhappy, Julia? Please tell me. It pains me to see you like this. I'm so sensitive to tears. What is it?

130 **Julia.** Only once since I've been here have I ever been given any money and that was by your husband. On my birthday he gave me three rubles.

**Mistress.** Really? There's no note of it in my book. I'll put it down now. (*She writes in the book.*) Three rubles. Thank you for telling me. Sometimes I'm a little lax with my accounts . . . Always shortchanging myself. So then, we take three more from fourteen . . . leaves eleven . . . Do you wish to check my figures?

**Julia.** There's no need to, ma'am.

140 **Mistress.** Then we're all settled. Here's your salary for two months, dear. Eleven rubles. (*She puts the pile of coins on the desk.*) Count it.

**Julia.** It's not necessary, ma'am.

**Mistress.** Come, come. Let's keep the records straight. Count it.

**Julia** (*Reluctantly counts it*). One, two, three, four, five, six, seven, eight, nine, ten . . . ? There's only ten, ma'am.

**Mistress.** Are you sure? Possibly you dropped one . . . Look on the floor, see if there's a coin there.

**Julia.** I didn't drop any, ma'am. I'm quite sure.

150 **Mistress.** Well, it's not here on my desk, and I *know* I gave you eleven rubles. Look on the floor.

**Julia.** It's all right, ma'am. Ten rubles will be fine.

**Mistress.** Well, keep the ten for now. And if we don't find it on the floor later, we'll discuss it again next month.

**Julia.** Yes, ma'am. Thank you, ma'am. You're very kind, ma'am. (*She curtsies and then starts to leave.*)

**Mistress.** Julia!

[JULIA *stops, turns.*]

**INFER**

Re-read lines 126–132, where Julia explains why she is crying. What does her explanation reveal about her?

_____

_____

_____

_____

_____

_____

_____

**INTERPRET**

**Irony** occurs when the outcome of a situation is the opposite of what we had expected. In line 136, the Mistress says she is "always shortchanging" herself. What is ironic about this statement?

_____

_____

_____

_____

_____

_____

_____

_____

_____

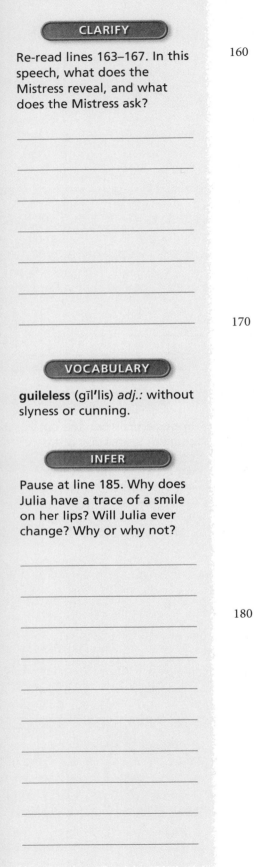

**CLARIFY**

Re-read lines 163–167. In this speech, what does the Mistress reveal, and what does the Mistress ask?

_____

_____

_____

_____

_____

_____

_____

**VOCABULARY**

**guileless** (gīl′lis) *adj.:* without slyness or cunning.

**INFER**

Pause at line 185. Why does Julia have a trace of a smile on her lips? Will Julia ever change? Why or why not?

_____

_____

_____

_____

_____

_____

_____

_____

_____

Come back here.

160      [*She goes back to the desk and curtsies again.*]

Why did you thank me?

**Julia.** For the money, ma'am.

**Mistress.** For the money? . . . But don't you realize what I've done? I've cheated you . . . *Robbed* you! I have no such notes in my book. I made up whatever came into my mind. Instead of the eighty rubles which I owe you, I gave you only ten. I have actually stolen from you and you still thank me . . . Why?

**Julia.** In the other places that I've worked, they didn't give me anything at all.

170      **Mistress.** Then they cheated you even worse than I did . . . I was playing a little joke on you. A cruel lesson just to teach you. You're much too trusting, and in this world that's very dangerous . . . I'm going to give you the entire eighty rubles. (*Hands her an envelope.*) It's all ready for you. The rest is in this envelope. Here, take it.

**Julia.** As you wish, ma'am. (*She curtsies and starts to go again.*)

**Mistress.** Julia!

[JULIA *stops.*]

Is it possible to be so spineless? Why don't you protest? Why
180      don't you speak up? Why don't you cry out against this cruel and unjust treatment? Is it really possible to be so **guileless,** so innocent, such a—pardon me for being so blunt—such a simpleton?

**Julia.** (*The faintest trace of a smile on her lips*) Yes, ma'am . . . it's possible.

[*She curtsies again and runs off. The* MISTRESS *looks after her a moment, a look of complete bafflement on her face. The lights fade.*]

# The Governess

**Scene Chart**    In drama, many elements, including **props, scene design,** and **costumes,** play a part in creating a scene's effect. Fill in the chart below. You'll be able to find details from the play to complete the top category. For the final two categories—scene design and costumes—there is no specific information in the play. Use your imagination to complete these categories.

| Props (items used by the play's characters) |
| --- |
| |

| Scene Design (room furnishings that are not part of the action) |
| --- |
| |

| Costumes |
| --- |
| |

# Standards Review

## TestPractice  The Governess

Complete the sample test item below. The box at the right explains why three of these choices are not correct.

| Sample Test Item | Explanation of the Correct Answer |
|---|---|
| Based on information in the play, what can you **infer** about the Mistress's past?<br><br>**A** Her husband has died.<br><br>**B** She has employed other governesses before.<br><br>**C** She herself was a governess.<br><br>**D** She was always afraid of people. | The correct answer is *B:* she refers to her other governesses.<br><br>*A* is incorrect: references to her husband indicate he is alive. There is no reason to believe *C,* that she ever was a governess. As for *D,* although outwardly bold people are sometimes inwardly afraid, the play does not explore this aspect of her character. |

**Reading Standard 3.1** Articulate the relationship between the expressed purposes and the characteristics of different forms of dramatic literature (e.g., comedy, tragedy, drama, dramatic monologue).

**Reading Standard 3.10** Identify and describe the function of dialogue, scene designs, soliloquies, asides, and character foils in dramatic literature.

**DIRECTIONS:** Circle the letter of each correct response.

1. The **conflict** of this play is between—

   **A** the Mistress and Julia

   **B** Julia and the children

   **C** the Mistress and her husband

   **D** the two governesses

2. From the **stage directions,** you can infer that Julia is—

   **F** greedy

   **G** bossy

   **H** angry

   **J** meek

3. The **set** and **props** of the play include all of the following *except*—

   **A** an account book

   **B** coins

   **C** a telephone

   **D** a desk

4. At the play's end we learn that—

   **F** Julia is looking for a new job

   **G** Julia has always been taken advantage of by employers

   **H** Julia has been fooling the Mistress all along

   **J** Julia was paid more than she deserved

# Standards Review

**TestPractice** **The Governess**

## Connotations

**DIRECTIONS:** Put a check mark next to each correct answer.

1. Which of the following synonyms for *guileless* has a more positive meaning?

   _____ honest          _____ simple

2. If you wanted to create a negative impression of the Mistress, you could describe her as—

   _____ thrifty          _____ cheap

3. If you wanted to create a positive impression of the Mistress, you could describe her as—

   _____ proud          _____ snobbish

4. Which term describing Julia's position sounds more positive?

   _____ servant          _____ employee

**Reading Standard 1.2** Distinguish between the denotative and connotative meanings of words and interpret the connotative power of words.

## Vocabulary in Context

**DIRECTIONS:** Complete the paragraph below by writing the correct word from the word box in each numbered blank.

> ### Word Box
> inferior
> discrepancies
> discharged
> guileless

The wife said to her husband, "You know, our nanny is so

(1) _____, it's easy to fool her. This morning, I pretended

to find (2) _____ in my account book. I told her I owed

her less than I did. But she would not insist on her rightful pay. It made

me feel (3) _____ to her, because she was so saintly.

I (4) _____ our last nanny for her carelessness, but this

one I'll keep."

**Before You Go On . . .**

Check your Standards Mastery at the back of this book.

# Part Two

## Reading Comprehension

# Informational Materials

## Academic Vocabulary

These are the terms you should know
as you read and analyze these selections.

――――――

**Source** A person, book, or document that provides information on a topic.

**Elaboration** The addition of ideas to support the ideas already presented in a work.

**Synthesis** The merging of information gathered from more than one source.

**Argument** A series of statements designed to persuade the reader to accept a claim, or opinion.

**Claim** An opinion on a topic or an issue, which is often stated as a generalization, a broad statement that covers many situations.

**Evidence** Support for an idea. Evidence includes facts, statistics, examples, anecdotes (brief stories about real people), and quotations.

**Credibility** The believability of an argument or a statement.

> ### For Further Information . . .
>
> Be sure to read about the following in *Holt Literature and Language Arts:*
> - **Generating research questions,** pages 187, 366.
> - **Primary and secondary sources,** pages 88, 632–633.
> - **Synthesizing sources,** pages 21, 411.
> - **Evaluating arguments,** pages 284–285, 577–578, 881.

**Reading Standard 2.3** Generate relevant questions about readings on issues that can be researched.

**Reading Standard 2.4** Synthesize the content from several sources or works by a single author dealing with a single issue; paraphrase the ideas and connect them to other sources and related topics to demonstrate comprehension.

**Reading Standard 2.5** Extend ideas presented in primary or secondary sources through original analysis, evaluation, and elaboration.

**Reading Standard 2.8** Evaluate the credibility of an author's argument or defense of a claim by critiquing the relationship between generalizations and evidence, the comprehensiveness of evidence, and the way in which the author's intent affects the structure and tone of the text (e.g., in professional journals, editorials, political speeches, primary source material).

# Shipwreck at the Bottom of the World

## by Jennifer Armstrong

**Reading Standard 1.1**
Identify and use the literal and figurative meanings of words and understand word derivations.

**Reading Standard 2.3**
Generate relevant questions about readings on issues that can be researched.

### BEFORE YOU READ

In this informational article, you'll read about the heroic expedition of Ernest Shackleton and his crew to the most hostile place on earth—the Antarctic. Think of questions that you'd like answered after learning about the details of this epic journey to the "bottom of the world." You may want to do some research on Shackleton after you read about his amazing ordeal.

### INFORMATIONAL FOCUS: HOW TO GENERATE QUESTIONS

When you start to do a research project, your first step is to think of questions that will help you find the information you're looking for. Here are some guidelines for asking useful research questions:

- **Check the subheads** of an informational article to locate ideas for a limited topic to research.
- **Focus on one aspect** of your subject, and limit your questions to a narrow topic. Try to focus your questions on the main idea of your topic.
- **Ask the *5W-How?* questions**—*who? what? where? when? why?* and *how?*—about your topic. Be sure to ask reasonable questions that you can find answers to.

### READING SKILLS: MAKE A KWL CHART

Practice asking and answering questions by completing a KWL chart like the one below. Fill in the first two columns of the KWL chart *before* you read the article. In the first column, list what you know about the Antarctic, Ernest Shackleton, or other expeditions to cold places. In the second column, list questions you would like answered as you read about this voyage. Then, *after* you read the article, fill out the last column. Some sample items are given below.

| What I Already KNOW | What I WANT to Find Out | What I LEARNED |
|---|---|---|
| The Antarctic is frozen and hard to get to. | How did Shackleton and crew get there? How long did the journey take? | |
| There is not much food or fresh water in the Antarctic. | How did they survive? | |

# Shipwreck at the Bottom of the World

## Jennifer Armstrong

### The Boss

Imagine yourself in the most hostile place on earth. It's not the Sahara or the Gobi Desert. It's not the Arctic. The most hostile place on earth is the Antarctic, the location of the South Pole. When winter descends on the southern continent, the seas surrounding the land begin to freeze at the terrifying rate of two square miles every minute, until the frozen sea reaches an area of seven million square miles, about twice the size of the United States. Just imagine yourself stranded in such a place. In 1915, a British crew of 28 men *was* stranded there, with no ship and no way to contact the outside world. Fortunately they were led by Ernest Shackleton, a polar explorer famous for bringing his men home alive.

10

GENERATE QUESTIONS

Ask at least two questions about the title of this article.

_____

_____

_____

_____

_____

_____

IDENTIFY

Re-read lines 1–8. What makes the Antarctic "the most hostile place on earth"?

_____

_____

_____

_____

_____

_____

_____

*Ernest Shackleton.*

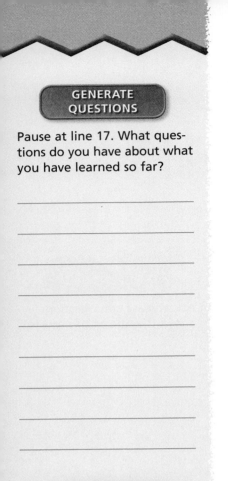

**GENERATE QUESTIONS**

Pause at line 17. What questions do you have about what you have learned so far?

_____

_____

_____

_____

_____

_____

_____

**TEXT STRUCTURE**

Maps and photographs provide much of the information in this article. As you read, stop from time to time to trace the expedition's route on the map of Antarctica.

_____

_____

_____

_____

_____

_____

_____

_____

_____

_____

The crew was somewhat in awe of Ernest Shackleton, whom they all called Boss. Shackleton was a master at keeping his crew working together. Whenever he found two men who had quarreled and were not speaking to each other, he told them, "Stop and forget it," and made them shake hands.

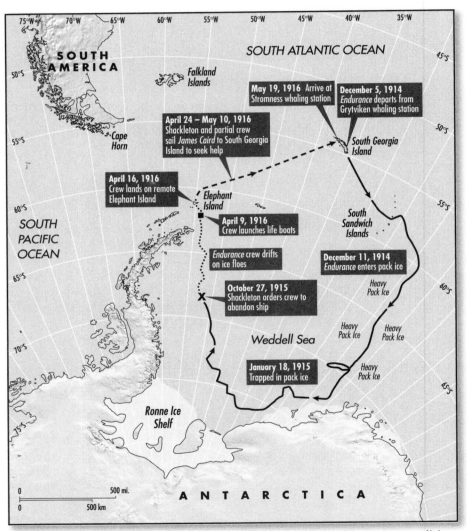

_The route of Shackleton's expedition._

## Shipwreck: Stuck in the Ice

The last stop the expedition's ship, *Endurance,* made before taking
on the challenge of the Antarctic was a whaling station on South
Georgia Island. Soon after leaving the station on December 5,
1914, *Endurance* was caught in pack ice in the Weddell Sea and
then frozen in place for the winter. All the crew could do was wait
and hope that the drifting ice pack, which was slowly moving
north, would carry them closer to land.

Toward the spring, great masses of ice pushed by the wind
first toppled and then crushed the ship, forcing the men onto
the ice. They tried to drag their three lifeboats toward land, but
the boats weighed a ton each and enormous slabs of ice jutted
out of the pack at all angles, blocking their way. Instead they
made a camp and waited for the ice pack to break up. More
than a year after *Endurance* first became stuck in the ice, the
crew was able to row the lifeboats into the open ocean. At this
point their lives depended on their making land at either
Elephant or Clarence Island, the tiny islands at the tip of the
Antarctic peninsula. If they missed the islands the nearest land
was South America, and they would almost certainly die at sea.
After six horrific days in the lifeboats, they reached Elephant
Island on April 16, 1916. But the island was barren and many of
the men were near collapse. It was clear that somebody would
have to try to reach the whaling station on South Georgia Island
before winter set in.

## Shipwreck: The Open Boat Journey

Shackleton handpicked five men for the relief party he would
lead. The ship's carpenter refitted one of the lifeboats, the *James
Caird,* for the journey. The men loaded it with bags of stone to
keep it steady, boxes of food, a hand pump, a cook pot, a camp
stove, two kegs of drinking water and six reindeer-skin sleeping
bags. As they shoved off, the 22 men left behind cheered and
waved. "Good luck, Boss!" they shouted.

**IDENTIFY**

Re-read lines 26–33. When
and why were the men
forced onto the ice? How
long did they wait for the
ice to break up?

_____

_____

_____

_____

**IDENTIFY
CAUSE & EFFECT**

Circle the description of
Elephant Island in line 39.
Read on to line 42, and
underline the action the
men were forced to take.

**GENERATE
QUESTIONS**

Pause at line 50. Suppose
you were researching
Shackleton's expedition.
What questions does this
paragraph raise?

_____

_____

_____

_____

_____

_____

_____

Endurance *trapped in pack ice.*

The living arrangements on board were uncomfortable and cramped. It was a tossup which was worse—being pounded up and down in the bow of the boat in a sorry excuse for sleep, or huddling in the cockpit as icy seas swept across thwarts and gunwales. The men were dressed in wool, which got wet and stayed wet for the duration of the voyage. With temperatures below freezing, and no room to move around to get their blood stirred up, they were always cold. Miserably cold. Waves broke over the bows, where bucketfuls of water streamed through the
60    flimsy decking. The bottom of the boat was constantly full of water, and the two men on watch who weren't steering were always bailing or pumping. The reindeer-skin sleeping bags were soaking wet all the time, and beginning to rot. Loose reindeer hair found its way into the men's nostrils and mouths as they breathed, into their water and food as they ate.

On their seventh day at sea, the wind turned into a gale roaring up from the Pole; the temperature plummeted. The men began to fear that the sails would freeze up and cake with ice, becoming heavier and heavier until the boat toppled upside
70    down. With the gale howling around their ears, they took down their sails.

Throughout the night, waves crashed over the *James Caird* and quickly turned to ice. At first the crew was relieved, since it meant the flimsy decking was sealed against further leaks. But when they awoke on the eighth day, they felt the clumsy, heavy motion of the boat beneath them and knew they were in trouble: 15 inches of ice encased the boat above the waterline, and she was rolling badly.

The ice had to come off. Taking turns, the men crawled on
80    hands and knees over the deck, hacking away with an ax. "First you chopped a handhold, then a kneehold, and then chopped off ice hastily but carefully with an occasional sea washing over you," one of the men explained. Each man could stand only five minutes or so of this cold and perilous job at a time. Then it was the next man's turn.

### WORD STUDY

Lines 51–55 have four words that may be unfamiliar to you: the *bow* (bou) is the front of a boat; the *cockpit* holds the helm, or steering wheel; *thwarts* are the rowers' seats; *gunwales* (gun'əlz) are the upper edges of the boat's sides. What do these words indicate about the crew's main tasks?

_____

_____

_____

_____

### CLARIFY

Briefly explain what happened during the seventh and eighth days at sea (lines 66–85).

_____

_____

_____

_____

_____

_____

_____

_____

_____

_____

**INFER**

Re-read lines 93–97. What does the paragraph reveal about Shackleton's personality?

_____

_____

_____

_____

_____

_____

_____

_____

**IDENTIFY**

Re-read lines 98–108. Underline the danger the men faced after the gale ended.

**DRAW CONCLUSIONS**

Pause at line 114. Why didn't the men drink the water that had salt in it?

_____

_____

_____

_____

_____

By the time the gale ended, everything below was thoroughly soaked. The sleeping bags were so slimy and revolting that Shackleton had the two worst of them thrown overboard. Exposure was beginning to wear the men down. They were cold,

90 frostbitten, and covered with salt-water blisters. Their legs were rubbed raw from the chafing of their wet pants, and they were exhausted from lack of sleep.

When someone looked particularly bad, the Boss ordered a round of hot milk for all hands. The one man he really wanted to get the hot drink into never realized that the break was for his benefit and so wasn't embarrassed, and all of the men were better off for having the warmth and nourishment.

The night after the gale ended, Shackleton was at the tiller, hunched against the cold. He glanced back toward the south and

100 saw a line of white along the horizon. "It's clearing, boys!" he shouted. But when he looked again, he yelled, "For God's sake, hold on! It's got us!" Instead of a clearing sky, the white line to the south was the foaming crest of an enormous storm wave bearing down on them. When the wave struck, for a few moments the entire boat seemed to be submerged. Then for the next hour the men frantically pumped and bailed, laboring to keep the water from capsizing the *Caird*. They could hardly believe they had not foundered.

On the twelfth day out from Elephant Island, they dis-

110 covered that salt water had gotten into one of the two kegs of drinking water. Shackleton reduced the water ration to half a cup a day. The water had to be strained through gauze to remove the reindeer hair that had gotten into it—the hair had gotten into everything.

On their fifteenth day out from Elephant Island they reached South Georgia Island, but it was obvious they were in for a storm. By noon the gale had blown up into hurricane force, lashing them with snow, rain, hail, and sleet. The howling winds were driving them straight toward the rocky coast.

120    Their only hope lay in trying to sail out of reach. The boat began clawing offshore, directly into the onrushing waves. Each wave now smashed into the *Caird* with such force that the bow planks opened and lines of water spurted in from every seam. All afternoon and into the night, the punishment continued.

   Finally the hurricane began to decrease. With the storm over, the first watch crawled into the bows to try to catch some sleep. A meal was out of the question: the water was gone, and their mouths and tongues were so swollen with thirst that they could hardly swallow. When the sun rose, the men stared bleary-
130  eyed at the coast of South Georgia. They had to land that day. Shackleton thought the weakest man among them would probably die if they didn't.

## Shipwreck: The Rescue

They landed that evening, but they were on the wrong side of the island, the side opposite the whaling station. Afraid to take the battered boat to sea again, the three strongest men—Shackleton, Worsley, who was captain of *Endurance,* and second officer Crean—set out to cross the mountains that lay between them and the station. They stumbled into the station on May 19,
140  1916, 17 months after they had begun their expedition. They were so changed by their experience they were not recognized.

**FLUENCY**

Read the boxed passage aloud with the quick and smooth delivery of a newscaster.

**GENERATE QUESTIONS**

Pause at line 141. What questions might you ask about the men's arrival at the whaling station?

Notes

GENERATE
QUESTIONS

What questions would you ask the men left behind on Elephant Island? Think of two or three.

_____

_____

_____

_____

_____

_____

For the next four months Shackleton tried desperately to get a rescue ship to Elephant Island, where the men who had been left behind were huddled in a hut made of the remaining two lifeboats. Each time, the winter ice turned him back. Finally on August 30, more than four months after the *James Caird* had sailed away, the rescue ship arrived at the island. As soon as a boat lowered from the ship got within shouting distance, Shackleton called out, "Are all well?" "Yes!" someone shouted back. "We knew you'd come back," one of the men later told Shackleton, who said it was the highest compliment anyone ever paid him.

150

*Rescue is at hand as Shackleton and his men return to Elephant Island.*

# Shipwreck at the Bottom of the World

**5 W's and H**     Imagine you are doing research on the Shackleton expedition. Think about the information you learned from the article. Then, use the investigation guide below to focus your research.

Ask *who? what? where? when? why?* and *how?*—the *5W-How?* questions—about your topic. Remember that you can ask more than one of each type of question.

## Investigation Guide

| | |
|---|---|
| **Who?** | |
| **What?** | |
| **Where?** | |
| **When?** | |
| **Why?** | |
| **How?** | |

# Standards Review

**TestPractice**

## Shipwreck at the Bottom of the World

Complete the sample test item by circling the correct answer. Then, read the explanation to the right.

| Sample Test Item | Explanation of the Correct Answer |
|---|---|
| What is the topic of "Shipwreck at the Bottom of the World"?<br><br>**A** Ernest Shackleton<br><br>**B** the wreck of the *Endurance*<br><br>**C** survival in sub-zero temperatures<br><br>**D** preventing shipwrecks | *B* is the correct answer. Although Shackleton was the leader of the expedition, the article does not focus on him (*A*). Survival in sub-zero temperatures is also not the main topic (*C*). *D* is not correct because no information is given on preventing shipwrecks. |

**DIRECTIONS:** Circle the letter of each correct response.

**Reading Standard 2.3**
Generate relevant questions about readings on issues that can be researched.

1. Which research question would generate the most useful information for a report on Ernest Shackleton?

   **A** What percentage of Earth's surface is covered in ice?

   **B** When was Shackleton born?

   **C** How did Shackleton learn survival skills?

   **D** What route did Amundsen take to the South Pole?

2. Which of the following research questions is *not* directly related to topics discussed in this article?

   **F** What is the area of the Antarctic?

   **G** What route did the Shackleton expedition take?

   **H** How does a whaling ship operate?

   **J** How did Shackleton select his crew?

3. Under which subhead would you likely find information about the *James Caird*?

   **A** The Boss

   **B** Stuck in the Ice

   **C** The Open Boat Journey

   **D** The Rescue

4. For research on Shackleton's career, which question would generate the most relevant information?

   **F** What animals live in the Antarctic?

   **G** What other expeditions did Shackleton lead?

   **H** What would be needed to grow food in the Antarctic?

   **J** How many siblings did Shackleton have?

# Standards Review

## Shipwreck at the Bottom of the World

VOCABULARY DEVELOPMENT

### Synonyms

Synonyms are words that have the same basic meaning. Circle the letter of the word or phrase that is the best synonym of each underlined word from "Shipwreck at the Bottom of the World."

1. Something that is <u>hostile</u> is—

   A friendly

   B unwelcoming

   C sick

   D warm

2. A <u>drifting</u> ice pack is one that is—

   F melting

   G wet

   H tall

   J moving

3. <u>Enormous</u> means—

   A hungry

   B scary

   C huge

   D sickly

4. When the temperature <u>plummeted</u>, it—

   F rose

   G dropped

   H froze

   J changed

5. <u>Duration</u> means—

   A length

   B strength

   C preparations

   D meanwhile

6. A job that is <u>perilous</u> is—

   F well paying

   G worthwhile

   H dangerous

   J difficult

7. A boat that is <u>submerged</u> is—

   A leaky

   B under water

   C secret

   D damp

8. When the men <u>frantically</u> pumped, they did so—

   F quickly

   G as a team

   H carefully

   J desperately

**Reading Standard 1.1**
Identify and use the literal and figurative meanings of words and understand word derivations.

### Before You Go On...

Check your Standards Mastery at the back of this book.

# Iceman: Mummy from the Stone Age; The Iceman Ate-eth Meat; Iceman of the Alps Was Slain, X-ray Shows

**INFORMATIONAL ARTICLES**

## BEFORE YOU READ

In 1991, two mountain hikers discovered a body frozen in the ice. Scientists soon realized that the body was that of a man who had died about 5,300 years ago. The three articles here describe some of the things scientists have learned about the Iceman so far. You'll be surprised at how much information was buried in the ice along with him.

### INFORMATIONAL FOCUS: SYNTHESIZING SOURCES

When you research a topic, you collect information from several sources. Once you have read all your sources, you need to **synthesize** what you've learned—put it all together to better understand the subject. Here are some guidelines for synthesizing sources:

- **Find the main idea** of each source.
- **Compare and contrast** the ideas presented in each source. What do they have in common? How are they different?
- **Connect** the ideas to related topics and other articles you've read. To make connections, gather together main ideas and supporting details in a chart like the one below.
- **Connect the main ideas.** Now, consider all your sources as a group. What **conclusions** can you draw from your sources?

| Source 1 | Source 2 | Source 3 |
|---|---|---|
| Main Ideas | Main Ideas | Main Ideas |

**Synthesize: What I think (or know) about issue or topic**

### READING SKILLS: PARAPHRASING

To help you understand a source, try paraphrasing its ideas, which means restating them in your own words. A paraphrase includes all the information in the original. Here's an example:

| Original Text | Paraphrase |
|---|---|
| Archaeologists speculate that the Iceman, Ötzi, met his demise in late summer. | Archaeologists think that Ötzi, the Iceman, died in late summer. |

**Reading Standard 1.1** Identify and use the literal and figurative meanings of words and understand word derivations.

**Reading Standard 2.4** Synthesize the content from several sources or works by a single author dealing with a single issue; paraphrase the ideas and connect them to other sources and related topics to demonstrate comprehension.

# ICEMAN:
## MUMMY FROM THE STONE AGE

### *from* Discovery Channel.com

### The Iceman's Body

On September 19, 1991, Ötzi (the name given to him by scientists)
was found at about 10,500 feet in the Ötztal Alps on the border
between Austria and Italy. His body was so well-preserved that
the hikers who found him and the first investigators assumed
he had been dead for a relatively short time.

So archaeologists were not immediately consulted, and
Ötzi remained frozen on the mountain for four more days, his
upper body protruding from a glacier. The lag allowed curious
10  onlookers to poke around, including one member of the Alpine
Rescue Service, who inadvertently damaged the left hip and
buttock with a pneumatic hammer, trying to dig the corpse
from the ground.

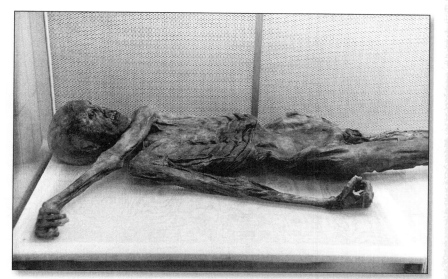

*The Iceman, Ötzi.*

**IDENTIFY**

Pause at line 6. Underline
the name that scientists
gave to the Iceman. Circle
the information that tells
where the body was found.
From the **context,** what do
you think *well-preserved*
(line 3) means?

**WORD STUDY**

*Archaeologists* (är′kē·äl′ə·jists)
(line 7) are scientists who
study ancient peoples and
their cultures.

**WORD STUDY**

What does *inadvertently*
mean (line 11)? (Hint: Would
a rescuer do damage on
purpose?)

**INFER**

Pause at line 18. Underline the details that describe Ötzi's appearance and clothing. Why did scientists think that he "was no modern European"?

_____

_____

_____

_____

**IDENTIFY**

Re-read lines 19–20. Underline where Ötzi's body is kept today.

**DRAW CONCLUSIONS**

Pause at line 24. Why do you think Ötzi is taken out of storage for no more than eleven minutes at a time?

_____

_____

**PARAPHRASE**

Pause at line 32. Restate the theories scientists made after studying the broken arrows and unfinished bow found with Ötzi's body.

_____

_____

_____

_____

_____

As Ötzi's body began to thaw from its icy grave, it became apparent that this was no modern European. About 5 feet, 4 inches tall and dressed in three layers of furs and grass clothes, he wore well-lined shoes, a belt from which to drape his loincloth and suspend his leggings, a jacket, a cape, and a bearskin hat.

Today, Ötzi resides in a cold-storage vault in the
20 Archaeological Museum of Bolzano in Italy. The vault temperature remains at a constant –6° C, with a relative humidity of 96 to 98 percent. For investigational purposes the body is removed from storage and put in a laminar flow box for no longer than 11 minutes at a time.

## Bow and Arrow

The Iceman's bow and arrows have been the subject of considerable speculation among the experts who have studied his remains. The fact that he carried mostly broken arrows and a bow under construction (but no usable bow in his possession)
30 has led to theories that Ötzi had recently met with a violent encounter—either with other humans or a wild animal—and perhaps had fled high into the mountains in retreat.

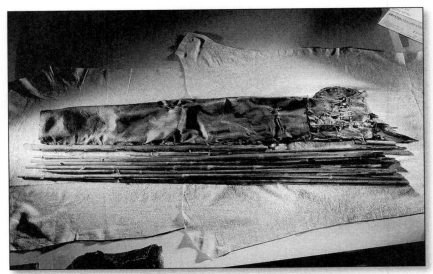

*The Iceman's quiver and arrows.*

They assume that he found a suitable piece of wood from an evergreen yew trunk and was working on it at night while resting at camp. Perhaps he was even working on it before falling asleep the night he died.

Ötzi's fur quiver, where he kept his arrows, contained 12 blank shafts and two finished arrows, which were broken. His bow was more than 6 feet long. The yew wood from which he

40 worked was ideal for bow-making; it's tough and elastic, almost never splinters, and has no resin.

The quiver contained two arrows ready to be shot (with flint arrowheads), 12 partly finished arrow shafts, a coiled string, four bundled stag-antler fragments, an antler point, and two bundled animal sinews. The antler fragments could have been used to carve at least eight arrowheads, although the completed arrowheads were carved from flint, which was probably the preferred material.

# THE ICEMAN ATE-ETH MEAT [1]

Archaeologists are divided over whether
a prehistoric man had the salad or the steak.

## Jessa Netting

### TONE

Re-read lines 1–4. A real
food fight occurs when
people throw food at each
other. How is the expression
used here? How does the
term help create the author's
**tone,** or attitude toward
her audience and subject?

_____

_____

_____

_____

_____

_____

### COMPARE & CONTRAST

Pause at line 8. Underline
the contrasting views people
have about Ötzi's eating
habits.

### IDENTIFY

Re-read lines 9–13. Underline
the information that con-
tains facts and details you
already learned from reading
"Iceman: Mummy from the
Stone Age." Circle a new
detail presented here.

A food fight is raging in the field of archaeology. The food in
question last saw the light of day 5,300 years ago, just before
being swallowed by a man who then hiked into the Ötztal Alps,
died, and was sealed within a glacier for millennia.

Now, thousands of years after his last meal, researchers are
debating the diet of the Tyrolean[2] Iceman, also known as Ötzi.
A year after one group decided that he was vegetarian, another,
citing different tests, is suggesting that Ötzi had a taste for meat.

Ötzi's incredibly well-preserved body melted out of a

10 mountaintop glacier just inside Italy in 1991. His unusual state
of preservation—skin, clothes, tattoos, and all—gave archaeologists a rare chance to reconstruct the lifestyle of a European who
trekked the mountains long before people kept travel diaries.

Among the murkier aspects of Ötzi's lifestyle is what he ate.
In spite of the hard climb, on the day he died the Iceman headed
into the mountains without provisions and had last eaten eight
hours before he died.

Last year, researchers looking at the chemical composition
of Ötzi's hair suggested that he was primarily vegetarian or even

20 vegan, eating little if any meat or milk.

---

1. **Ate-eth Meat:** The writer is making a humorous **allusion,** or
   reference, to a play by Eugene O'Neill (1888–1953), *The Iceman
   Cometh,* which is unrelated to the Iceman in the article. The *–eth*
   ending was used in English hundreds of years ago.
2. **Tyrolean** (ti·rō′lē·ən) *adj.:* from the Austrian and Italian Alps.

This came as a surprise to University of Glasgow botanical archaeologist James Dickson. "I could hardly believe it," says Dickson, who with colleagues from several institutions now presents evidence to challenge the claim.

The Iceman's innards, they contend, reveal that Ötzi was much more of a gourmand. His last supper included fire-cooked flatbread, herbs, and meat. Dickson and his colleagues make the case for omnivory in the *Philosophical Transactions of the Royal Society of London B.*

30    Their argument centers on the contents of Ötzi's colon, which included grain, moss, pollen, the eggs of a parasitic whip-worm, and muscle fibers from meat.

They also take issue with previous analyses of the chemicals in Ötzi's hair. The team's interpretation of the hair data suggests that meat may have made up as much as 30% of the Iceman's diet, bringing his tastes in line with modern hunter-gatherer societies.

But archaeologist Stanley Ambrose of the University of Illinois in Urbana feels that both sides of the argument have problems. "The controversy seems to be inflated," he says.

40    Ambrose says that the results of the hair analysis do not translate into a diet that was one-third meat. He thinks that meat probably made up about 10% of Ötzi's food, supporting the earlier team's vegetarian claim.

The two theories are not mutually exclusive, concedes Stephen Macko of the University of Virginia, who led last year's vegetarian camp. Hair records diet over as long as a month. Microscopic gut examination picks over a single meal.

"For a portion of his life he was equivalent to what we call a vegan today. But he was clearly opportunistic," says Macko.

50    If nothing else, this latest twist shows the advantages of analyzing both hair and gut contents. Researchers are about to probe the diet of 550-year-old Kwaday Dän Sinchi (meaning "Long Ago Person Found"), the first North American Iceman.

**IDENTIFY**

Re-read lines 30–32. Underline the reasons scientists believe that Ötzi was an omnivore (someone who eats both plants and animals).

**PARAPHRASE**

Pause at line 47. "Two theories are not mutually exclusive" means they may both be true. Restate the last two sentences of the paragraph. (Hint: *Records* [ri·kôrdz'] is a verb here.)

_____

_____

_____

_____

_____

_____

**IDENTIFY**

State the **main idea** of the article.

_____

_____

_____

_____

_____

_____

_____

_____

# ICEMAN OF THE ALPS WAS SLAIN, X-RAY SHOWS

## Richard Boudreaux

ROME—It took about 5,300 years to find the body and 10 years to perform the autopsy, but researchers in Italy say they know what killed the Iceman: He was shot with an arrow and likely died in agony.

Who fired the arrow—a rival hunter, perhaps, or a warrior in battle—is being investigated as scientists work to reconstruct the life and death of the Bronze Age's best-preserved mummy in search of precious knowledge about that prehistoric time.

The mummy's caretakers announced the discovery yester-
10 day at a news conference in Bolzano, Italy. X-rays "revealed a sensation: a flint arrowhead is visible in the left side of the thorax," said Bruno Hosp, president of the South Tyrol Museum of Archeology.

The Iceman's frozen corpse turned up in the Alps in 1991 when two German hikers noticed it protruding from an Alpine glacier near the Italy-Austria border 11,000 feet above sea level.

The ice also preserved a treasure trove of prehistoric artifacts: the metal, wood, fruit, hay, grass, leather, and weapons that composed his worldly possessions.

20 When the Iceman, nicknamed Ötzi by researchers, was discovered, scientists speculated he may have fallen asleep and died in the snow or was possibly killed in a fall.

Since then, Ötzi and his stuff have been pored over by protohistorians, archaeologists, anthropologists, and students of anatomy, medicine, forensic dentistry, and nutrition from all over the world. They flock to his refrigerated, chapel-like room at the museum, where visitors can view him through a small window.

So far, researchers have learned from carbon dating that the Iceman lived early in the Bronze Age, which ran from 3500 to 1000 B.C. Microscopic analysis of a sample removed from his intestines last year revealed he ate meat, unleavened bread, and an herb or green plant for his last meal.

Pollen in that food tells scientists it was springtime and the Iceman had been in the valley hours before climbing to the heights where he died face-down in a large rock hollow. They have even calculated his age at death: 45 to 50.

But the cause of his demise had been a mystery because the fatal puncture wound was so tiny, barely visible on his shrunken skin.

The X-ray revealing the inch-long arrowhead was made last week using a technique called computerized tomography, which makes a multidimensional image.

The discovery came as scientists were taking new X-rays to study the Iceman's broken ribs, trying to learn how the ribs were bashed, in an attempt to zero in on the possible causes of his death.

Eduard Egarter Vigl, the mummy's chief curator, said the arrow was fired into the left side, shattering the scapula and tearing through nerves and major blood vessels before lodging just below the left shoulder near the lung. The Iceman suffered what must have been painful internal bleeding and paralysis of the left arm, the curator said, and probably survived no more than a few hours.

When Ötzi was discovered, scientists hailed him as startlingly well-preserved.

They said the body was in such good condition that pores in the skin looked normal; even the eyeballs were preserved behind lids frozen open. His body was discovered along with a copper ax, a bow, and some flint arrows with the same kind of arrowhead that some rival or aggressor fired at him.

**IDENTIFY CAUSE & EFFECT**

Underline why it was so difficult for scientists to find the cause of Ötzi's demise, or death (lines 37–39).

**PARAPHRASE**

Re-read lines 47–53. Then, restate the text in your own words.

IDENTIFY

Circle the information in lines 61–64 that helps you understand what was yet to happen in the rest of the world when Ötzi died.

IDENTIFY

State the **main idea** of the article in your own words.

_____

_____

_____

_____

_____

_____

SYNTHESIZE

Briefly explain how the three articles about Ötzi work together.

_____

_____

_____

_____

_____

_____

_____

_____

_____

_____

_____

_____

The death of the Iceman gives archaeologists and historians new insights into his times. He would have been slain 5,300 years ago, before the great Pyramids of Egypt were built and as Europeans were first experimenting with the wheel.

"This changes everything. Now the research on the Iceman starts over," said Alex Susanna, director of the South Tyrol Museum of Archeology.

"Maybe there was a combat, maybe he was in a battle," he said. "There is a whole series of new implications. The story

70  needs to be rewritten."

In September, the museum will host an international conference on the Iceman.

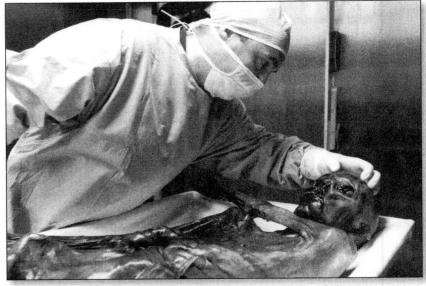

*A researcher prepares to take samples of the Bronze Age hunter known as Ötzi.*

# Iceman: Mummy from the Stone Age;
# The Iceman Ate-eth Meat;
# Iceman of the Alps Was Slain, X-ray Shows

**Synthesizing Sources**     Use this chart to consider all your sources as a group. Complete the chart by writing details from the three articles on the Iceman. Some of the boxes have already been filled in. When the chart is completed, draw a conclusion and write it in the box below.

| | Iceman: Mummy from the Stone Age (Internet) | The Iceman Ate-eth Meat (Magazine) | Iceman of the Alps Was Slain, X-ray Shows (Newspaper) |
|---|---|---|---|
| **Topics covered** | body found; weapons found with body | | |
| **How he died** | | not discussed | X-ray shows path of arrow; suggests painful death |
| **His last meal** | | same | |
| **What he usually ate: vegetarian or meat eater?** | | | doesn't say whether he was a meat eater or a vegetarian |
| **Purpose of article** | to provide background information | to discuss whether he was vegetarian or meat eater | to explain how X-ray revealed cause of death |
| **Main idea** | | | |

| Conclusion |
|---|
| |

# Standards Review

**TestPractice**

## Iceman: Mummy from the Stone Age; The Iceman Ate-eth Meat; Iceman of the Alps Was Slain, X-ray Shows

Complete the sample test item. Then, read the explanation at the right.

| Sample Test Item | Explanation of the Correct Answer |
|---|---|
| The three articles all agree that— <br><br> **A** Ötzi had nothing in his stomach <br><br> **B** Ötzi's body was well-preserved <br><br> **C** studying Ötzi's body is useless <br><br> **D** eating meat is important | The correct answer is *B.* <br><br> The stomach contents were studied, so answer *A* is incorrect. *C* is incorrect because the articles discuss what scientists have learned from studying Ötzi's body. *D* is not correct; none of the articles make this statement. |

**DIRECTIONS:** Circle the letter of the best response.

**Reading Standard 2.4**
Synthesize the content from several sources or works by a single author dealing with a single issue; paraphrase the ideas and connect them to other sources and related topics to demonstrate comprehension.

1. Which of the following best states the **main idea** of "Iceman: Mummy from the Stone Age"?

   **A** Icemen come from the Stone Age.

   **B** A prehistoric man was preserved in ice.

   **C** The Iceman wore fur and grass.

   **D** People used bows and arrows long ago.

2. "The Iceman Ate-eth Meat" concludes that Ötzi ate—

   **F** only vegetables

   **G** eggs and potatoes

   **H** only meat

   **J** some meat

3. Which article(s) would you cite in a research report on how Ötzi died?

   **A** "Iceman: Mummy from the Stone Age"

   **B** "The Iceman Ate-eth Meat"

   **C** "Iceman of the Alps Was Slain, X-ray Shows"

   **D** all of the above

4. Which of the following is discussed in all three articles?

   **F** Ötzi's discovery in the Alps

   **G** pollen in Ötzi's stomach

   **H** Ötzi's bow and arrows

   **J** Ötzi's village

# Standards Review

 **Iceman: Mummy from the Stone Age; The Iceman Ate-eth Meat; Iceman of the Alps Was Slain, X-ray Shows**

## Multiple Meanings

**DIRECTIONS:** Read the passage in each item below. Then, circle the letter of the answer in which the underlined word is used in the same way as it is used in the passage.

1. "As Ötzi's body began to thaw from its icy grave, it became apparent that this was no modern European."

   A  The doctor gave the patient grave news.

   B  Grave colors matched a gray day.

   C  The accent is called grave because it points left.

   D  As is usual, the grave was six feet deep.

2. "He was shot with an arrow and likely died in agony."

   F  Do you think I have a shot at making the team?

   G  Julio's shot of the sunset won first prize.

   H  The missile was shot from a submarine.

   J  The little girl cried when given a shot.

3. "For investigational purposes the body is removed from storage and put in a laminar flow box for no longer than 11 minutes at a time."

   A  The prizefighter loves to box.

   B  This kind of box turtle is very rare.

   C  Carefully place the box on the floor.

   D  The box camera was easy to operate.

4. "A food fight is raging in the field of archaeology."

   F  The baseman was unable to field the ball.

   G  I want a job in the field of health.

   H  The field was muddy from the rain.

   J  The students looked forward to their field trip.

**Reading Standard 1.1** Identify and use the literal and figurative meanings of words and understand word derivations.

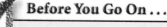 **Before You Go On . . .** Check your Standards Mastery at the back of this book.

# The Great Blizzard of '88 by Robert C. Kennedy;
# The Land Is an Ocean of Snow by Jim Murphy

## BEFORE YOU READ

Have you heard the expression "A picture is worth a thousand words"? In the selections you're about to read, both pictures and words are good sources of information. "The Great Blizzard of '88" includes a cartoon that offers a vivid image of a memorable snowstorm. That article and "The Land Is an Ocean of Snow" both describe some of the brave adults and children who refused to let a massive snowstorm get in their way.

## INFORMATIONAL FOCUS: PRIMARY AND SECONDARY SOURCES

When you do research on a subject, you collect information from a number of **sources.** Your sources may be magazines, newspaper articles, books, or information from the Internet. Sources can be divided into two types:

- **Primary sources** are firsthand accounts. They include autobiographies, eyewitness news reports, letters, diaries, photographs, and newsreels. In primary sources, writers present firsthand responses to and opinions about events they have witnessed or taken part in.
- **Secondary sources** are materials in which a writer summarizes, interprets, or analyzes events the writer did *not* witness or take part in. A writer may study primary sources and write articles or books based on information and ideas from these sources. The author may also express opinions about the information from the sources. Secondary sources include encyclopedias, textbooks, and biographies. The discussion of the cartoon and of related historical events in "The Great Blizzard of '88" is a secondary source, and so is "The Land Is an Ocean of Snow," a chapter from a book.

## READING SKILLS: IDENTIFY AND ELABORATE ON MAIN IDEAS

When you read primary and secondary sources to collect information on a topic, you look for main ideas. The **main idea** is the most important point made in a paragraph or passage. The rest of the paragraph provides support (usually facts) for the main idea. Identifying the main idea helps you follow the writer's discussion, as you stay alert for the major information and ideas that are presented.

**Reading Standard 1.1**
Identify and use the literal and figurative meanings of words and understand word derivations.

**Reading Standard 2.5**
Extend ideas presented in primary or secondary sources through original analysis, evaluation, and elaboration.

After you identify the main idea, you can elaborate on it. When you **elaborate** on a main idea, you make connections between the facts and ideas in the article and your own prior knowledge. You add details to the information you've read. To elaborate on an idea:

- Connect the information to your own experience.
- Ask questions about the ideas and information in the article.
- Jot down information that adds to your understanding of the subject.
- Make a list of your own ideas on the topic.

As you read the two articles that follow, use this chart to jot down your elaborations of some of the main points. An example is included to get you started.

| Main Idea | My Elaboration |
|---|---|
| Terrible snowstorm hit eastern U.S. in 1888 and caused 400 deaths. | Has my city ever suffered from a major storm? How can I find out? |
|  |  |
|  |  |
|  |  |
|  |  |
|  |  |
|  |  |

# The Great Blizzard of '88

## Robert C. Kennedy

### IDENTIFY SOURCES

The cartoon was drawn by someone who lived through the blizzard. Is it a **primary source** or a **secondary source**? Explain.

_____

_____

_____

_____

_____

_____

_____

_____

_____

_____

_____

_____

_____

_____

_____

_____

### INFER

Read the **caption** under the cartoon. Underline the name of the person the note was sent to; circle the name of the person who sent it.

On March 24, 1888, *Harper's Weekly* featured a cartoon about the Great Blizzard of '88.

"To Mayor Hewitt, New York:—

"Bismarck stands ready to give substantial aid to blizzard sufferers of New York. Let us know your needs."

"M. R. Jewell, Chamber of Commerce."

This *Harper's Weekly* cartoon shows Father Knickerbocker, the symbol of New York City, stranded shoulder-deep in the Great Blizzard of 1888. The young city of Bismarck, Dakota Territory (today, North Dakota), survivor of a blizzard which hit the plain states earlier in January, offers its assistance. The March blizzard blanketed the eastern seaboard from Maine to Washington, D.C., causing over 400 deaths and tens of millions of dollars in prop-

From "Little Bismarck to Father Knickerbocker" (retitled "The Great Blizzard of '88") as it appeared on *New York Times* website. Accessed February 25, 2002 at /http://www.nytimes.com/learning/general/onthisday/harp/0234.htm. Reprinted by permission of **The New York Times Company.**

erty damage. It was New York City's worst snowstorm since 1857, and took the metropolis almost two weeks to recover completely.

10    The weather in New York City on Sunday, March 11, 1888, had been rainy, but the early-morning edition of the March 12 *New York Tribune* optimistically forecast "clearing and colder, preceded by light snow." Most readers did not see that Monday headline, though, since their papers were buried underneath a mountain of snow. A low-pressure system from the west had collided with another from the south, while a frigid air mass from Canada held the fronts stationary.

Heavy rain on Sunday night turned to sleet, then to snow just after midnight, and continued for almost two days. Most
20    roads were impassable by sunrise on Monday morning, although gale-force winds, registering up to 60 m.p.h., cleared a few areas while piling snow up to second-story windows on other streets. At 7:00 A.M., the snowstorm gathered strength, as winds gusted to 75 m.p.h. and temperatures ranged from 11° to 1°. Almost 17 inches of snow fell on Monday, and four more on Tuesday.

New York City was virtually immobilized. Businesses, markets, and schools closed or never opened; few street transports operated; nine ferry boats were sunk, driven ashore, or otherwise abandoned; ice on rails and snow-clogged switches forced
30    the railroads to stop running (some in mid-trip); telegraph and telephone communications were cut; and the mayor (like most others) stayed home. One makeshift entrepreneur placed a ladder up to a stranded elevated car and charged passengers 50 cents to climb down.

The unlucky individuals who had left their homes early enough to make it to work found that the only way home was afoot or by paying exorbitant prices to the few cabdrivers braving the weather. Besides the cold, wind, and snow, the streets were littered with downed or falling electric wires, business signs,
40    barber poles, cigar-store Indians, and other debris. Hotels, lodging houses, and clubs were filled to capacity, even with

IDENTIFY

Pause at line 9. From the cartoon and the text, what geographic area will the article discuss in detail? Circle your answer.

IDENTIFY
CAUSE & EFFECT

Re-read lines 10–17. Underline the words explaining what caused the storm.

IDENTIFY

Circle the **main idea** in lines 26–34. Underline at least three details that support it.

IDENTIFY
CAUSE & EFFECT

Re-read lines 35–40. Why were so many people stranded?

_____

_____

_____

_____

_____

_____

_____

_____

_____

_____

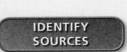

**IDENTIFY & ELABORATE**

Pause at line 51. Underline the main idea of the paragraph. How does this paragraph **elaborate** on, or add information to, the previous paragraphs?

_____

_____

_____

_____

**IDENTIFY & ELABORATE**

Pause at line 69. Circle the main idea of the paragraph. Then, briefly note how you would **elaborate** on a description in the paragraph.

_____

_____

_____

_____

**IDENTIFY SOURCES**

Is the text of the article a **primary source** or a **secondary source**? Explain.

_____

_____

_____

_____

corridors transformed into sleeping areas; the Astor House had to turn away 400 people who were seeking shelter.

Undeterred by a bit of snow was Roscoe Conkling, New York's former U.S. senator and one of the city's most prominent lawyers. The stubborn, tempestuous Conkling showed up Monday morning for a court hearing on a high-profile case involving the widow of A. T. Stewart, the department-store millionaire.

50  Conkling was aghast to find that the judge was snowbound and had rescheduled the hearing for Tuesday. Oblivious to the weather, he returned to his office and worked until 6 P.M.

After hailing a cab for the New York Club at Madison Square, Conkling indignantly refused to pay the $50 charge, so set off on foot. The two-and-a-half mile journey through the darkened, snow-packed city took him three hours, including one hour trying to extricate himself from a snowdrift into which he (like Father Knickerbocker) had fallen up to his armpits. Once inside the door of the club, exhausted and caked with snow and ice, he collapsed unconscious. The next day he was back in

60  court, even though the snow was still falling.

On Tuesday, the city began digging out, producing huge snow piles in the gutters. Sleighs appeared to carry groceries, coal, and other necessities, and the elevated railways began functioning again. That morning, an ice-bridge allowed thousands of people to walk across the East River between Brooklyn and Manhattan. On Wednesday, residents built bonfires to melt the gargantuan snowdrifts, and the trains to the suburbs resumed operation. By the end of the week, the streetcars were running and the sun was shining.

70  Roscoe Conkling continued working until March 30 when he took sick in court, complaining of a severe headache. Physicians determined that an abscess in his inner ear, high temperature (reaching $104\frac{1}{2}°$), and delirium were the results of his trek through the blizzard. On April 17, Conkling lapsed into a coma, and died at 2 A.M. the next morning.

# The Land Is an Ocean of Snow

## Jim Murphy

On Monday, March 12, people from Delaware on up to Maine, and inland as far as the Mississippi River, woke to discover a white and hostile visitor lurking outside. A blizzard was rattling their windowpanes and piling up snow against their doors.

A blizzard is defined as any storm where snow is accompanied by temperatures of 20 degrees Fahrenheit or lower, plus winds of at least 35 miles per hour. During the Blizzard of 1888, temperatures often went below zero, and winds were clocked at 75 to 85 miles per hour. Many newspapers nicknamed the storm the Great White Hurricane.

The exact origin of the word *blizzard* is disputed and debated. The English claim it came from the common Midland expression "may I be blizzarded," which, roughly translated, means "I'll be darned." The notion is that the astonished speaker has been knocked over by an icy blast. Others say the word is derived from the German *blitzartig*, which means "lightning-like."

In the United States, some insist the word came from an old western phrase "to be blizzarded," or struck many times by violent punches. And we do know that in Tennessee and Kentucky, the word is used to refer to a period of intense cold, even without wind or snow.

Whatever its origin, the word *blizzard* certainly fit what was happening to the northeastern coast that morning. As temperatures plummeted, the wet snow changed into tiny, sharp particles of ice that ripped at any exposed skin. A Philadelphia resident remembered how "the snow would follow breath into his lungs and fill them with water, nearly choking him."

---

**INFER**

Read the title and the first paragraph of the text. What do you think the subject of the text will be?

_____

_____

_____

_____

_____

_____

_____

_____

_____

_____

**IDENTIFY**

Circle the definition of *blizzard*, given in lines 5–10.

**IDENTIFY**

Re-read lines 11–21. Underline details that provide **elaboration** on the topic "blizzard."

Pause at line 31. Underline the quoted passage from a newspaper. Is the quotation a **primary source** or a **secondary source**? Explain.

_____

_____

_____

_____

_____

COMPARE &
CONTRAST

This text describes the blizzard in cities from Maine to Delaware. In what way does "The Great Blizzard of '88" differ?

_____

_____

_____

_____

_____

_____

_____

FLUENCY

Read the boxed passage aloud quickly and smoothly, as if you were a newscaster.

An Albany *Journal* reporter struggled through the howling wind and snow to his paper's offices where he wrote: "In truth
30 the land is an ocean of snow. . . . The city looked dead and was literally buried."

His city may have appeared lifeless, but in fact there was a great deal of activity going on. Monday was the beginning of the week, which meant work and school for hundreds of thousands of people. Bank presidents, chambermaids, store owners, factory workers, telegraph operators, students, schoolteachers and principals, Western Union messengers, blacksmiths, and newspaper deliverers alike set out that morning just as they did on any other workday. This was true in big cities such as Albany,
40 Boston, Buffalo, and New York, and in the many smaller towns and villages in between.

Milkman William Brubacker was one such person. When he awoke at 1:30 A.M. Monday morning, a hard, vicious snow was pelting his house in downtown New York City. But Brubacker never hesitated. His customers expected to find their bottles of milk and cream waiting as always, and he had no intention of disappointing them.

After hitching up his horse and wagon, Brubacker went to the Hudson River, where he crossed to Jersey City on a ferry.
50 There he met the milk train, loaded his wagon, and returned to New York City to begin his deliveries. By this time, it was 5 A.M. and Brubacker was already two hours behind schedule.

Dutifully, he followed his usual route, going up one slick cobblestone street and down another, making every stop just as he would on a normal morning. Often, the milk boxes were hidden by drifts of snow and sealed tight by ice, so William had to dig them out and chip away till the lids opened.

At 10 A.M. that morning, he had only covered about half his normal route when painfully cold ears and exhaustion forced
60 him to stop at a saloon to warm up. He gulped down a glass of whiskey and was preparing to leave when the bartender told him he looked awful. "He made me walk the floor for ten minutes

"The Perils of Union Square in the Midst of the Blizzard,"
(1888). Wood engraving.

DRAW
CONCLUSIONS

Why do you think the writer
included the account of
the milkman's experience
(lines 42–75)?

and I had another drink. I began to realize myself that I did not
stop any too soon."

At the time, a glass or two (or more) of whiskey was considered the best medicine to fight off cold and frostbite, and was
liberally administered to men, women, and children. Never mind
that it often left the patient intoxicated, or that the illusion of
warmth the liquor provided often prompted a drunk to stagger
70    back out into the storm.

Reluctantly, but wisely, Brubacker turned his horse and
wagon around and went home, where he stayed for the next four
days. Later, he would recall that long before he understood the
danger of the storm, his horse had turned toward the stable
three times. "He had more sense than I," William concluded.

Another group who made it to work were the men of the
New York City Weather Station. Sergeant Francis Long was the
first at the station, but soon his boss, Chief Dunn, and the
others arrived.

PREDICT

Re-read lines 76–79.
Underline the topic sentence,
the sentence that tells you
what the paragraph is about.
What will the next section of
text be about?

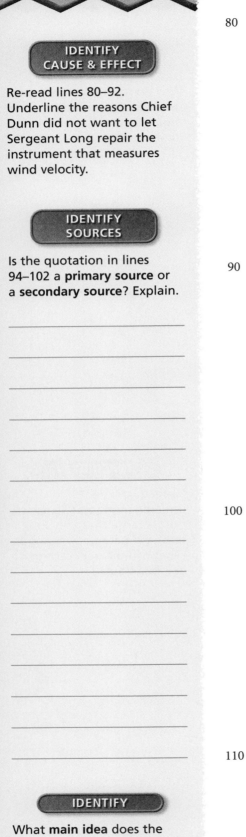

**IDENTIFY CAUSE & EFFECT**

Re-read lines 80–92. Underline the reasons Chief Dunn did not want to let Sergeant Long repair the instrument that measures wind velocity.

**IDENTIFY SOURCES**

Is the quotation in lines 94–102 a **primary source** or a **secondary source**? Explain.

_____

_____

_____

_____

_____

_____

_____

_____

_____

_____

_____

_____

_____

_____

**IDENTIFY**

What **main idea** does the writer introduce in lines 108–114? Underline it.

80    The day before, they had to deal with no communications from Washington or any of the other local weather stations. Today, they found that the machine to measure wind velocity, the anemometer, had frozen stiff. Fixing the instrument seemed out of the question. It was screwed to the top of a four-inch-wide pole that was affixed to the rooftop tower, nearly 200 feet above the sidewalk. Chief Dunn estimated that the wind gusts were "75 miles an hour in a driving spiculum of snow and ice."

Sergeant Long stepped forward and volunteered to repair the anemometer. At first, Dunn refused to let Long risk his life,

90    saying, "You are too heavy a man. The pole will snap and I will be responsible for a dead man." "Sir," Long replied, "it will be at my own risk."

After a few more minutes of discussion, Chief Dunn relented. "[Long] climbed that slim pole without any support," Dunn would say in a report, "adjusted the instrument and replaced some wiring with one hand. . . . The wind pressure was so great that it was most difficult for one to stand up, even by holding on, and impossible to get one's breath if facing the wind. Long was nearly frozen, but still he kept on until the instrument

100   was in proper working order. It was a most heroic act. . . . The principal record of the storm would have been lost had it not been for Francis Long."

Long never wrote about this incident, and he never spoke very much about it, either. He continued working at the weather station for another twenty-eight years, and eventually became chief forecaster. For Sergeant Long, climbing a wobbling pole in the face of a blizzard was simply a part of his job.

Even young children wouldn't let the obvious power of the storm get in their way. In Brooklyn, ten-year-old Rufus Billings

110   announced at breakfast that he intended to go to school. His parents tried to talk him out of this reckless adventure, and even hid his boots, but young Rufus was determined. He found his boots and plunged out into the storm before his worried parents could stop him.

A dozen other students were already at the school when Rufus arrived. The only problem was that the door was locked. No adults had made it—not the principal, teachers, or the janitor. Still, these children had no intention of giving up. They huddled at the front door for an hour and only went home when the principal finally appeared and officially proclaimed school closed for the day.

120

Another very determined child was ten-year-old Sam Strong, who lived in Harlem with his aunt and uncle, Mr. and Mrs. Charles Green. Sam didn't have to fight and argue to go outside. His aunt actually gave him a list of items she wanted him to buy at Brady's notion store before going on to school. Among the things he was to get were whalebones, dressmaker's chalk, and a large needle, so his aunt could sew herself a new corset.

Sam glanced out the front window and saw a man get blown over by the wind. He also noticed that the front gate was completely covered by a five-foot-tall snowdrift. When he said something about this to his aunt, she made him wear his high rubber boots, a heavy overcoat, woolen cap, gloves, and a muffler. "There," she said as she buttoned up his coat, "you could go to the North Pole in that outfit. Hurry up now, so you won't be late for school."

130

At first, Sam liked the experience of being outside in a wild storm, fighting his way through belt-high snow and fending off the wind. His aunt and uncle had instilled in him a strong sense of self-reliance and duty. He had been told to go to the store and then to school, so he was going to do both, no matter what the consequences.

140

Several blocks later, Sam came face to face with the violence of the blizzard. As he was crossing an intersection, the wind was on him like a wild animal. It picked him up and tossed him into a deep snowdrift.

Sam struggled and clawed to get free of the snow, but he was in over his head. The more he moved, the more snow fell on top of him. He shrieked for help, but no one heard him above

**IDENTIFY & ELABORATE**

Re-read lines 115–121. How did these students feel about going to school that day? Briefly note how you would **elaborate** on the passage.

_____

_____

_____

_____

_____

**ANALYZE**

**Anecdotes** (brief true stories) are a type of elaboration. They can add a personal note to a discussion. What effect does the anecdote starting on line 122 create?

_____

_____

_____

_____

_____

_____

**IDENTIFY**

Re-read lines 143–149. Underline details that show why Sam's trip to the store was so difficult.

PREDICT

Pause at line 154. Do you think Sam will give up and go home? Why or why not?

_____

_____

_____

_____

_____

_____

_____

_____

_____

_____

_____

_____

_____

_____

_____

_____

_____

_____

_____

_____

_____

_____

_____

_____

_____

150 the wind's mighty roar. His boyish romp had turned into a frightening trap in just seconds. Finally, just as his strength was about to give out, a policeman came along and yanked him free. "You hadn't ought to be out in this, Sonny," he recalled the policeman telling him. "You go straight home."

But Sam didn't go home. More determined than ever, he pressed on, going down 125th Street, past abandoned wagons and carriages. A cable car being pulled by four horses struggled at a feeble pace, while the few other people out that morning were hunkered over against the icy gusts. "When I could get down out

160 of the cutting wind behind a snowdrift, I was all right," the boy recalled, "but traveling took every ounce of power in my body."

"The Blizzard in New York: A scene on 26th Street," (1888). Woodcut.

When he finally reached Brady's, he discovered it closed, the front door and window covered completely by a giant snowdrift. Instead of giving up, Sam continued along the street for several blocks, hoping to discover a store—any store—open. There were none.

At this point, he stopped a fellow traveler to see if the man knew where he could purchase a corset needle. The man had no idea where to get the needle, but he did teach Sam something

170 else. "[I] learned a few new and attractive profane expressions to add to my already fair vocabulary of cuss words, and with his help I about-faced and started the homeward trek."

If anything, his return journey proved more treacherous. The drifts seemed to have grown enormously in height; the snow seemed sharper, the wind more cutting. Sam, like thousands of others, would later come to realize that as fatigue set in, obstacles he had handled fairly easily before were now much harder to deal with. Six times Sam got stuck in the snow and six times he had to be pulled to safety. Finally, at around noon, he clawed his

180 way up his front stairs and tumbled into the vestibule.

Neither his aunt nor his uncle—who had stayed home from work—said anything harsh to the boy. It was Sam who was upset. "Although I had fought the snow for more than four hours, I had failed in my mission. There were many tears. . . . I [went to] bed with glass bottles filled with hot water, a big slug of raw whiskey, and some food, and I was asleep, not waking until night and then only for more food and drink. I was exhausted."

**IDENTIFY CAUSE & EFFECT**

Re-read lines 173–180. Sam's trip home seemed more difficult. Locate and circle the cause—why the trip was so much harder.

**IDENTIFY & ELABORATE**

Underline the words telling what Sam was most upset about (lines 181–188). How might you **elaborate** on Sam's words?

# The Great Blizzard of '88;
# The Land Is an Ocean of Snow

**Elaboration Chart**     When you elaborate, you extend or expand on a topic by adding details, comments, and questions. Passages from "The Great Blizzard of '88" and "The Land Is an Ocean of Snow" appear in the left column of the chart. Elaborate on those passages in the space provided.

| Text Passage | My Elaboration |
|---|---|
| "Bismarck stands ready to give substantial aid to blizzard sufferers in New York." ("The Great Blizzard of '88," cartoon caption) | |
| "One makeshift entrepreneur placed a ladder up to a stranded elevated car and charged passengers 50 cents to climb down." ("The Great Blizzard of '88," lines 32–34) | |
| "Sergeant Long stepped forward and volunteered to repair the anemometer." ("The Land Is an Ocean of Snow," lines 88–89) | |
| "[Sam] had been told to go to the store and then to school, so he was going to do both, no matter what the consequences." ("The Land Is an Ocean of Snow," lines 140–142) | |

# Standards Review

**Test Practice**

# The Great Blizzard of '88; The Land Is an Ocean of Snow

Complete the sample test item below by circling the correct answer. Then, read the explanation to the right.

| Sample Test Item | Explanation of the Correct Answer |
|---|---|
| The text of "The Great Blizzard of '88" is a **secondary source** because the—<br><br>**A** writer presents his own experiences<br><br>**B** article contains an anecdote<br><br>**C** article has appeared on the Internet<br><br>**D** writer did not take part in the event | *D* is the correct answer.<br><br>The writer is not presenting his own experiences, so *A* is incorrect. *B* is incorrect; the article contains an anecdote, but both primary and secondary sources may include anecdotes. *C* is not correct because both primary and secondary articles appear on the Internet. |

**DIRECTIONS:** Circle the letter of each correct response.

1. The cartoon in "The Great Blizzard of '88" is—

   **A** a secondary source

   **B** a primary source

   **C** meant to make readers laugh about the blizzard

   **D** not related to the text of the article

2. The author's **purpose** in "The Land Is an Ocean of Snow" is to—

   **F** change the reader's opinion

   **G** brag about his writing

   **H** warn people about blizzards

   **J** present information about the blizzard

3. "The Great Blizzard of '88" and "The Land Is an Ocean of Snow"—

   **A** are examples of cause-and-effect articles

   **B** give conflicting information about a blizzard

   **C** provide historical details about a legendary blizzard

   **D** are not reliable historical sources

4. Which of the following is *not* an **elaboration** included in "The Land Is an Ocean of Snow"?

   **F** the anecdote about Sam's experience

   **G** the history of the word *blizzard*

   **H** a quotation from the mayor of New York City

   **J** paraphrases of original quotations

**Reading Standard 2.5**
Extend ideas presented in primary or secondary sources through original analysis, evaluation, and elaboration.

 TestPractice

## The Great Blizzard of '88; The Land Is an Ocean of Snow

### Prefixes

A **prefix** is a word part attached to the front of a word or root to change its meaning. For example, the prefix *un–* (which means "not") changes *happy* to *unhappy.* Understanding the meanings of prefixes can help you enlarge your vocabulary.

This chart gives several prefixes and their meanings, the languages they come from, and an example of a word for each prefix.

**Reading Standard 1.1**
Identify and use the literal and figurative meanings of words and understand word derivations.

| Prefix and Meaning | Original Language | Example |
|---|---|---|
| *inter–* (between) | Latin | interstate |
| *tele–* (far away) | Greek | telephone |
| *trans–* (across) | Latin | transfer |
| *pre–* (before) | Latin | predate |
| *un–* (not) | Old English | unlikely |

**DIRECTIONS:** Each word in the left column has a prefix. The right column lists definitions of the prefixes. Match each word with the definition of its prefix by writing the letter of the definition on the line.

1. _____ televise

2. _____ interplanetary

3. _____ unusual

4. _____ transport

5. _____ prearrange

a. across

b. not

c. far away

d. between

e. before

**Before You Go On . . .**

Check your Standards Mastery at the back of this book.

# Who Wrote Shakespeare?

by Terry Deary

## BEFORE YOU READ

Did William Shakespeare (1564–1616) actually write the plays that have his name on them? Some scholars argue that the plays were written by somebody else. Who was this Shakespeare-in-hiding? This article rates the top ten possibilities for the "real" Shakespeare. Do any of them get your vote?

### INFORMATIONAL FOCUS: AUTHOR'S ARGUMENT

In some informational articles, authors offer a **claim,** or an opinion, on a subject. A claim can often be stated in a sentence—for example, "Head Start has been a successful educational program." Claims are generally supported by an **argument**—evidence to persuade readers to accept the views.

There are two main types of arguments, also called **appeals.**
- **Logical appeals** use facts, examples, and opinions by experts on the subject.
- **Emotional appeals** are often just opinions—for example, "I know I can do the job." Emotional appeals include the use of loaded words, or words with strong emotional impact (such as *patriotism*), and anecdotes, or brief, true stories that may interest the reader but do not support the claim.

### READING SKILLS: IDENTIFYING AUTHOR'S PURPOSE AND TONE

An author's **purpose** is his or her reason for writing (to convince, to alarm, to amuse, to inform, and so on). **Tone** is an author's attitude toward the topic of his or her writing. An author may convey a respectful tone, a serious tone, or a lighthearted tone, for example.

An author's purpose may be stated directly; sometimes, however, you have to examine the author's word choice to arrive at his or her purpose. To identify tone, examine an author's word choice and its effect on readers.

You may want to fill in a chart like the one below as you read "Who Wrote Shakespeare?"

| Passage | Purpose | Tone |
|---------|---------|------|
|         |         |      |
|         |         |      |
|         |         |      |

**Reading Standard 1.1** Identify and use the literal and figurative meanings of words and understand word derivations.

**Reading Standard 2.8** Evaluate the credibility of an author's argument or defense of a claim by critiquing the relationship between generalizations and evidence, the comprehensiveness of evidence, and the way in which the author's intent affects the structure and tone of the text (e.g., in professional journals, editorials, political speeches, primary sources material).

# Who Wrote Shakespeare?

## Terry Deary

### IDENTIFY

Pause at line 9. Underline the **claim,** or opinion, the writer presents. Whose claim is the author presenting?

_____

_____

_____

_____

_____

_____

### CLARIFY

According to lines 10–11, who was the first person to question Shakespeare's authorship of the famous plays?

_____

_____

_____

_____

_____

_____

### IDENTIFY PURPOSE & TONE

Re-read lines 10–18. Circle the words that reveal a tone of mild disapproval.

Shakespeare wrote about great Roman characters like Julius Caesar, Mark Antony, and Coriolanus. He also wrote wonderful poetry. Over the years since Shakespeare's death, some academics and professors believed that a glover's son from Stratford could *not* have had the brains or the education to write these plays.

Someone else wrote them, they claim, and then stuck the name of a simple actor on the play. The actor was William Shakespeare, but the real writer of the plays was someone else. Who?

10    A priest called the Reverend James Wilmot started the trouble about a hundred years after the death of Shakespeare. The Reverend went to Stratford to investigate old records. He couldn't find any letters by Shakespeare, any books owned by him, or any mentions of "Shakespeare the play writer" by other Stratford people of the time. Wilmot also couldn't believe that a glover's son like Shakespeare could go on to become a favorite of a queen and a king. He started the suspicion that Shakespeare's plays weren't written by William Shakespeare.

"Who Wrote Shakespeare?" from *Top Ten Shakespeare Stories* by Terry Dean. Copyright © 1998 by **Scholastic Children's Books.** Reprinted by permission of the publisher.

American Delia Bacon was even more snobbish. She said

20 Will was, "A stupid, ignorant third-rate play-actor from a dirty, doggish group of players."

## Whodunit?

Here are the top ten possibilities:

### 1. Queen Elizabeth I

**Claim:** The queen loved drama. But women and upper-class people could not be seen to write something as "common" as a stage play. She had to disguise her efforts by

30 giving them to a young actor she fancied, William Shakespeare. Elizabeth had the education necessary to write the plays and backed Shakespeare's theater company for many years. Computer experts have matched Elizabeth's portrait with Shakespeare's and say they are the same person!

**Against:** She continued writing

40 the plays for eight years after her death. A clever trick if you can manage it.

**Score:** 1/10

HEY GORGEOUS, PASS THESE OFF AS YOURS, WILL YOU?

**IDENTIFY**

Locate and underline an opinion presented by the writer in lines 19–21.

**IDENTIFY**

Pause at line 38. In each entry, the word *claim* introduces an **argument** showing why a historical figure might have written Shakespeare's plays. How would you state the above claim in a sentence?

_____

_____

_____

_____

_____

**IDENTIFY PURPOSE & TONE**

Re-read lines 39–42. The queen died in 1603; Shakespeare probably wrote his last play around 1611. Circle the words expressing the writer's **tone**, or attitude, in the argument against the claim. How would you describe the tone?

_____

_____

_____

_____

## 2. King James I

**Claim:** The king was fanatical about witchcraft and about his own right to the throne. The play *Macbeth* is about witchcraft and kingship. Who better to write the play than James

50 the expert? He put a lot of his own money into Shakespeare's plays. So that Shakespeare would produce the plays written by the king?

**Against:** Shakespeare's plays were being written in 1590 while James was still in Scotland. And James wasn't all that bright.

**Score:** 2/10

## 3. Anthony Bacon

60 **Claim:** Brother of the famous Francis (see number 8). Anthony visited the French king's court in the early 1590s. When *Love's Labour's Lost* was performed in 1593 there were characters called Berowne, Dumain, and Longaville, almost the same names as French lords that Anthony would be mixing with.

70 **Against:** He wasn't in England much when the plays were being performed.

**Score:** 3/10

---

### AUTHOR'S ARGUMENT

What two basic details are given to support the claim that King James I wrote Shakespeare's plays (lines 45–53)?

_____

_____

_____

_____

_____

_____

_____

### AUTHOR'S ARGUMENT

Pause at line 69. Circle the words telling where Anthony Bacon was in the early 1590s. Then, underline the argument linking this information with Shakespeare's play *Love's Labour's Lost* in 1593. Does the link seem to be based on fact or on guesswork?

_____

_____

_____

_____

_____

_____

## 4. Henry Wriothesley, Earl of Southampton

**Claim:** A brilliant student who went to Cambridge University when he was just sixteen and a rich playboy who gave a lot of money

80 to Will Shakespeare. Shakespeare is supposed to have written poems like *Venus and Adonis* for young Henry. But what if Henry wrote the plays and Shakespeare agreed to have his name put on them?

**Against:** Henry enjoyed good living too much. Would he have had the energy to write plays?

**Score:** 4/10

90 ## 5. The Earl of Rutland

**Claim:** The Earl knew Shakespeare and there are records that he paid Shakespeare money. Money for Shakespeare's help in producing the Earl's plays? The Earl had been to several of the places where the plays are set—Venice, Verona, Padua—whereas William Shakespeare probably hadn't. The

100 Earl even went to the Danish court just before *Hamlet, Prince of Denmark* was written. He died in 1613 when the last Shakespearean play was written.

**Against:** There is no proof that the Earl of Rutland ever wrote a play.

**Score:** 5/10

### ANALYZE

Circle the **loaded word** in line 79. Is the word intended to praise or to ridicule the Earl of Southampton?

_____

_____

### IDENTIFY PURPOSE & TONE

Take time to study the cartoons that accompany the text. What **purpose** might the writer have for including cartoons in this article?

_____

_____

_____

_____

_____

_____

_____

_____

_____

### AUTHOR'S ARGUMENT

Re-read lines 91–104. Underline the facts. Circle the speculations (open questions).

## AUTHOR'S ARGUMENT

Is the argument in lines 110–121 based on facts? Explain.

_____

_____

_____

_____

_____

_____

_____

_____

## IDENTIFY PURPOSE & TONE

Read the footnote provided for this text. How would you describe its **tone**?

_____

_____

_____

_____

_____

_____

_____

_____

_____

### 6. William Stanley, Earl of Derby

110 **Claim:** A scholar dug up an old letter that said the Earl of Derby was "busy penning comedies for the common players." There is no record of a Stanley or Derby play ever being performed. So, if they weren't performed as Stanley plays, were they performed as Shakespeare plays? Derby had been to France as a young man and met 120 some of the real people who later appeared in the Shakespeare plays.

**Against:** There may be no record of a Stanley play being performed because they never were performed. Lots of people write plays that don't get performed. They are just too awful!

**Score:** 6/10

### 7. Edward de Vere, Earl of Oxford°

130 **Claim:** There were letters that said he wrote plays but, like the Earl of Derby, no list of his plays survives. However, one of his descendants now travels around the world giving lectures on how Oxford came to write the plays. There are many supporters of the theory that Oxford wrote the plays.

---

° Let's hope Oxford didn't write the plays. He was not a nice man. He murdered a kitchen lad with his sword in a fit of temper and gave his poor wife a very hard time.

140 **Against:** He died in 1604 and, like Elizabeth, must have written the greatest Shakespeare plays from the grave. Maybe he used a ghost writer!

**Score:** 7/10

## 8. Sir Francis Bacon

**Claim:** The writer of Shakespeare's plays knew a lot about law and a lot about the French king's court. Bacon's brother, Anthony, had been to the French court and written 150 home to Francis. Bacon's father had been Elizabeth's Lord Keeper and his mother had been related to Elizabeth's chief minister. Bacon was a poet.

**Against:** Bacon had no experience of the theater.

**Score:** 8/10

## 9. Christopher Marlowe

**Claim:** A brilliant young playwright 160 and a huge success when William Shakespeare arrived in London. However, he was in trouble for his spying activities. He had to fake his own death to save his life. In order to keep writing plays, he produced them under Shakespeare's name. Shakespeare was well paid so he didn't mind taking the glory.

**Against:** There is too much 170 evidence to show that Marlowe *was* murdered in 1592.

**Score:** 9/10

**IDENTIFY PURPOSE & TONE**

Underline the sentence in lines 141–142 in which the writer makes a pun, or wordplay. In what way is the pun suitable to the writer's **purpose**?

_____

_____

_____

_____

_____

**AUTHOR'S ARGUMENT**

Re-read lines 145–154. Underline the words explaining what the writer of the plays must have known. Circle the argument suggesting that Sir Francis Bacon wrote the plays.

**CLARIFY**

According to lines 159–168, why might Marlowe have needed someone to write his plays?

_____

_____

_____

_____

_____

## AUTHOR'S ARGUMENT

Pause at line 177. Underline the part of the argument that is a **generalization**. Circle the details in the other part that provide evidence for the claim.

## IDENTIFY PURPOSE & TONE

Re-read lines 190–196. Is the **tone** of the passage serious or playful?

_____
_____
_____
_____
_____
_____
_____
_____
_____
_____
_____
_____
_____
_____
_____
_____
_____
_____
_____

### 10. William Shakespeare

**Claim:** Everybody said he wrote the plays, including people like Ben Jonson and other playwrights that he was competing with.

**Against:** Not a lot.

**Score:** 10/10

180  The problem of "Who wrote Shakespeare?" was sensibly solved in the 1940s by a professor who paid a spiritualist to get in touch with the ghosts of Shakespeare, Oxford, and Bacon. The spirits told her that they *all* wrote the plays! Shakespeare did the plots, Oxford worked on the characters, and Bacon polished the poetry.

Dead men tell no lies, but spiritualists sometimes do! Believe that if you want.

190  Did you know . . .
Shakespeare's longest word is:
"Honorificabilitudinitatibus."
Rearrange the letters and you get the Latin phrase *Hi ludi F. Baconis nati tuiti orbi.* In English this means "These plays, the children of F. Bacon, are preserved for the world." Some writers have used this to prove that Bacon wrote the plays.

# Who Wrote Shakespeare?

**Argument Chart**    "Who Wrote Shakespeare?" presents various claims about the "real" author of Shakespeare's plays. Use this chart to identify the types of details used in the author's argument. Fill in the right-hand column with passages from the article that are examples of each type of persuasive detail.

| Type of Detail | Example Passage from Article |
| --- | --- |
| Claim | |
| Logical Appeal | |
| Emotional Appeal | |
| Generalization | |
| Opinion | |
| Speculation/<br>Open Questions | |

# Standards Review

**TestPractice** ## Who Wrote Shakespeare?

Improve your test-taking skills by completing the sample test item below. Then, read the explanation in the right-hand column.

| Sample Test Item | Explanation of the Correct Answer |
|---|---|
| What **claim** is presented at the beginning of the article?<br><br>**A** Shakespeare wrote about Julius Caesar.<br><br>**B** Shakespeare's father made gloves.<br><br>**C** Shakespeare wasn't smart enough to write the plays.<br><br>**D** Professors are good judges of plays. | The correct answer is *C*.<br><br>Because *A* and *B* are both statements of fact, neither item is the correct answer. *D* presents an opinion, but not one that is in the article. |

**DIRECTIONS:** Circle the letter of each correct response.

**Reading Standard 2.8**
Evaluate the credibility of an author's argument or defense of a claim by critiquing the relationship between generalizations and evidence, the comprehensiveness of evidence, and the way in which the author's intent affects the structure and tone of the text (e.g., in professional journals, editorials, political speeches, primary sources material).

1. Which of the following is an example of a **logical appeal**?

   **A** "Everybody said he wrote the plays."

   **B** "He had to fake his own death to save his life."

   **C** "Shakespeare wrote wonderful poetry."

   **D** "The Earl even went to the Danish court just before *Hamlet, Prince of Denmark* was written."

2. The **tone** of this article can be described as—

   **F** preachy

   **G** serious and scholarly

   **H** angry

   **J** gently mocking

3. "Anthony visited the French king's court in the early 1590s" is an example of—

   **A** a statement of fact

   **B** loaded words

   **C** an emotional appeal

   **D** a claim

4. The author of the article wants to persuade you that—

   **F** a glover's son could never write plays

   **G** Shakespeare had many friends and enemies

   **H** the idea that someone else wrote Shakespeare's plays is ridiculous

   **J** Queen Elizabeth I was smarter than Shakespeare

# Standards Review

**Test Practice** **Who Wrote Shakespeare?**

## Context Clues

**DIRECTIONS:** Use context clues to guess the meaning of each underlined word or phrase in the following sentences. Circle the letter of the correct response.

1. His suspicion about Shakespeare's ability to write was not proved to be true. In this sentence, *suspicion* means—

   **A** fear

   **B** doubt

   **C** excuse

   **D** superstition

2. Elizabeth I's portrait hung from the wall in the theater's lobby. In this sentence, *portrait* means—

   **F** goblet

   **G** rope

   **H** crown

   **J** painting

3. One of the Earl's descendants travels around, giving lectures on how Oxford, his ancestor, came to write the plays. In this sentence, *descendants* means—

   **A** things that hang

   **B** ministers

   **C** offspring

   **D** chariots

4. According to the article, King James I was very interested in, or fanatical about, witchcraft. In this sentence, *fanatical* means—

   **F** obsessed

   **G** unsure

   **H** scared of

   **J** neutral

5. Because Elizabeth I fancied Shakespeare so much, she gave him money and support. In this sentence, *fancied* means—

   **A** imagined

   **B** liked

   **C** envied

   **D** disliked

6. The scholar announced that through research he could prove that Shakespeare was indeed Shakespeare. In this sentence, *scholar* means—

   **F** person who studies

   **G** person who disproves

   **H** person who judges

   **J** person who cheats

**Reading Standard 1.1** Identify and use the literal and figurative meanings of words and understand word derivations.

**Before You Go On . . .**

Check your Standards Mastery at the back of this book.

# Consumer, Workplace, and Public Documents

## Academic Vocabulary

These are the terms you should know
as you read and analyze the selections that follow.

———

**Consumer documents** Documents used in the selling and buying of products. Many consumer documents, such as warranties, protect the rights of the purchaser and the seller. Other consumer documents include advertisements, contracts, instruction manuals, and product information.

**Public documents** Documents that inform the public. Public documents are created by governmental, social, religious, or news-gathering organizations. They include safety information, government regulations, schedules of events, explanations of services, and newspaper articles.

**Workplace documents** Documents used in offices, factories, and other work sites to communicate information. These include business letters, contracts, instruction manuals, memorandums, and safety information.

**Technical documents** Documents used to explain or establish procedures for using technology, such as mechanical, electronic, or digital products or systems. Technical documents include how-to instructions, installation instructions, and instructions on carrying out scientific procedures.

**Functional documents** Any documents prepared for a specific function, such as consumer, public, workplace, and technical documents.

---

### For Further Information ...

- Be sure to read Chapter 11 in *Holt Literature and Language Arts,* beginning on page 907.

# Jobs in Computer Animation

**BEFORE YOU READ**

Suppose you've just gotten a job as a character animator at a company that creates computer graphics. Some workplace documents can help you settle in. An organizational chart will tell you how your job relates to other jobs in the company, and your job description will let you know what's expected of you. Good luck in your new position!

## FOCUS: WORKPLACE DOCUMENT

The purpose of most workplace documents is to present accurate information as briefly and clearly as possible. The documents you will read next fulfill that purpose.

- The organizational chart uses a graphic format to show how jobs are ranked and how they relate to each other. The job titles are set in boxes, with positions of greatest responsibility at the top and those of least responsibility at the bottom. Connecting lines show the paths of supervision.
- The job description uses an outline structure to present information. Boldface and numbered headers clearly identify aspects of the job. Lowercase letters introduce duties, which are listed in point-by-point sequence.

## TERMS TO KNOW

**Boldface**—dark, heavy type.

**Format**—the design of a document.

**Graphics**—visual elements that illustrate, demonstrate, or highlight the text, such as art, photos, drawings, and diagrams.

**Header**—a label or heading that begins a section of a document.

**Point-by-point sequence**—a sequence that lists items in no particular order.

**Step-by-step sequence**—a sequence that tells what to do first, second, third, and so on.

**Reading Standard 2.1** Analyze the structure and format of functional workplace documents, including the graphics and headers, and explain how authors use the features to achieve their purposes.

# Jobs in Computer Animation

## *from* Ed-Venture Films/Books

### TEXT FEATURES

This chart presents information in a graphic format that is easy to read and understand. What is listed in the boxes on the chart?

_____

_____

_____

### TEXT FEATURES

What do the graphic lines from one box to another indicate?

_____

_____

_____

_____

_____

_____

_____

### IDENTIFY

Put a checkmark in all boxes showing positions supervised by the Computer Graphics Supervisor.

## Organizational Chart

Visual Effects Supervisor

Digital Effects Supervisor

Visual Effects Animation Supervisor

Computer Graphics Supervisor

Character Animator

Technical Effects Animator

Technical Director

Compositor

3D Modeler

Match Mover 2D/3D

Rotoscoper

Painter— 2D/3D

Concept Artist

Matte Painter

Digital Editor

Film Scanner

Film Recordist

Maintenance Technician

"Job Descriptions: Visual Effects Animation Supervisor, Computer Graphics Supervisor, Character Animator" from *Job Descriptions for Film, Video & CGI* by William E. Hines, SOC. Copyright © 1999 by **Ed-Venture Films/Books.** Reprinted by permission of the publisher.

# Job Description

## CHARACTER ANIMATOR

1. **Responsibilities:** The **Character Animator** is directly responsible to the **Visual Effects Animation Supervisor,** is responsive to the **Computer Graphics Supervisor,** and is responsible for creating and animating the character(s) developed for the production in order to assure seamless integration of the work with live action and other digital elements.

2. **Duties:**

   a. Reading and annotating the script for meaning, emotion, action, continuity, plot, and character development, as necessary;

   b. Reviewing the storyboard to determine the type, placement, and number of technical effects required;

   c. Examining film or tape plates, clips, and stills of the background and/or principal action, as available;

   d. Suggesting the type, and where and how effectively computer generated animation and modeled imagery might be applied to the production;

   e. Preparing tests of proposed animation to show to the **Visual Effects Animation Supervisor** and the **Computer Graphics Supervisor** for approval;

   f. Getting approval from the **Visual Effects Animation Supervisor** of all CG character animation and modeling elements being developed at each stage of development.

   g. Conferring regularly with the **Visual Effects Animation Supervisor** and the **Computer Graphics Supervisor** to apprise them of the progress and synchronization of the character animation and modeling work;

   h. Otherwise carrying out the duties normally required of this classification.

10

20

30

**TEXT FEATURES**

Circle the job title **header.** What are the four main sub-heads under the job title?

_____

_____

_____

_____

**FORMAT**

Read item number one. What elements are printed in **boldface** type?

_____

_____

_____

**SEQUENCE**

Numbers and letters sometimes indicate a step-by-step sequence, which tells you what to do first, second, third, and so on. However, in this document, the numbers and letters are part of an outline format. What type of **sequence** are the items listed in?

_____

_____

_____

_____

3. **Considerations:** When one (1) or more of the above duties are required, a **Character Animator** is called for.

4. **Requirements:** The **Character Animator** must be experienced in traditional forms of animation and in CG animation work and must have a thorough working knowledge of the UNIX and Mac platforms, the SGI and Sun workstations, and of the various proprietary software programs utilized in CG work—principally, the 2D/3D packages by: Alias/Wavefront, Softimage, and Side Effects (Houdini and Prism); the 2D packages: Parallax and Discrete Logic (Flint, Flame and Inferno); and Adobe (Photoshop).

40

*Inside an animation studio.*

# Standards Review

 **TestPractice** · **Jobs in Computer Animation**

Complete the sample test item below. The box at the right explains why three of these choices are not correct.

| Sample Test Item | Explanation of the Correct Answer |
|---|---|
| Graphic elements of the Organizational Chart are— <br><br> **A** the title <br> **B** the boxes <br> **C** job titles <br> **D** headers | The correct answer is *B*. <br><br> The boxes are visual, or graphic, elements. *A, C,* and *D* are incorrect because the title, job titles, and headers are all text elements or features. |

**DIRECTIONS:** Circle the letter of the best response to each item.

1. In the Organizational Chart, the lines represent—

   **A** how to get from one job to the next

   **B** family relationships

   **C** routes between offices

   **D** paths of supervision

2. In the Organizational Chart, which jobs have the most responsibility?

   **F** those at the top

   **G** those at the bottom

   **H** those at the left

   **J** the ones with the most lines

3. In the Job Description, in what order is the information presented?

   **A** step-by-step sequence

   **B** point-by-point sequence

   **C** chronological sequence

   **D** no particular sequence

4. How are job titles highlighted in the Job Description?

   **F** They are turned into headers.

   **G** They are printed in boldface.

   **H** They are placed in parentheses.

   **J** They are printed in regular type.

5. The Organizational Chart and the Job Description are both—

   **A** consumer documents

   **B** public documents

   **C** workplace documents

   **D** graphic documents

**Reading Standard 2.1** Analyze the structure and format of functional workplace documents, including the graphics and headers and explain how authors use the features to achieve their purposes.

**Before You Go On . . .**

Check your Standards Mastery at the back of this book.

# Scanning Images by Tim Harrower

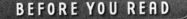

## BEFORE YOU READ

Would you like to send a photo of yourself to a friend by e-mail? Here are some handy technical directions for how to scan your picture into your computer. Once you have done that, you can enlarge or crop the photo, send it out over the Internet, or incorporate it into any document you want. You could even make it into a poster for your campaign for class president!

### FOCUS: TECHNICAL DOCUMENT

The following document gives directions for scanning images into your computer. Look for these graphic features, which will help you find the information you need.

- Drawings and photos illustrate the text.
- Boldface headers clearly identify scanning procedures and terminology.
- A numbered list presents directions in a step-by-step sequence.
- A bulleted list shows rules of thumb in a point-by-point sequence.

### TERMS TO KNOW

**Boldface**—dark, heavy type.

**Bullets**—dots, diamonds, squares, or other shapes used to introduce lists in point-by-point sequence.

**Caption**—text that labels, explains, or describes an illustration, a diagram, or a photograph.

**Drop-out type**—type set in white on a dark background.

**Format**—the design of a document.

**Graphic**—visual elements that illustrate, demonstrate, or highlight the text, such as art, photos, drawings, and diagrams.

**Italics**—type that slants to the right.

**Point-by-point sequence**—a sequence that lists items in no particular order.

**Step-by-step sequence**—a sequence that tells what to do first, second, third, and so on.

**Reading Standard 2.6**
Demonstrate use of sophisticated learning tools by following technical directions (e.g., those found with graphic calculators and specialized software programs and in access guides to World Wide Web sites on the Internet.

# Scanning Images

## Tim Harrower

How do you get photos and artwork into your computer? It's easy. All you need is a *scanner,* a machine that captures images electronically—*digitizes* them—so you can adjust them, store them, or print them later.

To the casual observer, scanners look and perform much like photocopying machines. Here's how the scanning process works:

**1** **Preparing to scan:**

*Take your original image—a photo, a drawing, some type—and lay it*
10 *face-down on the scanner's glass surface. Special software will allow you to crop the image, resize it— even adjust its contrast.*

**2** **Scanning the image:**

*The scanner lights up like a photo- copying machine as it duplicates the image electronically, converting it into microscopic dots or pixels (picture ele- ments). The more dots the scan uses,*
20 *the finer the resolution will be.*

**3** **Importing the image:**

*Once it's scanned, the electronic image can be imported into a page-layout program, where you can further adjust its size and shape. The image can then be printed alone or as part of a finished design.*

"Scanning Images" from *The Newspaper Designer's Handbook, 4th Edition,* by Tim Harrower. Copyright © 1998 by **The McGraw-Hill Companies, Inc.** Reprinted by permission of the publisher.

---

**TEXT FEATURES**

What is the purpose of the cartoonlike **illustrations**?

_____

_____

_____

_____

_____

_____

**SEQUENCE**

Numbers and boldface headers introduce the steps in scanning. What is the **sequence** of these technical directions?

_____

_____

_____

_____

_____

_____

_____

_____

PURPOSE

What is the purpose of the boldface type and the italic type in the **captions** for the three photos?

_____
_____
_____
_____
_____
_____
_____
_____
_____
_____

FORMAT

In the "Scanning Terminology" list, why are the terms in **boldface** type?

_____
_____
_____
_____
_____
_____
_____
_____
_____
_____
_____

## Scanning Terminology

Since scanning software is generally user-friendly, you won't
30  need years of training to get good results. But it *will* help to
know some basic terms:

**A grayscale image** *uses shades of gray.*   **A line art image** *uses only solid black.*   **A low-resolution image** *uses fewer dots, which means it's less detailed.*

**Grayscale:** A scan of a photograph or artwork that uses gray
tones (up to 256 different shades of gray, to be exact).

**Line art:** An image comprised of solid black and white—no
gray tones.

**Image size:** The physical dimensions of the final scanned image.

**File size:** The total number of electronic pixels needed to create
a digital image, measured in kilobytes. The more pixels an
image uses, the more detail it will contain.

40  **Dots per inch (DPI):** The number of electronic dots per inch
that a printer can print—or that a digital image contains.
The higher the dpi, the more precise the image's resolution
will be—up to a point, anyway.

**Lines per inch (LPI):** The number of lines of dots per inch in
a halftone screen. The higher the lpi, the more accurate the
image's resolution will be.

**Resolution:** The quality of digital detail in an image, depending
upon its number of dots per inch (dpi).

**TIFF:** One of the most common formats for saving scans
50      (an abbreviation of *Tagged Image File Format*).

**EPS:** Another common format for saving scans, especially
illustrations (short for *Encapsulated PostScript*).

**Moire (*mo-ray*) pattern:** An eerie pattern that's formed when
a previously screened photo is copied, then reprinted using
a new line screen.

## Scanning Rules of Thumb

- **Name and store your scans carefully.** Think about it this way: When you import an image into a page-layout program, you might think you're looking at the *actual scan* when you see it on your screen—but you're not. You're only looking at a low-resolution rendering of the actual scan. (Which is a clever idea, actually; otherwise, a page loaded with real scans could involve millions of megs of memory and become impossibly heavy and slow.)

  When you finally decide to print that page, however, your computer traces a path back to that original image and uses *that information* for printing. Which means two things: You need to store all scans until they're finally printed. And you need to store them in a consistent place, so that your computer will be able to find them when it's time to print.

- **Allow for dot gain.** When printed, images often appear darker than their scans. Find out how your screen dots will behave when the ink hits the paper—and learn to compensate consistently every time you scan.

- **Keep your file sizes as small as possible.** Unnecessarily large scans waste memory, slow down your software, take longer to print—and don't always mean higher quality output, anyway. As a rule of thumb, small black-and-white images (a few square inches in area) usually consume fewer than 200K; big color images, on the other hand, can range from one to 20 megabytes.

- **Consider using low-resolution scans for big jobs.** You'll save time in the long run if you scan those complicated images *twice:* a low-resolution version that won't slow you down while you work on the page, and a high-resolution scan that you can import when you're ready to print.

- **Crop and scale images as you scan.** You can save memory by scanning only that part of the image you plan to print. Remember, too, that if you plan to enlarge an image when

60

70

80

**FORMAT**

Why does the "Scanning Terminology" section come before "Scanning Rules of Thumb"?

_____

_____

_____

_____

_____

_____

_____

_____

**SEQUENCE**

The rules of thumb for scanning are in a bulleted list, in **point-by-point sequence.** Why is that type of sequence appropriate for this information?

_____

_____

_____

_____

_____

_____

_____

_____

_____

## IDENTIFY

What two categories of information does the chart show?

_____

_____

## PURPOSE

The chart gives information in a highly visible form. What is its purpose?

_____

_____

_____

_____

_____

90   you import it, you should scan it at a higher resolution; if you plan to reduce it, scan at a lower resolution.

Yes, image resolution can get confusing—all those *dpi's* and *lpi's* mean different things at different stages of the scanning and printing process. If you're unsure how to measure "high" or "low" resolution, consult the chart below.

**Using the chart below:** *If, for instance, you need to print a high-resolution photo, you'll need to scan it as a 300-dpi grayscale, then print it using a 150-line screen on a printer that prints at least 1200 dpi. If at any point in the process you used lower numbers,*

100   *your quality would drop. Or, another way to use the chart: If you're printing at 600 dpi, there's no need to scan grayscales any higher than 150 dpi—your printer won't be able to reproduce all the detail in a higher-resolution scan.*

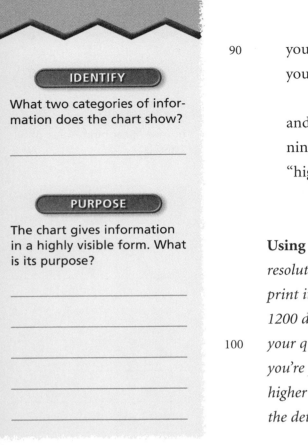

| | INPUT | | OUTPUT | |
|---|---|---|---|---|
| | Grayscale images (measured in dpi) | Line art images (measured in dpi) | Screens for photos (measured in dpi) | Printer quality (measured in dpi) |
| **HIGH RESOLUTION** (slick catalogs, books) | 300 | 1200 | 150 | 1200–2400 |
| **FAIR RESOLUTION** (magazines, newspapers) | 150 | 800 | 85–100 | 600–1200 |
| **LOW RESOLUTION** (newsletters, fliers) | 75 | 300 | 65 | 300–600 |

**TestPractice** Scanning Images

Complete the sample test item below. The box at the right explains why three of these choices are not correct.

| Sample Test Item | Explanation of the Correct Answer |
|---|---|
| Which of the following steps do you do first when you scan an image?<br><br>**A** Crop the image.<br>**B** Place the image in the scanner.<br>**C** Run the scanner.<br>**D** Put the image in the page layout. | The correct answer is *B*.<br><br>*A* is incorrect because cropping happens after an image is scanned. *C* is incorrect because the image has to be in the scanner before you run it. *D* is incorrect because images are put in the page layout after they are scanned. |

**DIRECTIONS:** Circle the letter of the best response for each item.

1. What is the purpose of the three cartoons with the scanning directions?

   **A** to make you laugh

   **B** to fill up the page in an interesting way

   **C** to look really sharp

   **D** to illustrate the three steps

2. Why are the scanning instructions presented in **step-by-step sequence**?

   **F** The sequence doesn't matter at all.

   **G** The order of the steps is important.

   **H** You have to take each step.

   **J** The steps can be done whenever you want.

3. In what order are the scanning rules of thumb presented?

   **A** point by point

   **B** step by step

   **C** chronological

   **D** order of importance

4. Which part of the article gives **technical directions**?

   **F** the list of scanning terminology

   **G** the point-by-point list of tips for scanning

   **H** the step-by-step instructions for scanning

   **J** the input–output resolution chart

**Reading Standard 2.6** Demonstrate use of sophisticated learning tools by following technical directions (e.g., those found with graphic calculators and specialized software programs and in access guides to World Wide Web sites on the Internet.

**Before You Go On . . .**

Check your Standards Mastery at the back of this book.

# Teen Driver's Guide and Permit Application

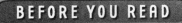

## BEFORE YOU READ

Are you looking forward to getting your driver's license soon? Besides the road test, you'll have to get through a lot of written materials. The following documents include information on how to apply for a permit and a copy of an application form. (To apply for your license, you must get an original form DL 44 from the Department of Motor Vehicles.) Both documents are meant to be easily understood. Do they seem clear and logical to you?

### FOCUS: FUNCTIONAL DOCUMENT

The information guide and application are both essential functional documents for teenagers who want to get their driver's licenses.

- To make the information clear and accessible, a variety of text features are used, such as blocks of type, boldface headers, numbered and bulleted lists, and boxes to check.
- Information is presented in the logical sequence most appropriate for clear understanding, such as step-by-step or point-by-point sequence.
- Sections of text are separated by horizontal and vertical lines and black bands with numbered headers.

As you read the documents, decide whether you think the information is presented clearly or if it might be improved to prevent any possible reader misunderstandings.

### TERMS TO KNOW

**Boldface**—dark, heavy type.

**Bullets**—dots, diamonds, squares, or other shapes used to introduce lists in point-by-point sequence.

**Cross-reference**—words, often in parentheses, telling you to look at a different section of the text or a different text entirely.

**Logical sequence**—a sequence that makes sense.

**Point-by-point sequence**—a sequence that lists items in no particular order.

**Step-by-step sequence**—a sequence that tells what to do first, second, third, and so on.

**Reading Standard 2.7**
Critique the logic of functional documents by examining the sequence of information and procedures in anticipation of possible reader misunderstandings.

# Teen Driver's Guide and Permit Application

## *from* California Department of Motor Vehicles

**How to Apply for a Provisional Permit if You Are Under 18**

To apply for a provisional permit if you are under 18, you must:

- Be at least 15, but under 18 years of age
- Visit a DMV office (make an appointment for faster service)
- Complete the application form DL 44 (An original DL 44 form must be submitted. Copies obtained by xeroxing, faxing or other methods will not be accepted.)
- Have your parents' or guardians' signatures on the application form DL 44
- Give a thumb print
- Have your picture taken
- Provide your social security number
- Verify your birth date and legal presence
- Submit the proper form(s) for Driver Education and/or Driver Training (see below for details)
- Pay the $12 application fee (This fee entitles you to three exams of any type within the 12-month period and pays for both the instruction permit and the driver license. If all requirements are not met within the 12-month period, the application becomes void and **all** steps must be completed again.)
- Pass a vision exam
- Pass a traffic laws and sign test. There are 46 questions on the test. A passing score is at least 39 correct answers. You have three chances to pass the test. If you fail, you must wait 7 days before taking it again.

10

20

---

**SEQUENCE**

How do you know the items in the bulleted list are in **point-by-point sequence?**

**TEXT FEATURES**

What kind of information is given within parentheses (lines 4; 5–7; 15; and 16–21)?

## Driver Education and Driver Training Form Requirements

If you are 15 to 15 1/2 years of age, you will need to submit:

30

- Form DL 356 or OL 237 (Completion of Driver Education) with form DL 391 (Driver Training Enrollment ) if your school has a contract with a driving school

**OR**

- Form DL 356 and a letter on company letterhead signed and dated by the driving school owner stating the student is currently enrolled in driver training. The letter must identify the student and list the class date, the school license number, the driving instructor's name and license number.

**OR**

40

- Form DL 356 or forms OL 237 and OL 238 (Completion of both Driver Education and Driver Training)

**OR**

- Submit form DL 391 or OL 239 (Simultaneous Enrollment in Driver Education and Driver Training)

If you are over 15 1/2 but under 18 years of age, you will need to submit:

- Form DL 356 or OL 237 (Completion of Driver Education)

**OR**

- Form DL 391 or OL 239 (Simultaneous Enrollment in

50

Driver Education and Driver Training)

If you are over 17 1/2 but under 18 years of age, you may get your permit without the driver education and driver training certificates; however, you will not be able to take the driving test until you turn 18.

Once you pass your written test, you will be issued a provisional permit. You can be issued a permit at age 15, but you cannot take the drive test or be issued a driver license until you are 16 years of age.

---

**TEXT FEATURES**

There are four **bulleted** items that list what you need to submit if you are 15 to 15 1/2 years of age (lines 29–43). Do you need to submit all the items? Why or why not?

_____

_____

_____

_____

_____

**IDENTIFY**

Look over lines 27–54. In what order is the information presented?

_____

_____

_____

_____

_____

**EVALUATE**

What would you do to make the section from lines 27 to 54 easier to understand?

_____

_____

_____

_____

_____

60 A parent, guardian, spouse or adult 25 years of age or older, who has a valid California driver license, must be with you when you drive. They must sit in a position that allows them to take control of the vehicle, if necessary. **It is illegal for you to drive alone at any time.**

Before being eligible to take your driving test you must:

- Be 16 years old

  **AND**

- Have possessed your permit for a minimum of six months

  **AND**

- Have completed driver education

70 **AND**

- Have completed 6 hours of professional driver training

  **AND**

- Have completed 50 hours of practice with an adult 25 years or older. The adult must have a valid California driver license and certify to the 50 hours of practice. At least 10 of the 50 hours must have been done at night.

You will also need to show proof of insurance for the vehicle you will be taking your drive test in.

After you pass your drive test you will be issued an interim
80 license valid for 60 days until you receive your new photo license in the mail. Double check your address before you leave DMV and tell the DMV representative if you have moved or if your address is incorrect. If you have not received your license after 60 days, call (916) 657-7790 and they can check on the status for you. Have your interim license with you to provide information when requested.

If you fail your drive test, you must wait two weeks before you can take the test again. You have three chances to pass.

**SEQUENCE**

Lines 55–86 use both **step-by-step sequence** and **point-by-point sequence**. Explain how you can tell the difference.

## FORMAT

Look over the application form. How is it made clear that there are seven separate sections?

_____

_____

_____

_____

_____

_____

## SEQUENCE

In section 1, check the box for a teenage driver permit. Why is it important to fill in this section first?

_____

_____

_____

_____

_____

_____

_____

## FOLLOW DIRECTIONS

For practice in filling out an application form, complete the information requested in section 2. If you do not have a state-issued ID card, leave those sections blank.

90    If driver education and driver training were taken in a state other than California, DMV will accept either a To Secondary Schools Other Than California Schools form DL 33 completed by the out-of-state school, or a letter on the out-of-state school's stationery signed by a school official stating that the courses are equivalent to California's requirements. Instructional permits issued by another state are not acceptable.

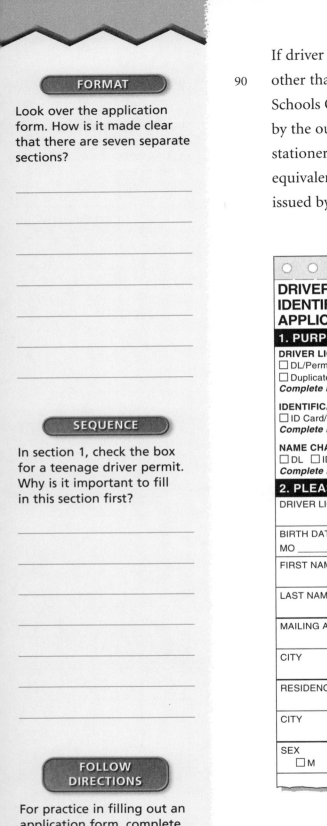

*(continued on next page)*

(continued)

## 3. LICENSING NEED: ✔ all boxes that you need.

**BASIC LICENSE**

☐ Basic Class C  ☐ Motorcycle

See explanation in California Driver Handbook.

*If basic license only, go to Part 4.*

| NON-COMMERCIAL LICENSE | FIRE FIGHTER | |
|---|---|---|
| ☐ Class A | ☐ Class A  ☐ Class B | ☐ **Ambulance Certificate** |
| | | ☐ **Verification of Transit Training** |

### COMMERCIAL DRIVER ONLY

**(SSN is verified before any original commercial driver license application is started.)**

**COMMERCIAL LICENSE**

☐ Class A
☐ Class B
☐ Class C

**Endorsements**

☐ Passenger Transport    ☐ Tank
☐ Hazardous Materials/Waste    ☐ Air Brakes
☐ Doubles/Triples

I certify that the motor vehicle in which I am taking the driving skills test is representative of the type of motor vehicle I expect to operate. I am not subject to any disqualification, suspension, revocation, or cancellation as contained in Title 49 of Federal Regulations, Part 383.51, and I do not have a driver license from more than one state or jurisdiction.

ACCORDING TO PART 391 OF THE FEDERAL MOTOR CARRIER SAFETY REGULATIONS

☐ I plan to operate in foreign or interstate commerce and I meet the qualifications.

☐ I do **not** plan to operate in foreign or interstate commere and I am **not** subject to Part 391.

## 4. QUESTIONS: Please answer the following questions.

A. Have you ever applied for a driver license or ID card under a different name(s):

☐ No  ☐ Yes  If yes, list name(s) here _____

_____

Question B is for the confidential use of the DMV. *Please review the "Medical Information" on the back of this form before answering.*

B. Have you had any health or vision problems that could affect your ability to drive safely?

☐ No  ☐ Yes  If yes, briefly explain: _____

_____

## 5. DO YOU WISH TO REGISTER TO VOTE OR CHANGE YOUR VOTER ADDRESS?

**CHECK ONE BOX ONLY. Complete the attached form if you check box "Y" or "C" only.**

Y ☐ First-time voter registration or a voter registration change (i.e., name change or political party change).

N ☐ I do not wish to register to vote or to change my voter registration address.

C ☐ Please update my voter registration address record to a **new** county.

S ☐ Please update my voter registration address record within the **same** county.

## 6. FOR DRIVER UNDER 18, PARENT/GUARDIAN SIGNATURES REQUIRED: If both parents/guardians have joint custody, *BOTH MUST* sign.

I/We accept liability for this minor.

| MOTHER'S/GUARDIAN'S SIGNATURE | DATE | DAYTIME PHONE NUMBER |
|---|---|---|
| | | |
| FATHER'S/GUARDIAN'S SIGNATURE | DATE | DAYTIME PHONE NUMBER |
| | | |

## 7. CERTIFICATION: I have read and agree to all the certifications on the back of this form and I have made no false statements. I certify under penalty of perjury under the laws of the State of California that the foregoing is true and correct.

*STOP*  **Do not sign until instructed to do so by a DMV employee.**

| SIGNATURE OF APPLICANT | DATE | DAYTIME PHONE NUMBER |
|---|---|---|
| X | | |

**TEXT FEATURES**

A **cross-reference** instructs the reader to look at another document or another section of the same document. Circle the cross-reference in section 4.

**INFER**

In section 7, why do you think you are instructed not to sign the application form until told to do so by a DMV employee?

# Standards Review

## Teen Driver's Guide and Permit Application

Complete the sample test item below. The box at the right explains why three of these choices are not correct.

| Sample Test Item | Explanation of the Correct Answer |
|---|---|
| In the Teen Driver's Guide, what kind of information is provided in parentheses?<br><br>**A** things to do first<br><br>**B** illustrations<br><br>**C** sequences<br><br>**D** tips and extra information | The correct answer is *D*.<br><br>*A* is incorrect; although some of the parentheses contain tips, they do not tell what actions to take first. No illustrations or sequences are provided in the parentheses; therefore, *B* and *C* are also incorrect. |

**DIRECTIONS:** Circle the letter of the best response for each item.

**Reading Standard 2.7**
Critique the logic of functional documents by examining the sequence of information and procedures in anticipation of possible reader misunderstandings.

1. What is the main, overall **logical sequence** of the Teen Driver's Guide?

   **A** age order

   **B** time order

   **C** order of importance

   **D** no particular order

2. The Teen Driver's Guide includes all of the following **text features** *except*—

   **F** bulleted lists

   **G** boldface headers

   **H** graphic illustrations

   **J** information in parentheses

3. The Permit Application form separates items with—

   **A** horizontal lines

   **B** logical sequence

   **C** careful descriptions

   **D** confusing directions

4. The purpose of a **cross-reference** is to—

   **F** illustrate the text

   **G** refer you to other information

   **H** grab your attention

   **J** make you cross

**Before You Go On...**

Check your Standards Mastery at the back of this book.

# Citing Internet Sources: Teen Drivers

BIBLIOGRAPHY

## BEFORE YOU READ

Before you start driving, it might be a good idea to learn more about teen drivers. You can use your school, library, or home computer to search the Internet for databases, public service sites, and commercial sites that will furnish the information you want. If you prepare a report on your research, you'll need to include a bibliography or works cited list.

### FOCUS: DOCUMENTATION

- The following *Works Cited* is a listing of Internet resources on the topic of teen drivers.
- The citations are listed alphabetically by author or title, following the style of the Modern Language Association.
- The electronic address (URL) is listed last in each citation.
- The date the Web site was accessed comes right before the URL.

### TERMS TO KNOW

**Bibliography**—a list of sources of information on a subject, also called *Works Cited*.

**Citation**—an entry in a list of sources of information on a subject.

**Database**—a large collection of information on a computer, organized so that it can be expanded, updated, and retrieved rapidly for various uses.

**Source**—a book, document, or person that provides information.

**URL**—Uniform Resource Locator; a site's Internet address.

**Reading Standard 2.2** Prepare a bibliography of reference materials for a report using a variety of consumer, workplace, and public documents.

# Citing Internet Sources: Teen Drivers

## Works Cited

American Automobile Association. "Teen Drivers: A Guide to California's Graduated Driver License." 30 Jan. 2002. 9 Mar. 2002. <http://www.csaa.com/global/articledetail/ 0,8055,1004040000%257C1274,00.html>

Chen, Li-Hui, et al. "Carrying Passengers as a Risk Factor for Crashes Fatal to 16- and 17-Year Old Drivers." Journal of the American Medical Association 22–29 Mar. 2000. 9 Mar. 2002. <http://www.jama.ama-assn.org/>

10  CNN. "Death Risk for Teen Drivers Soars When Other Teens Ride, Study Shows." 21 Mar. 2000. 3:59 EST. 11 Mar. 2002. <http://www.cnn.com/2000/HEALTH/children/03/21/ teen.driving/>

Direnfeld, Gary. "Reducing Injury and Death in Teen Drivers." Journal of Trauma Nursing Jan.–Mar. 2001. 9 Mar. 2002. <http://www.parentsassociation.com/health/ i_promise_program_trauma.html>

DriveHomeSafe. "Teen Driver Training Chart for Parents." Advertisement. DriveHomeSafe, 2000, 2001. 1 Apr. 2002.
20  <http://www.drivehomesafe.com/ teendriver_trainingchart_for parents_page1.htm>

Insurance Institute for Highway Safety. "Black and Hispanic Children, Teenagers Are at High Risk of Motor Vehicle Crash Death." 14 Dec. 1998. 9 Mar. 2002. <http://www.hwysafety.org/news%5Freleases/1998/pr121498.htm>

Insurance Institute for Highway Safety. "Does Your Teenager Drive a Safe Car? Vehicle Choice Is Particularly Important for Young Drivers." 21 Sept. 1999. 9 Mar. 2002. <http://www.hwysafety.org/news%5Freleases/1999/pr092199.htm>

30   Insurance Institute for Highway Safety. "Driver Death Rate Among 16-Year-Olds Has Nearly Doubled While Going Down Among Other Drivers, Even 17–19 Year-Olds." 14 Apr. 1998. 9 Mar. 2002. <http://www.hwysafety.org/news%5Freleases/1998/pr041498.htm>

Insurance Institute for Highway Safety. "Fatality Facts: Teenagers." Oct. 2001. 9 Mar. 2002. <http://www.hwysafety.org/safety%5Ffacts/fatality%5Ffacts/teens.htm>

Memmer, Scott. "Young Drivers at Risk." Teen Driver Safety Series: Part One. Edmonds.com. 9 Mar. 2002.
40   <http://www.edmunds.com/ownership/driving/articles/44908/article.html>

Safeway Driving Center. "Teen Drivers Education Course." Advertisement. Safeway Driving. 1 Apr. 2002.

### IDENTIFY

Are the Insurance Institute for Highway Safety citations **public, consumer,** or **workplace documents**?

_____

_____

### TEXT FEATURES

**Databases** are underlined in a *Works Cited* list. Circle the database in lines 38–39. What item in this citation indicates that more information on teen drivers is available?

_____

_____

_____

### EVALUATE

Do you think an advertisement for a teen drivers education course (lines 42–43) is a useful citation for a *Works Cited* list on teen driving? Why or why not?

_____

_____

_____

_____

_____

_____

_____

# Standards Review

**TestPractice** ### Citing Internet Sources: Teen Drivers

Complete the sample test item, and then read the explanation at the right.

| Sample Test Item | Explanation of the Correct Answer |
|---|---|
| The first piece of information in a **bibliographic citation** is the—<br><br>**A** title of the work<br>**B** URL<br>**C** author's last name<br>**D** date of access | The correct answer is *C*.<br><br>*A* is incorrect; the title is listed second. *B* is incorrect; the URL is listed last. *D* is incorrect; the date of access is listed before the URL. |

**DIRECTIONS:** Circle the letter of the best response for each item.

**Reading Standard 2.2**
Prepare a bibliography of reference materials for a report using a variety of consumer, workplace, and public documents.

1. In a *Works Cited* list, citations are listed—

   **A** by URL

   **B** by electronic publication date

   **C** by the date the article was accessed

   **D** alphabetically by author and title

2. What is the name of the database in the following citation?
   Memmer, Scott. "Young Drivers at Risk," Teen Driver Safety Series: Part One. Edmonds.com. 9 Mar. 2002. <http://www.edmunds.com/ownership/driving/articles/44908/article.html>

   **F** Scott Memmer

   **G** Teen Driver Safety Series: Part One

   **H** Edmonds.com

   **J** 9 Mar. 2002

3. In a bibliographic citation, the date an article was accessed goes—

   **A** after the title of the work

   **B** before the author's name

   **C** after the URL

   **D** before the URL

4. Which of the following is most likely to be a **consumer document**?

   **F** American Automobile Association. "Teen Drivers: A Guide . . ."

   **G** Chen, Li-Hui, et al. "Carrying Passengers as a Risk Factor . . ."

   **H** DriveHomeSafe. "Teen Driver Training Chart. Advertisement . . ."

   **J** Insurance Institute for Highway Safety. "Does Your Teenager Drive a Safe Car?"

**Before You Go On . . .**
Check your Standards Mastery at the back of this book.

# Word List

Keep track of all the new words you have learned by filling out the
following chart. Review these words from time to time to make sure
they become part of your permanent vocabulary.

| WORD | |
|------|--|
| DEFINITION: | _____ |
| _____ | |

| WORD | |
|------|--|
| DEFINITION: | _____ |
| _____ | |

| WORD | |
|------|--|
| DEFINITION: | _____ |
| _____ | |

| WORD | |
|------|--|
| DEFINITION: | _____ |
| _____ | |

| WORD | |
|------|--|
| DEFINITION: | _____ |
| _____ | |

| WORD | |
|------|--|
| DEFINITION: | _____ |
| _____ | |

| WORD | |
|------|--|
| DEFINITION: | _____ |
| _____ | |

| WORD | |
|------|--|
| DEFINITION: | _____ |
| _____ | |

| WORD | |
|------|--|
| DEFINITION: | _____ |
| _____ | |

| WORD | |
|------|--|
| DEFINITION: | _____ |
| _____ | |

| WORD | |
|------|--|
| DEFINITION: | _____ |
| _____ | |

| WORD | |
|------|--|
| DEFINITION: | _____ |
| _____ | |

**WORD**

DEFINITION: _____

_____

**WORD**

DEFINITION: _____

_____

**WORD**

DEFINITION: _____

_____

**WORD**

DEFINITION: _____

_____

**WORD**

DEFINITION: _____

_____

**WORD**

DEFINITION: _____

_____

**WORD**

DEFINITION: _____

_____

**WORD**

DEFINITION: _____

_____

**WORD**

DEFINITION: _____

_____

**WORD**

DEFINITION: _____

_____

**WORD**

DEFINITION: _____

_____

**WORD**

DEFINITION: _____

_____

**WORD**

DEFINITION: _____

_____

**WORD**

DEFINITION: _____

_____

**WORD**

DEFINITION: _____

_____

**WORD**

DEFINITION: _____

_____

**WORD**

DEFINITION: _____

_____

**WORD**

DEFINITION: _____

_____

**WORD**

DEFINITION: _____

_____

**WORD**

DEFINITION: _____

_____

**WORD**

DEFINITION: _____

_____

**WORD**

DEFINITION: _____

_____

**WORD**

DEFINITION: _____

_____

**WORD**

DEFINITION: _____

_____

**WORD**

DEFINITION: _____

_____

**WORD**

DEFINITION: _____

_____

**WORD**

DEFINITION: _____

_____

**WORD**

DEFINITION: _____

_____

**WORD**

DEFINITION: _____

_____

**WORD**

DEFINITION: _____

_____

**WORD**

DEFINITION: _____

_____

**WORD**

DEFINITION: _____

_____

**WORD**

DEFINITION: _____

_____

**WORD**

DEFINITION: _____

_____

**WORD**

DEFINITION: _____

_____

**WORD**

DEFINITION: _____

_____

**WORD**

DEFINITION: _____

_____

**WORD**

DEFINITION: _____

_____

**WORD**

DEFINITION: _____

_____

**WORD**

DEFINITION: _____

_____

**WORD**

DEFINITION: _____

_____

**WORD**

DEFINITION: _____

_____

| WORD | | WORD | |
|---|---|---|---|
| DEFINITION: _____ | | DEFINITION: _____ | |
| _____ | | _____ | |

| WORD | | WORD | |
|---|---|---|---|
| DEFINITION: _____ | | DEFINITION: _____ | |
| _____ | | _____ | |

| WORD | | WORD | |
|---|---|---|---|
| DEFINITION: _____ | | DEFINITION: _____ | |
| _____ | | _____ | |

| WORD | | WORD | |
|---|---|---|---|
| DEFINITION: _____ | | DEFINITION: _____ | |
| _____ | | _____ | |

| WORD | | WORD | |
|---|---|---|---|
| DEFINITION: _____ | | DEFINITION: _____ | |
| _____ | | _____ | |

| WORD | | WORD | |
|---|---|---|---|
| DEFINITION: _____ | | DEFINITION: _____ | |
| _____ | | _____ | |

| WORD | | WORD | |
|---|---|---|---|
| DEFINITION: _____ | | DEFINITION: _____ | |
| _____ | | _____ | |

**WORD**

DEFINITION: _____

_____

**WORD**

DEFINITION: _____

_____

**WORD**

DEFINITION: _____

_____

**WORD**

DEFINITION: _____

_____

**WORD**

DEFINITION: _____

_____

**WORD**

DEFINITION: _____

_____

**WORD**

DEFINITION: _____

_____

**WORD**

DEFINITION: _____

_____

**WORD**

DEFINITION: _____

_____

**WORD**

DEFINITION: _____

_____

**WORD**

DEFINITION: _____

_____

**WORD**

DEFINITION: _____

_____

**WORD**

DEFINITION: _____

_____

**WORD**

DEFINITION: _____

_____

# Checklist for Standards Mastery

Each time you read, you learn something new. Track your growth as a reader and your progress toward success by checking off skills you have acquired. You may want to use this checklist before you read a selection, to set a purpose for reading.

| ✓ | California Reading Standard (Grade 8 Review) | Selection |
|---|---|---|
| ☐ | **1.2** Understand the most important points in the history of English language and use common word origins to determine the historical influences on English word meanings. | |
| ☐ | **1.3** Use word meanings within the appropriate context and show ability to verify those meanings by definition, restatement, example, comparison, or contrast. | |
| ☐ | **3.1** Determine and articulate the relationship between the purposes and characteristics of different forms of poetry (e.g., ballad, lyric, couplet, epic, elegy, ode, sonnet). | |
| ☐ | **3.4** Analyze the relevance of the setting (e.g., place, time, customs) to the mood, tone, and meaning of the text. | |
| ☐ | **3.7** Analyze a work of literature, showing how it reflects the heritage, traditions, attitudes, and beliefs of its author. (Biographical approach) | |

| ✓ | California Grade 9–10 Reading Standard | Selection |
|---|---|---|
| ☐ | **1.1** Identify and use the literal and figurative meanings of words and understand word derivations. | |

| ✓ | California Grade 9–10 Reading Standard | Selection |
|---|---|---|
| ☐ | **1.2** Distinguish between the denotative and connotative meanings of words and interpret the connotative power of words. | |
| ☐ | **1.3** Identify Greek, Roman, and Norse mythology and use the knowledge to understand the origin and meaning of new words (e.g., the word *narcissistic* drawn from the myth of Narcissus and Echo). | |
| ☐ | **2.1** Analyze the structure and format of functional workplace documents, including the graphics and headers, and explain how authors use the features to achieve their purposes. | |
| ☐ | **2.2** Prepare a bibliography of reference materials for a report using a variety of consumer, workplace, and public documents. | |
| ☐ | **2.3** Generate relevant questions about readings on issues that can be researched. | |
| ☐ | **2.4** Synthesize the content from several sources or works by a single author dealing with a single issue; paraphrase the ideas and connect them to other sources and related topics to demonstrate comprehension. | |
| ☐ | **2.5** Extend ideas presented in primary or secondary sources through original analysis, evaluation, and elaboration. | |
| ☐ | **2.6** Demonstrate use of sophisticated learning tools by following technical directions (e.g., those found with graphic calculators and specialized software programs and in access guides to World Wide Web sites on the Internet). | |
| ☐ | **2.7** Critique the logic of functional documents by examining the sequence of information and procedures in anticipation of possible reader misunderstandings. | |

| ✓ | California Grade 9–10 Reading Standard | Selection |
|---|---|---|
| ☐ | **2.8** Evaluate the credibility of an author's argument or defense of a claim by critiquing the relationship between generalizations and evidence, the comprehensiveness of evidence, and the way in which the author's intent affects the structure and tone of the text (e.g., in professional journals, editorials, political speeches, primary source material). | |
| ☐ | **3.1** Articulate the relationship between the expressed purposes and the characteristics of different forms of dramatic literature (e.g., comedy, tragedy, drama, dramatic monologue). | |
| ☐ | **3.2** Compare and contrast the presentation of a similar theme or topic across genres to explain how the selection of genre shapes the theme or topic. | |
| ☐ | **3.3** Analyze interactions between main and subordinate characters in a literary text (e.g., internal and external conflicts, motivations, relationships, influences) and explain the way those interactions affect the plot. | |
| ☐ | **3.4** Determine characters' traits by what the characters say about themselves in narration, dialogue, dramatic monologue, and soliloquy. | |
| ☐ | **3.5** Compare works that express a universal theme and provide evidence to support the ideas expressed in each work. | |
| ☐ | **3.6** Analyze and trace an author's development of time and sequence, including the use of complex literary devices (e.g., foreshadowing, flashbacks). | |
| ☐ | **3.7** Recognize and understand the significance of various literary devices, including figurative language, imagery, allegory, and symbolism, and explain their appeal. | |

| ✓ | California Grade 9–10 Reading Standard | Selection |
|---|---|---|
| ☐ | **3.8** Interpret and evaluate the impact of ambiguities, subtleties, contradictions, ironies, and incongruities in a text. | |
| ☐ | **3.9** Explain how voice, persona, and the choice of a narrator affect characterization and the tone, plot, and credibility of a text. | |
| ☐ | **3.10** Identify and describe the function of dialogue, scene designs, soliloquies, asides, and character foils in dramatic literature. | |
| ☐ | **3.11** Evaluate the aesthetic qualities of style, including the impact of diction and figurative language on tone, mood, and theme, using the terminology of literary criticism. (Aesthetic approach) | |
| ☐ | **3.12** Analyze the way in which a work of literature is related to the themes and issues of its historical period. (Historical approach) | |

# Index of Authors and Titles

# Vocabulary Development

**Pronunciation guides,** in parentheses, are provided for the vocabulary words in this book. The following key will help you use those pronunciation guides.

As a practice in using a pronunciation guide, sound out the words used as examples in the list that follows. See if you can hear the way the same vowel might be sounded in different words. For example, say "at" and "ate" aloud. Can you hear the difference in the way "a" sounds?

The symbol ə is called a **schwa.** A schwa is used by many dictionaries to indicate a sort of weak sound like the "a" in "ago." Some people say that the schwa sounds like "eh." A vowel sounded like a schwa is never accented.

The vocabulary words in this book are also provided with a part-of-speech label. The parts of speech are *n.* (noun), *v.* (verb), *pro.* (pronoun), *adj.* (adjective), *adv.* (adverb), *prep.* (preposition), *conj.* (conjunction), and *interj.* (interjection). To learn about the parts of speech, consult the *Holt Handbook.*

To learn more about the vocabulary words, consult your dictionary. You will find that many of the words defined here have several other meanings.

---

at, āte, cär; ten, ēve; is, īce; gō, hôrn, look, tool; oil, out; up, fur, ə *for unstressed vowels, as* a *in* ago, u *in* focus; ' *as in* Latin (lat''n); chin; she; zh *as in* azure (azh'ər); thin, the; ŋ *as in* ring (riŋ)

---

# Picture Credits